SIMENON: A CRITICAL BIOGRAPHY

A Georges Simenon amicalement

Bernard Buffet 57

SIMENON
A CRITICAL BIOGRAPHY

by
Stanley G. Eskin

McFarland & Company, Inc., Publishers
Jefferson, North Carolina, and London

Frontispiece: portrait of Simenon by Bernard Buffet, 1957

Library of Congress Cataloguing-in-Publication Data
Eskin, Stanley G.
Simenon, a critical biography.
"Bibliography of the works of Georges Simenon": p. 275.
Secondary bibliography: p. 289.
Filmography: p. 287.
Includes index.
1. Simenon, Georges, 1903–   .
2. Novelists, Belgian — 20th century — Biography.
I. Title.
PQ2637.I53Z625   1987   843′.912 [B]   86-43084
ISBN 0-89950-281-4 (acid-free natural paper) ∞

McFarland & Company, Inc., Publishers
Box 611, Jefferson NC 28640

For Barbara

"One holds it a bit against him, for he spoils a marvelous subject; out of haste, and, one might say: out of impatience."

André Gide on *Touriste de Banane*

"I was impatient to write something else."

Simenon, on being forced to learn to write in first grade, having already learned in nursery school.

TABLE OF CONTENTS

TABLE OF CONTENTS

PREFACE

Throughout his entire career Georges Simenon experienced an uncertainty about his literary enterprise which was echoed by the public and critical response to his work. He has always been a writer needing to be "placed," as countless reviewers, critics and well-wishers have attempted to do for half a century. This book undertakes to define the problem and perhaps bring it to rest by an examination of Simenon's life and works and a valuation of his œuvre. He is worth a good deal more than the widespread, perfunctory view of him as the creator of Maigret, but perhaps not quite as much as some of his more hyperbolic admirers have proclaimed (these include André Gide, François Mauriac, Jean Renoir, Jean Cocteau, Henry Miller, Charles Chaplin, Thornton Wilder, Anaïs Nin, Federico Fellini, and a multitude of other prominent but less famous figures). He invites consideration of the relationship between commercial literature and serious art, but one finds that he is a rather idiosyncratic case. He maneuvered himself into his perennially ambiguous position because of deep-rooted drives, needs, interests and phobias that constitute the texture of his life and his books. One tries to identify the threads of his public and private selves and weave them into a pattern that, with luck, provides clarification and corresponds to reality.

The information comes mostly from documents, supplemented by interviews with various persons concerned, beginning with Simenon himself. In addition to letters, published and unpublished, there is Simenon's own mass of autobiographical writings, some presented with narrative continuity, but most of it scattered helter-skelter. The major autobiographical works, none of which is systematic or comprehensive, need to be explained.

[xi]

The last is the very long *Mémoires intimes* of 1981, which attempts to draw many threads together and provide some continuity, but is skimpy on the early life and spotty on much of the adult life, providing extraordinarily minute detail for some things, but passing lightly over others—most notably his writing. It is predominantly an accounting of his family life—his love for his children and strife with his second wife. The *Mémoires* were preceded by 21 volumes of dictated reflections and reminiscences (1973–79), quite rich in random details, particularly of his childhood and his old age. Also dictated is *Lettre à ma mère* (1974), a discussion with his mother, in the second person, not long after her death at the age of 91—a further installment of an inner monologue—often a diatribe—which he carried on throughout his life. Earlier, there was a handwritten diary, *Quand j'étais vieux*, written in 1960–63 but not published till 1970, recording miscellaneous incidents in his life past and present, and thoughts on his mind. Much earlier, in 1938, he wrote *Trois Crimes de mes amis*, vaguely fictionalized, but quite dependable as autobiography and dealing with certain episodes in his late adolescence.

The most important sources for his early life are two books, *Je me souviens* and *Pedigree*, which are closely linked with each other. They originated in 1940, when a radiologist misread a chest x-ray and told Simenon he had no more than two years to live. The result was that Simenon wrote a private account, addressed to his three-year-old son, Marc, intended to provide him in the future with a description and evaluation of the Simenon background—the kind of folks he came from—in the form, mostly, of Simenon's detailed memories of his childhood. The running title of this memoir was "Pedigree of Marc Simenon."

Simenon sent a part of this manuscript to André Gide, with whom he was at that time in frequent correspondence. Gide was impressed, but urged him to stop immediately writing a straightforward memoir in the first person and to turn the project instead into an autobiographical novel in the third person. Simenon accepted Gide's advice, and, over several years, rewrote as fiction what he had already composed as memoir, and continued the fictional narrative considerably beyond the point where he had left off the memoir.

In 1945, Simenon published the original memoir under the title *Je me souviens*. In 1948 he published three volumes of the fictionalized version under the overall title of *Pedigree*. He left his fictional alter ego, whom he gave the name of Roger Mamelin, at age 16. His intention may have been eventually to carry on beyond that point, but, unfortunately, libel suits by some touchy *Liégeois* who recognized themselves in certain unflattering descriptions discouraged him from continuing *Pedigree*.

We are then left with *Je me souviens*, which gives us many details about Simenon as a small child and about his family; and with three volumes of a fiction which is so verifiably close to autobiography in most parts as to qualify as a source — of descriptions, episodes, factual details, general atmosphere, the "mood of the times," etc. As evaluation and interpretation of events and people, it must be used more critically. But then so must also the straight autobiographical works.

In any case, the earlier part of *Pedigree* corresponds very closely with *Je me souviens*. Sometimes even the wording is identical. Many episodes in the latter part of *Pedigree* (beyond the time span covered in *Je me souviens*) correspond to autobiographical statements elsewhere. Consequently, it is reasonable to use *Pedigree* as authentic documentation. As regards proper names, Simenon chose to be inconsistent: in many instances, the name is changed. In the fiction, Simenon changed his mother's first name from Henriette to Elise, while his father's name remains Désiré in both books.

All translations are my own.

I am grateful for the cooperation of Georges Simenon in granting interviews, responding to letters, and giving permission to quote passages and use photographs. I also wish to thank Mme. Tigy (Régine) Simenon and Mme. Denyse Simenon for their willingness to talk to me, as well as Mme. Joyce Pache-Aitken, Mr. Kenneth McCormick, Mrs. Helen Wolff, M. Claude Nielsen, M. Gilbert Sigaux, and M. Robert Toussaint. At the "Centre d'Études Georges Simenon" at the University of Liège, Professor Maurice Piron, Mme. Colette Delruelle-Brahy, Mme. Christine Swings, and M. Paul Goret were especially helpful. I wish also to thank Mr. Yousuf Karsh for permission to use a photograph of Denyse Simenon. M. Claude Menguy's generosity in making available his immense collection of Simenon materials and his detailed bibliographical and biographical knowledge, and granting permission to use his bibliographies, was invaluable. For their help and comments on the manuscript at various stages, I wish to thank Ronald Sanders, Irvin Stock, Nicholas Delbanco, Robert Pickering, Howard Lewis, and my wife, Barbara.

Shady, N.Y., November 15, 1986

I

INTRODUCTION

At the Gare du Nord in Paris, a tall, very thin young man, two months short of twenty years, stepped off the night train from Belgium. He wore a cheap raincoat, his shoes were worn, and all his possessions were packed in two synthetic leather suitcases, one kept closed by a precariously buckled strap. His longish blond hair, broad-brimmed black hat and breezy neckerchief suggested something of a bohemian.

Paris, on December 11, 1922, was not at its most inviting. It was cold, raining and dark. The young man's feelings were mixed, but leaned toward disillusionment. The train had approached the Gare du Nord through the interminably gray façades of dingy Parisian suburbs, where a few windows were lit up: the little people washing and breakfasting, while the streets were mostly deserted in the feeble predawn light.

Disappointment and depression — and yet the sense that, rain or shine, this *was* nonetheless Paris: "What counted was finally to be in Paris. What also and above all counted was, come what may, to keep one's head above water, earn a living, and try to eat more or less every day." He quickly displayed prudence by taking a cheap attic room in Montmartre, then exuberance by devouring, to the astonishment of other customers, a dozen croissants at a café.

It was the young Belgian, Georges Simenon — then mostly known to friends and public alike as Georges Sim — who thus arrived in Paris on that bleak December morning. He had been to Paris briefly twice before as a very young reporter, and would return to his native Liège a few months later to pick up a wife, which, his bohemian side notwithstanding, seemed

[1]

to him, somehow, a necessary appurtenance for a Paris début. Nonetheless December 11, 1922, serves quite well as the date of Georges Simenon's "official" entry into Paris, and, thence into "the world."

Five years later, he was, if not rich, doing very well writing stories, articles, and, mostly, pulp novels of adventure, crime, romance, sex and humor, which he turned out with astonishing speed and published under some 18 different pseudonyms. In time, he was able to buy boats, cars, horses, English-tailored suits, to travel incessantly, and to establish residence in a variety of interesting places in and out of Paris which he bought, rented, fixed up or—it appears sometimes—virtually invented.

Ten years later he was publishing a series of detective stories starring Maigret, a commissaire of the French Police Judiciaire, which became an overnight success and made him—this time—squarely rich and quite famous.

Twenty years later he was still writing Maigrets but had also written an impressive number of "straight" novels which brought him considerable critical encouragement, both in the press and privately from a number of notable literati. This opened up the vexed question, bandied about for subsequent decades, of Simenon's relationship to "higher" literature. He kept on writing both Maigrets and non–Maigrets at his usual phenomenal rate, and responded amicably—occasionally enthusiastically—to his admirers. But toward "literature" he adopted a complicated stand, as often as not a combative one. At various times he expounded theories about the seriousness of his literary enterprise, as if asking himself what he was up to.

Thirty years later, Simenon was living as a country squire in an elegant estate in Connecticut. He spent ten consecutive years in the United States. His reputation and his problematical literary status remained more or less steady. On one level, he always had trouble—has trouble to this day—getting away from the Maigret image. Throughout much of his career, one review out of two began with something like, "The creator of the famous Commissaire Maigret now turns his attention to a different subject...." To this day, in Paris bookstores which should know better, no matter what kind of Simenon the client is asking for, he is automatically directed to the detective shelves. Even some professionals do odd things. An American bibliographer entitled a monograph "Georges Simenon: A Checklist of his 'Maigret' and Other Mystery Novels and Short Stories in French and in English Translation." Half of the items listed have nothing to do with "mysteries"; some are not even fiction.

Forty years later, getting richer and richer, with people talking about "the Simenon industry," he had moved back to Europe, eventually to Switzerland, where he still resides.

Fifty years later, seventy years old, he brusquely decided to abandon fiction, even taking the trouble of bringing his passport to the Belgian consulate to have the designation changed from "writer" to "without profession." He expressed repeatedly how relieved he was, and published nothing but musings which he dictated into a cassette recorder and called "Dictées," until 1981, when he published a long autobiographical memoir, written by hand.

Throughout his career Simenon was a man pursued by statistics (even though he declared once that he was allergic to statistics): How many books has he written? How many pages could he turn out a day? How many pseudonyms did he use? How many languages has he been translated into? How much money did he make?

Money—with some early exceptions—he categorically refused to discuss with anyone in detail, except publishers and producers. There are no reliable statistics. He made a lot and he spent a lot. This he readily acknowledged and it is perhaps the only significant generalization to be made on the matter.

How fast he wrote? He claimed that in his heyday as a pulp novelist in the twenties he would write up to eighty typewritten pages a day. Later, with the Maigrets and the regular novels, his oft-described procedure was to write a chapter a day. Most of his novels are short, so that meant, more or less, eight days to two weeks. Eleven seems to have been the average. Ferociously, he almost always refused to revise anything. It was almost a kind of negative obsession, the causes and consequences of which are complex. A *New York Times* review of *Les Volets verts* quotes him as saying, "I write fast because I have not zee brains to write slow."

How much has he written? Probably no one will ever know exactly. As regards published novels, a rapid calculation yields one juvenilium, 190 pulps under pseudonym, and 201 novels under his own name. That comes to 392 novels. Many are quite short, while the longest, *Pedigree*, is virtual autobiography. There are 25 straight autobiographical works and one work of literary criticism–history, making a total of 418 entire *books* (that is to say, not collections of shorter pieces).

As for shorter pieces, there are thousands: short stories, magazine articles, newspaper articles, and a few speeches and essays. There are many collections of *some* of these; many more are uncollected. One should add the very numerous interviews that Simenon gave throughout his career, which were published in everything from scholarly journals to Sunday scandal sheets.

As for women, though the statistics are even less precise, Simenon jauntily left himself open for speculation when, in a published dialogue with his friend Federico Fellini in 1977, he stated, off the top of his head, that he must have slept with about ten thousand women in his lifetime. He declared

[3]

elsewhere that he began at 13, and that at age 70 he learned to become monogamous with his companion of many years, Teresa. That provides 57 years of polygamous sex life, which averages out to a different woman about every other day. (That remark in *L'Express* occasioned a call to Simenon's secretary by an English journalist who asked, "Did he really say *ten thousand?*") It is not unlikely that Fellini was spoofing his friend in the grotesque character of Dr. Zübercock in *Città delle donne*, who is celebrating his ten-thousandth conquest in his luridly appointed mansion with a gigantic cake studded with 10,000 candles.

Unlike the books, there are no catalogues in this domain, and in respect to 9,997 of the women, Simenon has been admirably discreet. In respect to his two wives and to the companion of his later years, he has been quite voluble — especially as regards his second wife, with whom from the mid-sixties to 1982 he carried on an increasingly public, detailed, and acrimonious dispute about money, children, alcohol, mental health and character evaluation. The statistics point to a libidinal frenzy which he always chose to interpret as an exuberant thirst for experience, but which was also an obsession born of resentment toward his mother, and which, like his compulsive changes of domiciles, pointed to persistent dissatisfaction. Women were objects of constant desire, and also threats of constant disappointment. Whether or not frustration was directly experienced in life, the threat of it was channeled into fiction, where a large proportion of his characters are frustrated, though not necessarily in a sexual context.

If statistics have plagued Simenon, that has been partly his own fault, and they are not of course what is important. What is important are his books, and, for that reason, the nature of the man who wrote them. The books are almost all flawed, except maybe the pulp fiction which he learned to turn out with great expertise. Yet among these flawed books are a half dozen or so near-masterpieces, several score of talented, interesting books, a quantity of middling ones, and a complement of duds. He created an enduringly appealing detective who, like all great fictional detectives, acquired a life of his own and a relation to the public separate from his creator's.

The nature of the man? Like most interesting personalities: multiple, paradoxical, complex. Simenon is an immensely successful man, who in one way or another frequently tends to recant his success. He has repeatedly dissociated himself from the appurtenances of success, cultivating an image of himself more as a man of the people than a multimillionaire moving in classy circles. He is clearly sincere both in his occasional exuberant relish of his success and its benefits, *and*, in another mood — or even simultaneously — in his dismissal of it all, and in his sense of self-reintegration with "the little people." He has recanted his success also in his extremely unstable attitude toward the importance or significance of his works, as well as in the curiously unartistic instincts that governed his method of composition.

Simenon is a man of paradoxes: a man of success whose most widely recurring fictional subject is failure; a man of order and discipline, yet fascinated by and sympathetic to the phenomenon of the dissolution of will; a self-described rebel writing constantly about other rebels and dropouts, who nonetheless usually gives the impression of being harmoniously at ease with his surroundings. Simenon is a highly organized, aimless wanderer — in life as well as in literature.

He came to be a self-assured, disciplined, adventurous, healthy man of the world, inside of whom, however, hid a "little man" — oppressed, frightened, frustrated, resentful, will-less, impotent. This little man was in large part fiction, but in some part one of Simenon's potential selves. Inside the little man hid an artist, who made superhuman efforts just barely to articulate the little man, each time falling back exhausted from the effort. He almost never reached the outside man: the worldly, self-assured one. The artist was indeed *inside* and had to struggle outward. He never did such things as "soaring above" or "taking a step back to contemplate the whole."

What complicates the issue is that Simenon's discipline has been applied to the production of literature; his credentials as a man of the world are literary ones; and his success has come from his books. Furthermore, the literary production which has thus been the effective cause of the "outer" man (the successful, worldly one) is itself sharply divided into at least two dimensions, possibly more. There has been "popular" literary production, which "caused" popular success, lots of money, and the worldly self that was the outward Simenon; and there has been a "literary" literary production, which was the "cause" of a different kind of success, namely, esteem among the literati — being taken seriously by Gide and the rest. Finally, as a further complication, this second kind of success turned out to be not at all incompatible with the other kind: it has provided just as much money, worldly stature, and fame. On the other hand, what it neither has provided nor is derived from is self-assurance about his writing.

In his early teens, Simenon began writing — in school and on his own — because he was good at it, and because he was a precocious and avid reader: writing fell into his lap, became part of his personal environment. This was the beginning of his serious writing. A little later he fell in with a bohemian, arty crowd which might have been expected to nourish the idea of serious writing but instead had the opposite effect: sniffing out a depressing odor of failure among the bohemians, he kept his distance and went his own way. His own way by then was mainly journalism, which he had stumbled into and which brought him rapid local success. When he was 16, one branch of his journalistic work — humor — overflowed into fiction:

he started his novelistic life as a verbal caricaturist, and maintained that momentum for some years in Paris with bawdy stories, ill-paid but which he could turn out so fast there was money in it. He had discovered commercial literature, which had not been at all part of his calculations as a teenager, but which he soon expanded into every conceivable form of pulp literature.

Except for occasional scribblings in notebooks, serious literature lay dormant and had nothing to do with the commercial work: he wrote for money because he found he could do it successfully, but might as well have been doing anything else for money. He had always intended to reconnect himself with serious literature, but had never thought of it as a way of making a living; that it turned out to be so was something of an accident — which did not keep him from making the most of the accident, by promotion, public relations and advantageous contracts.

Somewhere along the line — between his early teens and his taking up serious fiction when he was close to thirty — he made a gradual discovery: that literature was a mode of exploration of experience, and a mode of knowing. He did not put it in these terms, but that is what it was. He probably had felt intuitively that the great writers he admired as a youth were doing just that, but never seems to have considered he might do the same. He never made a firm connection between his own literary enterprise and that of anyone else. He came to understand his literary project as a delving into man, which he found exhausting and anxiety-provoking.

His explorations in literature paralleled his explorations in life, and came from the same impulses — probably curiosity and discontent, which, in fiction, often became curiosity about discontent. The parallel between life and literature turned out, in his eyes, to be a conflict, and in his work, a disadvantage; he came to see literary labor as that much effort drawn away from the business of living, and was impatient to get it over with and go back to life. His underlying conviction when he wrote novels was not that he was composing works of art but that he was exploring life, and that there were more gratifying ways of doing so. For several decades he mulled over the problem with varying degrees of clarity or confusion. Money very quickly became part of life; he got used to it and no more envisioned giving it up than giving up any other aspect of life. Aggressive negotiations and literary empire-building were part of life, but not of literature. Money was always incidental to literature, and literature incidental to money. Some readers found the books striking and recommended them; many more found them entertaining and bought them. Some found them both, and some neither. Simenon, at various times and in various moods, cared a great deal or not at all about any of his categories of readers.

I I

THE SIMENONS
AND THE BRÜLLS

Georges Simenon was born on February 13, 1903, in a small third-floor apartment at 18, rue Léopold, close to the heart of Liège, where a plaque now marks the event. He was born at ten minutes past midnight. His mother was alert enough to ask what time it was and to realize that it was now Friday the thirteenth, and superstitious enough to plead with the midwife not to reveal the time of his birth to anyone. The next morning his father duly went to the city hall to register the birth, on February *twelfth*, of Georges Joseph Christian Simenon.

"Liège est une ville pluvieuse" (a rainy city) — a small, busy port with a population that grew with the century from something above 100,000 to something below 200,000. It is an important river harbor on the Meuse, which is navigable by sizable ships. It is a steelmaking center and has long been noted for its small-arms manufactures. It had its heroic moment in 1914, when it held out for 12 days against the German onslaught, a matter which Simenon, unimpressed by military grandeur, has made virtually nothing of in his recollections of Liège during World War I. Otherwise, the dominant tone of Liège is sturdily bourgeois, its cultural resources provincially respectable, and its language unequivocally French (if Walloon be included as a branch of French).

Georges Simenon was the first child of Désiré Simenon and Henriette, née Brüll. Désiré met Henriette when she was a salesgirl at one of Liège's department stores, *L'Innovation*. Simenon never knew exactly how they met

[7]

but speculated that Désiré walked by *L'Innovation* from time to time, somehow was attracted to the young salesgirl, and made a habit of walking by even more often. Henriette and her best friend, Valérie, began noticing the tall, slender young man who kept walking by with a measured stride "as regular as a metronome." It was Valérie who first noticed him and would nudge Henriette: "I'm sure it's on account of you he comes by." Eventually Désiré approached her. Eventually they were married.

But this was mostly speculation: "My parents never talked about those things." It is probably also speculation that, during Henriette's labor, Désiré was pacing up and down the rue Léopold, frequently interrogating the corner policeman about the exact time, explaining with an apologetic smile that, "at any moment now.... You see, officer ... it's such an important event in your life...." Simenon was more sure that, after the birth, Désiré approached Henriette and, in tears, told her that she had just given him "the greatest joy that a woman can give a man."

The Simenon family and the Brüll family were very different, and the difference turned into an almost mythic polarization in Georges Simenon's consciousness, which he frequently described, analyzed, and brooded about, and which is often reflected in his fiction.

The Simenons were classical petit bourgeois, doubtless with many of the faults of the "little" bourgeoisie, but also with its virtues, which, for psychological reasons of his own, Georges chose to emphasize. They were (generally) dependable, scrupulous, moderate, and modest. They were diligent, but they also knew how to take it easy and enjoy themselves. Most important, perhaps, they felt at home in their environment and in their own skins; they were well settled; they "belonged." The Brülls, for their part, did *not* belong. Some were social climbers, others dropouts, and in between were many who, on the surface, pursued the same kind of petit-bourgeois activities as the Simenons, but who, in Simenon's eyes, were malcontents, complainers, *mal-mariés*, and, especially, alcoholics. One thing which the Simenons and the Brülls did have in common was lots of children, and coincidence made both Henriette and Désiré one of 13 siblings: Désiré the next to the eldest, sometimes cast in the role of eldest because he was considered the brains of the family; Henriette by far the youngest, in itself a disconnecting factor.

Simenon's paternal grandfather, Chrétien, left the ancestral farm to become a hatmaker, and, after a travelling apprenticeship through Europe, establishing his shop on the rue Puits-en-Sock, married Marie-Catherine Moers, and provided humble but decent circumstances in which to raise their 13 children. He had the true artisan's sense of pride in his craft, and once refused to sell a larger-size derby to a customer who considered the one chosen by Chrétien too tight: "That's how a derby is supposed to be and I won't sell you another one." Simenon remembers his grandfather as a tall man with white hair and a large moustache, who stood firmly erect into his eighties—a man of few words, with a serene, often motionless expression. One of his daily joys was to stand in front of his shop every morning with Mr. Kreutz, the dollmaker next door. The two men, in a daily ritual, would look at the morning activity of the rue Puits-en-Sock, then, at a given moment, would glance connivingly at each other, go to the back of the shop, and, saying little or nothing, down a minuscule glass of the local brandy and get to work.

Chrétien Simenon turned into a petit-bourgeois King Lear when, after the death of his wife, he was persuaded by some members of the family into shaking off the cares and business of his age and dividing up his goods. His Cordelia was his daughter, Georges's Aunt Céline, who took over the shop with her husband but unfortunately died not long after, leaving the disconsolate old man in the hands of his son-in-law and the son-in-law's new wife, whom Simenon describes as a "vieille punaise de confessionnal" (an old cockroach of the confessional).

There is some chronological confusion about Simenon's paternal grandmother who, by some indications, died when he was two years old, yet elsewhere is described as someone he knew throughout much of his childhood—perhaps a blur between things experienced and things told about. Grandmother Simenon was a diligent and uncomplaining housekeeper with an emotionless expression and a severe personality that frightened the young child. She was particularly appreciated for the fine bread she baked for her children into their adulthood—a tradition which Simenon later adduced as an example both of the Simenon sense of belonging—the closeness of the family—and of the Simenon sense of craftsmanship—the good bread baked in an enormous, specially made oven. Grandmother Simenon disliked Henriette, and, on one of her rare visits, to take a look at the newborn Georges, her only comment (in Walloon patois) was, "Que laid enfant!" (What an ugly child!)

The oldest member of the Simenon clan was Grandmother Simenon's father, Guillaume Moers. Simenon was amazed at having sat on the knees of a man who had witnessed the insurrection that brought the Kingdom of Belgium into existence in 1831. "Vieux-Papa" had been a miner and gone through a harrowing experience in a mine ensevelment. He was blind in his old age, and one of his few remaining pleasures was nibbling raw onions, which he was forbidden for medical reasons. Blind as he was, he would sneak down the cellar steps to the onion bag, swipe one, and go on his stroll happily munching his onion, greeted by all the shopkeepers. Since he lived to the age of 85, the onion warning seems to have been a false alarm.

Few of the other Simenons were memorable. There were Aunt Céline,

[9]

married to a locksmith, who had taken over the household when her mother died; Arthur, a jolly man with a pretty wife, and a capmaker ("casquettier") by trade; Uncle Lucien, the carpenter; Aunt Françoise, wife of a sacristan, whose ultraquiet house, where normal speech sounded like a roar, it was a particular ordeal to visit; and Uncle Guillaume, who ran an umbrella store in Brussels, dressed modishly, was married to a divorced woman, and was frowned upon by the rest of the family as some sort of defector. Most of the Simenons — four generations from "Vieux-Papa" to Georges's own — formed a solid clan that gathered together from time to time in its multitude, gatherings where in-laws — notably Henriette — felt excluded. Many of the sons visited the rue Puits-en-Sock daily, to pick up a loaf of Grandmother Simenon's celebrated bread, eat a meal, or get their shirt collars washed.

In describing his paternal heritage, Simenon sometimes tends to present the qualities he esteems in general and abstract terms, while the concrete details of character and behavior are not always so impressive. "Those kinds of artisans," he wrote, "are happy people, at peace with themselves." However, it is not difficult to picture the grandfather as a henpecked old man stultified into near-total silence, the grandmother as a cold fish whose only words to a young mother are about how ugly her child is, and the men as sissies incapable of breaking the umbilical cord — except for Uncle Guillaume of Brussels who gets dumped on for doing so. What is significant is not the real quality of the Simenon clan, but the mythic shape it took in the author's mind to emerge in his fiction later on.

In the case of his father, general virtues and specific descriptions that demonstrate them cohere better. Désiré Simenon was a trained accountant, in contrast with the shopkeepers and artisans, and for all his adult life was one of five employees in a small insurance agency owned by a certain M. Mayeur (Monneyeur in *Pedigree*).* Early in his career he was given the choice of handling fire insurance or life. He chose fire, which was a mistake: life was where the action was, and his colleague who handled that branch got increasingly larger commissions with the years, while Désiré never earned more than 180 francs a month — less than the wages of the average blue-collar worker. Henriette never forgave him the life-insurance decision, and, ironically, also nagged him about not taking out life insurance for himself, until, in 1918, he had a heart attack and revealed that he had known all along about the heart condition which made it impossible for him to get life insurance.

Not an artisan, Désiré nonetheless had the artisan job sense. He took pride in his efficiency and in his reputation for rapid, invariably correct arithmetic. He was meticulous, orderly and punctual. Indeed, he had a

For names and documentary status of Pedigree, *see Preface.*

mania about clocks, and would wind up the office clock immediately upon arrival, before taking off his overcoat. There was a clock in his father's house (the tick-tock of which Georges Simenon could still hear in his seventies) which Désiré had expected to be his share when the old man distributed his goods. By this clock Désiré set his watch. It was one of the disappointments of his life that he inherited a coffee mill instead.

His orderliness, Simenon believed, was a source of joy to him: his punctual, half-hour's walk to the office; washing his hands at the office sink; setting his double-keyboard typewriter; arranging his pencils and erasers; and, a special pleasure, eating his bread and butter in the office by himself while the others went out to lunch. Apart from work and the almost daily visits to Simenon headquarters at the rue Puits-en-Sock, he participated in various civic activities: Civil Guard drill, sharpshooting tournaments (where he once won a silver watch which Simenon was so ashamed later of having used to pay the fee of a magnificent black prostitute), amateur dramatics, and volunteer work for "Les Pauvres Honteux" — a benevolent society to help low-level white-collar workers, like himself, who fell into difficulties. At home, Désiré liked best to sit in his wicker armchair and read his newspaper.

Simenon saw him as a happy man whose happiness lay in little pleasures. He had a cheerful serenity which came from not demanding much of life, but relishing what was there. In *Les Quatre Jours du pauvre homme*, Simenon's cameo of the elder Lecouin (whose very name suggests someone quietly sitting in his corner) must be a direct recollection of his father: "He manufactured little joys for himself alone." Like the other Simenons, Désiré was a belonger at heart and managed as well as he could to establish a territorial center of his own. Offered a promotion to Brussels, he turned it down, saying, "I was born in this neighborhood; I know everybody." He stayed, but, as Simenon sees it, it was a constant struggle for him to maintain his serene territoriality, a struggle mostly against his wife, who functioned with different imperatives. Lecouin is in the same situation, as is the elder Rico in *Les Frères Rico*, and other Simenonian couples featuring dominant wives and meek husbands. Simenon, all his life, venerated his father and, as a child, tried to imitate his gestures and demeanor. Many critics, and Simenon himself, have said that his father was the model for Maigret. Furthermore, the social and personal ideals which he considered embodied in his father play a major role in his fiction — albeit most often by their absence, or in counterpoint to the main themes that are the opposite of those ideals.

Simenon repeatedly attributes another, more ambiguous, trait to his father, and to most of the other Simenons, as well as to himself. This is what he calls the Simenon "pudeur," a sense of discretion, a reluctance to manifest

[11]

emotions, a reserve, a kind of bashfulness. It was "pudeur" that made the only form of address between Désiré and Georges "Père" and "Fils," and which prompted Désiré to respond to Henriette's complaint that he never said "I love you": "But you are there!" When someone in 1951 sent the celebrated author a study of religious sentiment in his work, the study felt to him like a probing into intimacies, and elicited a long letter, the first paragraph of which is wholly devoted to the Simenon "pudeur" and to his father, "for whom, if I am not mistaken, any display of emotion was incongruous." This Simenon reserve was an ambiguous quantity, even in Simenon's own mind. If he saw it as a charming quality in his father, and an explanation for some of his own attitudes and behavior, and, in some contexts, described a warm closeness to his father—sometimes indeed a sense of conspiratorial solidarity against his mother—in other contexts he expressed twinges of regret at the walls of incommunication erected by "pudeur." The need to communicate became a major theme of Simenon's fiction, as did obstacles against communication. The paternal "pudeur" heritage had much to do with it. In his old age, Simenon was to overcome "pudeur" in a curious avalanche of intimate autobiographical writings.

Désiré lived out his life with his inbred reserve and his little pleasures, his space increasingly violated when Henriette moved the family to a larger house and took in boarders. When he was 41 he had his first heart attack, and chest pains would oblige him to stop on the street. Perhaps it was "pudeur" too that made him pretend to be looking at store displays. He died in 1921, in the little insurance office where he had always taken pleasure in keeping objects and figures in such good order.

As for the maternal Brülls, they were, for Simenon, the antithesis of the paternal clan. Their most notable characteristic was social instability: some rose to become wealthy, some fell to become derelicts, some see-sawed, and some, stuck at lower echelons than they wanted, never ceased to strive to rise a little bit higher in the bourgeois hierarchy, and lived in constant dread of slipping lower. This last was Simenon's view of his mother, to whom he attributed an insecure class-consciousness, an obsequious deference to certain kinds of gentry, a pinched disdain for certain others, and a snobbish paranoia toward everything vaguely proletarian—a sort of gathering of the skirts and pulling the children to safety.

The Brülls were outsiders, not only in that they were not Liégeois, but not Walloon (French-speaking). Henriette's father, Guillaume Brüll, who died when she was five years old, seems to have been half German and half Dutch and came from a region where all three countries met. At one time he was a "dyjkmaster" (dikemaster), holding a post of some importance, and perhaps also burgermeister of the German village of Herzogenrath, near Aachen. Later he moved to Belgium and became quite wealthy as a farmer, a wood dealer, and or a barge owner. Then came the decline: whether he started to drink because he went bankrupt or went bankrupt because he was drinking (as Simenon believed) is uncertain. He was ruined when he put up security for a friend who then defaulted and left Guillaume Brüll penniless, soon degenerating rapidly into alcoholic oblivion.

Henriette's mother, Maria Loyens, is an even more obscure figure. The only two things that Simenon knew about her were that, after the bankruptcy, she was so proud that, even if there was nothing to eat in the house, as soon as somebody knocked at the door she would hurry to put pots of water to boil on the stove to make it appear that a big dinner was in the works. The other thing was that she never, ever went out of the house without her hat and gloves.

Whatever the moral qualities by which the Brülls might be distinguished from the Simenons, Henriette's relationship with her family was much more ambiguous, changeable and insecure than Désiré's with his. Her father was lost to her five-year-old memory, and, for some reason, her mother, who died when she was 21, seems equally lost. Her brothers and sisters — Simenon's *other* dozen uncles and aunts — were a very mixed bag. There were the rich ones, like Albert, who was in lumber, grains and fertilizers in Hasselt and came in from time to time to Liège for the stock exchange, but never visited Henriette, who had married a lowly insurance employee, except once, when he took away the valuable antique furniture that was her share of the family heritage and substituted ugly modern pieces for it. (He may be identical to Henri, who later acquired a château and called himself Henri de Tongres, and who refused to lend Georges 500 francs for his father's funeral.)

Also rich was her sister Marthe, married to Jan Vermeiren (Hubert Schroefs in *Pedigree*), a wholesale grocer. Marthe was an alcoholic who periodically locked herself up in her room to go on a drinking binge (a "neuvaine"). Occasionally her husband would call Henriette to coax her sister out of her retreat and reward her with some tidbit from his warehouse, like a can of sardines. Marthe eventually died in an insane asylum.

On a lower economic level and equally bad off emotionally was Félicie, married to a café owner named Coustou but nicknamed Coucou because of his habit of sneaking up on people and scaring them by saying "Coucou!" Jealous and brutal, he forbad her visits to or from her family, and once received a two-year sentence for wife-beating. Henriette, from time to time, would sneak into the café when Coucou was away, and the two sisters would bemoan the burdens of life. Félicie took to drink too, and one day was hauled off from the café to an asylum, a scene which Simenon remembered well since it was somehow considered appropriate that he be present for the ceremony. For some time throughout his childhood he had recurring anxieties that the same thing was going to happen to his mother. Félicie, three days later, died of delirium tremens.

Anna (or perhaps Maria; Louise in *Pedigree*), the eldest of the Brüll sisters, was still lower on the economic scale, but slightly higher on the emotional. She had married an amiable, deaf, old widowed weaver named Lunel Croissant, and ran a canal shop on the commercial wharves. (Canal-shop settings occur frequently in Simenon's fiction.) There was a period in Georges's childhood when visits to Aunt Anna's shop were de rigueur every Sunday, during which her daughter Lina regularly played the piano and sang "Au temps des cerises" for them. Georges fidgeted on the chair where he was forced to sit until Uncle Lunel woke up; but the smell of Norwegian tar, spices, and "genièvre" left pleasant memories. Sensory joys, in Simenon's life and fiction, were often a kind of redemption from otherwise disagreeable circumstances.

As to maternal uncles, the only one who played a significant role in Simenon's consciousness was Léopold, who was the black sheep of the family, a total dropout. "J'avais un oncle clochard," Simenon wrote—"I had a hobo uncle." The "clochard" became a recurring character in Simenon's fiction in a variety of incarnations. Léopold was a genuine eccentric. He seems to have attended university, did a stint in the army, and married the canteen-keeper. Afterward, he worked at various odd jobs, travelled abroad a bit, then declined into alcoholism and listless eccentricity, with, it seems, occasional forays into vaguely political anarchism. He had disappeared for years when Henriette, on an evening walk with the family, discovered him urinating against a wall. He became a regular, if secretive, visitor at the apartment. Once he appeared with a little painting he had made of the "dyjkmaster" house where Henriette was born. Later he dropped out of sight again, and died of cancer, survived only by a few weeks by his faithful wife, Eugénie, who was found starved to death. "C'était le type le plus sympathique de la famille," Simenon asserted: "The most likeable guy in the family."

Léopold was the eldest of the 13 Brüll children, Henriette the youngest. She was born in 1880 and her early life remains obscure. For a time as an adolescent she lived with the Vermeirens, who treated her like a servant, and where she had to resist the lewd advances of the wholesale grocer. At 16, pretending to be 19, she became a salesgirl in the lingerie department of *L'Innovation*. It was there that Valérie became her best friend, and "Le Grand Désiré" made his approach to her. Simenon envisioned her, in those days, as "un oiseau pour le chat " (a bird for the cat), a Belgian expression for frailty surrounded by danger, which occurs frequently in Simenon's work and was used by his second wife, in reference to herself vis-à-vis Simenon, as the title of her book.

Henriette feared the degenerate streak in her family, and she feared insecurity. She put up a fight against both with a tense determination—perhaps a stubbornness—that was another of her characteristics. The effort sometimes led to momentary fits of hysteria (hence Georges's anxiety that she might be carted off like Aunt Félicie), which Désiré would handle with his native serenity. During one of these outbursts she knocked Georges down and stomped up and down on him.

She worried about everything: about Désiré doing the housework immediately after the birth of Georges, about the baby carriage that the people downstairs complained of, about liquor (she kept none in the house), about impressing some people and avoiding others. Once, when a friend who had just bought an automobile took Désiré for a ride, Henriette had the two boys on their knees praying for his safety. She felt out of place in the Simenon clan, but the Brülls—disparate, neurotic, and busy with their own worries about status—were not a feasible alternative. Her dream was of being well established in the lower bourgeoisie—owning a little shop, for example—and, fired with visions of herself behind the counter of a prosperous patisserie, hoped Georges would become a pastry cook. Terrified of penury in old age, she saved money centime by centime, which she kept in a soup tureen and deposited once a month in a savings account.

She complained a lot: complaint was the subject of the talk with her sisters and friends:

> She always complained. On my mother's side I always heard the women complain when they got together—my mother and her sisters.
> I used to call that tear parties. They wept. They loved to weep.

She complained about having to make do with what she kept calling "le strict nécessaire." But she was also proud of it, for she was a proud woman. She had her little vanities, like insisting that Désiré be referred to as an "accountant," not an "employee," and her little snobberies. In *Pedigree* Simenon effectively, and maliciously, dramatized imaginary inner conversations he envisioned her having with neighbors. She supposes the rich Mme. Lorisse, observing her from her balcony, to be saying, "How tired she must be! How proud and courageous she is! We must show our good will, smile at her son who has such thin legs," while Elise (i.e., Henriette) says to herself:

> "You have understood me. I do all I can, even though I have available to me only 'le strict nécessaire.' You are the richest people on the block, and yet you make signs to me from your balcony. The proof that I am not ungrateful and that I am well educated is that I pet your dog, who frightens me so much every time he comes close to Roger [i.e., Georges] and who, with his habit of licking faces, could give him worms. Thank you, thank you very much. Do believe that I appreciate."

She was proud in various other ways throughout her life. She received money periodically from her now rich and famous son, but kept it all and returned it all to him. Then there was the corset affair. When Mme. Simenon came to visit her son and his second wife, Denise, in Connecticut, Denise discovered that the old lady had only a threadworn old corset. She bought her a new one and threw the old one in the garbage. During the night, Mme. Simenon *mère* made her way to the garbage bins and retrieved the old corset.

Some time after Désiré's death, Henriette married a man surnamed André, and for a while took to signing herself "Mme. André Simenon." (In *La Folle de Maigret* the widowed Mme. Antoine adopts her first husband's name in the same way, here out of pride in her first husband.) The marriage turned sour after a few years and Simenon felt that she developed a much warmer relationship with an enormous parrot his brother Christian had brought her from the Congo than with her husband. Eventually the couple refused to speak to each other and communicated only by writing little notes. André died first. Henriette died in 1970 at the age of 91.

Simenon was at her bedside when she died, and three and a half years later wrote a letter to her: *Lettre à ma mère*. But that was only the latest, and most compact, form of a monologue about his mother that probably began not long after his first words and continues to this day. He has said that Balzac once defined a novelist as "a man who doesn't like his mother." If the attribution is correct, it only partially suits Balzac, but it suits Simenon totally. If one placed all his remarks about his mother end to end they would add up to a tremendous, endless harangue. The "Letter" is in the second person, but he was already addressing her in the second person as far back as *Je me souviens*. The "Letter" is often interpreted as his coming to terms with his mother, but is only a slightly attenuated mode of the lifelong harangue. He felt her to be pretentious, snobbish, prejudiced, sentimental, self-pitying, disloyal, shallow, whiny; weak where it mattered, but headstrong and domineering where it didn't; emotionally unstable but insensitive to others' emotions. What he admired most about her was an abstraction: that she came from the "little people" — the *petites gens* that became such an integral part of his personal myths and of his fictional world.

What was *her* attitude toward him? Evidently little warmth (but no less than that given by Simenon's father). A great deal of complaining to him as a child, often in the form of a sort of blackmail: you're acting so badly, and here I am with my organ problems; if you go on like this I'll go straight to the hospital (she evidently did have gynecological problems). Her stance toward him as an adolescent was more complaining, and despair that he would ever amount to anything. When he became an adult, her attitude was predominantly one of suspicion: she never seems to have been quite sure just what it was he did for a living, and, when she visited one of his mansions, would ask the servants if "all this" was really paid for. She once said that he was very proud, but, "you see, it was a misdirected pride." He always felt she favored his younger brother, Christian, and seems to be right if his evidence is correct. He was always being blamed when his little brother cried: "What did you do to him *now*?" Worse, when Christian died in his early forties, after a career as a colonial functionary in the Congo and a collaborator during the war, she told Georges, "What a pity it was *Christian* who died." The story of two brothers, one getting the better of the other, recurs in Simenon's fiction — *Pietr-le-Letton, Le Fond de la bouteille, Malempin* — perhaps a transposed reflection of Henriette's favoritism. He wonders whether she ever once held him on her lap, and claims that she always looked at him like "a hen who sees a duck hatching among her eggs." Simenon felt repeatedly betrayed by her — for selling the mahogany table on which he wrote his first novel, for example, and by her remarriage and her desire to be buried in "Père André's" vault rather than with Désiré. Yet he had moments of tenderness toward her, when he saw her as the frail, oppressed little five-year-old making her way in a hostile world: "l'oiseau pour le chat." She always wanted a singing canary, and when she finally got one, it was a female, which doesn't sing (another motif that recurs in Simenon, as in *Maigret et l'homme du banc*). In retrospect she looks like a strong woman, and Simenon occasionally acknowledges that side of her. Yet at any given point, what he usually described, particularly in scenes of the early days, was a weak woman.

Simenon's multifaceted sense of having been failed by his mother colored his relationship with women all his life and his depiction of them in his fiction. If his abnormally strong libido sent him on a frenzied search for satisfaction, his maternal experience led him also to expect disappointment, and to get it, until, one day, he found himself a substitute mother, who turned out to be the perfect woman. Disgruntled by his mother, he turned to his father, but Désiré was self-effacing and died young, bequeathing to Georges more of an idealized image than an actively useful model. Simenon emerged with an ideal vision of domestic harmony, ever frustrated: a myth of family and antifamily that pervades his serious fiction.

III

T H E C H I L D
1 9 0 3 - 1 9 1 4

Georges Simenon, then, was born on February 13, 1903, on the rue
Léopold. In August of that year, Henriette and Désiré moved to a two-room
apartment at 3, rue Pasteur, across the Meuse, where Christian was born
in 1906, and where Georges's first conscious memories come from. He had
a reputation for being a weak child. When Grandmother Simenon found
him ugly as a newborn infant, she added that he looked "green," and the
Simenon clan accused Henriette of having "weak milk," which led him, on
the advice of Dr. Van Donck, to be put on the "Soxlet" formula. Though
he continued to look "green," and to vomit a lot, he became healthy at some
point and remained so most of his life. The only childhood infirmity that
stayed with him was sleepwalking, which, he has speculated, is related to
creativity.

He has claimed that the first words he heard were "money, money,
money," but that is presumably more antimaternal hyperbole. He also
thinks one of the first words he heard was "caca," as in, "Get your hands off
that, it's caca." In both cases, these words betoken attitudes to rebel against:
financial pettiness, forbidden things.

> The floor was of white wood, and my mother scrubbed it with sand
> once a week, every Saturday . . . Also of white wood were the mas-
> sive kitchen chairs . . . I used to overturn one, using the back as
> shafts. I would push it, not without some effort, across the room,
> shouting, "Potatoes, twenty-five centimes a kilo! Antwerp mussels,

fifty centimes a liter." I see all this in a room bathed in sunshine. Liège certainly has plenty of rainy days, but, God only knows why, my memories are almost always sunny.

The toddling market hawker initiates a lifelong love of markets which often made its way into Simenon's fiction — always on the rare "sunny" side of his fiction — and reaches its literary apogee in *Le Petit Saint*. Marketing was one of the few areas in which he expressed gratitude to his mother "for having taken me with her to market since I was three years old," only to withdraw the gratitude later in an implicit contrast between Henriette's mercenary concerns and the child's (or the remembering adult's) appreciation of the market spectacle:

> Henriette doesn't come here because it's the loveliest spectacle in the world, in the still discreet, early morning symphony of blue and gold. She doesn't sniff the smell of moist greens; . . . even the fruit market, a veritable riot of odors and colors — strawberries, cherries, plums and nectarines — all that translates for her into centimes: centimes saved, centimes lost . . .

Simenon as a child had an unusually active sensory apparatus, and a sensory memory which served him well in creating the celebrated "atmospheres" of his fictions, and which remained very active throughout his life. In the "Dictées" of his old age, images from childhood constantly and unexpectedly welled up from his deep memory and were duly recorded on the cassette:

> Houses, in those days, had each its own smell, largely according to what was being cooked in the kitchen . . . I knew, as soon as I walked into the hallway, what we would be eating, for there was the smell of mussels (which I particularly relished), of red cabbage, turnips, the Sunday roast garnished with cloves, etc.

Christmas (Saint-Nicolas) brought two particular odors: the living room, with *pain d'épice* and oranges; and the kitchen, with the smell of oilcloth on the table and soup simmering on the stove. These were winter smells. There were summer smells of manure and of hay under the summer sun during countryside outings, the warm feel of the wheat, the sight of red poppies and young girls (cousins) in floppy straw hats and long dresses, the sound of birds, and, at a distance, the crackling of the weekly amateur sharpshooting match. Indoors, when it rained, he could spend hours watching "the unpredictable zigzags of the water drops on the window panes." One side of his childhood personality was clearly contemplative:

"Why don't you go play?"

"I *am* playing."

He *isn't* playing. He is contemplating that marvelous mist of golden dust [as his mother is beating mattresses] that rises from the room and is slowly, irresistibly, absorbed by the moist air of the street.

When Simenon was four years old, the family moved again to a house on rue de la Loi, which Simenon later evaluated as one of the ugliest places he ever lived in, with pretentious assembly-line pseudoantiques and dreadful wallpaper "with those eternal, gradually fading roses, those garlands, or else those more or less pastoral images." On a typical summer evening Georges and Christian would be sent to bed at eight while their parents sat in front of the house to chat with neighbors as the sun set. Henriette peeled potatoes or mended socks, and Désiré was jolly and playful. Whenever there was a ripple of laughter, Georges knew that his father had said something funny. He envied grownups who could sit on the sidewalk, chatting, telling stories and laughing; "Such were the joys of those times, the joys of the little people who went to the theater once a year and to town only for shopping."

This idyllic side was not predominant. Disagreeable scenes with his mother and rebellious hostility toward relatives were more common. Preparations for Sunday outings, with Henriette increasingly flustered and working up to hysteria, were typical. Hypersensitive, Henriette accused Désiré and all the Simenons of lack of feeling. His failure to bring a present home from a trip other than a champagne cork, for example, would cause "a paroxysm of indignation, of pain . . . which Désiré will bear as his burden, heavier each year, till his death bed." Désiré's serenity contrasted with Henriette's anxiety. When a general strike broke out in 1913 and Désiré's national guard unit was called out, she expected a cataclysm, an invasion, a flood, while he came back with jaunty accounts of urinating against Bellanger's store front: "We all went at it, one after another." Henriette's fear of the general strike was related to that snobbish attitude toward the working class with which Simenon reproached her so ferociously. He was always being told things like, "Don't put your fingers in your nose . . . like a brat from the community school."

Georges's relations with his brother, Christian, who was born at the rue Pasteur in 1906, were not warm. (In *Pedigree* there is no brother.) He discovered that Christian talked in his sleep and, if questioned softly, would divulge all sorts of little secrets. At Christmas Christian would hoard his presents "like a suspicious young puppy." The only memorable episode occurred when they were ricocheting stones on the river, and Christian fell in. Georges jumped in and, with some difficulty, brought him back to shore, thus earning his first and only medal for heroism (which he soon discovered to be of false bronze). The only reason he tells this story (on several occasions) is that he was forced by the school director to alter his account so as not to make it appear that they were loitering "like little hoodlums from the free school.... And I received my medal for that, for a false story. That's why, since then, I have never believed in decorations." Christian never meant much to Georges at any time, though relations with Christian in later life were not quite as bad as Georges made them out to be. It has recently been revealed that Christian was a collaborator during World War II and appealed to his brother for help at the end of the war, who arranged for him to escape into the Foreign Legion, where he died in Indochina.

As for other children of his age from the preadolescent period, there was Albert, with whom he played marbles, and whom he admired and envied because he was handsomer, richer, and more charismatic than the others. He admired him even more because of his mother, who was what was known in those days as a kept woman ("une femme entretenue"), and whose image remained in Simenon's consciousness as that of one of "the most attractive, the most truly feminine women" that he has ever known. Other than Albert, Léon Thoorens of Liège, in his little book on Simenon, says that he knows a certain "André" who remembers that Simenon used to beat him up and, Thoorens adds cryptically, that it was because of this André that Georges probably had his first contact with the police.

There is the boy called Armand in *Pedigree*, who was memorable, maybe enviable, because he had a father who had killed his mother; and the one called Ledoux who tried to illuminate Roger-Georges on copulation by thrusting the index of one hand into a thumb-index circle of the other. This demonstration merely puzzled Georges, but the idea of parental sex caused him discomfort — "un malaise indéfinissable" — when he used to go kiss his parents in the morning and smelled "l'odeur du sexe." Perhaps his first sexual experience was in bed with his brother one night, when he became aware that his penis was rubbing against Christian's thigh, and Christian grabbed it for a few seconds. He was impressed, if perplexed, by the antisexual fulminations of the brothers at school, especially the ones that condemned "evil thoughts."

The early hostility and rebelliousness against his mother extended often to other relatives:

> When I was a child, I was against ... grownups ... I ... hated my aunts and uncles. They were imposed on me. I felt no bond between them and me, and I bristled at their condescendence, their artificial gestures of affection.

The afternoon gatherings of uncles and aunts, pressed together in somebody's kitchen or dining room, made him claustrophobic. Then there was the episode of Uncle Guillaume, who had brought him a splendid red outfit from Brussels and was profoundly thanked. But as soon as he had left, Henriette broke out in lamentation. Georges's patron was the Virgin Mary, whose color is blue: for him to wear red would be sacrilegious. Not only that, but meanwhile he had peed in the red pants. Could the stain be washed out? Could they exchange the suit at *L'Innovation?*

Such were life's little tragedies.

The move from the rue Pasteur apartment to the house on rue de la Loi in 1907 was a victory for Henriette Simenon. Désiré was content with the way things were and kept saying, "What more do we need?" But for Henriette, a two-story house with boarders signified a rung or two up the social ladder.

This was the beginning of the boarder period. Reading Simenon's autobiographical works, one tends to assume that the boarders arrived when he was older, but he was four years old when the house was invaded. "Invaded" is the correct word: the title of the second volume of *Pedigree — La Maison envahie —* bristles with a sense of resented intrusion. He recurringly evokes images of Désiré displaced, dispossessed of his space and his privacy; of himself and his brother constantly sent out on the street "so you don't disturb Mlle. Pauline."

The first lodger, however, was not Pauline but Frida Stavitskaia, a surly, stiff, ascetic Russian medical student and radical, who, it seems, eventually became a Soviet commissar. At the beginning of her stay at the Simenons she would mostly lock herself in her room, reject all attempts at communication, and slam doors whenever she went in or out. She lived on a pittance and Henriette, taking pity on her, ventured to offer her a bowl of soup, and to put some flowers in her room, which resulted only in the following exchange:

"What's *that?*"

"I thought that maybe a bit of hot soup . . ."

"Did I ask you for anything?" . . .

"I took the liberty — to cheer up your room — of putting a few flowers . . ."

"I detest flowers."

This charming girl once locked herself up for several days and nights. The family doctor, summoned by the alarmed Henriette, reassured her by explaining that the lodger was a hysteric.

Pauline Feinstein arrived a little later: a Polish-Jewish student of mathematics from a well-to-do family in Warsaw. She had the best room, received frequent packages of Eastern European goodies, did a lot of studying at home, where she would appropriate the best space and stick her fingers in her ears to concentrate. About the same time a certain M. Saft took a third room. M. Saft was also Polish but not Jewish; when Henriette introduced him to Frida Stavitskaia, expecting that Poles and Russians were more or less the same thing, she was dismayed to find them staring at

The Child

each other with savage ethnic hatred. Since M. Saft was as antisemitic as he was anti-Russian, Henriette was even more confused, and the household bristled with tensions.

In subsequent years, boarders came and went. A flighty and flirtatious Mlle. Lola inherited Mlle. Pauline's room and was the object of a good deal of teasing, by Désiré among others. Among the others was a Belgian medical student who is called M. Bernard in *Pedigree*, who used to chase the giggling Lola up and down the stairs and into her bedroom, and once put a skeleton borrowed from medical school in her bed. He seems to have been less enthusiastic about his studies than about Lola, and Henriette had instructions from his parents that he was to be locked up in his room to keep him at his books. It is partly to this "M. Bernard" that we owe Simenon's decision not to continue *Pedigree*, for in the original edition he appeared under his real name and took offense at the way he was depicted — particularly at the allegation that he never made it through medical school and became a dentist instead.

It appears that Simenon was mistaken, and that "Bernard" *did* manage to get through medical school. He sued Simenon and Marcel Baufays — the publisher of a Belgian magazine where parts of *Pedigree* were serialized — for 100,000 francs. On appeal he got 6000. (The proceedings may be found in the judiciary archives of Liège: November 13, 1950, for the first trial; May 5, 1952, for the appeal and final judgment. The disagreeable dentist with medical pretentions in *Maigret se défend* is probably another swipe at "M. Bernard.")

The boarders period (other boarders came and went) was important because it was partly from it that Simenon derived his fictional concern with alienation — with people struggling, and often lost, in an alien environment. The East European students in particular provided him with recurring character types in whose social and, even more, psychological situation he took special interest. In both life and fiction these character types are frequently Eastern European but blend in with similar types from anywhere (Uncle Léopold is one of them). The range of Simenon's attitude toward them is wide: from caricatural ridicule, to condescending disdain, to condescending sympathy, to compassion, and almost to heroicized idealization.

In this connection, Chapter 15 of *Je me souviens* is quite remarkable. After two pages of superb descriptive writing about the child's return from school to home, "home" dissolves rapidly into "boarders." They are viewed at first in the satiric tone with which they had been introduced earlier:

> Possessed of a haughty, condescending niceness, Pauline Feinstein, who has the best room, is the richest.
> ... Frida Stavitskaia has become almost domesticated. For that to

happen, threats were needed: "Look, Mlle. Frida, you can't go on eating in your room. There are bread crumbs everywhere. It's not clean."

The Russian-Polish fiasco is described:

M. Saft bristled like a cat stroked in the wrong direction, and he nearly left the house. Henriette had to run after him in the corridor. Explanations had to be made.

But then the tone changes to compassion:

M. Saft is poor. His mother lives on a meager pension in a two-room flat in Crakow . . . Frida is poor too. Her father is a school teacher in a village of tiny wooden houses.

And even Pauline Feinstein, excluded from the compassion earlier because she is too rich, is admitted a few pages later because of "the narrow little store, lit by smoky oil lamps, where her father and mother earned their little fortune by selling ready-to-wear garments." The tone has changed to epic — the epic of the *petites gens* struggling — in a manner which in America became proverbial — to provide a better life for their children. Furthermore, the epic of the little people, in this chapter, turns out to include Simenon's mother, and her sister Anna of the canal shop — both exactly like the struggling Eastern European students:

Aunt Anna hungers for dignity and sacrifices, immolates herself every day, smiling to her drunken clients . . . Henriette is tormented by an acute need for security. She has known poverty only too well with her mother, when there was nothing in the pot but water.

Frida has seen her father humiliated, harassed by the Czar's officials, despised by the Kulaks . . . M. Saft works for the liberation of Poland . . . All hunger for betterment, all have intimations of a different life . . .

Unexpectedly associated with this sense of struggle is a brief but energetic description of political agitation — the sweating, grimy steelworkers, who sometimes stage a protest demonstration broken up by the police and the Civil Guards — the very Civil Guards that Désiré told funny anecdotes about when they were called out to quell civil disorder. For here it is against Désiré's "inertia" that Henriette has had to "to struggle for years in order to get her boarders" — which is to say the boarders who, on the one hand, provide her with a supplement to a meager income, and, on the other, with whom she finds herself associated, in a kind of collective unconscious of the "petites gens," in the struggle for a better life. There has occurred a momentary rectification of values that has much to do with the Simenon myth of the little people.

In real life, at least two of the Eastern European boarders were very successful: Frida became a commissar and Pauline a student of Albert

Einstein. Yet, in the fictions, the little people, with rare exceptions, are failures and outcasts, despairing and miserable. Throughout his career, Simenon maintained a double-tracked view of the little people: an enthusiastic view of their heroic and colorful attributes, proclaimed in interviews and autobiographical works, and a more condescending, if compassionate, view of their misery and, often, sterility, incarnate in his fiction. Perhaps his mother's snobbisms had something to do with his complex perspective.

Simenon's formal education began at Soeur Adonie's "pouponnière," a nursery school run by an "enormous nun who smelled like vanilla and had the most reassuring of smiles," where, precociously, he learned to read and write. He attended primary school at the Institut Saint-André, directly across from his house, run by the Petits Frères des Écoles Chrétiennes. Credits from Soeur Adonie were not transferable, and he was forced, tediously, to learn his letters one by one all over again. Throughout primary school he was always at the top of his class in all subjects, except for one year when he was beaten out by a certain Van Hamme, "who spends his life studying, his head on his hands, and who has never been seen to play." Van Hamme became a civil servant and a good family man, and died prematurely.

Georges graduated from the Institut Saint-André in 1914 with a 293.5/315 average. Not only was he first in class, but also teacher's pet ("le chouchou des Frères"), the one who had the key to the water tap in the courtyard, who got to ring the bell for the eight-thirty prayer, etc. He always remembered with particular pleasure the school vegetable garden where, at recess, the youngsters, bare knees in the fresh earth, helped weed; and at Épalinges, the palatial home he built in 1964, he reproduced the garden of the Petits Frères. Yet in the Institut Saint-André was concentrated an unusually high proportion of chicanery, prejudice, hypocrisy and silliness. Some of the friars indulged a penchant for little boys (an account of which was left out of *Pedigree* under threat of further lawsuits). In the wake of labor unrest, the school organized reactionary skits in support of the newly formed Christian-Democratic Party, in which Simenon later was not proud to have been cast in a starring role as drum-major of a paramilitary force, who, from a ladder, declaimed an aggressive call to crush the labor movement.

He was also a choirboy at the Hôpital des Bavière, where he received fifty centimes for officiating at absolutions for the dead. On a good day there might be two or three in a row: he wished these old folks no harm, but fifty centimes was fifty centimes. He would get up at five-thirty in the morning and either tiptoe past his parents' bedroom or go in to kiss them goodbye (Simenon contradicts himself—possibly a contradiction of psychoanalytic interest since it might have to do with parental sex; see page 21 above. The corresponding episode in *Pedigree* has him waking up his mother, but there is no mention of sex.) The hospital was not far from home, and in the winter darkness he was afraid and would make a dash for it down the middle of the street — a memory he used with great effectiveness in one of the Maigret short stories, "Le Témoignage de l'enfant de choeur."

In the summer, the early rising for choir duty was a source of joy rather than fear — vibrant exultation in the bright morning sun. Simenon was an early riser all his life and always felt the need "to throw myself into life" as soon as possible after awakening. He often used to go for a quick morning swim in the Meuse before school, even in cold weather — with his grandfather, no less. This Simenon zestfulness accounts perhaps for his tendency to remember Liège scenes as bathed in sunlight, even though much of the time there must have been no sun ("Liège est une ville pluvieuse"). Darkness is repressed, to emerge, on a different memory track, in fiction.

Especially memorable in this vein were summers at Embourg, just past the edge of the city, where Henriette and her two sons went for summer outings, and the boys were left for longer periods. As regards sunniness, the difference between the Embourg described in *Pedigree* and the Embourg evoked in the memoirs of the seventies is astonishing. The Embourg of *Pedigree* is mostly about his mother, and mostly about what a snob, nuisance, and fuss-budget she was at Embourg. In the other Embourg "it was warm. Everything smelled good. Everything was innocent. *Tout était joie de vivre.*"

Nor was Henriette absent from this Embourg, but blended into the idyllic setting: "While my mother, who still wore her hair in a bun, sewed or knitted, my brother and I constructed dams in the brook." The favorite outing was to a spot known as "Les Quatre Sapins," where there were two pine trees, and where the earth, "warmed by the sunshine, had an odor quite different from any I have ever known, especially when it blended with the odors of the pine needles." It is a pleasant coincidence that "Les Quatre Sapins" is the exact spot where now stands the house of Professor Maurice Piron, emeritus of the University of Liège and director of the Simenon archives at the University Library.

As for his cultural and intellectual life, Georges had a brief bout with violin lessons, but quit because his teacher forced his fingers against the strings so hard that they ached, and, besides, had bad breath. He preferred painting, and his favorite and recurring Christmas present was a paint set. He often expressed regrets that his talent lay in the verbal rather than the visual arts, for he would have preferred more palpable, less intellectual materials, and, like his father, had an obsession with the tangible tools of his craft: well arranged and sharpened pencils, paper in the right spot, typewriter checked for mechanical problems, etc.

The Child

More important than either music or art for the future writer of 392 novels were his reading habits. One of the things he did with the fifty centimes earned at absolutions was to buy a weekly called *Le Petit Illustré*—not exactly a comic book, but stories for children or childish adults with lots of pictures. The only story he identifies was a serial called "Onésime Pourceau, sportsman." He read Jules Verne and the Comtesse de Ségur, and, on a higher level, was exceptionally fond of a book called *Voyage autour de ma chambre* by Xavier de Maistre, though it is not clear at what age he was reading this. It is a rather mannered series of reflections on nature, man, life and the like, purportedly by a young count as he is lying in bed, with a recurring allegory of the soul and "l'autre" (i.e., the body), and how the soul goes off on its own projects, leaving the body doing weird things.

Essentially, *Voyage* is a glorification of "the imagination," reflecting a late eighteenth-century sensibility—a sort of very genteel and jejune Laurence Sterne. Its importance in relation to Simenon is that it is "fine writing" and probably gave him a sense of the possibilities of verbal expression, of style, and of the imagination; by the same token, it may be one of the sources of his subsequent lifelong allergy to "fine writing." Finally, a childhood interest in insects led him to read the books of the entomologist Jean Henri Fabre, and of his compatriot, Maeterlinck, on bees.

Simenon's childhood provided him with an enormous cast of characters that reemerged in various guises in his fiction. He used to say that he had written *Pedigree* to get rid of these so as to progress to other things. But that is not what happened. Whatever progress there was—before or after *Pedigree*—never left very far behind some aspect or other of the dramatis personae that strutted and fretted upon the stage of the child's consciousness.

In his childhood also lay the source of a divided self, between acceptance of his surroundings and rebellion against them, which recurred in various forms throughout much of his life and informed significant aspects of his fiction. It is the rebellious side that produced the predominant "dark" mood of his books, and is also related to the loneliness which he often felt in childhood and to which he once attributed the underlying theme of all his serious work. But the acceptance side *also* stayed with him throughout his life, which was not the life of a rebel, and played a role in his work. The dichotomy is particularly visible in the contrast between the content and the tone of *Je me souviens*: the content largely depicts conformity to his surroundings, while the tone is one of unremitting rejection of large areas of these same surroundings. Simenon was himself perfectly well aware of this division:

> When I was very young I already had a tendency toward what is today called protest ["contestation"] ... which created a few explosions

between me and my mother. But in fact they were of short duration, for I had understood that it was useless to utter certain truths (or what I took to be truths), and I kept my mouth shut.

He repeatedly expressed amazement at what a conformist he always had been, whereas in fact, as he saw it, he had an innately rebellious spirit. The question, of course, is: which is the "real" inner self, and which is the outward pretense? Which is the conformist and which the rebel? But then again, that's not the question, because both are real and "inner," both come from his childhood experience, and both make their way into his books.

IV

EARLY ADOLESCENCE
1914-1919

"J'ai attendu toute mon enfance le moment de m'échapper" (Throughout my childhood I waited for the moment to escape). Simenon's escape took many forms. The more definitive one came at the end of adolescence, when, like James Joyce finding Liffey worth leaving and heading for Paris, he left Liège for the same destination. Meanwhile, during adolescence, escape took the form, variously, of bohemianism, sexual adventurism, spurts of cynicism, getting drunk, and, of course, railing at his mother. At the same time, these rebellious tendencies continued to confront their opposites: conformity, social and economic ambition, and, in certain contexts, the Simenonian sense of health and vigor. Later, getting a job was both an act of rebellion and of conformity. During those adolescent turbulences, a multifaceted sense of literary vocation germinated.

The reference to Joyce is not haphazard. Simenon was as hostile, listless, and ambivalent toward his Liège as Joyce-Stephen, his Dublin.

Solitude, sometimes anguish. Yet should one go about avoiding solitude?

Life is elsewhere, he knows not yet where. He seeks it outside, and he will continue to seek it.

Like Stephen's (in *Ulysses*) refusing to be drowned by a clinging family, Simenon repeatedly sought to dissociate himself from mediocrity and hollowness. Fights with his mother proceeded unabated. He was often disoriented and dissatisfied, hanging around seedy billiard halls with the uninspiring friend called Stievens in *Pedigree*, or, for lack of money, lying awake in the dark all evening, "a prey to rancorous thoughts." Simmering with teenage listlessness, he took to wandering about the city, drinking, slumming, seeking sexual adventures, and feeling guilty.

His sexual development started early and proceeded rapidly, though his first love, at age 11, for a pale, blue-eyed girl who lived at the other end of the rue de la Loi, was platonic, secret and mystical. He felt for her the same ecstasy he felt for a statue of the Virgin Mary during a short-lived mystical period. He never addressed the girl, but would write "I" "Love" "You" on separate pieces of paper which he would drop on the sidewalk.

He lost his virginity, together with his mysticism, at Embourg in the summer of 1915, to an enticing 15-year-old who is called Renée in *Pedigree*. The affair started with a wheelbarrow, in which she had hurled herself backward, legs in the air, as he wheeled her about, and ended in the bushes around the "Quatre Sapins." He was mortified that fall to find her in the arms of a youth two years older than he, but he did not pine away long, and other girls followed, seemingly in geometrical increments. A good deal of adolescent sex was a matter of prowling about disreputable neighborhoods, getting drunk in dubious bars, picking up girls, assuaging desires — or not assuaging them — either way with, often, the same emotional hangover later. Movies, with embracing couples scattered about, became a source of sexual excitement. Silhouettes of lovers glimpsed in the night behind drawn curtains aroused envy and a painful sense of exclusion.

Prostitutes, early, became an important part of his sex life and remained so in subsequent decades. The first one cost him two marks (German currency was used during the occupation). He sold books to pay for prostitutes, and the gold watch from his father, which went to pay "a splendid black girl." Simenon quickly became a sex expert, and by the time he was 16 or 17 was explaining to a 25-year-old colleague the difference between clitoral and vaginal orgasms. Oddly enough, his confidante for some of his sexual activities was his Aunt Céline, who took a truly prurient interest in the details of his sex life, and uttered comments like, "But, Roger, you were only twelve and a half! It's not possible." She would express ironic pity for his mother, who was continuing to pray daily for his virginity; and she swore to keep his secrets, but betrayed him to his mother before she died.

As for alcohol, that issue too, inherited from the Brülls, came into Georges's personal life in his teens. It is a recurring subject in many of his works, and, in his life, it was, off and on, a problem. Around age 14 he tried out the grain alcohol Henriette used to seal her jam: he kept watering the alcohol until none was left, and everyone assumed it had somehow vaporized. Later, he specialized in English pale-ale at the Café de la Bourse and went on periodic binges with his friends, many connected with his search for sex and his slumming tendency.

Adolescence, however, was not all gloom and guilt and thoughtless sexuality. The description of the binge that closes chapter six of *Pedigree* is immediately followed by a sort of *aubade* that opens the next chapter, celebrating the Simenon "morning spirit," market and all. Walks through the city were not all lugubrious prowlings;

> When I had an hour free I went into one neighborhood or another and walked up the first street I encountered, quite like an explorer venturing into wilderness. There isn't a neighborhood in Liège that I don't know.

A "perfect day" in those days consisted of reading a book in a corner by himself, eating, and drinking coffee while smoking his pipe (he had started smoking a pipe at the same time he lost his virginity, and has never stopped). It was also in those days that he developed a passion for fishing which remained with him for much of his life, and which he passed on to Maigret.

Nineteen fourteen was the beginning, not only of the Great War, but, for Simenon, also of secondary school. For one year he attended the humanities-oriented Collège de Saint-Louis, where his mother got him in at half tuition, on the ground that he was headed for the priesthood. This wasn't altogether fraudulent, since he was in his mystical period and was considering a clerical career seriously, if briefly. (Elsewhere, however, Simenon has repeatedly said that he considered the priesthood because he took it to be a profession that would allow him plenty of leisure to write; and later considered a military career for the same reason.) He got high grades in French, poor grades in Flemish, and middling ones in everything else. He had lively discussions with his French teacher, Père Renchon, about Lamartine, Victor Hugo, and other French writers.

He also studied German, where, allowing his mind to wander, he would frequently be brought back to attentiveness by a request from the teacher such as, "conjugate the separable and the inseparable verbs." What actually interested Simenon about the German teacher was not his subject but his demeanor and character. Simenon discovered that he had a secret: he was poor, and furthermore he was ashamed of his poverty. This discovery came from close observation and led to further close observation — a process of some symptomatic significance as regards the future novelist. It's a sort of paradigm of an important aspect of Simenon's literary stance. All his life, he was acutely interested in people, and curiously uninterested in art. Separable and inseparable verbs may not rank high as art, but the pattern involved is a striking one. Not only that, but his German teacher turns out to be another of the archetypal "little people," and Simenon felt that the overt hostility between them masked a deep secret communion, each "furious at finding his own image reflected in the other." That German teacher had many incarnations in Simenon's novels (though rarely as a teacher).

After a year he transferred to the science-oriented Collège Saint-Servais, because that was the summer of his escapade with Renée, and she went to Saint-Servais. It is ironic, possibly unfortunate, that he lost not only the girl but the humanities as well. Who knows? He might have turned out a different kind of writer had he stayed at the Collège Saint-Louis. As it was, except for the diction prize for 1915–16, his record was undistinguished. He seems to have lost interest in school. Life, including intellectual life, was elsewhere.

World War I and the disruptions of occupation added to the turbulences endemic to adolescence, though it seems unlikely that he personally felt the degenerative effects of the war as intensely as he describes them in the autobiographical *Trois Crimes de mes amis*. The three principals are all real people, bearing their real names (except for "K"), though "friends" seems perversely hyperbolic. They are friends, perhaps, in the sense that he, like them, suffered moral damage, the point being that he survived it while they didn't. The three crimes are "K's" suicide by hanging after a sinister session of hypnotism and cocaine (the basis for *Le Pendu de Saint-Pholien*); Deblauwe's killing of his prostitute-mistress when she took up with another man; and Danse's murder of his mistress and his mother in France, followed by his return to Liège to murder an old priest, Père Roux. (Père Roux, incidentally, who was deaf, was at one time Georges's confessor.)

In spite of *Trois Crimes'* somewhat chaotic structure, its basic purpose is quite clear: to examine the underlying cause of these crimes, and of many other symptoms of moral decay, which is World War I and its demoralizing aftermath. The most vivid parts of the book are the vignettes of the cheating, brutality, profiteering, and selfishness that infected everybody — even Désiré, who would grab an extra hard-boiled egg on his way to work. Henriette took in German officers as boarders, over Désiré's objections, insisting they were well-bred gentlemen. Young Georges himself was not above his own kind of trafficking: mixing industrial alcohol with a variety of dubious syrups which he and his cousin Gaston sold as "Chartreuse," "Benedictine," etc.

It was in the last year of the war that Désiré's heart condition was diagnosed and Georges that very day quit school and set out to make a living. He briefly yielded to his mother's ideal and became an apprentice pastry-cook, but couldn't stand all that flour. He lasted a bit longer as a bookstore clerk, where he tried to be a model of deference and propriety, but still got into trouble because the owner resented his superior knowledge of books and fired him.

Meanwhile, his writing vocation was incubating. His first art was painting, nourished by increasingly sophisticated paint sets at Christmas, and leading, by the time he was 12, to an abundant production of idealized landscapes associated with his mystical Virgin Mary period. He gave up painting and mysticism (as well as a humanist education) after making love for the first time. Was Georges Simenon sublimating his artistic impulses into sex? Did he continue to do that? Years later, when he was writing those 11-chapter best-sellers, he would often recuperate from the 11-day ordeal by having a fling with prostitutes. Sex instead of a second draft? In any event, it was around this time that the idea of "becoming a writer" germinated. He must have been encouraged in writing—or encouraged himself—in a way that he was not in painting, though his own evaluation of his early writing was no higher than of his painting.

In a 1963 television interview he was asked "When did you establish the firm intention of becoming a writer? Did it come from your own reading?" He answered, "Yes, certainly. I would not have had the idea of writing..."—which remains an unfinished sentence and is followed by a remarkable, meandering explanation:

> I think that the need to write came to me the day I felt myself at once belonging to my milieu and outside of it, against it ... Around twelve, twelve and a half, I suddenly realized that those people—I mean my relatives, my uncles, my aunts, all that—were victims, and I said to myself: *No, I do not want to be a victim too. I don't want to have their fate. I want to get out, to be outside.*

Thus, recognizing but skipping over the notion that the impulse to write books came in the first instance from reading them, he suggests that writing is a mode of simultaneously acknowledging and escaping one's environment. He concludes by adducing his notion of the "raccommodeur de destinées" (the mender of destinies) which he says here first entered his mind when he was 14. The idea is that unhappiness often comes from a slight psychological mistake, which, one thing leading to another, causes ultimate misery. The "raccommodeur" would either anticipate these mistakes, or somehow reverse destiny by bringing the subject back to the original mistake and giving him a chance to start over again on the right path.

Later, having become aware of psychoanalysis ("I did not read Freud until I was nineteen or twenty"), he acknowledged strong similarities between his "raccommodeur" and the analyst. His serious fictions are "mendings of destinies" in the sense that they trace back to its origin the woeful state of the protagonists. *In* the fiction, usually, nothing is mended, so that it would be the fiction itself that constitutes a mending. His own major autobiographical fiction, *Pedigree*, was, in a sense, the reverse of a mending of destiny; he himself saw it as the portrait of a young man who *should* have turned out badly. Somewhat later he had a much more concise explanation as to why he started writing:

> Writing was for me a sort of defiance of my mother. Whenever she saw me reading — I was reading at a very early age — she would say to me, "You'd be better off doing something than reading your trashy books." It was Dostoyevsky, Turgenev, Dickens . . .

It is difficult to tell what he read when: he started early and kept going. As regards "serious literature": Gogol, Chekhov, Dostoyevsky, Tolstoy, Turgenev, Conrad, Balzac, Dickens, Scott, Cooper, Dumas, Stendhal, Gorky, Pushkin, Chateaubriand, Flaubert, Maupassant, Hugo, Stevenson, Rabelais, Anatole France, Labiche, Augier, Mark Twain, Jerome K. Jerome. There were doubtless others. His very favorite, he has often asserted, was Gogol, and close after him, Dostoyevsky, Chekhov, and Conrad.

He acquired many books during his adolescence (when he was not selling them to pay for binges). He became interested in rare books when he was 14, and often acquired them from an ignorant bookseller by piling up a batch of books, including some current best-sellers, and offering, say, twenty francs. The shopkeeper, laughing, would say that the best-sellers alone were worth six francs apiece. Simenon, sighing, would put them aside and repeat the process a few times, offering twenty francs for the remaining old books and ending up with first editions of Balzac, Hugo, Stendhal, etc.

The majority of books that he read, however, were not bought but borrowed from the Liège library, where he was befriended and encouraged by the director, a gentle, kind, old Liégeois poet named Joseph Vrindts. Simenon has always expressed great gratitude to Vrindts, who discreetly but generously nourished the young man's sense of literary vocation, and facilitated his borrowing of books from the library. Vrindts had influenced him even before he knew him: as a child he would watch the poet strolling in the streets, with a wide-brimmed hat and a neckerchief flowing in the wind, and would say to himself, "What a wonderful thing to be a poet!"

For his part, Vrindts is reported to have said of the young Simenon, "Divins ses Crolés oûy's on léhève li malice," which in Walloon seems to mean something like "in his narrowed eyes one could read intelligence." Similarly, Simenon felt much affection and admiration for Théodore Gobert, an old archivist and historian of Liège, whose study, filled "with the smell of very old paper," seemed "an ideal universe" to him. The impulse to emulate men like Vrindts and Gobert, though soon abated, was not insignificant in the early formation of Simenon's literary vocation.

Simenon's reading was not all high literature. A downward move into popular literature was occasioned by his Aunt Céline, who had borrowed his high-class library books but didn't like them, and asked him to bring her books like *Chaste et flétrie* (Chaste and Abused). He dug up a lending library specializing in pulps, run by an illiterate woman he calls Mme. Pissier in *Pedigree*, who would identify books by their covers: "You mean the one with the vampire on the cover?" Before giving them to his aunt, Simenon would devour these books too. He seems also to have been familiar with the "Fantômas" series, and with nineteenth-century popular novelists a rung or two higher, like Paul de Kock and Alphonse Allais. As for detective stories, he has repeatedly claimed that he never read them, but did in fact absorb some French classics in his youth, like Gaston Leroux's Rouletabille series, and Maurice Leblanc's Arsène Lupin books. He also read medical textbooks, and, toward the end of the war, came across a number of bound volumes of the *Gazette des Tribunaux* — court records from the nineteenth century, where he discovered that many murders were of old men in rural areas, done in by relatives impatient for the inheritance.

As for writing, nothing has survived from before 1917, but there are signs that he was already "at work," in some measure, in his literary vocation. For instance, he was so good at French composition that his teachers exempted him from assigned topics and let him write anything he wanted. Significantly, he began signing his schoolwork "Georges Sim," the name with which he signed everything he wrote until 1930, except for what was signed with other pseudonyms. That "Georges Sim" gradually became his name in real life must be a sign of some complicated relationship between his life and his vocation. When he started signing "Georges Simenon," some people were confused. (As late as 1964 an Italian reviewer was explaining, "Georges Simenon, pseudonimo di Georges Sim.")

By around 1917 Simenon was writing poems, and probably "literary" prose pieces, in the unheated attic at rue de L'Enseignement, wrapped in a sort of bathrobe his mother had fashioned for him from an old red and yellow bedspread. Fragments of three poems survive, mostly in Simenon's bemused memory. One was a folksy, self-ridiculing portrait:

> Il était long,
> Il était maigre,
> Grands pieds, grand nez
> l'oeuil affamé
> Il était long
> Il était maigre
> Qu'il était ridicule, ô gué!
> (He was tall, he was thin, big feet, big nose, famished eye, he was tall he was thin, how ridiculous he was, hey ho!)

The "famished eye," perhaps, expresses his desire to devour life. In contrast, another poem expresses adolescent world-weariness: "Implacable, the days succeed each other, immutable always . . . and stupidly identical." The third, "Mélancolie du haut clocher," describes a church steeple looking down with envy upon the low houses surrounding it. In his own interpretation, he insisted that he identified himself not with the haughty steeple but with the lowly streets, "the dense crowd, the human warmth" — in short, the "little people." Yet it is in the very nature of the "little people" myth that he is both apart from them and close to them. Fascinated and sympathetic observation from outside, or from a height, is a recurring stance: in his frequent descriptions, for example, of travelling through Paris on bus platforms, relishing the bustling life around, or slightly "below." (Maigret is often in this situation.)

It was with this sort of literary baggage that Simenon was about to enter, almost simultaneously, the world of journalism and the world of bohemian artiness. These two worlds seem pitted against each other in his experience, while his soul somehow hovered lightly above both, committed to neither.

V

JOURNALIST AND BOHEMIAN
1 9 1 9 – 1 9 2 2

"I knew absolutely nothing about journalism," Simenon has asserted. He never read newspapers during his earlier adolescence. In those days, only the father in a family customarily read the paper, while the mother would cut out the serial at the bottom of the page. Nonetheless, in search of a job again in January of 1919, and somehow propelled by yet another line of the writing impulse, Simenon, as he was passing by the offices of the *Gazette de Liège* one day, ventured in, asked for a job as a reporter, and was hired on a whim by the editor-in-chief, Joseph Demarteau. Simenon did not realize that it was a reactionary, antisemitic, protofascistic paper, railing incessantly about Bolsheviks, anarchists and Jews — considered as more or less interchangeable categories. It was the kind of newspaper that in 1920 would report triumphantly from New York that jazz was dead once and for all because people now wanted "real music." Simenon, probably both naively and calculatingly, adopted, as far as his reportorial duties were concerned, the paper's ideological line without a murmur.

Starting out with the "chiens écrasés" (run-over dogs), a derogatory term for items of wholly local and minimal importance, he very quickly became an astonishingly successful 16-year-old reporter earning considerably more than his father, and stayed at the *Gazette* for three and a half years, living "one of the most exciting periods of my life." These *Gazette* days were full of sunniness and of a sense of youth and health. He thought of himself as a version of Leroux's very young reporter-detective, Rouletabille, and compared himself, to his satisfaction, with his editorial secretary, who had a perpetual cold and used to hang up his soaking handkerchiefs on a line strung across the office.

He quickly got off exclusively local assignments, and "Georges Sim" regularly appeared all over the paper. In addition to straight reporting, he did features, exposés, background articles, fiction, humor, and satire. He covered sports, visiting political figures and royalty, mining accidents, meetings of provincial and municipal councils, burglaries, murders, the Walloon regionalist movement, strikes (from the *Gazette*'s antilabor point of view), veterans' affairs, the cost of living, foreign affairs, the circus, gambling, architecture, literary criticism, painting, Jews, German inflation and Belgian profiteering, Bolshevism, scientific police methods, Braille workers, fishing, and the pollution of rivers.

One of his scoops was an interview with Marshal Foch, whose train was passing through Brussels on its way East. Demarteau instructed him to ask the Marshal if he would go to Warsaw. Without the slightest idea of the significance of the question, Simenon dashed to the capital, where a dozen reporters were unsuccessfully competing for an interview. As the train pulled out, the man from the *Gazette* jumped on the steps of the locked car. One of the aides-de-camp took pity on him as the train picked up speed and let him in. Foch granted him two minutes, and the young reporter managed to stammer, "Sir, will you go to Warsaw?" The Marshal hesitated an instant, then answered "Yes." Simenon got back to Liège, unhappy at the meager results of his first interview with an international celebrity, but Demarteau congratulated him and put out a special edition announcing that the Warsaw Pact was on.

He was soon writing his own feature column, "Hors du Poulailler" (Outside the Chickenhouse), short, satirical fictions, devolutions from the eighteenth-century "character" (the typical miser, the typical fop, etc.: the ultimate source of this sort of thing is Juvenal; in the case of Simenon, there must also be a bit of bargain-basement Gogol). A recurring structure — because of the rapidity with which it can get such a vignette under way — is the narrator meeting a long-lost friend, who tells him what's been happening. What's been happening, very often, are financial troubles and schemes for getting out of them, and these schemes in turn constitute satire or burlesque.

A typical piece has the narrator meeting a friend who bemoans the taxes that cut into his independent income and explains a money-making scheme for injecting artificial scents into artificial carnations (shades of the wartime liqueurs?). A variant is the portrait of the barber who sells an oral "Gazette capillaire," summaries of the news for his customers: four centimes for local news, eight for international, etc. In another, one of Simenon's early down-and-out figures (the "ratés"), having lost his lease on his apartment, decides the only place to go is jail. He accosts a man on the street and keeps repeating, "your money or your life," but the victim turns out to be deaf and dumb. There are vignettes of social life—for example, of a snobbish woman being stood up by an even more snobbish one in a watering town; and of domestic life, often in an antifeminist tradition that has become embarrassingly outmoded these days but has ancient roots in literary humor—in Rabelais, for example, whom Simenon knew well and who influenced much of his adolescent work.

The style of the "Poulailler" pieces tends to be arch and a bit pretentious: "Not long ago I was passing ＿＿ Street, when my retina was overwhelmingly ["magistralement"] impressed by a sky-blue façade..."; "If the fatty rotundities of the stomach in question stirred no memory within me, that was not the case of the countenance which topped it." This is definitely "fancy writing" of a kind that Simenon acquired very quickly, but later got rid of even more precipitously.

Some of his best writing for the *Gazette* was a delightful series on commercial fishing and river life—an early display of his talent for effective description and briskly dramatized settings.

On the other hand, a bad blotch on his journalistic career was a series on "The Jewish Peril" which he had the poor judgment to allow to be published over his signature. The stuff is mostly straight from the *Action française*, or equally disreputable sources. It has to do with Jews as agitators, revolutionaries, war profiteers, conspiratorial financiers, anarchists, and Bolsheviks. He plays cat-and-mouse with the virulently slanderous "Protocols of the Elders of Zion": even if they *are* forgeries, there may somehow be something to the ideas they express.

All one can say is that he was 17 years old, intellectually scatterbrained, willing to please by writing whatever he was told to write, and profoundly unconcerned with ideological questions. In primary school, Simenon had one Jewish classmate named Schoof, "gentle and shy," whom fellow students avoided on account of his smell, which had nothing to do with his Jewishness but with his family, which was in the salted fish business. He has claimed that "the antisemitism which prevailed in many countries, in particular in France, during and after the Dreyfus affair, was unknown to us kind." Yet there is no doubt that he came from a culture in which Jews were not customarily accepted and in which antisemitic attitudes rippled here and there.

The *Gazette* articles aside, Simenon himself occasionally manifested such ripples. One of his early satiric pieces includes a snide hint that Henri Duvernois, a once-popular French dramatist and short-story writer, is of Jewish origin. What is curious is that shortly afterward, or perhaps even then, Simenon admired Duvernois and felt intimidated by his talent. This is very early stuff. If one wants to press the matter one might point to occasional minor characters in his novels who are stock "Jewish types" — seedy old jewelry merchants emigrated from Poland and the like.

This issue, however, has already been raised, and Simenon has vehemently denied any antisemitic intentions in such portraits, adducing to his defense other works, like *Le Petit Homme d'Arkhangelsk*, in which Jews are treated with sympathy, understanding and admiration. The most reasonable conclusion is that Simenon (a) thoughtlessly wrote some antisemitic pieces in his youth; (b) retained unconsciously for a time some antisemitic vestiges from his culture, which cropped up marginally in his work; and (c) was rid of all such vestiges at some indeterminate point in his maturity. Perhaps the final word on Simenon and Jews is a sort of "imprimatur" by the American Zionist monthly, *Midstream*, in an article which, unaware of these long-past specks of antisemitism, praises his sensitive treatment of Jews and other outsiders.

To return to the *Gazette*: he made mistakes, then, of which this was the grossest. Others were in a lighter vein. Assigned to cover boring, unimportant meetings, he occasionally would fail to go and would manufacture a perfunctory report — until one day he reported the proceedings of a meeting that had been cancelled. Once, covering a banquet, some colleagues got him thoroughly drunk, and, for some reason, he stormed into the editor-in-chief's office, hurling a volley of insults. The next day, expecting to be fired and remembering nothing, he asked what he had said. Demarteau good-naturedly listed the insults and kept him on. Thus, the *Gazette de Liège* remained loyal to Georges Sim, and, for better or for worse, he to the *Gazette*.

Ever on the alert, he also sought out supplementary activities. Discovering that the French film trade publication, *La Cinématographie française*, lacked a Liège correspondent, he offered his services and briefly moonlighted for it. Toward the end of 1920 he became involved with the notorious Deblauwe of *Trois Crimes* in the scandal-blackmail sheet *La Nanesse*. *La Nanesse* really existed, as did Deblauwe, though the only information about Simenon's involvement is *Trois Crimes*. *La Nanesse* was full of little digs in the vein of "has anyone else observed that a well-known superior-court magistrate spends a great deal of time at the apartment of a certain lady on rue X?" The assumption was that said magistrate would then pay hush-money to prevent further revelations. What Simenon wrote were humoristic and satirical pieces of the kind he was writing for the *Gazette*. He used his experience with *La Nanesse* in a fictitious account of a similar journal, *La Cravache*, in *Les Quatre Jours du pauvre homme*, where he seems to know well the details of publishing a blackmail sheet, and also in *Maigret chez le ministre*.

Journalist and Bohemian

The *Gazette* engaged Simenon's conformist, success-oriented side—making it in the established social and economic environment—though he considered himself an "enfant terrible" on the staff and saw "a certain rebelliousness surfacing in my articles"—presumably the satirical thrust of some of the "Poulailler" pieces. His self-image is of a rebel hiding beneath a conformist, or an explosive, anarchic temperament which needs a particularly willful discipline to keep under control. When some interviewers visiting his mansion at Épalinges were struck by the orderliness of his set-up, he responded that, all his life, he needed a strong sense of order, security and solidity to counterbalance an equally strong tendency toward "letting go." The latter tendency was incarnated in the "clochard"—the carefree hobo ideal toward which he was repeatedly attracted. The former tendency was associated with such things as early rising, and with the numerous solid, well-organized dwellings he lived in—solid "afin de m'empêcher de 'foutre le camp'" (to keep me from getting the hell out).

In adolescence, the nonconformist side was reflected in his diffident association with the Liège art crowd, beginning not too long after the Armistice in the winter of 1919. Henri Moers, a fellow reporter on the *Meuse*, asked him if he would like to meet a group of artists. Simenon has tended to portray them mostly as wastrels, but they were *the* young art crowd of Liège—some more serious than others—and, knowing them well by reputation, he was most eager to accept Moers' invitation. Their leader was the twenty-year-old painter Lucien (Luc) Lafnet, "one of the most engaging persons I have ever known."

"I'll tell them you're a poet," Moers said as he shepherded Simenon to the attic room that was the group's meeting place. They had adopted the name "La Caque," a cask in which herring is tightly packed. Its emblem was a scorpion biting its tail. Most of them were students at the Académie des Beaux-Arts, with a contingent of miscellaneous aspiring writers, architects, poets and hangers-on. They met regularly, discussed philosophy, art and poetry, drank, got stoned, and played practical jokes. In his subsequent descriptions, Simenon's tone toward them is almost wholly contemptuous. He wrote a satiric portrait, circulated among them, called "Les Ridicules," which concludes, "The most ridiculous of them all is myself."

Whatever pride Simenon took in his allegedly rebellious temperament, he emphatically rejected the bohemian form of that rebelliousness. Especially in *Trois Crimes*, but elsewhere too, he is categorical in contrasting the morbidity of the bohemians with nature, health, ebullience and a vigorous society.

> To think that, for weeks on end, closeted in our "caque" and in our
> pretentious daydreams, we saw nothing of . . . the buds bursting forth
> on the trees of the square, nor those pretty girls in bright aprons,

with red or blue slippers, clutching their braided hair, running to the butcher on the corner!

The world of "Art" that invited young Simenon turned out to be, to him, totally uninviting: mere teenage frolicking which, taken too seriously, leads to morbidity and self-destruction. It seems probable that he made an existential choice of a life project in these days, and the choice was for success, achievement, worldliness. It may have been an accident that the particular path he followed was a literary one.

In a passage in *Pedigree* he alludes to the celebrated première of Victor Hugo's *Hernani*, whose romanticism shocked the conservative audiences of the eighteen-twenties. The avant-garde was vociferously present to defend its hero — most ostentatiously Théophile Gautier in his red vest. But it is not with him that Roger-Georges identified, but with Alexandre Dumas, who was also present, not as part of the flamboyant avant-garde in-crowd, but as a poor and obscure scribbler who had stood in line for his ticket: one of the "little people," in short — but who later became one of the wealthiest and most popular writers of his age.

Simenon, on the other hand, always denied worldly success as a motivation for his literary career. When he began to write he was convinced that, far from a profession, it was a vocation providing only personal satisfactions. Yet he has also declared, "I began to write, as an artisan, at the age of 16, always with the idea that some day I would achieve something." The "something" is serious literature as he knew it from his reading, while the artisanship is ambiguously a preparation for it and separate from it. The truth is that his literary intentions, consciously and unconsciously, were multiple, unclear to himself, and perhaps contradictory. Three categories — success, artisanship, and seriousness — jostled each other without fusing into a clear purpose; they never did.

His assertion that he did not think of literature as a viable profession was made in the context of discussing his first novel, *Au pont des Arches*, written when he was 16. It is a flimsy piece of humorous fiction in the vein of the humorous tidbits for the *Gazette*, introduced by an epigraph from *Gargantua* — the well-known remark that it is better to write of laughter than of tears because "le rire est le propre de l'homme." Thus his literary beginnings derive from his journalistic experience.

The story is a rambling account of young Paul Planquet's sexual initiation, abetted by his rich, sophisticated Uncle Timoléon from Brussels (Uncle Albert?), and Timoléon's subsequent help in saving the father from bankruptcy in his exotic scheme for mass-producing purgative pills for pigeons. The satiric thrust is against various kinds of pretentiousness: culinary, for example, in the opening scene of a catastrophic fancy dinner prepared for the rich uncle; or amatory, in Paul's flustered, inflated pride in having a mistress all his own. *Au pont des Arches* was published in 1921, subsidized by a woman who had taken a fancy to the young author.

The same fate would have awaited his second novel, *Jehan Pinaguet*, except that Joseph Demarteau, shocked at its bawdy, anticlerical episodes, told Simenon he would be fired if he published it, and Simenon opted for the *Gazette* rather than another stab at book publication. This was unfortunate, for *Jehan Pinaguet* is a better book than *Au pont des Arches*. Written also in 1921, it too is Rabelaisian, though with perhaps a touch of Gogol's Chichikov. It is an episodic, picaresque tale about an engaging young country bumpkin's adventures and education in the city. The writing is sometimes admirably vivid, as in the opening scene, describing the colorful hustle and bustle of an innyard, to which the delighted Jehan awakens:

> The cracking of the whips filled him with delight, and he could envision the heavy baskets groaning, piled high on the carts ... He looked down on the quai de la Goffe where the fruit baskets, the market women, and the carts jostled in a joyous chaos ...

There follows a lot of high jinks as Jehan tumbles down the inn stairs, tries to make out with one of the servants, and witnesses a rousing market squabble about an overturned fruit basket. He gets a job as a hack driver and delights at the sights and sounds of the lively, crowded streets which he can observe from his high perch: again, the enthusiastic Simenonian observer from on high. The part Demarteau disapproved of begins when Jehan accidentally knocks over a priest and helps him back to his presbytery. He gets a traffic ticket for this, which, incidentally, introduces us to Simenon's first police commissioner, a jolly type who settles the fruit-basket dispute somewhat in the manner of Sancho Panza in his judicial capacity (and, one notes, who smokes a pipe). Meanwhile, Jehan becomes friendly with the priest, a rousing *bon-vivant* in the lineage of Rabelais's Frère Jean, who drinks gin and praises sensuality.

Later the tone turns more serious as Jehan becomes a café waiter, participates in union organizing, and is moved to a positively Marxist feeling of compassion and solidarity: "An immense pity swelled up in him for that populace whose misery weighs more heavily since it has acquired a consciousness of its power and its right to happiness."

Such, with a fragmentary burlesque of detective fiction entitled "Le Bouton de col," was Simenon's adolescent production. His bent was for humor, and it was perhaps in reaction against it—the cultivation of an opposite self—that, for the most part, he so deliberately avoided humor in his serious work later. One should also add "Le Compotier tiède," published in 1922 in the *Revue sincère*, a small literary magazine to which he subsequently contributed several pieces from Paris. It is a somewhat sentimental but delicately written vignette of a young man contemplating a bowl of fruit stew, which becomes a symbol of the home where he is in danger of getting stuck, and which he is about to leave. Simenon has called this his "first truly literary text," and mused that, with it, he almost went the way of the little reviews—as if of a literary fate narrowly avoided.

If Simenon's bohemian connections had little to do with his literary career, they did lead, paradoxically perhaps, to his marriage. He had made the acquaintance of a young architect named Renchon, connected with the arty crowd of the Caque, who invited him and other members to a New Year's Eve party at his family home. Simenon's memory of exactly what happened is fuzzy since he started partying in the afternoon with his *Gazette* colleagues. By the time he was ready to switch from the journalism party to the art party he was quite drunk, managed his way up the stairs on all fours, and flopped into a chair, his head whirling. Out of synchronization, he became more sober as the others got drunker, and by four in the morning found himself quite lucid and deeply engaged in conversation with Renchon's sister, Régine, who was an art student at the Beaux-Arts.

The Renchon family made its contribution to Simenon's collection of Liège characters. The father was an orphan who had been left on the doorstep of the family which later became his in-laws. His father-in-law once patented a process for cleaning furnaces, and spent the rest of his life incubating his next invention, which never came: "Be quiet!" he would say, "I'm inventing." (Simenon used him as a model for a minor character in *La Folle de Maigret*.) The foundling married the inventor's daughter, and became a prosperous furniture dealer. He assigned professions to his children: the eldest an architect, the next a painter, and the third a musician. Thus Régine was sent to study painting at the Beaux-Arts.

Somehow, Simenon decided that Régine would make an appropriate wife: the "somehow" conveys the tone of his decision, at least as he viewed it many years later. He doesn't believe he was in love. She was three years older than he, and she was not pretty. Henriette, after meeting Régine, commented, "My God, she's ugly!"—perhaps some sort of oblique echo of her mother-in-law's comment on the newborn Georges. Simenon was attracted by her intelligence, knowledge, and lively conversation. She was a virgin, and he prided himself on the infinite care and patience with which he prepared her for sexual consummation.

Later, they became informally engaged, then more formally when M. Renchon came upon some compromising letters. He told Georges he would give him his daughter when he earned a thousand francs a month, and meanwhile forbade the young couple to see each other for a year—an injunction constantly circumvented. Simenon disliked her name and invented a new one, which she bears to this day: Tigy. He was more attracted to her 15-year-old sister, Tita, with whom he used to exchange glances of complicity; but she was too young, and it was Tigy-Régine that he became engaged to, playing, as he subsequently interpreted it, at being in love.

In 1921 Désiré Simenon died. Georges was on assignment in Antwerp and had passed the afternoon in bed with a beautiful girl — a distant cousin. Tigy and her father awaited him at the station with the sad news. He remained expressionless — true to his father's "pudeur" — and hurried home, where he gazed at the pale, serene face and brushed his lips on the cold forehead. At the funeral, he impulsively threw some of the flowers into the grave and was scolded by one of his cousins, to whom he retorted, "Are the flowers for my father, or to impress passers-by?" A five-franc gold piece was his only paternal heritage.

During 1921, and into 1922, Simenon led his astonishingly busy life, working for the *Gazette*, wooing Tigy, and gamboling about with his friends. Tigy wanted to go to Paris to start her painting career in earnest, and Simenon was not averse. He has insisted that he was not out to "tackle" the capital, though once there he acted very much as if he was. One obstacle to departure was impending military service, and he decided to anticipate his call. It only very momentarily interrupted his life style. He spent two months in Aachen, where he wrote long love letters to Tigy and peeled potatoes with a well-read recruit from Antwerp, while they recited Villon, Baudelaire and Lautréamont to each other. He requested reassignment to Liège and was assigned to a cavalry barracks three hundred meters from his home. He took up with the *Gazette* again and instructed his sergeant to get in touch with him there if he was needed.

By 1922, when he was 19, Simenon functioned quite squarely in a success ethos, and never ceased. He played at being in love with Tigy, and at being a rebel and a bohemian. Escape was a game too, not really predicated on a deep, rancorous sense of oppression and a desperate need to get away. *Presenting* it that way from time to time was also a game — which later became a literary game: dozens of his novels are about "little people" stifling in their environment and bursting out, usually briefly and tragically.

His own escape was jollier, sunnier. Those early Rabelaisian books reflect as real an aspect of his adolescence as the gloomier accounts in *Pedigree* and elsewhere. His escape was from one success ethos to another. Yet he was not ambitious in a readily identifiable way. It's almost as if he *found* himself in deep water, energetically and successfully swimming about. He had been on the way to becoming a big fish in a small pond, and in his nineteenth year decided — casually, not grandiosely — to head for a bigger pond. If Paris was Tigy's project, it was nonetheless Georges who went there, alone, on the night train of December 10.

[4 5]

V I

EARLY DAYS IN FRANCE
1922 - 1924

When Simenon left for Paris in December of 1922, he was not without precedent: everybody seems to have been leaving for Paris around 1922, from Dublin, Princeton, Kansas City, London ... Simenon was not even the first of the Liège contingent; the charismatic painter Luc Lafnet had preceded him by a few weeks. The Paris that they all found was crowded, eventful, beautiful, animated, creative, fashionable, and often frenetic. The "Belle Epoque" of the turn of the century had ended with World War I, replaced by "Les Années folles" of the twenties.

There was indeed such frenzy in the air that it might pass as madness. The franc was so low that Americans from Oklahoma or California ostentatiously lit their cigars with thousand-franc notes. Women wore very short dresses, with—a great novelty—pink panties of shiny artificial silk. They wore long pearl necklaces down to below the navel.

. . .

On the Grands Boulevards, you saw nothing but light little suits, dresses with flower designs, white or red hats, toques worn virtually over the ear from which disordered wisps of hair escaped.

Whatever the dollar exchange rate, one franc bought two packs of Gauloises, and three and a half francs a meal at a cheap restaurant. An average white-collar employee might make about a thousand francs a month. For the artists and sophisticates, Montmartre was on the decline and the Age of Montparnasse was just beginning—

. . . one of the high spots of the world, the carrefour Montparnasse, where the Rotonde and the Dôme faced each other across the boulevard, crammed with painters, models, artists, and philosophers, a generation in gestation, while, close by, the immense brasserie la Coupole was under construction.

. . .

. . . painters and poets who had come from all over the world, men whose paintings sell now for a million dollars, who at that time bartered them for a café-crème and a croissant.

The very rich could be found at the Ritz, the Crillon, and Maxim's. The Champs-Élysées was not "in," and still largely residential, except for Fouquet's, which is eternal, and which, for the young Simenon, was out of reach but would not remain so for long.

Simenon had come to write, to earn a living, and to succeed, but the three categories were unintegrated:

I came, if you wish, to "cut my teeth," but with no ambition of succeeding in any definite goal . . . [I was ambitious] just "to succeed" — to succeed in the novel, but still without attaching to the word "success" a specific meaning — financial, for example, or in terms of glory.

If his goals were vague, they would, somehow, have something to do with literature. He settled into a tiny attic room at the Hôtel Bertha in Montmartre and rented himself an old typewriter until he could afford to buy one. His dominant mood was of exploration, of absorbing an infinity of sensations, of drinking in the pied beauty of Paris.

I was hungry for everything, I was enchanted by everything, and it seemed to me that everything was different from other places — particularly from Liège . . . there was a buoyancy in the air, a buoyancy also in the way people talked, in their facial expressions.

. . .

To use my personal experience, "I was out hunting." Hunting humanity. Hunting life. Hunting women too . . . driven by the same electrifying curiosity.

An exceptionally mild February sharpened senses and desire: "A precocious spring made the buds of the chestnut trees burst out, and transformed women into so many irresistible temptations." "Partir en chase," "roder," "renifler," and "fouiller" (Hunting, prowling, sniffing, rummaging about) are the words he uses to describe his responses to Paris. Hunger was real, but also a metaphor for curiosity, as sexual consummation was for the penetration of Paris.

He was responsive to everything: pretty women, prostitutes, B-girls, but also "little old women, solitary old men, loud-mouthed housewives," and the swarms of "little people" in busy, colorful streets. He quickly developed his pastime of riding on bus platforms, pipe in mouth, observing the bustling street life; and walked all over the city, along the Seine, for example, as far as Charenton to "Lock Number One" (*L'Écluse numéro un*), which became the setting of one of the early Maigrets. He took in a wide range of cafés, bars, bistros, and nightclubs, sometimes slumming in the "guinguettes" on the rue de Lappe, where he once saw a client stabbed to death, or drinking "sur le zinc" (at the counter) chatting with the *patron* and the habitués.

The Moulin-Rouge became a favorite for a while, until he learned to join the in-crowd at Montparnasse: the Boeuf sur le Toit, the Dôme, the Coupole, the Jockey. He liked dancing and became a jazz enthusiast: "Armstrong was a god." He was swept off his feet by his first Bastille Day, which combined music, dancing, and the hubbub of popular street life. He and his friends covered most of Paris, going from one ball to the next, encountering at place de la République a young up-and-coming "chansonnier" named Maurice Chevalier.

Money was scarce during the first few months in Paris (even, off and on, for the first two years). To make ends meet, he sometimes took to selling his cleverly acquired first editions "to pay for the Camemberts of the faubourg Saint-Honoré or the girls of the boulevard des Batignolles." The Camemberts refer to his discovery that cheap Camembert swells up shortly after one has eaten a piece of it, and thus can be made to last several days. If his dominant mood was enthusiasm, he sometimes, at the beginning, also felt alienated:

> Right from my arrival in Paris I felt lumpish, awkward among the Parisians who gaily threaded their way through their city, breezily articulate with sharp banter.

At his first job he was teased for his belgicisms, like the compulsive use of "n'est-ce pas?" (similar to the compulsive New Yorkese "you know"). A piggy-bank was set up in which he had to drop ten centimes every time he used a Liégeois expression: "its contents repeatedly provided drinks for the whole office."

The gloomier aspect of his December arrival in Paris hit him hard two weeks later. Why he decided to move to Paris just before Christmas is not clear (he probably had an appointment), but the loneliness of Christmas Eve in a foreign city made a lasting impression on him:

> I know nothing more sinister than to be alone in Paris on such a night, with little money in your pocket, rubbing elbows with people enjoying themselves, or watching them through restaurant windows.

Nor would New Year's Eve have been cheerier for him, except that he picked up a girl named Pilar, who was staring, like him, at the display in the French Line offices on rue Auber. They had a drink, then spent a jubilantly passionate night together; though he considered himself well-versed in sex, she taught him, with "mischievous eyes, subtleties that astounded me"; it was she who could bring him to climax merely by batting her eyelashes against his. He fictionalized this incident at least twice — in *Les Anneaux de Bicêtre* and in *Le Passage de la ligne* — using the name "Pilar."

Simenon did not come to Paris without introductions. One was from a businessman named Georges Plumier, who had urged him to take the leap to the capital and put him in touch with a certain Binet-Valmer, a socialite and prolific writer of potboilers, whose greater prominence, however, derived from his presidency of the "Ligue des Chefs de Section et des Anciens Combattants," a veterans' organization concerned mostly with promoting right-wing causes and candidates.

Not long after his arrival, Simenon went to Binet-Valmer's, full of enthusiasm, under the impression he was being offered a job as secretary to a famous writer. But everything connected with this personage was a letdown. His headquarters was a dingy, one-story house where Simenon, instead of finding literary activity, found a couple of clerks loading cartons on trucks. Having been recommended by Plumier, he was immediately put to work loading the trucks: Binet-Valmer's latest brainchild was a Christmas-package project for "war-devastated" France.

After an hour of hauling cartons down the narrow stairs, Simenon was almost in tears with disappointment and ready to return to Liège. Nonetheless, he stayed for six months, stuffing and addressing envelopes, substituting for Binet-Valmer at ceremonial functions (particularly funerals on cold winter days), and delivering "urgent" messages to the 45 Parisian dailies. This last was more congenial: the long hackney-cab trips through the streets of Paris delighted him, and he came to know the anterooms of power — or rather a type of aristocratic power that was on the verge of disappearing. Binet-Valmer was a superficial political and literary operator, constantly jockeying for position among mediocrities in momentary positions of power — a mode of behavior toward which Simenon felt an immediate revulsion:

> It was not that kind of literary life that I had come to Paris for. I had no inkling of it in Liège. It was a whole side of literature which made me bristle, and I promised myself never to let myself be caught up in that kind of toadying.

In order to be closer to the Ligue headquarters and to the heart of the city, Simenon moved from the Hôtel Bertha and rented a room in the faubourg Saint-Honoré from an Englishwoman who, however, kicked him out when she found a particularly expansive Camembert oozing from under the fireplace screen. He moved nearby, to impasse Saint-Honoré, into a vaguely furnished room and a half, which was soon improved by the arrival of Tigy and some of her father's furniture. They were married in Liège on March 24, 1923. He remained in Paris until the last moment, taking the night train to arrive in Liège on the morning of the wedding. The night before, he celebrated his last day as a bachelor by picking up two voluptuous Dutch girls at the *Lapin Agile* and spending the night in their hotel suite. In Liège, he successfully maintained the fiction that he was now earning the 1000 francs a month stipulated by Tigy's father. He rode to the church with his mother, reciting cooking recipes to her to keep her from weeping. After the wedding, frisky with champagne, they took the night train back to Paris and set up their household at impasse Saint-Honoré.

Tigy painted a great deal, and in time was somewhat more successful than Simenon has made her out to be. In those days, however, she exhibited with the outdoor painters in Montmartre, where she did mostly portraits. Simenon would frame them and hang them on a cord between two trees on the place Constantin-Pecqueur, and stare intently at passers-by, hoping for a customer. Feeling he was scaring off buyers, Tigy would send him off for walks. One of his preferred ways of furthering her career was to go in search of women to pose for her, taking care to check them out personally before turning them over to her. The "chasse aux femmes," indeed, was a continuing activity.

Tigy, he has always insisted, was of a pathologically jealous temperament, for which he never forgave her: "During the more than twenty years that I stayed with her, I had to lie and hide." He picked up all sorts of women, from elegant hookers at the Café de la Paix, to the street walkers of the boulevard Montmartre and the rue de Lappe. His encounters were largely—but not exclusively—with prostitutes. When he collected money for his stories, he made a habit, if the sum exceeded 500 francs, of secretly appropriating twenty francs "for my personal pleasures." A little later, more prosperous, he became an habitué at an elegant establishment on the rue Brey run by a certain Mme. Hélène, "where, without having to waste one's time with tedious flirting and without compromising one's self, one found the most charming women of Paris." He was not sure what he was looking for in this frenetic search: sexual assuagement, to be sure, but also knowledge, communion—transcendence, almost:

> . . . it was a little bit like communing with a part of the universe. That is why I would have wanted them all. I suffered literally to know that there were millions of women in the world whom I would never know and who—every one of them—could have brought me something, could have increased a certain plenitude toward which I confusedly aspired.

For a while the Simenons frequented the little Liège expatriate circle that gathered at Luc Lafnet's Montmartre studio. Lafnet, like Simenon, had returned to Liège to pick up a wife, and the couple lived a precarious existence in their studio, where they recreated a Montmartre variation of the Caque. The dominant tone of Simenon's vision of them, as in Liège, was failure, weakness, and oblivion. Lafnet died young — in 1939 — though he was not, in fact, a total failure as an artist, and Simenon himself paid homage to him on the occasion of a retrospective of his work. Simenon felt more sympathy than — as he had in Liège — hostility, but was not of them.

With his women, his good looks and his jaunty energy, he remained, if momentarily broke, clearly within a success ethos. He tried to be fashionable. Having arrived with longish hair (à l'artiste), he soon changed his haircut to "à l'embusqué" (long on top, cropped at the back). He was proud of the first suit he bought in Paris because its material and cut manifested "a discreet fantasy"; but it was not a success: at the first rain it shrank and he arrived home with his trousers crawling up his ankles. A little later, he took to dressing quite flamboyantly: very wide, rosewood-colored trousers over yellow leather, square-toed shoes, "American style," and reversible coats bought on sale at a fancy English haberdasher — of high quality but extravagant colors. One was red-cabbage color with small checks; another, electric blue.

One of the heavy contributors to the Ligue was a certain Marquis Jacques de Tracy, whose father had recently died, leaving him several châteaux, an immense town house, rice fields in Italy, Tunisian properties and many bank accounts. He had also recently turned forty and gotten married, and to help him shoulder all these responsibilities he needed a secretary. Binet-Valmer one day called Simenon into his office and, screwing his monocle into his eye, told him solemnly about the Marquis's plight; he had recommended him for the secretaryship and he was awaited at eleven o'clock. He presented himself at the appointed time, was ushered through two valets to the Marquis, who received him in a wondrously disorganized study, wearing a silk dressing-gown and red kid slippers. "Your name is Sim?" he said. Simenon explained it was his journalism name but that his real name was Simenon. "I'll call you Sim," the Marquis pronounced, considering him as hired on the spot.

Simenon, who had had it with the Ligue, found the new job providential and celebrated by treating himself, for the first time, to one of the expensive girls of the Madeleine. He got along well with the Marquis de Tracy and stayed with him over a year, ostensibly straightening out the correspondence — some of which had not been read or answered for two years — and taking care of bills from jewelers, furriers, and the like. In fact, he had little to do, except follow Tracy from château to château. The longest period was spent in the immense château of Saint-Jean-des-Bois near the village of Paray-le-Frézil, while Tigy, who was not accounted for in his arrangement with the Marquis, lived in a hotel room in a village 18 kilometers away, where Simenon more or less secretly joined her by bicycle every evening. Occasionally the Marquis would dictate a letter "as if he didn't believe in it." Once, in one of the châteaux, Simenon discovered an extraordinary collection of rare books and offered to catalogue them, to which Tracy assented, also as if he didn't believe in it. He did everything as if he didn't believe in it, and his expression was generally of someone just awakened from a deep sleep.

Simenon, who always had a need for having much attention paid to him, relished the paternal interest that this otherwise aloof aristocrat took in him. Furthermore, life with the Marquis, as with Binet-Valmer, afforded him another glimpse into the arcane world of aristocratic life — astonishingly unreal and empty, but at the same time an exotic object of curiosity and another source of fauna for his collection. The most engaging figure from that world for Simenon was the bailiff at Saint-Jean-des-Bois, Pierre Tardivon, a tall, lanky, rough-hewn man who strode competently about the vast estate in boots and a velvet jacket. It was because of him that, later, Simenon made Maigret the son of a bailiff, fictionalizing Paray-le-Frézil as "Saint-Fiacre."

The Binet-Valmer and Tracy jobs were only detours on Simenon's literary path. He had approached Binet-Valmer in the first place in the expectation that he would be launched into the world of Parisian letters. If his functions were disappointing, he did brush elbows with some literary personalities and sent back sketches of some of them to the *Revue sincère* in Brussels: Henri Duvernois, Paul Fort, Maurice Barrès, Tristan Bernard. One of Léon Daudet, an antisemitic royalist, crushing his "siège fleur-de-lis" with his enormous posterior, perhaps makes amends for the antisemitism of the Duvernois piece.

These are the last pieces Simenon wrote for his Belgian market before launching into the Parisian. He eased into it writing in the vein he had already practiced with the "Poulailler" pieces and his juvenile novels: humor. Besides Binet-Valmer, he had another person to look up in Paris, a Belgian writer named Georges Ista, who prospered by turning out pulp fiction, mostly in a humorous-erotic vein.

Ista could carry on conversations only with the aid of a gigantic ear trumpet thrust at his interlocutor's mouth, and gave the young Simenon detailed advice on how to break into that branch of the Parisian literary scene represented by magazines with names like *Frou-Frou, Sans-Gêne*, and *Paris-Flirt*. Simenon did not know whether to laugh or cry at this notion of "literature," but he could hardly have been crying, nor surprised, to find himself a few weeks later churning out fiction — mini-stories known at that time as *contes galants* — for virtually all of the mildly raunchy Parisian magazines of this kind. The first of these pieces was sold in the winter of 1922–23 to a weekly called *L'Humour*, after which he branched out quickly.

Ista's advice — to pick his subjects carefully and think about them for several hours, had fallen on deaf ears. Simenon's method was to pace up and down for three or four minutes to consolidate an idea, then write the tale in less than an hour. For a while he was publishing several of these items a week in some fourteen different magazines: *L'Humour, L'Almanach de l'humour, Eve, Miousic, Gens qui rient, Le Sourire, Le Rire, Sans-Gêne, Frou-Frou, Paris-Plaisir, Le Merle blanc, Fantasio, Paris-Flirt* and *Mon Flirt*. Considering it indecent to use the same name for all of these — let alone his own — , he signed Aramis, Bobette, La Déshabilleuse, Luc Dorsan, Gemis, Gom Gut, Jean, Kim, Miquette, Misti, Pan, Plick et Plock, Poum et Zette, Sandor, Trott, and occasionally Sim.

Depending on the magazine, the stories might be soft-core pornography — sometimes hardly more than a dirty joke of embarrasing vulgarity — but most often turned on a more or less clever twist, a cute reversal, an ironic revelation. Sometimes, from raunchiness, they veered toward sentimentality. Some magazines wanted more sexual explicitness than others, and for all of them one had to be adept at euphemism.

One of the earlier ones, for example, published in *Sans-Gêne* of September 1, 1923, is about a naive young man who falls in love with a pretty girl and is troubled at learning that she is a nude performer at the Folies-Bergère. Visiting her in the dressing room and finding a dirty old man pawing at her, he utters his outrage and chases him out, but is rewarded only by his mistress' anger and rejection because the gentleman was an important dramatist who was about to give her a real chance on the stage. The young man is last seen sitting crestfallen day after day at the café where he and his true love had first met.

In another story for the same magazine three weeks later, we find a similar peripeteia without the sentimentality. A bounder in a park picks up a pretty woman, whom he takes to be the rich mother of two children cared for by a nanny, but who turns out to be the nanny's daughter and a part-time call girl requiring payment. Prurience, voyeurism, and exhibitionism play a large role in many of these tales, not only inherently in that they are designed to titillate voyeuristic instincts, but often in their content: they are *about* voyeuristic and exhibitionistic situations. An old man is caught in the bathroom, peeking at his mistress with her young lover. Or a young man sees a girl in a window across the street making erotic gestures, to which he responds, eventually undressing, thinking she's responding to him; but it turns out she's a professional dancer rehearsing, and he's arrested for exhibitionism.

The style is usually chatty and circumlocutory, and elicits a sense of collusion between writer and reader. A cocky narrative persona is very much present, often addressing the reader: "Ma foi, que vouliez-vous quelle [sic] fit...?" (Well, what would you want her to do...?) This stylistic tendency occasionally leads away from fiction into a kind of bantering reportage: "Would you like to make an amusing little experiment?"—and there follows an account of how orgies are organized, often ending up with a bunch of gentlemen showing up, but no women. Or, "Voulez-vous un tuyau?" (Do you want a good gimmick?) Then comes an account of things you can learn by pretending to operate a detective agency.

Not long after launching into erotic humor, Simenon began also to pursue another vein. Having met Henri Duvernois through Binet-Valmer, he admired his short stories, probably both because of their style and because they were regularly published in the wide-circulation *Le Matin*: Duvernois smelled of success and Simenon set out to emulate him. Soon, side by side with the "contes galants," he was trying his hand at a somewhat more delicate and serious mode of fiction.

The editor-in-chief of *Le Matin*, Henri de Jouvenel, was at that time the second husband of the celebrated novelist Colette, who served as literary editor of the newspaper. It was thus to Colette that Georges Simenon presented the short-short stories he hoped to place in *Le Matin*. He has described his encounter with Colette innumerable times, probably because it acquired in his life experience the status of something like an initiation myth. After briefly studying the fictional style of *Le Matin*, he submitted a couple of stories. The custom was to go to the literary editor on Wednesdays, when the author received either a check or his rejected manuscript. Simenon came back checkless a few times until, one Wednesday, he was told that Madame Colette wanted to talk to him. She impressed him immensely, sitting imperially in her editorial chair. Since his submissions were all signed "Georges Sim," she called him immediately "mon petit Sim," and said:

> *Mon petit Sim*, I've read your last story. That's not it. That's almost it, but that's not it. You're too literary. You mustn't write literature. No literature! Eliminate all literature, and it'll be O.K.

He simplified his style, submitted two more stories, and was told, "Still too literary, *mon petit Sim*. No literature!" He went home, tried again, and finally had two stories accepted. "Adorable Colette" he calls her, to have given him such good advice, to have drawn him away from literary pretentiousness and sent him gently on the path of simplicity and directness. Whatever role Colette may have played in the development of his career (it may not have been quite as pivotal as he subsequently made it out to be), it acquired its status in his personal mythology because her injunctions prefigure the plain, low-keyed style that characterizes much of Simenon's "serious" fiction (including the Maigrets). It also launched him into a higher level of Parisian literary journalism. The Colette myth, then, revolves around greater "realism," less "literature," and success.

There are no samples of what Colette rejected, so we cannot tell what modifications Simenon actually made in his style. The stories that he published in *Le Matin*, beginning with "La Petite Idole" on September 27, 1923, are written, on the whole, with a certain concision dictated by the brevity of the format, and with considerable grammatical elegance, particularly when compared with the deliberately flat style of his later fictions. They were all signed "Georges Sim" and generally came under the newspaper's standard rubric for short fiction, "Les Mille et un matins."

Many are unabashedly sentimental; pathos is the predominant tone. Some exploit a banal situation, quickly sketched out; some are more inventive; some are quite touching. There are many stories of unhappy love, often in a *Eugénie Grandet* vein: a woman's abandonment by an insensitive man; or sometimes inversely, a young man suffers unhappy love. The "little people" are a substantial presence in these early stories, prefiguring their central role in Simenon's serious work, but viewed mostly in a sentimental or tragi-sentimental mode, rather than the tragi-despairing or tragi-cynical mode of the major work. "Mélie" is about a self-effaced, sad woman who has worked all her life as a newspaper folder in a printing plant, who becomes pregnant, no one knows by whom, and finds joy in her impending motherhood.

Several stories pick up the "little people" theme on a collective, socioeconomic level: outsiders, marginal proletarians, like the Italian workers of "Le Chant du soir," whose alienated situation is effectively evoked in spite of a makeshift plot situation; or the Lacroix in the story that bears their name, outsiders in a region of small landowners who suspect them of a local crime and are disappointed when they are cleared; or the miners in "Le Grisou," which describes a mine accident with shameless sentimentality. Other stories evoke a more worldly context, like "Le Coup de feu," in which a seeming hunting accident is in fact a husband's revenge. For the aristocratic setting of this and other stories Simenon drew on his experience with the Marquis de Tracy. *Le Matin* was Simenon's principal outlet for short stories, though he sometimes published in other dailies. Dennis Drysdale's count of short stories is 25 for 1923, 204 for 1924, 276 for 1925 and 261 for 1926.

These Parisian literary beginnings were simultaneous with Simenon's jobs with Binet-Valmer and the Marquis de Tracy. When he worked for the former and lived in Paris, he wrote on a white table in a corner of the room at the impasse Saint-Honoré, while Tigy drew sketches in another corner. Sometimes he wrote in nearby bistros, under the eyes of curious locals, astonished at the furor of his writing pace. He took his products to editorial offices that ranged from the elegant headquarters of *Le Matin* to the dingiest of basements in back alleys. He submitted his material, collected his money, and met many of the literary hacks who were then his colleagues, "les tâcherons de la littérature," and the publishers, some of whom were in such a precarious business as to be likely, a year later, selling neckties on the street. In those early days, young Georges Simenon loved above all the hustle and bustle of the whole enterprise: "Everything was beautiful; I had the impression of discovering real life." When he became the Marquis de Tracy's secretary and travelled with him from château to château, he kept writing at the same rate. His markets were well enough established by then that submissions and payments could be handled by mail. Nonetheless, as he wrote more, earned more, and varied his outlets, the logistics became too complicated, and it was for this reason that he left the Marquis's service and returned to Paris to attend wholly to the business of literature.

VII

THE WIZARD
OF PULP FICTION
1924-1930

At the beginning of the summer of 1924 the Simenons moved into the apartment at 21, place des Vosges which was to be their headquarters for almost seven years. It consisted of the first, and later also the third, floor of a former townhouse, which Simenon decorated in the flamboyant new Art Deco manner introduced by the exposition of 1925. He chose black velvet for his curtains and his colossal couch, and gay, multicolored cubist designs in gouache for the walls. The centerpiece was an immense "American" bar, covered with frosted glass under which glowed electric lights. In front of it, bright yellow barstools with black leather seats were arrayed, while a stage light in a corner enabled Simenon to project a white, red, blue or yellow beam into any corner of the room. He painted SIM in large green letters on the front door.

His income was increasing rapidly, but he spent and overspent it all — on women, parties, nightclubs and restaurants; later, cars, boats and trips. At place des Vosges, parties often went on into early morning and turned into orgies, Simenon tending his bar and manipulating the stage lights. He himself was often more interested in observing than in participating, as if making a controlled experiment: what kind of behavior results when a couple of pretty girls take their clothes off? Some New Year's Eves were particularly tumultuous, with drunken guests strewn all over the floor, and the old woman on the second floor complaining of having met naked people in the hallway all night long. Simenon, however, Socrates-like, would regularly get up early after these parties, sit at his typewriter and put in his three or four hours of work—even if surrounded by "cadavers" who would gradually wake up one after the other.

He had numerous friends, or acquaintances. The Liège friendships lingered, then faded. At Montparnasse he came to know many painters—Vlaminck, Soutine, Paul Colin, Marcel Vertès, Kisling, Pascin, Fujita, and later Bernard Buffet. He knew Jean Renoir early, who, with his first wife, Catherine Hessling, could often be found at place des Vosges parties. Literary acquaintances were less prominent. He knew Georges Charensol, publisher of the *Nouvelles littéraires*, which subsequently could usually be counted on to give his serious work a good press; and he seems to have become fairly friendly with his early idol, Henri Duvernois, who, one day, confided to him:

> There comes a moment in life, Sim, when you can no longer make love: well, at that moment you find nothing more to write about within youself . . . I can admit to you that in the last three years I have been producing fake Duvernois . . . plagiarizing myself.

Simenon's response is not recorded, but forebodings of literary senility probably had little impact. He continued his obsessive pursuit of women—models for Tigy, prostitutes, adolescents in country inns, married women seeking adventures in bizarre Parisian establishments. It was in one of the latter that he was startled once to find the wife of a good friend, parading up and down on a podium with other naked women while gentlemen watched. Feeling that pretending not to recognize her and not picking her for himself would "give her a complex," he chose her.

Simenon's women are almost all anonymous. One exception from this period was Josephine Baker, who had lately arrived from America and swept Europe off its feet. He had met her among the increasingly worldly crowd that he and Tigy were hanging around with. They would often join her and others at a late-night spot called El Garrob where she would go after her show at a rue Fontaine nightclub. For a brief period in 1926, presumably out of friendship, he functioned as something like her secretary, helping her with her press clippings and her correspondence, along with Marcel Sauvage, who was a friend of Simenon's and much later helped Baker write her memoirs.

According to Simenon, "we fell madly in love"; it was *"le coup de foudre"*; she was the only woman until 1946 whom he felt inclined to give up Tigy for and marry. But he also was intimidated by her glory and her entourage, which included the likes of the Aga Khan. He was afraid that if he stayed with her he could only become "Monsieur Baker," and fled one night to the Île d'Aix, never to see her again, until she visited him thirty years later in Connecticut and said, "Georges! But why did you abandon me?" According to Sauvage, Simenon was not in love with her, and she was despondent when he left.

Concurrent with his up-to-date taste for Art Deco and jazz, Simenon developed a passion for movies — *not* the commercial stuff but the avant-garde films of the little art houses of the Left Bank. The first of these films he ever saw was the expressionist *Cabinet of Dr. Caligari*, "which opened new horizons to me," and he was enthusiastic about Jean Renoir's *La Petite Marchande d'allumettes*, René Clair's first film, *Entr'acte*, and *Le Chapeau de Paille d'Italie*, and Fritz Lang's *Metropolis* (he fell in love with Brigitte Helm's "sculptural body"). It is one of the complex ironies of Simenon's life that he felt this surge of excitement for the great films of the twenties, always disdained commercial cinema, lost interest in film altogether, was a close friend of several great filmmakers, made a fortune on movie rights, and presided over the Cannes Film Festival of 1960. (Not long before this last he was declaring that he only went to the movies for the peanuts, the ice cream and the ads.)

Not too long after he had begun to establish himself as a commercial short-story writer, Simenon decided to launch into longer fiction. He was already familiar — at least from the days of his Aunt Céline — with various types of popular subliterature, and in preparation for trying his hand, he now revived his knowledge by skimming through typical works to discover their gimmicks, their "ficelles." He had hit the metropolis at the right time to begin this career. In the subsequent decades the demand for such literature would be increasingly met by movies and radio, and later by television; but in the twenties that encroachment was only an explorative nibble.

In the preceding half-century the market for popular printed matter had soared. Expanded public schooling meant wider literacy. Printing and papermaking technology made progressively cheaper products possible. Increasing wealth, together with social and economic reforms in industrial countries, provided more leisure. Even the development of the railroad had a literary significance: a need for cheap, easy diversions to while away the hours on long journeys. In short, commerce was humming in the literary world: a mass market of consumers took shape, and industrious entrepreneurs fed it — publishers, editors, printers, booksellers ... and writers. Some of the latter, like Ista, were diligent hacks. Some were writers with higher achievements, aspirations or pretentions, temporarily slumming for quick income. Some were "popular" and "serious" alternately, or flowed imperceptibly from one to the other, and yet others produced works that simultaneously fit both categories.

[5 9]

The categories of literature, of course, have always been uncertain. They are clear at the extremes — Edgar Rice Burroughs is pop literature, Marcel Proust high literature — but often fuzzy in the middle. "Popular" is an ambiguous term, urged largely by French usage, in which "roman populaire" refers to the kind of cheap, throwaway ("pulp") product that is in question here. But it has varying connotations. It may mean "coming from the people" and relating back to them — opposed to "elite." Or it may mean shoddy, not arising from the true being of the creator, but dictated by, encouraging, and exploiting the shallow tastes of the mass public. Its antonym perhaps is "art." "Commercial" is a slightly more useful label, highlighting the chief determinant of the relationship between writer and reader, producer and consumer. The consumer wants to buy a known quantity, a specific product answering a specific need. The producer manufactures a product that fits that demand. While it is in the nature of the product to require variations, they are superficial. The basic product is standard, and it is most effectively written, as the phrase goes, "to formula."

The subjects of commercial fiction come mostly under three categories: crime, love and adventure. (The categories often overlap, and there are many subcategories, particularly under "adventure": Wild West, pirates, aviators, South Seas and other exotica, historical, etc.) The antecedents in literary history of this commercial literature are sometimes evident, sometimes obscure. Often, but by no means always, one can trace "lower" forms to "higher" ones: from Balzac, for example, to Eugène Sue to Paul Féval to Jean du Perry. Sue, in the latter half of the nineteenth century was an immensely popular writer of long novels full of adventure, mystery and suspense. Paul Féval was the most celebrated and prolific writer of cheap fiction in the decades before World War I. Jean du Perry was Georges Simenon.

Nineteenth-century French popular literature is a compendium of forgotten names — Pigault-Lebrun, de Kock — the last more memorable perhaps because Molly Bloom reads him ("nice name he has"). Among their antecedents Walter Scott, Dickens, Edgar Allan Poe, Alexandre Dumas are detectible, as well as the Gothic novel, the eighteenth-century sentimental novel, the exotic tale, and, further back, Renaissance romances, and behind them Greek romances, and much more. Characteristic, and foremost, among Parisian publishers of commercial fiction, was Fayard Frères, founded in the third quarter of the nineteenth century by Arthème Fayard *père*, and launching full force into the popular vein in the 1890's, beginning with the texts of popular songs in pamphlet form, passing through cheap collections of classics, popularized history, and encyclopedias, into a series of quick-selling fiction called "Le Livre populaire" and going for 75 centimes a piece. One of Fayard's first successes was *Chaste et flétrie*, the very book Simenon's Aunt Céline liked so much. Fayard published the Rouletabille series and the interminable Fantômas series — perhaps the biggest pulp success ever. Simenon was soon to become intimately connected with the firm, now under the leadership of Arthème Fayard *fils*.

Simenon's first try at a pulp novelette came about casually enough. One summer morning in 1924 he was hanging around the "Foire aux Croûtes," where Tigy was exhibiting her work. Tired of waiting for a sale, he retreated to a café not far off:

> I had discovered a little saloon on the rue Caulaincourt, very cheerful, very comfortable, very calm. One day, after having read several popular novels, I started one, on a marble-top table. It was called *Le Roman d'une dactylo —*

"The Story of a Stenographer": By lunch he had completed a novelette of between 2000 and 3000 lines — 79 printed pages in a very small format. He sold it for about 300 francs to one of the big pulp firms, J. Ferenczi & Sons, for the series called "Le Petit Livre," at 40 centimes a book. Pseudonyms like "Plick et Plock" being no longer appropriate, he signed it "Jean du Perry," which is the name of a street in Liège.

He got a quick and straight bead on his market, the nature of which is clearly revealed in the title: romantic stories for secretaries, salesgirls, housewives of the petite bourgeoisie, and the like — "romans à faire pleurer Margot," he called them, displaying nothing if not condescension toward what were, after all, those same "little people" he so mythicized in other contexts. *Le Roman d'une dactylo* pits the "little people," poor and innocent of heart, in the characters of Linette, the secretary, and her young beloved, Jean, against the corrupt rich — the sleazy banker she works for and the sleazier millionaire baron she is forced to submit to. The plot is quite simple: submit she must, because Jean has misused funds to buy her an engagement ring and will go to jail unless she saves him by bowing to banker and baron. Some years later, she shakes herself free of the despicable millionaires, and, in an accelerated finale, is reunited forever with Jean, who is now himself a successful businessman.

Having placed *Dactylo* without difficulty, he turned out another novelette in the same vein a few weeks later for Ferenczi, *Amour d'exilé*, followed shortly by *Les Larmes avant le bonheur*. This last was signed "Georges Simm" and was also addressed to the secretary market. The plot, more outlandish than *Dactylo*'s, involves a vacationing stenographer's love for a young count, momentarily frustrated by his lecherous father, whom she murders in self-defense. All ends well when the count takes her back, and, "for the first time, she truly surrendered herself." Simenon's experience with the Marquis de Tracy probably once again served him well for the aristocratic setting.

We are still in 1924. By 1925 the tap was wide open and pulp Simenons flowed out. This image is apt for all phases of his career: he writes a couple of pieces in a given vein, and the next thing we know an astonishing stream is flowing out. The profusion of pulps — together with the concurrent stream of short stories — accounts for the multiple pseudonyms: it would have been indecent to publish several stories, and a novel or two, week after week in a score of periodicals and by half a dozen book publishers, all under the same name. For the novels and novelettes, his principal pseudonyms were Georges Sim, Jean du Perry, Christian Brulls (combining paternal and maternal heritage), Georges-Martin Georges and Luc Dorsan. Claude Menguy lists 37 in all, but these include very slight variations, some probably due to his having misspelled his own pseudonym in the rush of it all. His normal pace, established in 1924–25, was to begin typing at six in the morning:

> I stopped around noon, took a short nap, then worked again for several hours, until exhaustion. I could manage thus up to eighty typewritten pages in a day ... A ten-thousand line novel took me about three days, a twenty-thousand line novel, a week.

When he went to work in the morning, he was able to pick up where he had left off, automatically, effortlessly, without notes, and without rereading the last paragraphs of the preceding day. He usually had a bottle of white wine by his desk and would take a sip from time to time. By his calculations 80 pages equalled two bottles. As more money poured in, he was reputed, on occasion, to deliver manuscripts to the pulp publishers in a Chrysler limousine with a chauffeur dressed as a sailor. The majority of his books were published by all three of the principal pulp producers: Ferenczi, Tallandier and Fayard. Simenon approached Fayard in 1927 with a novel called *Le Feu s'éteint*. Max Favelli, another writer of pulps, remembers Simenon's first appearance at Fayard, "solid on his legs, a short clay pipe firmly jutting out from between his beef-colored cheeks, dressed in a checkered coat, knickers, and a flat cap." Simenon impressed Charles Dillon, a senior editor at Fayard who had acquired a reputation as the genius of pulp editing. Dillon, whenever he needed something quickly, took to calling "Georges Sim," who invariably responded, "When do you need it for?"

"No man but a blockhead," goes Samuel Johnson's celebrated injunction, "ever wrote, except for money." Pulp fiction is paid as piecework and brings no royalties. A ten-thousand-liner fetched 100 to 1500 francs, a twenty-thousand-liner, 2000 francs at first, then, his prestige enhanced, 2500 francs. Shorter pieces, like *Dactylo*, paid less — as little as 200 or 300 francs. A contract of April 10, 1925, with one of the lesser publishers, F. Rouff, brought Simenon 500 francs for *Étoile de cinéma*, 78 pages long and selling for 60 centimes. Simenon, for the most part, knew what he was up to, and "popular" to him meant "commercial"—though on occasion he considered one of his inspirations to have been certain kinds of popular ballads sung by street singers, such as:

> Il était près du canal
> Dans le quartier de l'arsenal.
> Sa mère qui n'avait pas de mari
> L'appelait petit Henri,
> Mais on l'appelait la Filoche
> A la Bastoche —

a ballad about rough life, slums and poverty, not unlike certain songs of Edith Piaf and Maurice Chevalier. "Most of these songs were very somber, very cruel, like the popular novels I wrote subsequently." This association fits the other meaning of "popular"—having to do with "the people"—but in fact hardly relates to what he actually wrote, or to the spirit in which he wrote it. Generally, his definition of "roman populaire" was clear-cut:

> ... A work which does not correspond to the author's personality, to his need for artistic expression, but to commercial demand. The "roman populaire" is merchandise ... corresponding fairly closely to the range of goods found in a department store ... Thus the popular novelist is an industrialist or an artisan.

The pseudonyms underscored the absence of the author's involvement; "Sim," perhaps, was a reduced name for a reduced literature. He wrote these books to make money, calling them "littérature alimentaire." For him the product was without value, but not the producing of it. In addition to money, it provided some technical practice, and, especially, lessons in what *not* to do: it helped purge the writer, for example, of the temptation to stereotype.

Simenon contributed to all three of the main streams of the "roman populaire." He had started with sentimental love stories, and poured out many more. The basic formula almost always involved the trials of innocence at the hand of corruption—a devolution from Richardson and Laclos—with an ending that usually combined innocence, wealth, and happiness. *Le Roman d'une dactylo* and *Les Larmes avant le bonheur* are straightforward examples. In time, Simenon worked out variations.

The title of *A l'assaut d'un coeur* of 1925 points to the basic formula, but the plot is very complicated. The heroine-victim is (a) the widow of a French industrialist, (b) exiled from Soviet Russia, (c) the mother of a pretty teenage daughter, and (d) a successful dancer who, however, wishes to live a modest, unglamorous life. Nonetheless, she becomes helplessly drawn into the corrupt, decadent life of the wealthy archvillain Tessier and the toadies who surround him. A conspiracy develops to blackmail Tatiana so that her daughter will be delivered into Tessier's clutches on his yacht. Tessier's young secretary, Jacques, falls in love with Tatiana and saves her daughter in the nick of time when she has been lured onto the yacht and is about to be sacrificed to Tessier's evil lust, which "turns his cheeks crimson and makes his eyes shine."

In *L'Orgueil qui meurt*, also of 1925, innocence inheres mostly in the hero, whose beloved starts out in a dressmaking shop but, seduced by the world of glamour, becomes a movie actress, resists the advances of an American banker, is betrayed by the star she idolizes, but becomes a star herself and returns to her true love. *Les Adolescents passionnés* of 1928 opens with rural innocence (oyster gatherers in Brittany), proceeds with an inheritance that takes the heroine to corrupting Paris, and sends the *ingénu* hero off after her.

Not long after launching into the love stories, in canon, as it were, Simenon launched into adventure, with *La Prêtresse de Vaudoux*, published in 1925 by Tallandier and signed "Christian Brulls." Hot on its heels, in 1926, came *Se Ma Tsien, le sacrificateur*, a preposterous tale in which the hero goes to sea; finds a yacht on which everyone has been beheaded except a beautiful girl; goes with her in search of her father, a French colonel who is about to be sacrificed by a weird Oriental cult led by Se Ma Tsien; encounters a sinister Soviet agent who is somehow in cahoots with the murderous Chinese sect; and brings everything to a triumphant close in a fierce battle, at the end of which the colonel is saved, Se Ma Tsien escapes, and hero and heroine exchange kisses and declare their love.

Even more complex and equally fantastic, *Le Roi du Pacific* of 1929 is about a young couple sailing the South Pacific to capture a band of latter-day pirates, but are instead themselves captured, she becoming the prey of one of the pirate leaders. She is about to be massacred by the big chief, but is saved by a friendly native who is also in love with her.

Love stories and adventure stories intermingle, by tradition or by nature. An early piece, *L'Oiseau blessé* of 1925, is evenly balanced between them: a young aviator, whose squadron is being destroyed by a mysterious enemy, falls in love with a young girl from a country estate. The enemy turns out to be her father, a mad scientist intent on conquering the world. Behind this sort of thing Jules Verne is detectable; Ian Fleming's James Bond certainly follows it. In spite of his maniacal pace, Simenon had fun writing these things, particularly with the adventure stories. When one of these was called for, he would get up at dawn as usual, glance out the window at the beginning of early morning animation on the place des Vosges, then turn to his globe, twirling it around a bit until he had decided on an appropriately exotic setting.

I had treated myself to the Grand Larousse, and, to write *Se Ma Tsien le sacrificateur*, for example, I had to read everything that was written about Tibet and neighboring areas. A week later, I would be in the middle of the Congo, noting the names of plants, animals, various tribes. Then it would be the turn of South America, the Amazon. In this way, I travelled the whole world, seated in front of my typewriter, in a ray of sunshine generously dispensed by our tall windows.

Never again was he to have such a sense of adventure, even when he actually travelled to the regions he had written about from his encyclopedia: ". . . that period of my life is without doubt the one that I remember with the most tenderness, if not nostalgia."

As for the third category of pulp, crime, one might think it the most important for the future creator of Maigret, but in fact love and adventure were more up his alley than the standard detective story. He did produce some, starting perhaps with *Nox l'insaisissable*, published in 1926 in Ferenczi's detective series. It is in the Arsène Lupin tradition, and features a super-detective, Ansèlme Torres, pitted against a super-thief, Nox. Nox announces ahead of time that he will rob a certain banker, defying anyone to stop him (preannounced crimes occur several times in the Maigrets: *L'Affaire Saint-Fiacre*, for example, *Signé Picpus*, and *Maigret hésite*). Nox carries it off, but Ansèlme Torres confronts him, engendering a preposterous chase sequence and an inconclusive ending. Ansèlme Torres is a suave, worldly gourmet — another proto–James Bond.

A special place among the pulps should be reserved for those featuring Yves Jarry, because Simenon considered him the one character from these fictions invented with some degree of seriousness, with an "idea." The idea was of a man both desirous and capable of living a wide variety of different lives, in different milieus, different professions and different countries. Jarry is clever, self-confident and knowledgeable, showing up variously as criminal, detective, millionaire, adventurer — and, always, irresistible lover. He is a cross of Arsène Lupin, d'Artagnan, Lafcadio, and Simenon. Remembering him later, Simenon forgot that most of Jarry's "selves" are in the worldly, self-possessed adventurer mode, and thought of him as equally involved in manual labor, artisanship and slumming. He identified with him:

> I . . . had given him some of my desires . . . My ambition has always been (since childhood) to live several different lives, to be at the same time a farmer in the country, an elegant city-dweller, a deep-sea fisherman, etc. . . .

In the torridly titled *Chair de beauté*, published by Fayard in 1928, Yves Jarry is a writer who has become interested in Nadia, a glamorous dancer of African origin (Josephine Baker? Indeed, at the end of the first chapter, before Jarry has made his appearance, Nadia is calling out lovingly to a man named Georges). Georges, however, turns out to be the *ingénu* of the story, a young man whose desperate passion Nadia has just begun to reciprocate. Yves Jarry makes his entrance as, by coincidence, he is about to hire Georges's sister, rather carelessly named Yvette, as a secretary: "She felt bereft of her will. Or, rather she felt no other will than his." However, it's not she that counts in his life, but Nadia, with whom, in his own independent and undeclared way, he is in love. Being an expert on African art, he buys Egyptian masks that look like her. He turns detective for a while when Nadia is shot at during a nightclub dance (the attacker is revealed to be young Georges, crazed with jealousy), then, for the remainder of the novel, puts on his adventurer suit as he, Nadia and Yvette leave for Africa and complicated exotic entanglements in native uprisings, espionage and romance. At the end, Nadia and Georges are united, Jarry gallantly dropping out of their lives.

In *L'Amant sans nom* (1929), he plays the ardent lover in a 1920's gilded-age milieu. He is a criminal in this story, albeit a gallant and attractive one, involved in a complex story of stolen gold that unrolls in the South Seas, where he displays his extraordinary knowledge of the area. He is accompanied by his valet, François — a more or less comic figure in the Leporello vein — and pursued by a heavy-set, pipe-smoking detective, intuitive, slow and inexorably patient — clearly a precursor of Maigret.

In addition to love, crime and adventure, Simenon wrote a fourth category of pulp fiction, the humorous-erotic, at which he was an old hand. He published, in this period, a number of semipornographic books of the *Paris-Flirt* variety, but almost all of these are simply collections of short pieces of the kind already discussed. A young man with undulating black hair and a single white lock appeared one day at the place des Vosges apartment, announced he was a male prostitute, and proposed to tell Simenon his life story. Simenon accepted and turned out a colorful account of the man's bizarre experiences, which was published in 1929 as *Les Mémoires d'un prostitué*, with a cover photograph of the "young man with a white lock," seen from the back.

Simenon wrote "serious" work during these years, preserving its absolute distinction from "popular" work by never attempting to publish it, nor showing it to anyone except, occasionally, Tigy. He called it "writing for myself" and had been doing it since the Liège days, usually by hand in a notebook. They were brief, personal fictions, most of which came under one of two headings and were slipped into manila envelopes labelled accordingly: "Coïts," which expressed his overwhelming hunger for sexual experience; and "La Vie à deux," his yearning for the ideal couple that went back to adolescent glimpses of intimate couples in cozy, warm interiors, oppressing him with a sense of exclusion and envy.

This kind of writing was as agonizing as the pulp writing was easy. It required getting into a sort of trance and took so much out of him that after an hour of it he often got up and vomitted. The trance-like state and the anguish of composition were to remain fixtures throughout the main phase of his career. None of these pieces, unfortunately, has survived. There is reason to think they were cameos of impressionistic "fine writing" in the vein of "Le Compotier tiède." In addition, he would periodically interpolate a fragment of "real writing" — a sentence, a paragraph, a description — into the pulps, hoping no one would notice. If, in Liège, he could not envision literature as a profession, now he had his eye on a goal, however imprecise:

> I had not lost sight of the goal I had set for myself: to write novels.
> Not novels for a blue collection, or a red one or a green one. Novels
> that would express what I felt like expressing.

He considered these pseudonymous years as an apprenticeship, perhaps like his grandfather's tour to learn the hatter's trade. The Simenonian work ethic and sense of craftsmanship formed a continuum throughout his life, even if the craft did not. What he understood by "apprenticeship" was, ambiguously, practice in plotting and suspense provided by the pulps, and keeping his hand at serious work. "Gâcher le plâtre " (mixing the plaster), he called it. Sometimes he projected an ample ten years of "apprenticeship"; at other times he saw himself primarily as biding his time: "In two years I shall begin to really write."

Simenon is clearly a writer who juggles commercial modes with artistic ones. If he always insisted on keeping the two distinct, his subsequent career usually gives the impression of combining them. Are we to consider him like, say, William Faulkner, who went to Hollywood when he needed money, and then, when he had enough, came back to Oxford to do his art? Things did not work that way for Simenon, yet he wanted something like the same kind of distinction. Should we compare him to F. Scott Fitzgerald, who, also at certain points in his career, felt a sharp distinction between commerce and art, and would be annoyed that "a cheap story like 'The Popular Girl' written in one week . . . brings $1500 & a genuinely imaginative thing into which I put three weeks' real enthusiasm . . . brings not a thing"? But Simenon, who was in a similar position, never much resented the conditions that made his hack work salable and his "good" work unnoticed, and never had any trouble selling his "good" work once he decided he wanted to.

The inevitable comparison is with Balzac, who also began his literary career writing, under pseudonym, *his* era's version of pulp literature. His feeling that he was involved in "une véritable cochonerie littéraire" that paid well seems not unlike Simenon's sentiments. Like Simenon, but with a more

Napoleonic fervor, he aimed higher. Unlike Simenon, he had regrets about wasting his genius on garbage: "Now that I think I know my strength, I really regret sacrificing the flower of my ideas to these absurdities." Simenon never expressed such feelings about his stint at pulp writing. How Simenon as a "serious" writer compares with Balzac — or Faulkner or Fitzgerald — is another subject. As a commercial writer he was as exuberant as Balzac, and as condescending toward the commercial products he turned out. On the other hand, he did not, like Balzac and Fitzgerald, express a sense of wasted time. In this regard he was more like Faulkner, jauntily traipsing off to Hollywood to do his film scripts. But then again, the conditions — temporal, emotional and cultural — that structured the commercial-artistic relationship for Faulkner were very different from those that governed Simenon's career. In that respect, Simenon's situation was more complex, more problematical, more ambiguous.

In spite of the enormous success of his serious work, Simenon's inclination to view it as quite distinct from his commercial work was probably valid. Aesthetically, his commercial and "literary" impulses never mixed well, but remained in an unstable suspension, viable, in the final analysis, because of Simenon's disinterest in aesthetics, in art. The age of Balzac and Dickens was over, and in the world of twentieth century best-sellers, Simenon is a curiosity.

If Simenon's life in the twenties centered on Paris, there was also a deeply ingrained centrifugal force that sent him travelling constantly. Having settled into place des Vosges in 1924 and begun his spectacular accumulation of stories and novels, he and Tigy decided the following summer to take what he considered his first vacation (perhaps also his last: "vacation" is not a relevant category in Simenon's world). They went to the channel coast, partly because a friend with a villa there urged them, and perhaps also as a gesture of reconnection with his homeland. As a man of the north, he was always drawn to the south, but once in the south he would be drawn back to the north — a dialectic that perhaps accounts in part for his incessant movements.

Their friend lived in the little port of Étretat, near Fécamp — an area that was to provide the scene for many a novel. The villa was too small for guests, and they rented a big room in a farmhouse nearby in Bénouville, at first borrowing bales of hay to sleep on from Mme. Paumelle, their landlady. It was there that they met the 17-year-old Henriette Liberge, a neighboring farmgirl who used to come with her friends and watch them make love through the curtainless windows. They took her on as a maid and brought her back to Paris, where Simenon, somehow perceiving her face as getting rounder and rounder, rechristened her "Boule." They were strongly attracted to each other, but consummation was delayed by a deep diffidence he always felt about virgins, which he explained to her. A few days later she presented herself to him and said, "Now you can," having removed the obstacle by arranging to be deflowered. She fell in love with him — her "petit monsieur joli," as she called him — and remained his most faithful mistress for at least forty years, and his devoted servant for more.

The following year, in April of 1926, they headed south to the Mediterranean island of Porquerolles, a few kilometers off the coast, near Toulon. The genesis of his love affair with Porquerolles was not unlike that of his adventure novels. Tigy had sold her first painting, for a respectable sum, and they decided to take a trip. He looked at a map, trying to find the "ideal island," and somewhat haphazardly picked Porquerolles. They took the "Train Bleu" and woke up at dawn to a Provence abloom with almond trees, a joyful experience reproduced in *La Folle de Maigret* and *Mon Ami Maigret*. Simenon decided against the two hotels on the eucalyptus-lined central square, and instead shlepped baggage and typewriter to the other end of the island, followed by Tigy, Boule, and Olaf, the Great Dane.

At the Pointe du Grand Langoustier they found a two-room cottage with lovely verandas — the ideal house into which they moved instantly and stayed for several months. He immediately settled down to his crack-of-dawn routine to feed the presses of Fayard, Ferenczi, Tallandier, F. Rouff, *et al*. For a while there was a financial crunch, for the publishers were more leisurely about sending checks than Simenon about sending manuscripts. The situation got so tight that, for the only time in his life, he had to stop smoking for a week. Money finally came, and famine turned to feast as the Simenons and many new-found friends caroused in celebration.

Among the friends were Vladimir and Sasha, two sailors employed on the *Saint-Hubert*, a fancy yacht more or less permanently anchored at Porquerolles. Since its owner, a count who bore the same name as the yacht, hardly ever showed up, Sasha and Vladimir and their friends had frequent galas on board, as well as at the Simenons', at the beach, on the village square, at Hubert-Barbu's café (sometimes awakened in the middle of the night and persuaded to reopen), and at the Auberge de l'Arche de Noé, run by Maurice Bourgue, who remained for many years one of Simenon's local friends. Counterbalancing the late-night hoopla were more wholesome jollities like bowling on the green with the local residents, and fishing, a passion which Simenon developed further in Porquerolles and maintained for years afterward.

Those were golden days in 1926, prolonged in many subsequent stays. Porquerolles appears in many of Simenon's novels, often briefly as a symbol of relief and affirmation — in *Les Anneaux de Bicêtre*, for example, and *Cour d'assises*. It plays a major, more complex thematic role in *Le Cercle des Mahé*.

The Simenons were back at place des Vosges in September of 1926. They spent part of the following summer on the Île d'Aix, off the Atlantic coast, not far from La Rochelle. This is where he claims to have bolted to avoid marrying Josephine Baker. (The La Rochelle area subsequently played an important role in his life and in his books.) In the fall and winter of 1927–28 the Simenons stayed put at place des Vosges, where, in addition to the social whirlwind and the frenetic assembly line of paraliterature, he had a brief stint at magazine editing, and began supervising his career with exercises in promotion and public relations that he continued vigorously throughout most of his life. He began to be noticed as early as the mid-twenties. There is an interview, for example, in *Paris-Soir* of June 5, 1925, in which he says that he has come to Paris "pour faire de la littérature," and announcing his intention to write two novelettes a week of 1500 words each. "An extraordinary person," the interviewer comments. In another interview about that time he declared — probably reflecting Colette's advice — that he was seeking to achieve a "style . . . dépouillé" (a stripped-down style).

He became connected with the publisher of *Paris-Soir*, a flamboyant personage in Parisian journalism named Eugène Merle, erstwhile left-winger who, over the years, juggled a considerable variety of publications with which he cavalierly made and lost large amounts of money. In 1919 he founded a satirical journal whimsically named *Le Merle blanc* (to which Simenon contributed 11 stories in 1925), and, in 1923, the daily *Paris-Soir*, which, however, he lost control of four years later. In a different vein, he was also the publisher of *Frou-Frou*, where Simenon's early *contes gallants* were appearing with increasing frequency. Merle answered to several of Simenon's conflicting tastes. Simenon liked his irreverent, satirical personality, his origins among the "little people" of Marseilles's swarming "canebière," and his worldliness and high living.

> Merle had acquired an affection for me and spoke quite candidly to me: — "You see, *mon petit Sim*, there's only one thing in this world: money." The word shocked me . . . but I want to be sincere: that language began to rub off on me. It's because of Merle that, one day, in Liège, I said to my mother, "There are only two kinds of people in the world: the spankers and the spanked. I don't want to be among the spanked."

The image stuck in Simenon's mind and recurs in several novels: in *La Prison*, for example, where it is attributed to a weak-spirited, though successful, publisher of girlie magazines; and in *L'Horloger d'Everton*. If Merle felt money made the world go round, he had eccentric ways with it in business. He tended to pay his contributors with checks that often bounced, but evidently not often enough that they were worthless: Simenon found that he could sell them (to speculators?) at half the face value. From March to May of 1927 Simenon was the editor of a new, short-lived Merle enter-prise, *Le Merle rose*, which he ran virtually single-handedly and to which, under his multitudinous pseudonyms, he contributed the majority of the copy. *Le Merle rose* was a satirical and bawdy journal, much oriented toward reports of orgies and classified ads for sexual encounters. Simenon wrote an article on Josephine Baker, emphasizing her rippling laughter and pro-viding an elaborate description of the unique undulations of her buttocks: "c'est une croupe qui rit." There was a salacious question-and-answer sec-tion for which Simenon provided both questions and answers.

The best-known incident connected with Merle, retold innumerable times, is one that did not take place. In 1927, having lost *Paris-Soir*, Merle decided to try his hand instead at a morning daily, which was to have been called *Paris-Matin*, but which had to be changed to *Paris-Matinal* because *Le Matin* (of Colette fame) seems somehow to have copyrighted "matin." As a publicity gimmick Merle offered Simenon 50,000 francs to sit in a glass cage set up at the Moulin-Rouge and, for three days, compose a novel before the eyes of the public, which would then be serialized in *Paris-Matinal*. The cage was designed and the event resoundingly publicized. Unfortunately, Merle went bankrupt after a few issues and the great event was called off. For decades, however, people kept talking about the celebrated glass cage in which Georges Simenon wrote a novel; and even friends of his would tell him, "Remember when you sat in that glass cage and I came and tapped on the pane?"

Simenon's most extensive travelling in these years was by boat. Early in 1928 he bought a 15-foot boat called the *Ginette*, outfitted with a two-horsepower motor and, from May to September, toured the canals and rivers of central and southern France. The normal routine was to put-put along during the afternoon and moor at sundown. He and Tigy slept on the *Ginette*, turned into a cabin by removing the center board and stretching a canvass over a frame, while Boule and Olaf slept in a tent set up on the bank. The day began even earlier than usual, at four or five, when Boule would wake up Simenon and give him his coffee, after which he set immediately to work, either on the boat or taking over Boule's tent. His day's stint done, they would pack up and sail on to the next stopping point.

In small villages, arriving late in the evening, Simenon, still in swim-ming trunks, would go for bread and other supplies, startling the shopkeepers, who couldn't imagine where he had popped up from. Sometimes they docked in larger towns, or big cities, like Lyons, where Simenon began typing on deck at five o'clock in the morning and, after a few hours, would look up to the parapet above to see a congregation of amazed onlookers. They anchored off the beach at Grau-du-Roi, near Montpellier, where Boule would wade chest-high through the waves to bring Simenon his breakfast coffee. When he and Tigy went out at night, they would get back on board by taking their clothes off and swimming for the boat. Simenon acquired a thorough knowledge of canal life — the barge-people, the locks, the canal-shops (reminding him of his Aunt Anna's shop in Liège where he was so bored as a child). He registered everything, and it all came back later in innumerable novels. Those too were golden days:

> Life was slow. The barges going toward Bordeaux were loaded with wine. Coming back, they carried coal. At each lock the same little trading went on. The lockmaster would come with his jug to be filled with wine or his pail to be filled with coal. For his part, he offered goat cheese, a chicken, or a goat. As for wine, I obtained it at pumps which looked like gasoline pumps, where my keg was filled for a few francs. It was lazy. It was both warm and cool. You went constantly from shade to sun, and sometimes you had the impression of penetrating into a tunnel. A soft, silent world, which had the aroma of hazelnut trees and of the neighboring farms . . . Spots. Leaves in motion. Odors I have never found since. If the world could only be like that every day!

The following winter Simenon, more affluent, treated himself to a better boat. His bent was not for the high luxury of fancy yachts. Rather, early in 1929, he had a sturdy, seaworthy, 30-foot boat built of four-inch oak, along the lines of a commercial fishing vessel, with motor and sails. It was built in Fécamp, the Channel port that had attracted him three years earlier. He supervised construction, mingling with seafarers and dockhands, and plunged into a crash study of compass and sextant, logarithms, tide tables and advanced sailing techniques. He sailed it into the estuary of the Seine and up to Paris, where he moored it, prominently enough, at the pointe du Vert-Galant — the tip of the Île de la Cité. On a whim ("par coquetterie"), he persuaded the curé of Notre-Dame to christen it, "with great pomp."

The Simenons lived on the *Ostrogoth* for about two years, with some extended stays in Paris. Conditions were considerably more comfortable than on the *Ginette*: "I typed out my novels in a well-heated cabin where Boule did the cooking." The heat was necessary, for not only was it winter, but he decided soon to head north, eventually into Belgium, along his native Meuse, with a brief stay in Liège, where he had a party on board for old home-town friends. From Belgium, the *Ostrogoth* continued northward to Amsterdam, then into the Zuiderzee and the North Sea, often through thick fog, with Tigy or Boule working the hand-cranked foghorn. They followed the Dutch and German coasts, and put into Wilhelmshaven, where he was interrogated by the German authorities, suspicious because he was a Belgian flying the French flag, and because he was writing for a magazine called *Détective*.

"Why do you receive telegrams signed 'Détective'?"

"It's a magazine."

"You are a detective?"

"No. I write detective stories."

Expelled from German territorial waters, they backtracked and put into port at Delfizjl and Stavoren in Holland for extended periods, during which they returned to Paris or took other trips. One of these was a long trip by passenger ship up the Norwegian coast into Lapland: Bergen, Tromdjen, Kirkenes, and the Lofoden Islands. Way north, they undertook a trip inland, first, in a sort of protosnowmobile consisting of a wooden case on runners and hauled by a motorcycle with chains on its tires, then in a very low sleigh pulled by an eccentric reindeer who careened alarmingly over the expanses of frozen snow. The most dramatic experience was when the long darkness of winter came to an end, the sun made its first appearance, and the Lapps began to sing and dance.

Thus Simenon kept extremely busy in the second half of the twenties — exploring Mediterranean islands, sailing his boats up and down the waterways of France and northern Europe, partying, seducing women, editing *Le Merle rose* . . . and typing, typing, typing.

VIII

THE BIRTH AND TRIUMPH OF MAIGRET 1929-1932

In September of 1929 the *Ostrogoth* was in the little Dutch port of Delfzijl, whose houses and streets are constructed mostly of pinkish bricks, and which is surrounded by ramparts that are in reality dikes. The boat stayed in port much longer than planned, because Simenon discovered that some of its oak joints had been badly fitted and needed extensive caulking. He temporarily moved his "office" to a half-sunken barge, where he set up his typewriter on a big crate in the water, sat on a smaller crate, propped up his feet on two others, and kept typing. As usual, he worked from the early hours of the morning, his routine modified here by a morning break for a couple of shots of "genièvre" at a charming little bar, le Pavillon, where he quickly became an habitué.

This is where Maigret was and was not created. That he was created there is attested to by a statue of the famous detective commissioned by the Dutch authorities, and unveiled at the very spot in 1966 by his creator. The project was based on Simenon's long-standing account of how he invented Maigret: One morning in September, 1929, having come to the end of a project and seeking inspiration for the next, he sauntered over to the Pavillon, where he sipped two or three glasses of "genièvre" and smoked his pipe. Various images and seemingly random associations floated about in his head, and also a thought. The thought was that maybe his literary "apprenticeship" was ending:

[7 4]

What should I write next? For some time I had the feeling that my apprenticeship was drawing to a close . . . I was still hesitant to launch into a more difficult, if not more serious, vein.

The images were various: streets in Paris, where he had not been for many months; then the silhouettes of *rats de mer*—the wharfside bums one encounters in ports. Then he conjured up the vague outline of a portly, strong, stolid gentleman, which "it seemed to me, would do reasonably well as a police inspector." Musing further, he endowed his personage with some details: "a pipe, a bowler hat, a heavy overcoat with velvet lapels. And since a damp cold pervaded my abandoned barge, I provided him with an old cast-iron stove for his office." The result was *Pietr-le-Letton*, the first Maigret. It was, that is, the first "canonical" Maigret, the first "real" Maigret, and, indeed, the first "real" novel. The fact that it was the first piece of writing signed "Simenon" is significant, echoing his feeling that it was time to "move on" a bit in literature—though, curiously, he often described the decision to use his real name as an accident.

Simenon, however, provided this account many years after the event and almost certainly was confusing several different works. The *Ostrogoth* was berthed both at Delfzijl and at Stavoren for a very long time, including the period of the Scandinavian trip. He wrote many stories and novels in both ports, including, indeed, *Pietr-le-Letton*. What he was writing in his sunken barge in 1929 was detective pulp novels. The images of wharfside bums and Parisian streets correspond much less closely to *Pietr-le-Letton* than to a novel called *Captain S.O.S.*, featuring an Inspector Sancette, published by Fayard in 1929. On the other hand, he also signed a contract for another novel, entitled *Train de nuit* and signed Christian Brulls, at the end of September, in which a police commissaire named Maigret *does* appear. If this book was written in Delfzijl, which is quite probable, all is well: the statue, after all, belongs where it is, and Simenon's memory was merely blending different compositions into an anecdote charming enough to become enshrined.

Before the Maigrets, there were pre–Maigrets, which are of two kinds. One is a pulp crime story in which a policeman appears having some resemblance to Maigret, like no. 49 in *L'Amant sans nom*, Yves Jarry's plodding pursuer. Or *Fièvre*, which was not published until 1932 but may have been composed earlier, where a burly commissaire appears, bearing the name of Torrence (who in the real Maigrets is one of Maigret's chief subordinates) but acting more like a proto–Maigret, possessed, for example, of a gruff unpretentiousness, a love of fishing, a sense of emotional involvement with the criminal he is pursuing, and a wife who cooks nice little meals for him. The other is a pulp novel in which a policeman actually called "Maigret" appears, but bearing little if any resemblance to the famous commissaire.

Train de nuit, for example, is not even a detective story, but a love story turning, once again, on the corruption-innocence axis; some incidental crimes occur and are investigated by a Marseilles police commissaire named Maigret. Proto–Maigrets appear also in *La Figurante, La Femme rousse* and *La Maison de l'inquiétude* (this last published serially in 1930 in *L'Oeuvre*, rejected by Fayard, and published in 1932 by Tallandier).

The significance of these books lies less in their resemblance to the real Maigret than in pointing to a shift by Simenon in the late twenties toward more crime stories in proportion to love and adventure. He had dabbled at crime stories with things like *Nox l'insaisissable* and a few others. In 1928, probably urged by Fayard, he devoted greater attention to criminals and policemen. Under yet another pseudonym, J.-K. Charles, he published a series of brief, vaguely fictionalized accounts of police methods in a weekly called *Ric et Rac* (a Fayard publication), in preparation for which he read a number of works of modern criminology. In 1929, he contracted with *Détective* to write a series of very short detective stories, originally published under pseudonym but collected in 1932 under patronym as *Les 13 Coupables*, *Les 13 Énigmes*, and *Les 13 Mystères*, thus constituting the first works written to be published under the name "Georges Simenon."

These stories show Simenon taking one more turn toward the detective story, but in a mode quite contrary to the Maigret spirit, as if he were zigzagging toward Maigret and this were a last zag in the opposite direction. The "Thirteen" series are, so to speak, anti–Maigrets in being wholly, and frivolously, intellectual, in contrast with the intuitive Maigret, who keeps saying, "I never think." The detectives featured — Leborgne, Froget, and G-7 — are cerebral armchair types, whose exploits are usually reported by a first-person straight man in the manner of Dr. Watson and Archie Goodwin. Perhaps Simenon was exorcising a detective mode for which he had little affinity, or demonstrating his conviction that the cerebral mode is quite dull. His versions are, indeed, singularly uninteresting, and were in fact written as a sort of magazine game: the "mystery" was presented in one issue of *Détective*, readers invited to propose solutions, and the true solution revealed in the next issue.

By the late spring of 1930, Simenon, having decided to exploit the detective genre and tried out various approaches, settled on one of these: the heavy-set, slow-moving, unpretentious figure who had popped up in certain pulp works. At the same time, Simenon felt a need somehow to raise his literary level a notch or two, to begin to narrow the gap between commercial imperatives and the vision of a literary vocation that had germinated in his adolescence and gone underground subsequently. The result was *Pietr-le-Letton*. Having settled on a detective and conjured up a narrative starting point, Simenon wrote down the names of a few characters on a manila envelope he happened to have at hand, and which was to become a necessary part of his procedure for almost all the novels he wrote subsequently. Tempering the furious pace of the pulps, he took four or five days to finish the book, which runs to a little more than two hundred pages in a small format.

Simenon's sense that he was escalating some steps up the literary hierarchy was not unwarranted. *Pietr-le-Letton* is an interesting book, all the more remarkable in the flair with which Simenon established many of the traits of his celebrated commissaire that were to remain or be expanded. Of Maigret's accoutrements, the most insistent in this novel, from the first paragraph, is not his pipe but his stove. He has a mania for heat, perhaps because he spends several extended scenes — including the dénouement — soaking wet. The stove will remain, though rarely again so prominent, throughout Maigret's fictional career. So, very often, will the rain. In some other books, the rain will be sharply counterpointed with sunshine, which Maigret stolidly relishes.

Rain, sun and a humble, furiously overheated cast-iron stove — these are elements welling up more deeply than anything in the pulp fiction from a childhood in Liège, the *ville pluvieuse*. Maigret is 45, an age he more or less retains for forty years, except for a few flashbacks to his earlier career, and flash-forwards to his retirement. He is in command of the first "brigade mobile" (sometimes the "brigade criminelle") of the Police Judiciaire, a criminal investigation force roughly comparable to the F.B.I. or Scotland Yard, though French police organization makes analogies fuzzy. He has a high rank: a "commissaire" corresponds vaguely to "inspector" or "chief-inspector" in American police forces; the British call him "chief-inspector." (Terminology becomes all the more confusing because "inspecteur" in the French system refers to plainclothes detectives of various ranks, but below "commissaires." A commissaire has nothing in common with an American commissioner of police, which is not a rank but a civilian title.)

Maigret, in some stories, is designated as "Commissaire principal." He wears a bowler hat, an overcoat with a velvet collar, and reasonably well-tailored suits of reasonably good wool. His neckties tend not to knot quite properly and his pants to be a bit baggy: neither a dandy nor a slob, in short, but a man of the people. His abhorrence of worldliness and luxury is thoroughly established by the circumstances of this, his first story, much of which takes place in the lobby of the swank Majestic hotel, where his intrusive "otherness" is admirably sustained: "Le Majestic ne le digérait pas" (the fancy hotel finds him indigestible). We learn that he is a veteran and that he once was a medical student.

We do not actually meet Mme. Maigret until the end, when she reads newspaper accounts of the case to him, asks questions, gets grumbled replies and complains that it's hardly worth being the wife of a commissaire because one gets more information from the concierge. Her characteristic presence, however, is indicated earlier, when we learn that, if he were not so wrapped up in his investigation, he could go home any time and find a succulent stew waiting for him. The Maigret cast of characters is fragmentary. His principal collaborator is an Inspector Dufour, whose character is sketched out in some detail, but who is dropped in most subsequent Maigrets. On the other hand, the faithful Torrence appears and is murdered by gangsters halfway through the book, activating a sense of anger and revenge in Maigret rarely found later. Torrence is resurrected for the rest of the saga.

Judge Coméliau — the "juge d'instruction," something between a district attorney and a criminal-court magistrate — appears here, to remain a solid fixture and a principal ideological antagonist to Maigret. The basis of the antagonism here is very sketchy, but perceptible. It arises when Maigret explains the gnarled Eastern-European background of the principals, expressing psychological insight, understanding, and some sympathy, while Judge Coméliau's summing-up of the situation is, "What the devil are these foreigners up to in our country?"

The Maigret "method" is introduced sketchily, appearing here as the theory of the "fissure" — the crack in the criminal, who, until it appears, has been playing a game, but through which the real human being behind the game-player becomes manifest to the intuitive observer-investigator. Thus Maigret's understanding and sympathy are corollaries of the method: in finding the humanity behind the criminal situation, one's own humanity becomes activated, leading to the fellow-feeling the commissaire often develops with his quarry. Communion between police and criminals, on a variety of levels, is a familiar notion both in life and in detective fiction; but the Maigret version of that phenomenon has a tonality of its own.

The concluding scene of *Pietr-le-Letton* takes place in a hotel room where pursuer and pursued, soaking wet, talk things out, their mutual humanity asserted by the ill-fitting bathrobes lent to them by a good natured innkeeper. The pursued — the submissive, masochistic Hans impersonating his admired, strong-willed, sadistic brother, Pietr — describes his agitated, doomed life, confirming what Maigret had already intuited. *Pietr-le-Letton* is the first (in order of composition, not publication) of 19 Maigrets that constitute the "early" Maigrets, Maigrets of the first period — "Fayard" Maigrets, as they are sometimes designated, after their publisher. In these in general, and in *Pietr-le-Letton* in particular, Maigret's character and method are more roughly sketched than in later Maigrets, and his psychology, sociology, and criminology are embryonic. The early Maigret is not as benign or paternal as the later. By and large, he is a well-drawn outline, with some interesting or amusing details and much room for amplification and fine tuning. In short, by luck or design, a promising creation.

The promise was not lost on Simenon, who sensed he had a potential winner and was willing to bet on him heavily. It was to persuade Arthème Fayard to do likewise that he hopped on a train to Paris with the manuscript of *Pietr-le-Letton*. He showed it to Charles Dillon, who took it to Fayard with the comment that there was something gripping about the newly created commissaire. Simenon proposed "launching" Maigret with major publicity. Fayard's response, according to Simenon's frequently related account, was that (1) this was not a real detective story unraveling a mystery with unimpeachable logic, (2) his detective was neither infallible, nor young, nor sexy, (3) there was no clear-cut division between good guys and bad guys, and (4) there was no love interest, and everything turned sour at the end. Simenon held out his hand to have the manuscript returned, but Fayard said, "We're going to lose a lot of money, but I'll try it anyway."

He instructed Simenon to compose half a dozen Maigrets, which would then be published, with appropriate fanfare, at the rate of one per month. They argued a bit about pricing and design. Fayard wanted to market the books at five francs, but Simenon had made his own calculations and concluded that six would yield maximum profits. Simenon won, as he did with his proposal for photographed instead of drawn covers. He took his design seriously enough to engage André Vigneau, a prominent photographer, and even persuaded Man Ray to participate. Simenon himself went rummaging about the rue Mouffetard in search of an appropriate bum to pose for the third Maigret, *Le Charretier de la "Providence."* He also negotiated something above the normal 10 percent royalty, as he always did subsequently.

Simenon zipped back up to Holland and sailed the *Ostrogoth* back to France in the summer of 1930, mooring it at Morsang, upstream from Paris, where, in rapid succession, he composed three more Maigrets. In September he was in Paris at the Hôtel l'Aiglon (they had given up place des Vosges), where he wrote a fourth. He also backtracked to pulps, forced by a 30,000-franc advance from Fayard, who would not let him off the hook by deducting it from Maigret royalties, a parsimoniousness that later cost Fayard the loss of his most profitable author.

It was in this period that Simenon, caught between pulps and Maigrets and eyeing a higher notch on the literary ladder, developed his theory of the "roman semi-littéraire," or, more earthily, "semi-alimentaire." The theory was that he wrote pulps to bring home the bacon, was aiming at "straight" novels but felt strangely insecure, and took up the detective story as midway step. The pulp novel is easy to write because the writer is totally uninvolved, the "straight" novel difficult because he is wholly involved, to the point of exhaustion and nervous breakdown, and the detective story in-between, because, though involved, the writer has a set gimmick to structure his book and keep his reader interested: the crime to be solved and the detective who can come and go at will in solving it. It is curious to note that, at the very time he was mulling over theories of literary escalation, he ceased to read fiction.

In midwinter 1930–31 he was mostly in Paris, attending to the launching of the Maigrets with another category of "involvement." *M. Gallet, décédé* and *Le Pendu de Saint-Pholien* were chosen as the first two, and Fayard asked him under what name they were to appear. Various names were considered and rejected until Fayard asked him, "What *is* your real name, anyway?" "Simenon," Simenon answered, and they decided that would do. Simenon hustled to promote the project. On February 16, 1931, for example, a journalist friend did a jaunty interview in the daily *La République* describing the "semialimentary" theory and announcing the publication schedule of the first Maigrets.

The official release, on February 20, was a well-engineered extravaganza that was the talk of the town for some days and remained as much a part of the Simenon legend as the nonexistent glass cage. It took place at the well-known Montparnasse nightclub, the Boule Blanche, and was called a "bal anthropométrique," referring to police procedures for identifying and classifying criminals and suspects. The invitations were streaked with bloody fingerprints, and the guests themselves were fingerprinted at the door. The "Tout-Paris" was there, in detective-story outfits, the dominant motif being what was known as "Apache," a Europeanized Americanism of the twenties and thirties designating, by reference to ferocious Indians, tough urban hoodlums. Shortly after the start of the ball, three of Simenon's artist friends, illuminated by spotlights, rapidly sketched a series of criminal motifs on the walls.

In a corner, Georges Simenon was signing hundreds of copies of *Le Pendu de Saint-Pholien*. "To my friend . . . ," one columnist reports him as writing, and looking up: "please remind me of your name, Madame . . . Mme. Dupont! Thank you, *To my friend Mme. Dupont*. Next!" The showbiz and society columnists were all there, reporting each other's presence and that of long lists of in-crowd guests, almost all meaningless now. A few exceptions were Colette, who came to congratulate her erstwhile protégé; Francis Carco, the poet; Emil Pabst, the German filmmaker; Pierre Lazareff, who was then one of the society columnists but who later became publisher of *France-Soir* and a good friend of Simenon's; and André Thérive, the literary critic of *Le Temps*, soon to be one of Simenon's chief promoters for a higher literary niche.

As publicity, the "bal anthropométrique" worked splendidly and was reported everywhere in the press — sometimes, though, with some wry digs, as by *Le Canard enchaîné*:

> M. Georges Simenon wants to be famous at any price. If he doesn't reach fame with his "bal anthropométrique," he intends to walk around the pond at the Tuileries on his hands — while writing a novel.

The first four Maigrets were issued at the much-publicized schedule, and Simenon spent the spring of 1931 writing four more at Morsang on the *Ostrogoth* and at the nearby château of La Michaudière. In August he was chosen best-seller of the year by the publisher Hachette, who held a yearly book signing event at the classy Channel resort of Deauville, to which Simenon sailed the *Ostrogoth*, anchoring it among the luxury yachts that contrasted with it as the Hôtel Majestic with Maigret. From there, the Simenons proceeded to the more congenial Breton fishing port of Ouistreham, where they spent the fall and Simenon wrote three more Maigrets. Most of the rest of the first series were written in 1932, and the last two in 1933.

Simenon, as we have noted, has claimed that he read virtually no detective stories. He has also asserted that there is no such thing as the detective story. However, he did read at least a few of the French classics, and he must have read a few others when he was boning up on the pulps to get a handle on the genre. As for the genre, the evidence seems to be that it exists as much as any other genre, and that Georges Simenon, whether he likes it or not, played a significant role in its evolution. This role can best be identified as both a reaction against, and a modification of, what by the 1920's, had become the classical mode and the mainstream of the genre. In that sense he is parallel to the American "hardboiled" school of detective writing. The parallel by no means signifies direct influence in either direction; rather, it points to prevailing winds in a branch of literary history of which both he and the Americans are manifestations.

Most everyone agrees that the detective story was invented by Edgar Allan Poe in 1842 with "The Murders in the Rue Morgue" (though some commentators like to point to biblical, classical, and other antecedents). Poe's Chevalier Dupin is an eccentric snob with an astounding intellect that constantly dazzles his duller companion. The latter tells the story, and is the prototype of Sherlock Holmes' Dr. Watson, Hercule Poirot's Captain Hastings, Nero Wolfe's Archie Goodwin, and many others, including a variety of secondary characters in Simenon. In "Rue Morgue," Dupin concludes, by close observation and logic, that the murders, which occurred in a locked room with no evident means of ingress or egress, can only have been committed by an orangutan, which is indeed the case.

Edgar Allan Poe, we recall, was a moody, eccentric, unhappy, unsuccessful man who wrote extravagant poetry of a decadent, later romantic variety, and stories of fear and terror. It is perhaps in compensation for all this that he also cultivated a faith in human reason. Thus the detective story at its very birth, as well as in much of its subsequent development, celebrates the triumph of intellect over confusions and misleading appearances. If you're smart enough, you'll find the orangutan at the bottom of it all. One of the principal emotions aroused in the detective story is fear (a derivation probably from the Gothic novel), but it usually avoids exploring fear very deeply, or pushing it to the limits, as the emotion of love is, say, in *Romeo and Juliet*, or guilt in *Crime and Punishment*, or courage in the *Iliad*. The psychology of the detective story revolves around the opposite emotions of fear, engendered by the crime, and of security, inhering in the detective's infallible intellect which dissipates the murky shadows and restores the world to light and order.

After Poe, many factors contributed to the growth of the detective story. There was an increasing interest in crime, probably related to an actual increase in urban crime during the rapid development of industrial society. At the same time, a powerful middle class was establishing itself, with much wealth, property and privilege — all new, hence insecure and in need of protection, unlike the wealth and power of the firmly rooted aristocracy that preceded it. It was largely to serve the needs and allay the anxieties of this new class that modern police forces evolved. In England, the Metropolitan Police Act was legislated in 1829, and the detective department founded in 1842.

Other factors propitious to the growth of the detective story are those already noted in respect to popular literature in general: increased literacy, publishing technology, the railroad, and, one might add, the invention of the lending library. In France, the detective story developed in the wake of Poe, and interacted with its progress in England and, later, in America. One finds in France a greater interest in the criminal proportionally to the detective, often more sympathy with the criminal, and, on occasion, a certain intimacy between criminal and detective which is not without foundation in real life. For sympathy with the criminal, take Victor Hugo's *Les Misérables*, or Balzac's Vautrin, whose dynamism and energy shine brightly against the corrupt society around him.

Less distinguished but more important in the development of this subliterature is Emile Gaboriau, who, in the latter part of the nineteenth century, enthralled his readers with newspaper serializations of crude but exciting stories of the Paris underworld. There was also the bizarre Vidocq, first chief of the French Sûreté, who himself had a criminal background, left the police under a cloud of criminal accusations, and wrote memoirs which had some influence on the development of crime literature, particularly Gaboriau.

Meanwhile, in England, a young doctor having little success in his profession decided to try writing. In 1887 Arthur Conan Doyle published "A Study in Scarlet," featuring, in direct line from Poe, a private detective with a superhuman mind. Sherlock Holmes is mostly a reasoning machine, deliberately endowed with little eccentricities to give him more personality: cocaine, the violin, misogyny, misanthropy—a gambit imitated by many successors. As everyone knows, Conan Doyle got tired of Holmes and tried to kill him off, which the public would not allow him to do. Georges Simenon often identified with that phenomenon. Holmes, of course, had an enormous influence.

In France two writers whom Simenon *did* read are in the Holmes tradition, gallicized. With Maurice Leblanc's Arsène Lupin, we find the French, again, reversing, or being playful with, the detective-criminal roles. Arsène Lupin is a master criminal (theft), but his mind works exactly like Sherlock Holmes', and he repeatedly confronts another superintellect with a mind almost—never quite—equal to his. Sometimes he switches roles and becomes a detective himself. One of his antagonist-competitors is called Herlock Sholmès.

The other French offspring of Poe and Conan Doyle is Gaston Leroux, creator of the young reporter-detective Simenon once identified with, Rouletabille, who specializes in the "closed-room" mystery that Poe had initiated: the crime that seems impossible because there is no logical way by which the criminal could have entered or left the room.

Then comes what many historians and critics call "the golden age of the detective story," with its epicenter in England in the 1920's and 30's and many imitators in most major languages. Agatha Christie is the most complete embodiment of the golden-age mode. Her creatures, Hercule Poirot and Miss Marple, in the footsteps of Sherlock Holmes, are eccentric, self-assured, and capable of solving all crimes with infallible powers of observation and deduction.

The classic format is an unexpected murder among a fairly close-knit group of people, who, however, all turn out to have secrets from each other and from the reader, and who constitute a congregation of suspects. The detective, cooperating with but infinitely superior to the local police, interrogates the suspects and ferrets out clues. At the end, he convenes the suspects, describes his logical processes, and points to the guilty person, who is forced to confess by the irresistible power of logic.

It has been noted many times that the world of the classical detective story is a dream world. The stories are written in the 20's, the 30's and later, but most often take place in a stable, rural, aristocratic world that reflects—

if it reflects anything real at all—a society that disappeared forever with the First World War. It is a world of prelapsarian innocence; there is a crime, to be sure, but everything is safe, nothing has really changed, and the godlike detective restores an innocence we knew all along was never really lost. These stories were written during the Great Depression, during the coming to power of Fascism, Nazism and Bolshevism, during the Spanish Civil War and the Second World War: none of that ever enters into the secure, privileged world of the classic detective story.

The fact that the detective is usually an amateur rather than a professional policeman probably makes it easier for the reader to identify with him. We are not *really* involved in the world of crime and crime detection; we are all playing a little game together. The detectives are legion: G.K. Chesterton's Father Brown, Dorothy Sayers' Lord Peter Wimsey, Erle Stanley Gardner's Perry Mason, Frederick Dannay's and Manfred Lee's Ellery Queen, Rex Stout's Nero Wolfe, etc. (Rex Stout and Georges Simenon knew each other in the fifties, and Stout, asked whom he would choose to carry on if Nero Wolfe became incapacitated during an investigation, replied "Maigret.")

The modulation in the detective-story tradition that constituted a reaction against the "golden-age" mode took place in the late 20's and the 30's—that is, precisely during the period that Simenon was formulating and elaborating Maigret. The essence of this modulation might be summed up in one word, realism, if that were not the kind of word that creates more confusion than clarification. Certain writers decided that detective stories could be populated with people possessed of more flesh and bone, more blood, more character, and also more troubles, than the puppets and superintellects of the classical mode. They also felt that the detective story could provide a more accurate image of the contemporary world than did the idyllic, archaic settings of the golden-age stories.

This development meant more action in the story, and less logical reasoning. No armchair detectives, but men wandering about the artifacts and the populace mostly of large cities: bars, hotels, brothels, the mansions of the rich, the tenements of the poor, encountering severe obstacles at every step. It meant more violence: the obstacles frequently were rough characters from the criminal underworld, or corrupt policemen, or alcoholics, or psychotics, etc. Murder, no longer a formal pretext for the exercise of the detective's virtuosity, became what murder really is: brutality, violence, the crushing of bones and the flowing of blood. The major line of this kind of detective story is the American "hardboiled" school and its aftermath. However the term wandered from eggs to detectives, "hardboiled" has to do with the toughness of the detective, both physical and moral: his resistance to violent attacks upon his person, his almost negligent courage in the face of physical dangers, and his readiness to slug into oblivion a wide variety of hoodlums, thugs and racketeers.

The new detective hits hard; he's fast on his feet; he carries weapons and uses them if he has to. His language corresponds to his behavior and his character: tough, full of slang, usually laconic, frequently vulgar. He is the opposite of the sophisticated, elegant detective of the golden-age type. He is, most famously, Dashiell Hammett's Sam Spade and Raymond Chandler's Philip Marlowe. He is Humphrey Bogart, who played both. And he is Jean Gabin, who played Maigret.

Many things caused this development. For one, it was inevitable: there *had* to be a reaction against the implausibilities and absurdities of the classical genre, in the same way that there had to be a reaction against romances of chivalry, which gave us *Don Quixote*, a reaction against neoclassical formalism, which gave us romanticism, etc. There is the influence of Hemingway, Dos Passos, Sherwood Anderson, and, behind these, in America, of Mark Twain. Every time Spade or Marlowe utters one of his characteristic vulgarisms, he is echoing an American literary tradition that goes straight back to *Huckleberry Finn*.

There are social and historical causes, too, such as the emergence of organized crime in the twenties and thirties, with its famous gangsters like Dillinger and Al Capone, and all the little and big criminals who were spawned by Prohibition and who, at its end, went on to other illegal, violent and disreputable fields: drugs, extortion, blackmail, pornography. Although Maigret is very unlike Marlowe and Spade in many respects, he arises out of similar literary impulses, embodies variations of the same characteristics, and circulates largely in the same world. What Julian Symons has said of Raymond Chandler applies equally well to Simenon: "To accept a mediocre form and make something like literature out of it is in itself rather an accomplishment."

The 19 novels, then, from *Pietr-le-Letton*, written in 1930, to *Maigret* in 1934, constitute the first phase of Simenon's characteristic contribution to the modern detective story. Those stories manifest a Simenonian version of the new realism in the detective genre. Maigret's method of impregnating himself with the milieu of the case, which emerges as Simenon's celebrated "atmosphere," is nothing if not some mode of "realism." Maigret's search for the common humanity behind criminals, as well as other characters, is likewise a kind of psychological "realism." His refusal to pass judgment — hence his alienation from judges — is yet another kind of "realism," in asserting the facticity of legal-moral systems and evoking instead a more substantive realm of individual emotion and intuition. As Maigret develops, he demonstrates, as well as asserts, with increasing insistence, that, as a police officer, he searches out and arrests those who have broken the law, but that this civil function arrogates to itself no special dispensation, no special relationship to principles of justice or order; it is, in effect, a form of artisanship.

The second Maigret that Simenon wrote was probably *Le Pendu de Saint-Pholien*, for which he used the more sordid and destructive aspects of the Caque as the underlying causes of the crime Maigret investigates. The most sinister episode connected with the Caque, we recall, occurred when young Klein hanged himself after a dreadful night of alcohol, cocaine and hypnotism. In *Le Pendu* Simenon adds the murder of a supercilious, rich Jewish youth whom the rest of the Caque resents. Klein hangs himself out of guilt and despair. His roommate and best friend, Lecoq, a failed painter, leads a desultory, guilt-ridden life, carrying about with him in a suitcase the bloody clothes of the slain youth, which constitute damning evidence against them all.

The others have buried their past and are mediocre bourgeois, but Lecoq seeks obscurely to avenge Klein by blackmailing his erstwhile companions over the years. Shortly after Maigret encounters him he is killed, and Maigret spends the rest of the novel ferreting out the dismal story, guided by his intuition about the ex-bohemians he visits, and by a series of obsessive drawings of hanged men by Lecoq. Grafting to the detective genre his dim view of the fringe bohemianism he had experienced in his youth, Simenon ends up with a sort of minor Dostoyevskian tale. Maigret rummages around guilty consciences, hypocrisies and petty fears, and comes up with a common skeleton in all the closets. In a much later work, *Maigret tend un piège*, Simenon was once again to use arty decadence as background for crime, where the killer turns out to be a psychotic with a mother complex, and also a painter raté of "sad" and "morbid" paintings ("un cérébrale, un artiste").

The skeleton in the closet, a pervasive motif in Simenon's fictions, is endemic to the detective story. (An unattributed epigraph in *Les Soeurs Lacroix* declares, "Each family has a corpse in the closet.") A great deal of the time, the skeleton turns out to be a relative of skeletons in Simenon's own closet, from whom he kept his distance in life but readily conjured up in art: the woebegotten Brülls of his childhood, the seamier postures of his own adolescence, and a variety of later alcoholics, neurotics, nymphomaniacs, prostitutes, etc. It did not take much to steer these phantoms over the edge into some kind of criminality, bringing them into Maigret's embrace in the detective fiction, while, in other novels, pretty much leaving them stewing in their own juice. The autobiographical elements are not mere curiosities, but are a necessary contributing factor to the "realism" of the tale. If the result is sometimes imperfect, that is often because of a "bad fit" between autobiography and invention, due primarily to Simenon's rapidity of composition and distaste for revision.

The companion piece of *Le Pendu de Saint-Pholien* in the February launching, *M. Gallet, décédé,* is only moderately successful in working out an adequate plot to account for the posited situation: it all turns on a double identity and a somewhat implausible suicide made to look like a murder. *Le Charretier de la "Providence,"* on the other hand, which followed soon afterward, is a better story that fuses together many Simenonian motifs and experiences. The canal setting allows Simenon to activate his recent observations and enthusiasms, transferring them to Maigret, who noses out the secret by absorbing the canal-life atmosphere. The skeleton in the closet is the long-lost love of a young doctor for a jazzy, destructive woman who betrays him. The doctor goes overseas and returns years later as an inarticulate bargehand, one of Simenon's innumerable dropouts. Accident brings him in contact with his beloved, whom he murders. Solving the crime and finding pathos, Maigret displays his characteristic sympathy for a technical criminal, who dies at the end, obviating any legal questions of criminal justice.

Le Chien jaune, probably the fifth or sixth written in the series, is an excellent example of early Maigret. (It seems also to have struck the novelist Marcel Aymé's fancy, who wrote an appreciative preface for a 1962 reissue.) Unlike *Le Pendu de Saint-Pholien,* the foreground action has considerably more substance than the background action. Maigret's investigation in the little Breton port of Concarneau, terrorized by an unknown criminal, is a masterpiece of ambiance, suspense and sharp character description; the explanation behind it all is implausible and grotesquely involuted.

Simenon leads into the atmosphere and the foreground story with a terse style, verging sometimes on the telegraphic. "Friday 7 November. Concarneau is deserted." "In front of him, in the basin, a coastal vessel which has taken shelter that afternoon. No one on deck." "Leaning by the cashier, a waitress. At a marble table, two men finish their cigars, sitting back, legs stretched out." A sort of stage-direction style. Frequent predicateless sentences, no less effective on that account. The novel is rich in early examples of Simenon's atmosphere building, sometimes too specifically labelled as "atmosphere": "There was in the café's atmosphere something gray, dull that you couldn't put your finger on."

By and large, though, Simenon builds up a vivid sense of the quality of the town, the mood and sensibility of its denizens. A sense of rural sexual sordidness is pervasive, as well as small-town xenophobia and petty viciousness — as when townspeople throw stones at the hapless wounded dog of the title, while, in contrast, Maigret gently pats it. Individual corruption, as well as the town's disagreeable collective personality, are effectively echoed by the physical setting:

Maigret looked through the window panes. It was no longer raining, but the streets were full of black mud and the wind was still howling violently. The sky was livid gray.

In contrast with the bad weather — almost intruding on it — are bursts of good weather and of concurrent good humor, centering on Maigret but somehow spreading through the whole town:

> Maigret was in such a good mood that following morning that Inspector Leroy dared to follow him and chat . . . The sky seemed as if freshly laundered . . . The horizon seemed vaster, as if the celestial dome had been more deeply scooped out. The sea sparkled, punctuated by little sails that looked like the flags in a military map.

If bad weather is an emblem of human turpitude and misery, good weather is a way, not so much of counter-balancing it, as of getting a perspective on it, a way of wriggling momentarily into a Maigret-like serenity that embraces suffering and cruelty because it cannot neutralize them. Figures of speech are infrequent, as usual in Simenon's style. When they occur, they are either perfunctory, or else quite striking, as this one, describing Maigret and an associate observing from a rooftop the encounter between two young lovers in a room some distance away:

> It was imprecise, as blurry as a film projected when the houselights have been lit. And something else was missing: noises, voices . . . Again like a film: a film without the music.

One of the skills that Simenon developed as he escalated from a commercial to a more literary mode was to manipulate time, to move fluidly from present to past, to more distant past, and sometimes to future. In the early Maigrets, this is mostly a matter of flashbacks, usually toward the end, providing the explanatory background action. In *Le Chien jaune*, he experiments with some subtleties. In the course of the opening foreground narrative, another level of foreground is anticipated in dramatic juxtaposition:

> "It was only at that moment that I had the feeling that something had happened," the customs office would testify during the inquest.

As for Maigret himself, he is filling out his "first-series" personality. He still has his early brusque manner. "F---ez-moi la paix!" we find him shouting, using aggressive vulgarisms that he abandons later, and he has a rude way of staring at people without answering their questions. His gruff heaviness is used deftly to dramatize his sympathy for the victimized young waitress, Emma: ". . .he took her shoulders into his big paws and looked into her eyes at once gruffly and warmly." He still has his velvet-lapelled overcoat and his bowler hat, which he brushes on his sleeve. We find that he's already well known, as he remains throughout his career: people constantly recognize him. The famous Maigret method is both demonstrated and expounded. Simenon as author establishes the atmosphere which Maigret as detective immerses himself in, both drawing on their special skills in their respective crafts. The do-nothing aspect of the Maigret method—just sit back, observe, let it soak in—is laconically expressed:

"What do you intend to do?"

"Nothing at all." . . .

"I conclude from that . . ."

"Yes, of course . . . Only, for my part, I never conclude anything."

As for the detective-story tradition, *Le Chien jaune* builds up an impressive collection of suspects and brings them together for the dénouement in the best golden-age manner. There is a hint of the American hardboiled school in the background action, which has to do with how Emma's young lover, Léon, was seduced and betrayed by a corrupt group of local gentry in a murky bootleg-liquor operation across the Atlantic. And there is a touch also of the detective tradition's Gothic background in Léon's hideout in an ancient, abandoned coastal fortification, with a hidden staircase inside the walls (echoes of Arsène Lupin's "Aiguille creuse").

The other early Maigrets constitute a series of themes and variations. Simenon's preoccupation with Eastern European—often Jewish—alienated types who fall into criminality recurringly provides, as in *Pietr-le-Letton*, the background action. *La Tête d'un homme* (which was reissued in 1950 as *L'Homme de la Tour Eiffel*, which is also the title of the film made from it), centers on Radek, a sort of minor Raskolnikov who, blocked from realizing his ambitions legitimately, turns to criminal masterminding and involvement with despicable American millionaires and decadent habitués of the Rotonde. Radek's guilt psychology, intuited by Maigret, is what gets him caught.

Le Fou de Bergerac puts Maigret momentarily in the role of armchair detective because he is wounded in the opening chapter and conducts his investigation from a hotel bed through Mme. Maigret, whose first extended appearance is in this novel. Again Simenon is preoccupied with a small town gnawed by nastiness from the inside and terrorized by brutal murders from outside. The opening scene on a train is admirably brisk narrative, and much of the foreground story proceeds with a classical alignment of suspects.

The "femme fatale" recurs as the cause of crime, often in interaction with a weak-willed young man who falls for her: *Au rendez-vous des terre-neuvas*, for example, which takes Maigret to Fécamp unofficially (as is often the case) investigating an innocent young radio operator and an obsessed captain, both enthralled by the destructive sexuality of Adèle, a siren leading honest seafolks to disaster; and *Un Crime en Hollande*, which takes place, of all places, in Delfzijl, where, again, Maigret plays private eye to the Dutch police in investigating a murder revolving around another young *naïf's* obsession with a young farmgirl, seemingly healthy and lusty, but in whom

Maigret intuits a cynical femme fatale and a career as a vamp. (In this book
Maigret's theories emerge in extensive discussion on criminology with a
pompous young sociologist who happens to be hanging around, functioning
as one of the suspects.)

If *Un Crime en Hollande* brings Maigret back to his literary birthplace,
L'Affaire Saint-Fiacre brings him to his fictional birthplace, the little village
where his father had been a bailiff, and where he himself, like Simenon, had
been a choirboy, a fact that provides him with a fellow feeling for another
choirboy that helps him pursue his investigation. A disaffected nobleman is
at the bottom of it all, bringing the affair to a lurid climax partaking both
of the Gothic tradition and some of the ambiance of the Caque. *Le Port des
brumes* is as successful as *Le Chien jaune* and *Au rendez-vous des terre-neuvas* in
building up a small-town maritime atmosphere (the setting is Ouistreham
in Brittany, where he wrote several of the early Maigrets), though the plot
that Simenon contrives is highly uneven — a doggedly murky tale of passion,
provincial bourgeois snobbery and pettiness, respectability hiding evil, the
successful rebellion of a dashing black-sheep-of-the-family, and murder. It
is another story in which, violating the deepest tenets of detective fiction,
no criminal is caught at the end.

Simenon yielded several times to the temptation of infiltrating Maigret
into his own native north, and in *La Danseuse du Gai-Moulin* brings him to
Liège itself, investigating another vamp (again Adèle), an infatuated youth,
Jean, and his friend and corrupter, René, who carries on a sleazy affair with
Adèle. Jean and René are a recurring antithesis in Simenon: the guilt-
ridden, poverty-stricken, weak, awkward, provincial loser vs. the self-
assured, corrupting, cynical, worldly egoist. Both represent potential
sides — and potential dangers — of Simenon's personality. An unusually
bouncy and frisky Maigret, who likes international travel, saunters into the
story on the heels of a Greek millionaire, who is murdered, implicating
Adèle and her pals. Maigret plays very much the private-eye role here,
dancing circles about the bumbling Belgian police, even getting himself arrested, and, once again, acting the tough guy in physical fights.

Liberty-Bar takes place in Cap d'Antibes, on the Riviera, where
Simenon had been sojourning not long before writing it. We are still with
the early, gruff Maigret, whose common-folk gruffness once again puts him
in hostile opposition to the millionaire crowd and in communion with the
marginal, earthy, underworld types who hang around Liberty Bar and who
provide the "atmospheric" clues needed to solve the crime. The victim, to
make a long story short, had moved from the upper world to the lower — a
voluntary clochard who found life more interesting among picturesque
derelicts than uptight millionaires. A coverup at the end obviates criminal
proceedings: there *is* no criminal. Mme. Maigret is prominent at the end,

as Maigret, amusingly and in vain, tries to explain the tangled situation to her.

Remarkably few of the Maigrets take place in Paris, which is supposed to be Maigret's beat: part of *Pietr-le-Letton*, *La Tête d'un homme*, *La Nuit du carrefour* (on the outskirts). *L'Ombre chinoise* puts us in the heart of Paris, at Simenon's place des Vosges, with another murky family drama, contrasting again success and failure, but here with the successful Couchet as the attractive one, and the schlemiel Martin, as well as Couchet's weakling son, as disagreeable saps. In contrast with this dreadful antifamily, Mme. Maigret in the background, expecting relatives from her native Alsace, provides a pleasant sense of family coziness. *La Guinguette à deux sous* is a suburban story, featuring another femme fatale, Mado, and the many men about her, and also punctuated by notices from Mme. Maigret, who is *in* Alsace, urging Maigret to get on with it and join the family—which he does at the end. One of the last of the series, *L'Écluse numéro un*, is also set in Paris and features another attractive "strong" type, Ducrau, a no-nonsense, virile, open personality whom Maigret instinctively responds to because he is a bit like himself—and both a bit like Simenon—and in contrast with most of his family, who are despicable fools.

The Maigrets were an instant success. They were received by the press always with lively and widespread attention, and often with praise. The most favorable reviews saw Simenon as transporting the detective genre to a higher level, invigorating it with new energy, adapting it to more subtle and serious uses. The simplicity of his style and his descriptive powers were repeatedly praised, and the notion recurred that these were not *just* detective stories. Middling reviews saw him as a good craftsman in a minor subgenre, and he was repeatedly compared to England's prolific Edgar Wallace. An occasional bad review found him tedious. His writing pace and the publication fanfare occasioned recurring comments, often ironic.

The very first reviews, in March of 1931, predicted that Maigret would take an "honorable" place among fictional detectives, and that his stories would probably make good talking pictures. Another saw Simenon as "renovating this already conventional type," and recognized that Maigret "remains more a man than a policeman" and that his investigation is "enriched with more intimate emotions." *Le Matin*'s reviewer saw Simenon as taking up the succession of great crime writers. A little later, *Pietr-le-Letton* was received largely as a good thriller ("a skillfully constructed tale by a writer endowed with an abundant imagination"); *Le Pendu de Saint-Pholien* as "one of the best detective stories you can read"; and *Le Charretier de la "Providence"*, "a novel where imagination reigns." *La Tête d'un homme* was voted the best detective story of 1931.

By the fall of 1931, Simenon was clearly an "item." At least two longish essays dealt with the Maigrets in the aggregate. One found that "Simenon writes with an ease, an alert youthfulness that provides infinite pleasure," while the other discussed at some length how Simenon was "more" than a detective-story writer, finding in his work a combination of "intelligence and sensibility" that leads to "une manière d'oeuvre d'art." The *New Yorker*'s ever alert Janet Flanner ("Genêt") picked up on the Simenon item in her "Paris Letter" of October 24, 1931, making lots of mistakes but introducing Simenon to America. She anticipates "Simenon" will become his permanent pseudonym, recounts how he once started a novel in a glass cage, has him turning out Maigrets at the rate of four a month, and quotes him as saying, "My ambition is to arrive little by little in the class of a Jack London, or — who knows? — a Conrad"; but, "Genêt" gallantly states, "he is already in a class by himself."

By 1932 Simenon and Maigret were riding high. To be sure, not all the reviews were good. *Le Canard enchaîné* kept nagging ("M. Georges Simenon's profession consists in killing one person per month and discovering the murderer"); *L'Intransigeant*'s reviewer kept repeating that Simenon was o.k. to pass an hour on a train, but hardly worth more; and the *Cri de Paris* called him a "worthy tradesman" who had declined since he once undertook to write a novel in a glass cage in a week but now wrote only one a month. But the dominant tone was moderate to high praise:

> His work may well contain a subtle and very penetrating critique of current trends in the detective story.

> . . . Maigret, the detective invented by Georges Simenon, is on his way to becoming as famous as Sherlock Holmes.

> . . . the art with which Simenon creates a sordid and pitifully human atmosphere.

> . . . related more to the psychological novel than the detective story . . . confirms my appreciation for the art of M. Simenon.

> This young writer of detective stories has in him the makings of a great novelist.

> . . . an almost perfect success.

In a questionnaire on the ten best masterpieces since 1918, Roger Dévigne included *La Guinguette à deux sous*; and Jean Cassou wrote in *Les Nouvelles littéraires* that there was more poetry in Simenon's detective stories than in most works of poetry.

Robert Brasillach, the reputable critic of the less reputable royalist

Action française, took up Simenon in earnest in the August 11, 1932, issue, intelligently criticizing Simenon's sloppiness of construction while analyzing the genius for close observation that enables him to evoke such effective atmospheres. Brasillach was the first to use the word "cas" in respect to Simenon—Simenon as a problematical "case," which was the way many commentators would treat him in the future. For Brasillach, the "case" arises because Simenon is so gifted but takes so little care with his creations. "If M. Simenon ever acquires the literary education he lacks, we can be sure to expect something from him." Some years later Brasillach accurately identified Simenon's role in the development of the detective story as giving it "its counterweight of reality." Simenon, for his part, took it all in his stride, and by 1934 was writing a satirical piece on detective fiction for *Marianne*, expressing mock uneasiness with the subject because he has concluded that, since the detective story is now "in" and critics are anatomizing it, it must be dead.

The Maigrets were quickly translated into several languages, the earliest being English, Dutch and Norwegian. They received a mixed press in England and America in the early thirties, rarely, as in France, pointing to any potential beyond that of good detective writing. The *New York Herald Tribune* reported in 1932 that Simenon was "billed as the latest rage of Paris," and that, "confessing to 28 years, he has dashed off 280 detective stories," adding that they were "decidedly readable." The following year, the *Tribune* considered *Pietr-le-Letton* a "thinnish tale," and suggested he might "improve with time." The *Saturday Review*'s evaluation of *La Nuit du carrefour*, oddly, was that "the story is better than the detective." The *Boston Evening Transcript* was impressed largely by the fact that "Georges Sim has written 300 novels by age 30." The *Pittsburgh Press* found Simenon "an able writer"; the *Denver News* considered one of his books to have "literary importance because it is well written"; and the *New York Times* provided faint praise for his ability "to pack large gobs of mystery and excitement into a small number of pages."

In England, the *Sunday Dispatch* reported that "Simenon writes his stories in a yacht which he has made his home—at the rate of one every eleven days"; the *Times Literary Supplement* wrote of "well-told tales of ingenious construction"; while the Manchester *Evening Chronicle* sensibly objected to the constant comparison with Edgar Wallace, with whom Simenon shared little except quantity.

Maigret, as well as his creator, became famous. Very quickly, reviews began with something to the effect that "the famous commissaire Maigret confronts another mystery," etc. "Our old acquaintance, commissaire Maigret," began a review as early as Feb. 1, 1932. An American newspaper in 1933 headlined, "Inspector Maigret scores again"; and a British paper assured its readers that Simenon is "maintaining his reputation." Maigret, as we have seen, carries his fame into his fictions, where he is frequently recognized by taxi-drivers, concierges, passers-by, to say nothing of thieves, gangsters and the police forces of several countries. In Liège, meanwhile, an enterprising cousin was not long in getting on the bandwagon by opening a café "Chez Maigret." Maigret and his creator quickly became known also to the real French Police Judiciaire, whose director, Xavier Guichard, who had gained fame by arresting the famous "Bonnot gang," contacted Simenon and said to him something along the lines of: "Look, you write detective stories, but they're crammed with mistakes. I'd like to have you take a tour of the P.J." He did, and registered a large quantity of technical details on police methods and organization. In time, the P.J. was to issue an official badge in Maigret's name.

While the Maigrets were following their course, Simenon, as usual, was moving about a great deal and keeping very busy. He was busy, of course, writing more Maigrets, but also juggling other projects — perhaps insecure in his step up the literary ladder and wishing to keep in reserve his identity as a pop writer. In the summer of 1931 he embarked on a venture that struck him as having immense commercial potential: something called "phototexts." A young publisher named Jacques Haumont tried to launch a series of these — basically comic strips with photographs instead of drawings — and signed on Simenon as his principal writer, together with a photographer named Germaine Krull. The only phototext to see the light of day was a rather preposterous story called *La Folle d'Itteville*, about a writer of detective stories who goes along with Agent G-7 of the P.J. (and of *Les 13 Énigmes*) on a real investigation of a murdered doctor, whose corpse is substituted for another. G-7 has moments of irony: "If this were a novel, we'd have clues." The publication in August of 1931 was a minor replay of the "bal anthropométrique": an all-night signing party on the *Ostrogoth*, moored in the center of Paris, near the Bastille. As a result, and because it was signed "Georges Simenon," *La Folle d'Itteville* got some reviews, which is more than it deserved.

Simenon wrote two more of these phototexts on the *Ostrogoth*, for which Haumont paid cash as he picked them up personally. However, he went bankrupt shortly afterward, and Simenon came out on top by reselling the stories to Gallimard, which eventually published them in a collection called, of all things, "Les Chefs-d'oeuvres de la nouvelle." Simenon in the early thirties also produced some straight journalism, including a series of police articles signed Georges Caraman, and an account of French canals for the *Figaro illustré*, entitled "Au fil de l'eau," for which he retraced much of the route he had followed with the *Ginette* in 1928 in a black Chrysler imported especially from America, accompanied by a Czech photographer and a Yugoslav chauffeur named Jarko.

In the fall of 1931 the Simenons had settled in Ouistreham, where he felt at home among the sailors and fishermen, drinking with them and challenging them to Indian-wrestling matches. One morning, as he was typing on the deck of the *Ostrogoth*, Jean Renoir came roaring up in a Bugatti, shouted "At last, Simenon!" and asked excitedly if the rights to *La Nuit du carrefour* had been sold yet. Told that they were not, he offered 50,000 francs, which Simenon accepted on the spot. He was an admirer of Renoir and was very moved: he would have given the rights away just for the honor. They already knew each other but now became close friends, moved in the same circles in the thirties, and often lunched together at the restaurant Ramponneau in Paris. They remained intimate until Renoir's death: "He was for me like a brother," Simenon has said.

About this time, Simenon sold the *Ostrogoth*, packed up the Chrysler and drove to the Riviera, where he took up residence at Cap d'Antibes in an immense villa which was painted red and called "Les Roches Grises." There he worked on more Maigrets and Maigret filmscripts, and caroused in the evening at the casinos in Nice or Cannes, and, in the morning, with a pretty young secretary. Renoir joined him to work on *La Nuit du carrefour*, with Renoir's brother Pierre as Maigret — the best Maigret ever, according to Simenon, because he understood that Maigret was, in the first instance, a government functionary. Shooting was delayed by financial and emotional problems — Renoir's marriage with Catherine Hessling was breaking up and he was drinking heavily. As a result some key scenes were not shot, and, at prerelease screenings, some viewers reported difficulty in following the story, so that the producer offered Simenon another 50,000 francs to come on screen and explain the plot (an offer that was turned down).

The Renoirs were followed by the filmmaker Jean Tarride, who bought *Le Chien jaune* and signed Simenon on for the scenario and dialogues. But Simenon didn't get along with him and dropped out. Tarride was followed by a "big producer" who wanted Simenon not only to write but to direct *La Tête d'un homme*. He signed Harry Bauer on as Maigret, and put together a cast, but ran into more financial problems. His impression was that most movie financing in those days was done, in the manner of Eugène Merle, by bum checks, and his actors repeatedly stormed in waving worthless checks at him. Irritated and losing interest, he quit the project, which was taken over by the talented director, Julien Duvivier. Simenon was so soured by the experience that he rarely had anything more to do with film versions of his works, and embodied his jaundiced view of the movie industry in several novels, such as *Le Voleur de Maigret*.

Aside from one or two trips to Paris, the Simenons stayed in Antibes for about four months. In March of 1932 he had become bored with the Riviera, and, remembering with pleasure the countryside around La Rochelle from the days of the *Ginette* and the trip to the Île d'Aix, they packed up again, moved into the Hôtel de France in La Rochelle, and scoured the countryside for the "ideal house." They found it near Marsilly: a "gentilhommière"—a sort of little château with a turret, called "La Richardière," with which he fell immediately in love. Unable to persuade the farmer who owned it to sell it, he acquired a long lease on it, undertook all the improvements, and furnished it in sturdy French provincial. He raised horses and bought himself a forge, passing hours banging away on pieces of iron. Rustic and elegant, La Richardière served well for a time to combine Simenon's variable impulses toward simple (if comfortable) country life, and toward the worldliness which his success gave him access to: "I entertained a lot . . . We never knew at eleven o'clock how many guests we would have for lunch, nor at five how many for dinner"—the life of a country squire, in short, which he took to with combined pleasure and irony.

Throughout these years—the late twenties and early thirties—the poles of his existence were well enough represented by Indian wrestling with drunken sailors in Ouistreham on the one hand, and, on the other, driving up to Fouquet's on the avenue des Champs-Élysée in the pale green Delage convertible that had succeeded the Chrysler. La Richardière was in-between. Perhaps he was in part imitating Eugène Merle's lifestyle, for, in Paris, Simenon continued to frequent the dashing publisher and his circles. Merle too had his country estate at Avrainville, where he kept open house for a variety of classy Parisians, whom Simenon later remembered as mostly high-level business and government cynics discussing shady deals. Yet Simenon, whether at Avrainville or la Richardière or Fouquet's doubtless felt the zest of success, of in-crowd superiority. His old friend, the novelist Marcel Achard, rereading the early Maigrets years later, reminisced:

> What a joy to reread the early Maigrets, to find myself suddenly in 1930, in the days of Eugène Merle. ("We were the 'chacals,' we had no scruples". . .) and our youth that was beginning to triumph!

Simenon, for his part, retained a vivid image of Marcel Achard, strolling on the Champs-Élysée, in his idiosyncratic checkered suit, his broad-brimmed, pearl-grey, cowboy-like hat, and his "legendary neckerchief." Among other friends of those days were Renoir, Vlaminck, Jeanson, Marcel Pagnol, Maurice Garçon, who became a celebrated lawyer, Pierre Lazareff, and others. "We made no fixed dates, no weekly lunches. But the occasions for getting together were numerous, and always took place in joy." His friend the journalist Carlo Rim was writing in *Marianne* about them all: "To succeed! . . . That terrible and marvelous word is synonymous with hatred, incomprehension, and also spontaneous friendship and love." He added, perhaps with Simenon and La Richardière in mind, that Paris was where success was achieved, but the country where it was incubated. *Marianne* was a locus of developing friendships: Rim, Achard and Simenon all wrote for this weekly.

Thus, in the early thirties, Simenon was living a "brilliant," worldly life. In Paris he stayed at the Georges V or other "palaces"; the Delage was frequently parked in front of Fouquet's or at the Café de Paris, the most exclusive restaurant of its day. He had become part of the "Tout-Paris," and showed up at fancy events — like an haute-couture opening, for example, at the Grand-Palais at the beginning of December, 1933. In the summer of 1933 he could be found living it up on a 90-foot schooner with a crew of seven, the *Araldo*, on which he sailed the Mediterranean for several months. It too combined his luxury and tough-guy sides. Spacious enough, the *Araldo*, however, was not a yacht but had been used to transport marble, and at ports of call he and his men were in the habit of challenging the local bowling fans to a game of "pétanque."

Nor did he abandon his first Mediterranean love, his enchanted island of Porquerolles. He spent many periods of several months each there in the early thirties, renting for many years a house on the waterfront, "Les Tamaris," with a tower — a sort of minaret — for a study. They entertained a lot here too, and he thought nothing of bringing back an afternoon's haul of forty or fifty big fish for a mammoth bouillabaisse. One of his hobbies at that period was carrier pigeons. He carried one on board his boat and would send it back late in the afternoon with an estimate of the catch. If it was insufficient for the expected guests, Boule would scurry off to the fishmongers.

Simenon, in retrospect, cast a jaundiced eye on his life and identity in the thirties — ". . . a bad memory . . . a bad after-taste in my mouth":

> As for the thirties, I won't say they're a blank, but I don't recognize myself, and I don't feel myself living them ... The terrace at Fouquet's, for example. It happened sometimes that I would spend all my afternoons there at one of those tables, with hordes of actors and producers. What was I doing there? I don't know.

But this is Simenon in the seventies speaking. In the thirties, his lifestyle and public image bespoke an exuberance in his success that doubtless corresponds to aspects of his "real self," which he counterbalanced by a sense of irony and by sustaining a notion of himself as a rugged man of the people, fishing and arm-wrestling with the best of them. He did not know what he was looking for, but the uncertainty did not trouble him. He came to the conclusion that he wanted to try everything, and that, at bottom, what he was *really* looking for was an elusive entity he called "man," a search that took on increasing importance in his private mythology as he groped to understand what he was up to in his serious fiction.

IX

SIMENON MOVES ON
1932 – 1935

In June of 1933, Simenon wrote the "last" Maigret. He called it *Maigret*, a plain, straightforward title indicating a full stop: the end. He had been leading up to it in *L'Écluse numéro un*, written two months earlier, where much is made of Maigret's impending retirement, and the little house near Meung in the Loire valley where he intends to fish and garden. In *Maigret* he *is* retired but momentarily plucked away from his garden to investigate, again in a private capacity, a nasty professional gangster situation to which his successor at the P.J., Commissaire Amadieu, says the famous method is inapplicable. Maigret proves him wrong by getting his man — the cold, cerebral, cynical mastermind of the gang, who is caught precisely because, in the course of a long conversation with Maigret, he is momentarily humanized. Only momentarily: at the climax, which is exciting and effective, Maigret is fast on the trigger and relishes his triumph over the gangster boss — clearly still a Maigret of the first series, with affinities with the American hardboiled school.

Thus, soon after creating Maigret, Simenon phased him out. If he was hedging his bets as regards his financial future by keeping one toe in the pulp world, he was also clearly winding up for something else, and was perfectly sincere in his view of Maigrets as "intermediate" literature on the way from pulps to "real" literature. He had been practicing "real" literature, as we know, for a long time — indeed, from the days of his scholastic successes in French composition, through his admiration for the "fine writing" of Xavier de Maistre, his reading of the great classics, his own essays in "fine writing" like "Le Compotier tiède," and finally those "private" compositions that he turned to at the end of a day's work, or inserted surreptitiously into the pulps. More important than any of these was the deeply absorbed accumulation of personal experience which, by and large, plays little role in the commercial work, contributes significantly to the quality of the Maigrets, and lies in wait to dominate the future fictions.

It was not long after he had launched Maigret that Simenon began feeling his way into "non-Maigrets." First of all, he wrote two detective stories very early that might have been Maigrets, but do not feature the commissaire — as if Simenon were trying out what it was like to write a semiliterary work without Maigret. One is *Relais d'Alsace*, written in the summer of 1931, at the height of the Maigret momentum. A much less interesting detective, Inspector Labbé, investigates a much less interesting story than most of the Maigrets, centering on an international swindler (vaguely in the manner of Pietr) in search of his childhood and momentarily involved in a sordid affair of theft and seduction in an Alsatian country inn. The other, of higher quality, is *Le Passager du "Polarlys,"* which concerns a shipboard crime, with the captain acting as detective to unravel it. His Maigret-like humanity and understanding enable him to pierce through befuddling events — including a murder — to the psychological truth underneath: the perverse innocence of the seductive Katya and a hapless young officer's naive infatuation with her. It got some press attention: "A masterpiece of its genre," the *Nouvelle Revue critique* called it, though the *Mercure de France*, predictably, regretted the absence of Maigret.

The bulk of the Maigrets, first series, was written between the summer of 1930 and the spring of 1932. Only the last two were written later. Throughout the rest of 1932, while the Maigrets were making him famous, Simenon, in addition to everything else, began to write his first true "straight" novels. (He himself has called them variously "romans durs," "romans-roman," and "romans tout court," to distinguish them from both pulps and Maigrets.) He wrote four of them in a row in the fall and winter of 1932–33, interrupted himself for the last two Maigrets, then wrote five more in 1933. All of these, like the Maigrets and, indeed, all of Simenon's subsequent works, unfold in places that Simenon knew, often very well. On the other hand, not a single one of them evokes the way he was actually living, except for incidental glimpses of the ritzy life, viewed, as in the Maigrets, with a jaundiced eye.

Though none is a detective story, crimes occur in most of these nine novels. In most of them the central characters are — or become — outcasts, or drifters, or losers, or victims — or all of these. Many of the stories enact abortive rebellions against an oppressive environment, or an oppressive state of mind; some portray a grim — or a pathetic — knuckling under. What guarantees the seriousness of these works, though not necessarily their excellence, is that Simenon transposed their themes and psychological texture from the inlets and eddies of his own background: the Simenon clan, the disarrayed Brülls, the disturbances of childhood, the resentments of adolescence, the agitations of youth. They come from the "dark" side of Simenon, while his actual life was unrolling largely in the context of his "sunny" side. Tone and characters emerge from inner rumblings, while details of setting and behavior come from alert observation and memory. Flaws of structure and development result from restlessness of composition, from artistic insecurity. The only true importance of any correlation between Simenon's experience and his fictions is as a signal or emblem of seriousness of purpose. He had an overabundance of invention and creativity which he could avoid using trivially only by willfully reaching down into his guts. His need to vomit when he wrote "seriously" may have been an unconscious metaphor, as well as a description of emotional pressure.

If the preoccupations of Simenon's fiction are attributable to his personal experience and his particular sensibility, they are not alien to the spirit of the thirties. The Great Depression and the heightened social and political awareness of the period highlighted the "little people," their sufferings and their states of mind, variously interpreted. The Charlie Chaplin image was a particular concentrate of this current, echoed in film by René Clair's *A nous la liberté*, Renoir's *Le Crime de M. Lange* and *Boudu sauvé des eaux*, and many others. In fiction there were Dos Passos and Farrell and Steinbeck and a myriad more. The veneer of respectable society and the brutal forces of finance, beneath which struggled the "little people" in their various incarnations, were a recurring pattern of the art of this period. Simenon's ratés and clochards, without the whimsey of the Chaplin persona, were his darker vision of these currents, minimizing the larger social and political context, emphasizing individual misery.

It is impossible securely to determine the precise chronological order of the early straight novels. One of the very first may have been *L'Âne rouge*, which is unusually explicit in its transpositions from life. Its title is the name of a nightspot in Liège where the Caque used to congregate. Its protagonist, Jean Cholet, is a young journalist in Nantes, a provincial French city about the size of Liège. He works for the *Gazette de Nantes*, hangs around lurid bars (in particular the one that gives the book its title), drinks a lot, has a girlfriend but sleeps around. He is irritated by his mother, who is anxious, conventional and nagging, but he feels a quiet communion with his father, who works in an office and has a heart condition. In an early scene, he makes a drunken spectacle of himself in a nightclub, after which he insults the kindly editor-in-chief, M. Dehourceau.

All this, of course, and some other details, are direct transcriptions from Simenon's adolescence. Dehourceau is Demarteau of the *Gazette de Liège*; the friend who eggs him on in his spree is Deblauwe, as described in *Trois Crimes de mes amis*; Henriette and Désiré are obvious, as is Simenon as Jean Cholet. Equally, though more generally, autobiographical is the central theme of the novel: a young man's sense of suffocation and desperate need to break away. However, straightforward autobiography stops there and Simenon reimagined his own story in other terms. Until the end, it is a story not only of escape but of degeneration. Jean is falling apart, headed straight for failure or disaster — a lurid version of what Simenon thinks he was in danger of becoming, just as some of the characters in *Dubliners* serve the same function for Joyce. He has turned himself into one of his innumerable ratés — dropouts, failures, malcontents, and, in a curious twist, enlists, in a manner of speaking, his father in his downfall: the father has his heart attack not in the office but in a brothel. The end of the book is uncharacteristic of either Simenon's life or fiction: after lurking unsuccessfully in Paris, yearning feverishly to become a big shot, he reforms, returns home to resume work at the *Gazette*, and becomes a good citizen. In the earlier part of the novel, Simenon works his magic with atmosphere, particularly in the description of the fog that pervades Nantes, echoing a foggy psyche and a foggy milieu of alcohol, nightclubs and dispirited sex.

Le Locataire also draws from Simenon's early days, since much of the action takes place in a boarding house very like Henriette's on rue de la Loi (though located not in Liège but in Charleroi). The boarders, slightly transposed, are all there: the Polish Jew fights with the Polish gentile, and the Russian with the Pole; one is richer than the rest and gets fancy foods from home; and so on. There is a room for rent, which becomes occupied by the protagonist, Elie, a wandering Levantine Jew who has landed in Brussels, penniless after a business deal falls through, and involved with Mme. Baron's sexy and worldly, but blunt and good-hearted daughter, who sends him to hide out in the boarding house. He falls into an unreal yet totally compelling sense of coziness and belonging. The escape-from-home myth of *L'Âne rouge* (and so many other Simenons) turns into escape-into-home, with Elie's neurotic ensconcement brilliantly rendered. He even takes over M. Baron's chair when the latter is absent (he is a trainmaster: shades of Henriette's second husband). An alien among aliens, he invents for himself the homiest of homes. That his futile dream should take the form of Henriette's boarding house suggests a complicated transposition in Simenon's imagination from life into fiction.

"Home" is a major category in Simenon's fiction: getting away from it, getting back to it, yearning for it, being excluded from it, conjuring it into existence, putting up with it, destroying it. In *Les Suicidés*, the escape is from provincial and wintry Nevers to Paris, by Emile and Julie, a mediocre, mousy, pathetic Romeo and Juliet, who overcome the class barriers that separate them only by a degeneration into sordid hotel rooms and a suicide pact in which she dies but he is too cowardly to carry through. Emile is the first of many particularly ill-humored young men in Simenon who get into trouble and maltreat their women. Julie is pure masochism, Emile whiny moroseness too feeble to rise to sadism: very depressing.

L'Évadé is about a different kind of raté: one who builds a cozy, quiet life, mildly unhappy until a dark secret from long ago topples it all. J.P.G. has spent fifteen years as a German secondary school teacher and family man in La Rochelle, until a loose woman of the world from his lurid past shows up to destroy his cloistered domesticity, not because of anything she does but because something just "snaps" in his psyche. One hears echoes of Simenon's old German teacher at the Collège Saint-Louis, whose secret, less sensational, was that he was poor. J.P.G. makes an abortive escape back to a more flamboyant and luxurious world, which turns out to be not so glamorous after all: he's been a raté all along.

Simenon declared his first "roman dur" to have been La Maison du canal, either because it was the first published, or because he forgot that he had written others before it. It is set in rural Limburg, where some of his ancestors came from, notably grandfather Brülls who had lost all his money and sunk into alcoholism. The novel evokes not so much specific characters and episodes from Simenon's life as a general Brüll-like sense of decay and disharmony. The heroine, Edmée, comes from Brussels to live with her country cousins and finds a tottering patriarchy: the old man has just died; one of the sons, Fred, is a skirt-chasing wastrel, while the other, Jef, is an interesting Quasimodo type who falls in love with her. In a highly original scene, he catches and skins a squirrel before her, and the creatural vividness of the act somehow establishes an unspoken bond between them. His bizarre, intense naïveté, however, gets him nowhere, and Edmée is seduced by the rural playboy, Fred.

The plot crisis comes when they're all apprehended by a farmboy who laughs at them and is beaten up by the infuriated Fred, who involuntarily kills him. The three bury the boy in a drained irrigation canal, establishing a dark secret between them. The burial echoes the squirrel-skinning episode in its brutal creatural realism, as does an extended description of a canal-barge accident and drowned horses. A sense of grim physicality threads its way through the book, uncontained by the flimsy structure that the family has become. Damp and cold are the predominant sensations, with warmth associated largely with sex: a symbolic pattern which, in a more careful reworking, might have effectively helped to structure a novel that, in spite of some brilliant conceptions, remains lumpish.

Les Fiançailles de M. Hire turns the family motif into a hopeless potentiality which provides the book's ironic title. Monsieur Hire is perhaps the most downtrodden, alienated and miserable of Simenon's early creatures. He lives out a pathetic daily existence in the dismal suburb of Villejuif, among "little people" with whom he yearns to be integrated but who keep their distance. Deeper pathos comes when he falls in love with a servant girl across the courtyard. She, however, is committed to a brutish hoodlum who murders someone and manages to have suspicion fall on the hapless Hire. From the role of outsider, Hire sinks to that of victim, which he adopts with a measure of Christ-like masochism. In a sensational ending, he is betrayed by the girl, assaulted and abused by an angry crowd, climbs to a rooftop, and jumps to his death. (In this episode, Simenon drew on a case in Liège he had himself reported in the *Gazette*.) Of Simenon's early novels, it most reflects, as Quentin Ritzen has observed, the influence of his favorite, Gogol—though, one should add, without Gogol's whimsey.

Many of these "romans durs" could be regarded as detective stories in reverse. That is, there is a crime, but it takes place in the middle or at the end, and its investigation is never the point. It is easy to visualize all of these being reworked into detective stories, with the foreground action turning into background explanation of the crime with which the story would then have started. When the police arrive, it is not benign, as in the Maigrets, but hostile, sometimes corrupt (in *M. Hire*, the investigating inspector tries to make the girl: Maigret, where are you!).

Thus, one of the obvious differences between the Maigrets and the "romans durs" is that the latter, without the benevolent figure of Maigret, mender of destinies, provide no comfort: the protagonists are left with little more than a dose of existential *Angst*. Similarly, *L'Homme de Londres* could easily be a detective story, but isn't. Maloin, a dock crane operator, sees one man kill another on a wharf and lose a briefcase in the struggle, which Maloin recovers and finds full of money. The background story is uninteresting, but Maloin's reaction to the money is sensitively imagined. At first he becomes a big shot, freely dispensing money, as well as leers, nudges, allusions and winks. Subsequently he becomes more and more anxious about the whole situation, an anxiety compounded when he finds the killer hiding out in a shed near his home. Nagged by his anxiety, he rather mindlessly kills the man. In the last phase of the novel, the judicial process engulfs him, with police and magistrates equally obtuse, and uncomprehending of his complex, murky psyche. Maloin, who started out as a proletarian tough, acquires a certain dignity as a victim of class prejudice and of the superficial mechanisms of the judicial process. It is a minitragedy of fate in a Hardyesque vein.

Le Haut mal puts us again in the midst of rural decadence, disharmony and depression. Mme. Pontreau, a fierce, overbearing woman, who doubtless comes from some of the domineering women in Simenon's background (Grandmother Simenon has been suggested), kills her epileptic son-in-law and drives her three daughters to distraction or to escape in the colonies. Oppressive, she herself is oppressed by the hostility of the community and by her own grimly isolated ego.

Simenon's sense of escalation from "semiliterary" to "literary" works was marked, significantly, by a change of publishers in the fall of 1933. He was approached by Gaston Gallimard, head of the prestigious firm with the famous N.R.F. imprint ("Nouvelle Revue Française") and drew up a contract with him in October. Gallimard was probably interested in a best seller with potential on the side for literary prestige. Simenon, annoyed at Fayard for holding him to his pulp contracts, was ready for a new publisher and happy to find one who would so pointedly signal a rise in literary level.

Simenon was clearly riding high. The early Maigrets were at the peak of their success, and the early straight novels were just appearing—a conjunction that acted effectively as mutual support: the Maigrets were shown to be more than *just* detective stories, while the straight novels were off to a flying start because they appeared under an already famous name. It was a conjunction, however, which, in the long run, also caused some confusion in Simenon's reputation, and, in his sense of artistic identity, perhaps some harm. The transition from Maigrets to straight novels did not pass unnoticed by the press, which took both approaches: that is, Simenon the detective-story writer applying his already considerable talents to a higher genre; or, now that he is writing straight novels, we can see clearly that Simenon's detective stories transcended the genre all along. The move to Gallimard is noted:

> M. Georges Simenon, after publishing 27 novels with Fayard, now enjoys the hospitality of the Nouvelle Revue Française and has taken his place in this publisher's catalogue alongside Marcel Proust, André Gide, Paul Valéry, André Malraux, etc., etc.

Simenon took some pains to publicize his change of level: "Recently, he has announced his intention of abandoning detective novels to write psychological ones." A critical game begins about this time and goes on for a decade or two, which consists of announcing time after time that this or that novel constitutes a breakthrough. For one reviewer, it is *Les Fiançailles de M. Hire*, which, "although the plot revolves around a crime," is not a detective story but "a remarkably well worked out psychological study." For another, it is *L'Âne rouge* which marks a departure from the "roman policier" to the "roman tout court." Robert Kemp, reviewing *Les Suicidés*, speaks of Simenon's novels as "half-popular, half-detective," adding that "they seem to me to have great merit." The reviewer for *Le Rampart* pinpoints *Le Coup*

de lune as Simenon's emergence from being "an industrialist of literature."
Le Matin's review of *Les Clients d'Avrenos* sees Simenon as "more and more
committed to character studies and less and less constrained by the plots of
detective stories." *Europe* considers *Les Pitard* as Simenon's farewell to the
detective story: "For the first time he writes a straight novel."

Thus, by and large, Simenon got a good press for his first straight
novels. *La Maison du canal* is praised for his sense of atmosphere, as is *Le Coup
de lune; Les Suicidés* is written with "an inexorable realism"; and Kemp speaks
of "that astonishing story-teller, M. Simenon." As early as 1932 rumor had
it that he was being considered for the Prix Renaudot. In 1933 the critic Lucien Descaves thought the Goncourt should have gone either to Céline or
to Simenon. In 1933 someone was already lecturing on the work of Georges
Simenon. In 1934, Simenon was third on a list of the most read authors.

Simenon's most important critical breakthrough was actually *Les Pitard*
of 1935, an uneven but sometimes very powerful sea story, with a superlative
description toward the end of an attempted rescue of a trawler floundering
in a hurricane. The "mythic" action is that of the doomed voyage, like *Au
rendez-vous des terre-neuvas* before it and *45° à l'ombre* after it; or *Moby Dick, The
Rime of the Ancient Mariner, Mutiny on the Bounty, Lord Jim*, and others. To the
myth Simenon has added a struggle of class and temperament between Lannec, an old sea dog, and his wife Mathilde, née Pitard, whose family has
invested in Lannec's ship: a money-grubbing world intruding on a world of
honest seamanship. On the surface, this yarn reflects little of Simenon's
Liège background (more of his experiences on the *Ostrogoth*, in Fécamp, and
in the northern seas); yet the image of a domineering, money-minded
woman given to fits of hysteria, in contrast with a simple, pipe-smoking man
with a strong sense of his craft seems a likely transformation of Henriette
and Désiré, Brülls and Simenons. Lannec is a heightened figuration of
Simenon resistance against intrusion, chaos and cupidity.

Shortly after the publication of *Les Pitard*, the prominent critic of *Le
Temps*, André Thérive, devoted a substantial essay to Simenon's status as
a serious novelist, which begins: "I believe I have just read a masterpiece
in its pure state, in its basic state" ("à l'état pur, à l'état brut"). He
acknowledges that he has had a highbrow prejudice against Simenon, the
popular writer, and has now given in and joined the acclaim. He analyzes
"le cas Simenon" with some subtlety, pointing out that many writers
establish their reputation with "serious" works and then, riding on it,
publish all sorts of money-making trivia. Simenon has gone about it the
other way around. If Simenon were making his début with *Les Pitard* or even
Les Suicidés, "there would be great enthusiasm in the republic of letters." As
it is, Simenon's wide audience had had nothing to do with the literati; yet
they have begun to pay attention, often going about it with a certain kind

of paradoxical snobbism, like classy gourmets who admit to a penchant for one particular little roadside restaurant. Thérive squarely takes an anti–Maigret stand: there is no continuum for him between the pulp-and-detective writer and the serious writer. Of *Les Pitard* he wrote, "Pathos . . . reaches a mode of the sublime. No romanticism, no didacticism, an astounding power to make the truth felt," and defended Simenon's often attacked style.

Thérive's praise was echoed in other journals, though Paul Nizan, Jean-Paul Sartre's friend, took issue with Thérive in *L'Humanité*:

André Thérive has honored him as a great writer. M. Simenon has undertaken to write novels without detectives. One suddenly realizes that he was a passable writer of detective fiction, but that he is an extremely mediocre writer of just plain fiction.

The notion of a "cas Simenon" recurs:

Is it realized that there is a Simenon case? A young man begins by writing, with astonishing facility, a succession of popular novels . . . , then launches into detective fiction . . . Then he introduces into his fiction extravagant, or obsessively mournful landscapes . . . Soon, the essence of his books is the atmosphere which prevails around his characters . . . *Les Pitard*, which he has just published, illustrates this evolution very well.

These reviews went a long way in confirming Simenon's hold on a higher rung up the literary ladder. Everyone talked of a progression, even if, as in the case of Nizan, it was considered illusory. In addition to the press, there were also private responses. The poet Max Jacob was moved in 1933 to write to Simenon that his last book (unidentified) pleased him immensely, and that he had been an admirer of his for several years. It can also be assumed, judging from later correspondence, that many of Simenon's friends in the arts—Vlaminck, Renoir and the rest—were praising his early straight novels. Simenon, having aimed higher, had arrived higher, and was being firmly encouraged.

If Simenon was moving on in the republic of letters, he was moving on also geographically. Tired of the Marsilly-Paris circuit, he and Tigy took a long trip into Africa in the summer of 1932. The voyage began at the Hôtel George V in Paris, where they were staying while Brennan, his tailor, fashioned very lightweight outfits for him, and a specialist in tropical medicine recommended a long list of medical supplies. The latter arrived in a large box that contained, among other things, a quantity of little green boxes with a syringe and something called "Stovarsol," which they packed into one of the numerous trunks. It turned out that the doctor had meant to prescribe two vials to be used in case of malaria, but the pharmacist had understood two "complete treatments" against syphilis—a misunderstanding which cost them some funny looks from the Egyptian customs officials, who wished them a most enjoyable trip. On the other hand, they found the venereal disease situation in Central Africa such that all the little green packages came in handy as house gifts for their hosts.

They sailed from Marseilles, toured Cairo, took the long train ride to Aswan (where, overpowered by the heat, Simenon spent several days in a sweat in a seedy hotel), and proceeded in rickety planes across the Sudan to the border of the Belgian Congo. To continue on to Stanleyville, they bought an old Fiat and were accompanied by a young Belgian colonial who objected to Simenon's taking photographs of natives until they got well into the Belgian Congo, when the young man proudly announced that now those were *"our"* natives and worth photographing.

The Congo is Pygmy territory, and Simenon had instructions on how to approach these elusive people. He supplied himself with a quantity of salt bricks and cheap cigarettes and enlisted the help of a local chieftain. After several hours' wait, there was a rustle in the trees, and little by little the Pygmies approached. Once the salt and cigarettes were distributed they lost their shyness, allowed themselves to be photographed, danced for their visitors and fêted them for several hours. The road to Stanleyville was still being built, and at one of the work sites Simenon encountered what his driver reported to be anticipated cannibalism: a roadworker's legs had been crushed by a boulder, and since the nearest medical help was hundreds of kilometers away, fellow workers were awaiting his death to eat him. Further down the road, they reached the first Belgian outpost, with two administrators living in posh villas in the middle of nowhere, unable to socialize with each other because of hierarchic constraints.

Simenon attended a meeting of chieftains, presided over by the two administrators in all their bored glory. The meeting became a sort of small-claims court for the natives, who, Simenon concluded, were taking the whole thing as a joke and inventing complicated disputes for the sheer fun of it. Further along, they encountered a variety of horror stories: the colonialist who suspected his "boy" of trying to poison him and hung him upside down, dipping his head into a water barrel, until he drowned; the man, bored to distraction, sitting on the banks of the Congo, shooting at swollen corpses as they floated by. Further along, they watched the antics of an American cinema outfit making an exotic film, with their own American blacks to play the natives.

At Stanleyville they sold the car and proceeded down the Congo to Léopoldville on a Mississippi paddle wheeler that had been shipped over and reassembled, then by rail to the estuary port of Matadi, where his brother Christian, unforewarned, was astonished at their arrival: "How in the world did you get here?" Georges never much liked Christian, though their relations were somewhat more frequent and cordial than he has sometimes made them out to be. He was delighted to find that Christian's designation in the native language as "the white man with the beautiful voice" was a *double-entendre* that meant also "the white man with the big mouth." Simenon evinced as much contempt for Christian as for the rest of the colonials, and for his wife, who, according to him, spent her days in a hammock, calling for her tuxedoed boy to bring her drinks and cigarettes.

Bringing this family reunion to a quick close, they boarded a French cargo heading for Bordeaux, making numerous, leisurely calls at ports along the coast of French West Africa. Simenon always ventured ashore, rarely with much pleasure:

> The main street? I had the misfortune of starting up it by myself. I was looking for a café . . . Not a spot of shade. You walk. You sweat. You feel the back of your neck burning. After five minutes, I wondered if I would survive.

This is Port-Gentil on the coast of Gabon. He reached the café and got a drink, but otherwise found nothing but depressing talk about economic crisis, bankruptcies, and the days when lumbermen used to sit at the terrace drinking champagne all day long. Further up the Gabon coast, the ship made a longer stop at Libreville, where Simenon stayed at a little hotel on the edge of town eyeing Mme. Mercier, the attractive widow who owned it, and observing the brutish lumbermen who, here, *did* drink cases of champagne whenever they had made a sale, after which they would go woman hunting—which meant staggering into native huts, kicking out the husband, and making love with his wife.

In short, Simenon came back from Africa with mostly disagreeable impressions, which he wrote up in the early fall of 1932 for a series of articles in Gallimard's new magazine *Voilà*. The articles were anecdotal and offhandedly judgmental. By and large, the underlying judgment—though it was not the one Simenon in later years chose to remember—was that Africa was one hell of a lousy place: "I left Africa hating it." He eschewed all notions of "the picturesque"—as he always did in his travel comments. He was very proud of having picked up the title of a publicity film made by Citroën—*L'Afrique qui parle* (Africa Speaks Out)—and turning it into "L'Afrique vous parle et elle vous dit merde," which may be understood roughly as, "Africa speaks out to you, and it says, screw you."

Simenon later interpreted these experiences as prophetic of what came to happen in Africa in more recent times—presumably the militant anti-imperialism of the postcolonial period. But in the original *Voilà* articles a version of these words is put into the mouth of a soured old settler and has to do not with the Citroën film, but with the old man's dislike of young reformist bureaucrats. Simenon viewed the colonial experience as a moral, emotional, mental and physical catastrophe. He reserved a distant admiration for a few tough old curmudgeons who had turned their backs on Europe and savagely ensconced themselves in the Dark Continent. The rest became either fops — like his brother — or brutes or raving maniacs. Or corpses. He documented many instances of maltreatment and injustice, but the tone was more of distaste than of moral outrage. In later years he incorporated his African experience into his frequently described quest for "l'homme nu" (naked man) which posited that, underneath it all, men are all alike. But much of what he reported on his African experience points to the opposite conclusion: that "Africa" is alien and "other," that its inhabitants are "other," and that those who go there lose their identity.

Disagreeable or not, his impressions were numerous, often sharp, and well-stored in his capacious memory to engender future fictions, or provide quantities of marginal details. The first "exotic" novel was *Le Coup de lune* of 1933, in which Simenon, an early admirer of Conrad, tried his hand at his own *Heart of Darkness* — set in Libreville. He most effectively establishes the debilitating, sullen, sultry atmosphere that was "Africa" for him, bringing into it one of his archetypal "ratés," the young Joseph Timor. Joseph becomes embroiled with the woman who owns the hotel, Adèle, a sort of tropical Lady Macbeth who has killed her husband but has made certain that a hapless black has been accused of it. Discovering that her acquittal was a fraud, Joseph testifies against her; but by this time, heat, sordidness, penury and despair have sent him over the edge, and he is shipped back home muttering wildly that there is no such thing as "Africa."

Although this was fiction, and resemblance to persons living or dead was purely coincidental, Simenon, jotting names of characters and places on his manila envelope, made the mistake of calling Adèle's hotel the Hôtel Central, feeling safe since the hotel he remembered in Libreville was on the edge of the city. It turned out, however, that it *was* called the Hôtel Central in real life — as real, at any rate, as life could be in Libreville. He had picked up quite a few details and plot developments for his novel from local gossip, from the police commissioner — who gave him official and unofficial information about the Mercier case — and from Mme. Veuve Mercier herself.

The local colonialists had already been irritated by Simenon's articles in *Voilà*, feeling — not without justification — that he made them out to be nincompoops. When *Le Coup de lune* was published and widely reviewed, the locals, deciding that enough was enough, urged Mme. Mercier to sue for slander and took up collections to pay her expenses. Colonial newspapers everywhere attacked Simenon and wished Mme. Mercier success. She was either very courageous, however, or very stupid, for the lawsuit, after all, was predicated on her choosing to recognize herself as the original of the deeply unsavory Adèle.

Simenon's friend, the prominent lawyer Maurice Garçon, pleaded for the defense and made mincemeat of Mme. Mercier. "I doubt," he told the jury, "that . . . you have ever seen a woman come almost three thousand kilometers to tell you: 'it's true that for a long time I was a whore at place des Ternes. It's true that my jealous husband threatened me because I was sleeping, among others . . . with one of our servants. It's true that I killed my husband. It's also true that the prosecutor, with whom I slept once a week, decided not to press charges against me. It's true that I normally wear no underwear, but how did this man . . . manage to know it? He did not even take the trouble to change the name of my hotel?'" The trial took place in May, 1934. When a long summary of the plot put one of the magistrates to sleep, Carlo Rim whispered, "It's the first time I've seen someone fall asleep over a Simenon." Mme. Mercier lost her case and went home; Simenon promised himself to take greater care in the future to fictionalize proper names.

The African trip took up most of the summer of 1932. The following year, Simenon went on two long journalistic trips, both to the east. The first, for a series in Le Jour, was a comprehensive tour of central and eastern Europe, perhaps to satisfy a curiosity about the homelands of those boarders at rue de la Loi. Chance brought him into contact with one of them in Vilna, a Jewish woman who had evidently had a crush on Christian, now married and with a baby improbably named Christian. Her brother took Simenon to a brothel where his chosen prostitute, after taking off her clothes, found out that he was "French" and burst into a furious tirade, accusing the French of callously sending cannons to Poland, when food was what was needed. In compensation, in Warsaw, he met a young blonde on the street who took him to a cozy flat where he experienced "the strongest sexual emotion of my life."

The second trip of 1933 took him to the eastern Mediterranean, mostly in Turkey, with a brief sojourn across the Soviet border in Batum. In Istanbul he succeeded in interviewing the world's most prominent political exile, Leon Trotsky, who lived in a secluded villa on the island of Prinkipo and rarely talked to journalists at that period. About half the report, which was rushed to Paris and published in Paris-Soir the following week, is "atmosphere": crossing the Bosphorus, the busy water traffic, Trotsky's study. Trotsky told him that present conditions were favorable to fascist dictatorships, which constituted an underestimated danger, but that in the long run the Hitlers and Mussolinis could only interfere with, not stop, the inevitable evolution of society toward socialism.

Simenon also researched low culture in Istanbul for a few articles that came out as something between bawdy stories and exposés. Among other antics, he went to a preposterously staged harem set up to steal the wallets of rich Americans, took hashish and cocaine, and concluded that Turkey was rotten to the core. The Turkish experience engendered two minor novels featuring chumps done in by sexy women: *Les Clients d'Avrenos*, and, more interesting, *Les Gens d'en face*, about the sad and lonely Turkish consul in Soviet Batum who falls in love with the GPU-assigned secretary spying on him and slowly poisoning him — not, one assumes, one of the novels that has so endeared Simenon to the Soviets.

The thirties, together with the *Gazette* years of 1919–22, were Simenon's most active periods of journalism. His travels were usually linked with journalistic contracts that paid for them: northern Europe, eastern Europe, the Mediterranean (a series called *Mare Nostrum* for *Marianne*, which paid for the *Araldo*), and around the world. In addition, as might be expected, the fame of Maigret led to many occasions for crime writing: the Mafia, drug traffic, the Police Judiciaire. The most successful of these was a series in *Paris-Soir* that briskly described the gamut of events Paris municipal police dealt with on a typical day, which later became the source of his short story "Sept petites croix dans un carnet." By and large, his attitude toward crime was a straightforward law-and-order posture, in curious contrast with the charitable instincts he attributes to Maigret. An article of 1934, for example, attacked a law passed the previous year restricting police powers and giving the accused more rights.

When the Stavitsky affair began to rumble in 1934, Jean Prouvost, the publisher of *Paris-Soir*, urgently plucked Simenon away from Porquerolles to investigate the tangled threads of the scandal. He started out by sitting in a bistro in Montmartre, letting it be known he was ready to pay for information. This produced mostly phony tips, but eventually got him onto some real clues that led to high government echelons, where he got into trouble. He discovered that one of the young reporters assigned to help him was in fact a secret agent of the ministry of the Interior. Yet the minister himself had advised Simenon to carry a gun at all times. Once, in a dense crowd on the rue Royale, he felt a gun barrel pressed against him and was surprised to find a high police official in front of him, who, it so happened, was one of his regular guests at La Richardière, but whom he had listed in the previous day's article among the names of functionaries who should be investigated. "Look here, my dear little Georges," the man said, "I'm fond of you but won't hesitate to shoot if you don't promise to amend yesterday's article and leave my name out in the future." Through his coat pocket, Simenon shoved his own automatic at his friend and refused.

Simenon took on a variety of other press assignments. In 1933 he was in Berlin, running into Hitler in the elevator and analyzing the Nazi takeover. He published some sketchy socioeconomic analyses of Depression problems, a series on agriculture, on the French customs system, on bailiffs, luxury hotels, steerage travelers, a comparative study of brothels throughout the world, and more. Though he began, and continued off and on, as a journalist, and though he was successful enough at it, Simenon's gifts did not lie in journalism. At best, his journalistic work may have a certain snappiness — as in the municipal police series — and one can cull a few vivid descriptions, a few striking character sketches. But on the whole it is very superficial. It suffers from the carelessness born of extreme rapidity, but, unlike the mature fiction, unredeemed by the flash of imaginative recreation. Even though Simenon is nothing if not observant, in his journalism he often gives the impression of passing over his own observations, choosing the banal, preferring hearsay. His talent was for perception stored and retrieved, not for the articulation of present experience. It was, in short, the talent of the novelist.

Simenon's father, Désiré, and grandfather, Chrétien Simenon; and his mother, Henriette, with Désiré.

Simenon at 2 and at 11.

Simenon with Josephine Baker, 1925.

Above: The *Ostrogoth* in Paris, ca. 1928. Opposite: Simenon's bar at place des Vosges, 1926.

Simenon and Marc at Fontenay-le-Comte, 1941 or 1942.

Régine (Tigy) and Simenon, boulevard Richard-Wallace, 1936.

Denyse Ouimet (©1945 Yousuf Karsh).

Andre Gide reading *Monsieur La Souris*. The photo is inscribed "pour mon cher G. Simenon — son vieil ami."

Simenon with Count Keyserling and the Count's son, 1930s.

Simenon in Arizona, 1948.

Above: Simenon at Cannes with Fellini, about 1960 (woman is unidentified). Opposite: At Épalinges, about 1966.

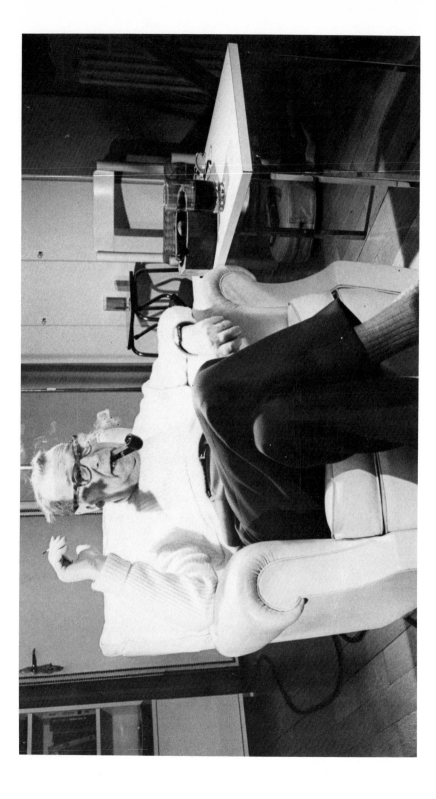

Above: Teresa, about 1980. Opposite: Simenon in Lausanne, 1980.

Simenon and "Mister," 1962.

X

THE SERIOUS NOVELIST
1934 - 1939

In the thirties, failure became as entrenched in Simenon's fiction as success and its appurtenances buoyed him up in life. It was still the old Liège antithesis between rebellion and conformity, which had always been correlative with failure and success: the explicit rebellion of the bohemian crowd and the implicit rebellion of the Brüll misfits connoted failure; the belongingness of the Simenons and of the *Gazette de Liège*, success. By the thirties, all this had become transfigured, but not erased. The fictive failures can mostly be identified as rebellions in one sense or another; the failure is, among other things, the failure of the rebellion. As for success, the buoyancy of high living may have displaced the solidity of bourgeois institutions, but not radically. Instead of the insurance office and the *Gazette*, it was Fouquet's and the Café de Paris; and against these too Simenon rebelled. The success, backwardly, was first solidly financial, then, in the course of the thirties, *d'estime*.

By the mid-thirties, money flowed in and out torrentially. Gallimard regularly provided him a fifty-thousand-franc advance for each book, and most of them appeared in prepublication serials, usually for another fifty thousand. His average prewar income is reported to have been over a million francs a year. Much of it went into real estate, furnishings, and paintings, which, as we have seen, were also antirebellion measures: solid houses to keep him from getting the hell out — from becoming a bum, risking failure. But the residences shifted frequently, were acquired on a whim and often sold at a loss — or not at all. This is where, with unfeigned insouciance, he placed much of his money. What he did not do, for the most part, was invest it. Unlike Balzac, who lost fortunes in chaotic business ventures, Simenon had no taste for speculation.

Once, in the winter of 1936–37, on a train to Innsbruck to go skiing, he shared the sleeping-car compartment with a well-dressed, extremely nervous gentleman, who turned out to be a well-known, if shady, banker named Oustrick, fleeing France after a burst financial bubble. For three hours, after downing the contents of Simenon's cognac flask, he unburdened himself to Simenon and, in gratitude, offered a hot tip on African mining stocks. Notwithstanding skepticism born of his firsthand observation of African enterprises, Simenon, reaching Innsbruck, decided to give it a whirl and bought some of these shares at 150 francs. They began to drop and continued until they reached ten centimes, where they remained forever.

> Such was my first contact with finance. It remained the only one. Money does not interest me. Certainly, I like my comfort, I like a certain number of pleasures that it makes possible. But I refuse to play with it, so to speak . . . I want to live from my novels, only from my novels, and only with those am I successful. The rest doesn't matter to me.

There is no reason to doubt his sincerity. He repeatedly asserted his contempt for capitalism, for the principle of money breeding more money, and his respect only for money earned. The lifestyle may have been high-flown, but the petit-bourgeois work ethic was not far beneath the surface:

> A biography might give the impression of a tumultuous and brilliant life. Nothing could be more false. It's true that I've travelled a lot. I have lived in a certain number of countries, houses, châteaux. Everywhere I followed the same schedule. Each hour had its function.

He did travel enormously and expensively but, on longer journeys, let newspapers foot the bills in return for his off-the-cuff reports. Early in 1935, the time had come for a trip around the world, and he made his usual circuit of newspaper directors — Noël Bailby at *Le Jour*, Jean Prouvost at *Paris-Soir*, and others — to draw up contracts and collect advances for travel articles. He and Tigy sailed on the United States Lines for New York late in January. In contrast with his subsequent love for America, he records little enthusiasm on his first visit, and in his articles reports only trivia and thoughtless clichés about Americans. The next leg of the trip was to Panama, where he roamed about for a period which may have been fairly short but looms large in retrospect because he absorbed an enormous quantity of details of Panamanian life and acquired a concentrated feeling for the ambiance which stimulated fictive reincarnations for years to come. He took the opportunity to locate a shady publisher in Panama City who had been issuing pirated editions of his work, forcing him at gunpoint to pay him royalties due.

After a brief foray into Costa Rica they set sail for a second go at the tropics: Colombia, Ecuador and Peru, short visits where he again registered a multiplicity of impressions soon to find their way into fiction. In his newspaper reports, the tone is similar to the African report: South America is a hopeless quagmire, engulfing the hapless Europeans who have the misfortune to come too close to it.

The French Line took them across the Pacific, stopping at the Galápagos Islands, and dropping them off for a good look at Tahiti, which seems to have been the brightest part of the trip — the single experience on which he reported favorably in his articles and about which he repeatedly reminisced in later writings. He found the natives beautiful, friendly, generous and charmingly innocent. The easy-going sexuality of the Tahitian girls impressed him, and once, while he was cavorting with one of them, she suddenly bolted for the window, stark naked, and jumped ten feet to the ground, having heard Tigy's footsteps; and Simenon has always remembered with gratitude such discretion and understanding of his wife's jealousy.

They sailed on from Papeete, calling at Fiji, the New Hebrides, New Caledonia, Australia and New Zealand. On a British ship from Australia to Bombay, he fell in love for the first time since Josephine Baker with a 16-year-old British girl. He became fiercely possessive and got into a fistfight with a young Englishman who had asked her to dance. She spoke no French and he, at that time, no English. Though she had a cabin next to her parents', he would slip in, pajama-clad, very early in the morning or late at night, not to make love but to woo her with the aid of a pocket dictionary. He was determined to marry her as soon as they got back to Europe, but nothing came of it. She seems, astonishingly, the only one of his innumerable liaisons that Tigy was aware of.

The rest of the journey, through the Indian Ocean, the Red Sea, Suez, Malta and Marseilles, was uneventful. The trip yielded a plethora of articles, a few of which were published in book form in 1938 as *La Mauvaise Étoile*, presenting depressing portraits of tropical dropouts — what he called "les ratés de l'aventure" — distinguishing and analyzing that particular breed of lowlife from the general species that so often preoccupied him. Another spinoff of the trip was one of his first public lectures, to Parisian students in 1937, entitled "Adventure is dead."

Shortly after their return they left La Richardière and settled closer to Paris, in the forest of Orléans, in a former Cistercian priory called Cour-Dieu. For a short period, he rented 25,000 acres of hunting grounds and organized semiweekly hunts in the grand manner, though he himself never took to the sport. At the first hunt, he wounded a deer and was forced to finish it off, which brought him to tears. He has killed nothing since then, except, "God only knows why," mosquitoes. He rode horseback a great deal in his woods, but otherwise found Cour-Dieu lugubrious: "It rained under the pine trees, and I was very bored."

Dissatisfied, but attributing to Tigy even greater dissatisfaction and a chronic "arty" desire to live in the capital, the following summer he rented a posh apartment on boulevard Richard-Wallace, across from the Bois de Boulogne in a building filled with theatre and cinema people. He hired an interior decorator, who provided them with floor-to-ceiling ebony bookcases, pigskin furniture, a dining-room of Brazilian rosewood and a bedroom with walls in bright yellow silk and furniture covered with genuine parchment. (It is probably unconsciously, but not by accident, that the apartment of the unsavory gangsters in *Maigret et l'indicateur* is draped in yellow silk.)

He considered it really *her* apartment, felt like a visitor there, and was out constantly, at theatre or movie openings, parties that went on all night, or the fancy restaurants he continued to frequent. At the Café de Paris in particular he would observe all sorts of VIP's, like Baron Edmond de Rothschild, who had his own salon reserved there every day, and Georges Mandel, the Minister of the Interior and Clémenceau's former secretary (of whom the great man is reported to have said, "When I fart, it's Mandel who stinks," a witticism prominently used in Simenon's fictional portrait of Clémenceau in *Le Président*). Dignitaries of this species were unattractive to Simenon, who continued to find them as cynical and dishonest as he had earlier at Eugène Merle's posh weekends. His congregation of particular friends now included a number of prominent personalities from the world of drama and cinema: Renoir, of course, from earlier days, Sacha Guitry, Raimu, and, a little later, Jean Gabin and Jean-Pierre Aumont. (It was Aumont who precipitated one of Simenon's few theatrical ventures, a dramatization of *Quartier nègre*, devised by the two — and by a wealthy Belgian named Lucien Fonson who produced the project in Brussels — during one long afternoon of heavy drinking at Fouquet's. The text has disappeared, but two songs survive, written by Simenon in halting English for a black American singing troupe.)

If he hobnobbed principally with actors and painters, he had some literary friends, though he always compulsively avoided literary "circles." In addition to Marcel Achard from before, he came to know the writer-adventurer Blaise Cendrars, because they both wrote for *Paris-Soir*, Marcel Pagnol, Jean Cocteau, and, a little later, Pierre Benoit, another habitué of Fouquet's, who remained a lifelong friend. There were counterpoints to the ritzy life—rebellions, if you wish—such as his walks from boulevard Richard-Wallace, when he gravitated not toward the swank strollers in the Bois de Boulogne, but across the Seine to the busy neighborhoods of Puteaux. Since he habitually started the creative process with a walk, several novels of this period must have germinated among the "little people" of Puteaux. And there were periodic flights away from it all: not only long trips and whimsical departures from the Paris airport at a moment's notice, but also humbler escapes, such as his stay in a cozy little hotel in Port-en-Bessin in Normandy, with home cooking and no uniformed personnel or elevators, where he wrote *La Marie du port* in 1937 (and where a café now stands bearing that name).

The years 1936–38 were exceptionally restless, even by Simenonian standards. Though officially residing at the Richard-Wallace apartment and still keeping a foot in Cour-Dieu, they in fact spent much of their time elsewhere. They were at Porquerolles longer than anywhere else in 1936 and 1937. In December of 1936 they were skiing in the Tyrolean Alps: part of the summer of 1937 back in Paris; August on an island in Lago Maggiore; October in search of the simple life in the little hotel in Normandy; December in another little hotel in Saint-Thibaut (Oise). By this time Simenon was definitely fed up with the swank Parisian life; "I suddenly had a fit of revolt against my surroundings, against the puppet role that I was playing in a world of puppets." He told Tigy, "I want to go work elsewhere, in a little house to my size, far from tourists, near the sea."

They would have bought Les Tamaris or La Richardière, but neither was available. They packed the car, drove straight north and rummaged about Holland, then back down the Norman and Breton coasts, repelled by the crowds. In March of 1938 they were back in Porquerolles, then around the Dordogne valley, stopping long enough in the little town of Beynac for him to write *Le Coup de vague*, and a month later back at old haunts in La Rochelle, where, listlessly, he decided to try detective fiction again, producing a flood of short stories and reviving Maigret. Then, miraculously, he found exactly the little "grandmother's house" he was dreaming of at Nieul-sur-mer, a stone's throw from the sea, by oyster beds. Knocking out outer layers, he discovered that he had once again bought an old priory. He had the garden landscaped, ordered cast-iron gates, and scoured antique dealers from one end of France to the other for furniture appropriate to his state of mind—i.e., as different as possible from the decorator-designed apartment.

> I began to dress normally again, without playing the English gentleman, and, when I went to Paris, I often forgot the five-o'clock rendez-vous at Fouquet's.

Happiness returned, and sunshine prevailed: "Sunshine streamed into our house through all the windows, and I must have written a novel in my new study, where I felt like a god" (the novel was probably *Les Inconnus dans la maison*). A new secretary, Annette de Bretagne, provided just the right touch:

> ... young, with big, gay eyes, and a gluttonous mouth, for she was gluttonous of everything, not just of food, but of sunshine, movement, colors; and I can still visualize her, one afternoon, bringing wheel-barrows-full of warm manure from the farm next door which we were spreading on our flower-beds.

With contented enthusiasm, he plunged once again into the role of gentleman farmer, tending his crops, gardens and livestock, riding horseback, talking farm-talk with his neighbors, and hobnobbing with local fishermen, oyster-growers and mussel-gatherers. The pretty secretary aside, Nieul activated his mythology of domestic settledness and genera-tional continuity. If it was a "grandmother's house," he had a revery of it also as a grandchildren's house, himself as patriarch receiving his loving prog-eny. The sense of family had been a major dimension in his past, and was a complex and paradoxical one in his fiction and his ideology. In his fiction, the sense of family is prominent by its negation: family as something yearned for, usually vainly; or family as sterile and destructive—the antifamily.

It was at Nieul that he and Tigy decided to have a child—paradoxically, since the decision was made after his realization that the mar-riage would not last. He pinpointed that realization to his infatuation with the British girl on the ship to Bombay, and attributed the same realization to his wife: "For the first time, I think, she felt confusedly that I was a stranger to her, or, more precisely, that she was a stranger to me." His rela-tionship with Tigy, though enduring, had always been tenuous—from the beginning, when his engagement had a curious quality of arbitrariness, of marrying for marriage's sake, Tigy in particular being a whim or an acci-dent. "I realized almost immediately that it 'wasn't it.'" He reproached her for not wanting children, for lacking tenderness, and for being jealous, but he did appreciate her companionship.

> She was for a long time an excellent comrade, always ready to leave at the drop of a hat for anywhere in the world. I might even say she would have been perfect had she not been prey to a constant jeal-ousy.

The separation predetermined in 1935, delayed, presumably, by the arrival of a child, by the war and perhaps also by inertia, was precipitated—though not completed—a few years later. The proximate cause was his being caught making love to Boule—oddly, since he had had almost daily intercouse with her since she joined the Simenon household. He was in the habit of taking an afternoon nap, and Boule of coming to wake him for a romp: "One sunny afternoon, Tigy burst in, stiff and pale, and beckoned me to come out with a gesture worthy of the Comédie-Française." She demanded that Boule be fired immediately, and, when Simenon refused, said that either she or Boule had to leave. Neither left, and he proposed that, henceforth, he and Tigy should each have his freedom.

The arrangement, as he saw it, was that, from 1943, he and Tigy continued to live together but granted each other "full freedom." After 1946 they no longer lived together; in 1950 they were divorced. On the other hand, Simenon's dream of Nieul as an ancestral home of Simenons came partly true, for he ceded the house to Tigy, who lives there to this day, occasionally receiving children and grandchildren.

Such was the couple, who, later in 1938, decided to have a child. Shortly after the conception, domestic peace was shaken not only by domestic tension, but by international turmoil as well. As the clouds of war gathered toward Munich, Simenon decided to weather out the crisis in Belgium, but, "peace in our time" having been declared, soon returned to Nieul. About this time he became associated with an abortive movement called "Sans-Haine," engendered with his friend the journalist Lucien Descaves, and proposing little more than urging people to be nice to each other. They distributed pins with a dove logo to various notables, and Descaves wrote a couple of articles, but nothing much else came of it. It was about as close as Simenon ever came to political *engagement*, an area that was not up his alley. Meanwhile, Simenon's enthusiasm for impending fatherhood was indisputable, and, afraid of appearing too old to his future child, he embarked on an intense exercise program. Fretting about optimal medical care, he took Tigy (together with Boule and Annette) to Strasbourg in March of 1939 where a clinic had been recommended. But world events intervened again. Hitler had occupied the Sudetenland, was making ugly noises about Poland, and carrying on alarming troop movements. Some kind of homing instinct and futile sense of Belgian "neutrality" sent Simenon rushing to Brussels, where Marc Christian Simenon was born on April 19. Once again the war clouds appeared to subside, and Simenon brought his family back to the homestead at Nieul.

Between 1934 and the end of 1939 Simenon wrote 30 straight novels (if one includes *Trois Crimes de mes amis*). The preoccupations and patterns of the earlier novels recurred and ramified, mingling ghosts from the past with the whirlwind of recent experience. His unabated literary fertility quickly accumulated an oeuvre abundant enough for the typical to become readily identified, the exception and the variation noted. The Simenonian themes have been repeatedly classified and commented. There are alienation, flight, return, destiny, justice, destructiveness and self-destructiveness,

[1 1 9]

desire, despair, hate, tenderness, envy. There are the couple, the family, the siblings, the parent and child (often father-son), the clan, the town, society, mankind, "them." Behind these, or beyond, there is solitude.

Most Simenonian characters are radically alienated, either from the start or because something happens to dislocate them from their surroundings. The ubiquitous flight motif frequently ensues from this dislocation: in one day the protagonist abandons all, hops on the train and gets the hell out. Sometimes, without leaving physically, he is nonetheless in the same state of flight as his *semblable* on the train. Rather often, the flight is from a socially integrated situation to an alienated one, where the protagonist feels more at home, and finds his real self; yet a constituent element of the alienated situation is a longing for what one is alienated from — that is, what one has fled from. There is a painful sense of exclusion, a sort of sad gazing into warm and cozy interiors from a cold outside. Some want out, some want in; wanting out and succeeding means being where, by definition, you want in.

Often, Simenon's characters try to build something, which turns out to be a house of cards on shifting sands; or they discover that such a structure is where they've been living all along. Add the closets, put in the skeletons, and you have the basic Simenonian habitat. The exceptions and alternatives are dotted around it, isolated specks in a sparsely populated region. The majority of Simenon's protagonists are propelled by inexorable destiny, as in classical tragedy, but with a stronger inmixture of futility and helplessness, and a glaring absence of heroic resistance. Destinies are mostly carried out alone, occasionally in small groups. Rarely are the latter successful or harmonious, though some are enduring in their disharmonies.

Unhappy families are all alike in Simenon, and consist of people hating but stuck with each other: antifamilies, anticouples, antipartners. Sometimes Simenon likes to experiment with extreme, test-tube situations compounding deep hostility, tight proximity, and isolation: islands, jungles, ships at sea — though an equally radical isolation can arise in city apartments or French provinces. Instances of love, tenderness, loyalty, respect and responsibility sometimes provide relief from this bleak landscape, but serve more often to define it.

Throughout the thirties Simenon elaborated his vision, by accumulation more than by refinement, by repeated "takes" rather than sharper focussing — but always with his customary energy and innate imagination. During this period the critical response to his books reached higher levels, and the debate on his situation in the republic of letters — the Simenon "case" — became a recurring topic among the citizens of the republic. The novels of this period constitute the major phase of the "Gallimard period," succeeding Fayard and preceding Presses de la Cité.

Simenon followed up on the tropical vein initiated with *Le Coup de lune* of 1933 with several other stories drawing from the African trip of 1932 and the round-the-world trip of 1935. In *45° à l'ombre* another of Simenon's doomed ships proceeds from West Africa to France, threatened by leaks and an epidemic of yellow fever among the miserable Orientals in steerage. The ill-fated ship echoes the ill-fated young protagonist, Huret, fleeing the tropics and dealing with life with futile aggressiveness and resentment. Reflecting Simenon's own categories of spankers and spanked, Huret sees eaters and eaten, himself among the latter. His malign destiny is perceived by the fatalistic, opium-smoking Dr. Donadieu, with whom, as Lucille Becker suggests, a father-son relationship develops, but to no avail: no mender of destinies, Donadieu can only be paternally sympathetic as he observes the catastrophe.

In *Quartier nègre*, set in Panama, Dupuche escapes from his pretentious bourgeois wife to a high-spirited, sexy, local adolescent, Véronique, who calls him "Puche" and raises his spirits—but not sufficiently to keep him from sinking into lethargy and indifference. In the background is a mother who had egged him on and to whom he is afraid of writing of his Panamanian failure. Henriette Simenon, we recall, tended to expect failure from her elder son, and never firmly believed in his success. Dupuche in particular, and all Simenon's ratés in general, are perhaps, in part, a way of dealing with this maternal suspicion, as if he were saying, "You thought you had a failure on your hands: well, here you are!"

In *Long Cours* Mittel and Charlotte flee into the tropics as stowaways on another doomed ship whose captain, Mopps, becomes infatuated with her and paternal toward him. Simenon's maritime enthusiasm provides vivid tableaux of shipboard life and realistic details about everything from machinery to freight financing. For the long and powerful second section of the novel, Simenon drew from the account he had heard during his world trip and described in *La Mauvaise Étoile* of the engineer sent to run a nearly inaccessible gold-mine in the Colombian jungles, where he is virtually abandoned by the fraudulent company that sent him and begins to go mad as he fights off rats and disease. In *Long Cours* he is called Plumier and is joined by Mittel and Charlotte, forming a Simenonian anticommunity of people living at close quarters in hostility, cut off from the rest of the world.

Ceux de la soif, utterly bizarre, yet, it seems, closely following a true story much in the news of the day, is about the baronne de Wagner (fictionalized as the comtesse de Klébert), an eccentric German aristocrat who led a whirlwind life in Paris, then took off for the Galápagos Islands, intending to found a hotel, or a colony, on a desert island, where she eventually went crazy, proclaimed herself empress and died of thirst. She is one of Simenon's uppercrust alcoholic nyphomaniacs, surrounded by panderers and corrupting everyone in sight. At the center of his version of her story, however, Simenon has put an even more outlandish personage: a professor Müller, philosopher and former doctor, who has left wife and children in Berlin to live in uncontaminated nature, has had all his teeth pulled out to avoid the temptation of eating meat, and is working on a comprehensive philosophical treatise. He is perhaps Simenon's vision of the intellectual at work as dropout: depicting intellectuals is not Simenon's strong point. Some of the older of the tropical fugitives — Müller among them — tend toward the clochard character, reflecting Simenon's interest in men turning their backs on professional and social accomplishments. They sometimes attain fragments of clochard whimsey, serenity and humorous abandonment, but more often fail in their cultivation of failure. The younger ones are mostly straightforward ratés. Dupuche in *Quartier nègre* tries for clochard, but remains raté. The tropics provide occasional glimpses of a communion-with-nature notion, quickly undermined.

An exception to tropical futility is *Le Blanc à lunettes*, one of the rare novels with a clear-cut happy ending. Set in the Congo, it incorporates many details from Simenon's African trip: the airplane journey through the Sudan, the automobile ride into the Congo, the salt-bricks for the natives, the farcical small-claims tribunal, the two lone Belgian administrators grimly separated by hierarchy. The protagonist, Graux, is a coffee-plantation owner modelled on an entrepreneur briefly described in *La Mauvaise Étoile*. Graux's plantation is well planned, well ordered: in Graux, Simenon embodied the sense of competence that he cultivated in himself, and which is related to the heritage of Simenon craftsmanship. Such constructiveness is usually crushed by the all-destructive tropical nightmare; with Graux, miraculously, it thrives, with the help of Graux's devoted, courageous fiancée, also an exception in Simenon's fiction, where strong women tend to be unpleasant, if not evil.

Simenon's most ambitious project of this period, though by no means the best, is *Le Testament Donadieu*, which occasioned considerable critical comment and which is the only novel to which he wrote a sequel. In a letter to Gilbert Sigaux in 1960, commenting on Quentin Ritzen's book about him, he rejected Ritzen's contention that *Le Testament Donadieu* and other novels of that time constitute a "Balzacian" period. He riposted that it had nothing to do with Balzac, but with the fact that he was friendly at that time with some big shipowners in La Rochelle and exploring their milieu, and also that its length was dictated by *Le Petit Parisien*, in which it was serialized. To André Gide in 1939 he explained that *Donadieu* had not been written, like most of his books, in one burst of sustained momentum, but that he let himself be interrupted by fishing and socializing, which accounts for its rambling quality.

Gide, for his part, had read *Donadieu* by 1939, when he wrote Simenon to praise the construction of his novels, *except* for *Donadieu*. Ten years later he had forgotten that he had read it and was enthusiastic to "discover" it: "How can such a book have passed by unnoticed? . . . a substantial book . . . I am amazed. . . ." Gide's second response stresses the multiplicity of plot and characters, unusual in Simenon, that made some critics hail *Donadieu* as (once again) his first novel. Gide's earlier response, criticizing poor construction, seems more to the point. André Rousseaux in *Le Figaro* expressed perplexity as regards Simenon's talent, suggesting only that an unformed masterpiece lurked beneath the sloppy style and construction. Thérive abandoned him with *Donadieu*, on similar grounds. Emile Henriot, on the other hand, to whom Simenon had sent a copy, wrote back that it was a masterpiece and Simenon a master novelist.

The center of the novel is the rise of Philippe, a ruthless young man on the make, whose principal stepping stone to power is seducing Martine Donadieu, of a powerful shipping family in La Rochelle: a third-rate Rastignac penetrating third-rate Buddenbrooks. A younger Donadieu brother, Oscar, provides the sequel, *Touriste de bananes*. In the first novel, he is a potentially interesting *naïf*—a possible Benjy or Mirsky—who rebels against his suffocating environment and ends up as a laborer on an American dam in a place called Great Hole City. *Touriste de bananes* is another tropical novel, with Oscar another hapless young fugitive to Tahiti, seeking regeneration in the tropics, but instead finding despair. In Simenon, such salvation-through-nature is only a glimpsed possibility (rare at that), quickly excluded.

Another novel whose publication was accompanied with particular resonances was *La Marie du port*, which Simenon publicized as marking a new stage in his development. For twenty years, he declared, in spite of some "clowning about" and some purely "alimentary" activity, he was "searching for a human truth beyond psychology, which is only an official truth." Gide, who had received a packet of books from Simenon, among which only *La Marie du port* was inscribed, assumed that Simenon attached special importance to it, but responded that he found all the books very good, and this one not particularly worthier than the others. Simenon answered:

> If I appear to have given a certain importance to *La Marie du port* that is for purely technical reasons. It is the only novel which I succeeded in writing in an entirely objective tone.

Simenon's remarks lack precision, and Gide's instinct that he was somewhat arbitrary in singling out this book is probably correct.

The significance of Simenon's declarations is more general: he was conscious of further literary escalation, and groping, uncomfortably, toward a

[1 2 3]

conceptual context for his aspirations. He asked to be judged, not on his past production, but on a new cycle that begins with *La Marie du port* — a request firmly supported by André Thérive: "If this novel appeared under an unknown name, everybody would be shouting 'masterpiece!'" As for the novel itself, it is doubtless one of Simenon's better ones but by no means a sharp demarcation of an entirely new style or level. It is essentially a comic novel, written, it should be recalled, when he impulsively left the high life in Paris to rub elbows with the rugged folk of the little Breton port of Port-en-Bessin, where the action takes place.

It's a courtship story, in which Chatelard, a young café owner from Cherbourg, reluctantly falls in love with the sexy, headstrong Marie, a waitress in Port-en-Bessin. He incarnates popular vigor, roughness, vulgarity and egotism: "il était peuple." She gets under his skin, he roughly seduces her, but is piqued and humiliated when, though yielding to him, she remains cold and passive. Disgruntled, he sidles toward marriage; in a marvelously comic scene he asks various of his employees how *they* went about getting married. Actually, it's she who is making plans to hook him as a desirable, status-providing bachelor. There are some splendid little vignettes as Chatelard, big shot from Cherbourg on the make, needles the country hicks; upon leaving a bar, for instance, he pats Marie's thigh and hops in his car before she has a chance to respond: "He hadn't taken the trouble to close the door. It was the nearest client who kicked it closed, violently, relieving his own annoyance." The opening paragraphs describing Port-en-Bessin are as fine an example of Simenonian descriptive artistry as one can find from this period. *La Marie du port* was widely praised in the press.

Among the nontropical "flight" novels of the period ("fugue" is the term French critics most often use), *L'Homme qui regardait passer les trains* is perhaps the most archetypal. Kees Popinga, a middle-level Dutch executive, learning one morning that he is ruined, takes flight almost instantly for Amsterdam, where he looks up his boss' jazzy mistress, tries to seduce her, strangles her when she laughs at him, and takes flight again for Paris (where he arrives at the Gare du Nord in a way very reminiscent of Simenon's arrival in 1922). His flight is not the result of a cause; the apparent cause is merely an occasion. It is not because he is ruined that he flees, but because the bankruptcy reveals what he always knew: that his ordered, bourgeois life was a lie. Similarly, the murder of the girl is a sort of accident, and the occasion of his flight to Paris.

In a brilliantly conceived but imperfectly realized action, Popinga keeps reading about himself in Paris newspapers and responds by writing letters to rectify the distorted image of him that the press is constructing. Yet it is ambiguous whether the image he himself so desperately seeks to affirm is any more real, for he is going insane. He ends up in the hands of psychiatrists, who become, not menders of destiny but antagonists, and, as he brilliantly plays chess with one of them (but also mischievously dropping a pawn into the doctor's teacup), the reader is teased into considering whether, underneath it all, he is not sane after all. At the end, Popinga is writing a memoir; but when the psychiatrist picks up the notebook and finds that all it contains is a title — "The Truth about the Case of Kees Popinga" —, Popinga looks at him "with a constrained smile" and murmurs, "There is no truth, is there?"

Le Suspect also records a two-stage flight by Chave, a gentle, unsuccessful young Belgian, first into an anarchist group — disagreeable and dangerous malcontents whose literary antecedents are *The Secret Agent* and *Under Western Eyes* and *The Possessed*, and whose biographical derivation is clearly Henriette's boarders — then to Paris where he succeeds in preventing a bomb attack. His true yearning is for family life, however dubious the family structures he knows may be, and, in the end, he returns to Belgium to pick up the pieces of his own rickety little household.

Bergelon is structured as a double flight. The first is Bergelon's, a small-town doctor, suddenly embroiled in a nasty malpractice affair that becomes the occasion (again, not the cause) of a sexual escapade and the temptation of flight to the tropics, rejected in favor of mediocrity at home rather than abroad. The other flight is young Cosson's, whose flight does lead to the tropics: he disappears into a gold-digging venture in Africa, having rapidly declined from well-behaved petit bourgeois to alcoholic dropout. The role of alcohol is significant in both protagonists, as it often is in Simenon's novels. Simenon, who frequently thought he might have liked to have had a medical career if things had worked out differently, depicted many doctors in his fiction, and often cast them as failures, not so much in their professions as in their lives. Malempin is another example in the novel that bears his name. The true "action" is his delving below a flimsy domestic and professional life into a murky, haunting childhood and heredity. The narrative is in the first person (for the first time in Simenon), and his musings, prompted by his son's illness and triggering reflections on his own father, constitute as much a flight as Bergelon's or Popinga's, though he does not physically go anywhere: he is running in place. Dolefully, he "comes home" at the end, having learned that there is no communication with his family, past or present, and never has been: most men are strangers to one another. In a touching scene near the end, he feels excluded from whatever communication there is, as he catches a snapshot vision of his wife and the child smiling at each other.

The "flight-by-running-in-place" motif is as frequent in Simenon as actual "fugues." *Le Bourgmestre de Furnes* is another instance, and another critical success of this period. Simenon also set special store by it, writing to Gide in 1939, "I think I have reached a new stage with *Le Bourgmestre de Furnes*.... To use Thérive's term, it might be my master production ['oeuvre de maîtrise']." The character in flight, this time, is a strong one: Terlink, cigar manufacturer, mayor of a Flemish town, and domestic, social and political tyrant. The triggering event for Terlink's "flight" is his refusal of a loan to a young employee with a pregnant mistress, who then commits suicide after first trying to kill the girl, Lina. Terlink's flight has two aspects. One is his search for Lina with obscure intentions — perhaps reparation. But Lina turns out to be a sexy little vixen, and Terlink falls into a psychologically complex obsession with her. He is like so many other Simenonian characters in enacting a troubled discovery of "sex" — but in an idiosyncratic way that corresponds to his complex character. The second aspect of his flight is his alienation — almost ostracism — in the town, in spite of his powerful personality. The flight, one might say, is the town's from him. Losing the town's sympathy, he acquires the reader's, as a certain rugged, no-nonsense side of him comes out in contrast with his more pretentious peers.

L'Assassin is a simpler version of the "flight-in-place." The fleer, unlike Terlink, is a weak man — another troubled doctor like Bergelon and Malempin. The triggering event ("le déclic") is Dr. Kupérus' discovery of his wife's infidelity, and his subsequent murder of her and her lover. The metaphysical situation, so to speak, is very much like Popinga's in *L'Homme qui regardait passer les trains*: it is not so much a question of cause and effect — infidelity leading to murder leading to flight — as of occasion for discovery. The discovery is exactly the same as for Popinga or Bergelon or Malempin: the meaninglessness of domestic and social structures carefully erected and cultivated for decades. For some reason it all bursts like a pricked balloon: for some reason, any reason; infidelity and murder, like bankruptcy or malpractice, are incidental. Considering the incidents that occasion the narrative, Simenon notably underplays the moral dimension in *L'Assassin* and other similar novels, placing his characters in a world determined by metaphysical poles, with relatively little of the "moral." In this respect he is quite in the mainstream of modern French literature; the world he conjures up is morally more like that of *La Nausée* or *L'Étranger* or even *Waiting for Godot* than it is like *Cousin Pons* or *L'Assommoir*.

All of these flights, of course, lead to radical alienation, at home or abroad — occasionally, as for the repentant anarchist of *Le Suspect*, with a fragile reintegration at the end. *L'Outlaw* murkily dramatizes the flight and alienation of Stan, a desperate young Pole in Paris embroiled with a brutal Polish gang. *Faubourg*, another novel for which Gide expressed high praise, is a flight in reverse, a homecoming after flight, the return of a prodigal son who forthwith escalates his prodigality. His real name is Chevalier, which he has literally translated into de Ritter, and he pops up in his hometown after twenty-five years of wandering about as a small-time swindler, mostly in the tropics, or in jail.

De Ritter's childhood background is familiar: a mother who complains, whose life dream is to have a little store, whose best friend was a salesgirl she used to work with; an aunt who was taken to an insane asylum, another who is an alcoholic; a grandfather who committed suicide, and an uncle caught urinating against a wall—in short a veritable catalogue of Brülls. The father was a low-level clerk in poor health. De Ritter's surly rebellion twenty-five years earlier has the exact tonality of the darker aspects of Simenon's adolescent discontent. In a whimsical transposition, Simenon has his protagonist embark on a journalistic career *after* his return home, acquiring prestige with peppy articles about his exotic adventures. Though in his forties, he behaves like one of Simenon's bad boys—those arrogant, disagreeable young men, usually pampered by one or more maltreated women, who start in trouble and end up in more. In this book, it all devolves into utter depravity: destructive elements Simenon had well observed for three decades and felt occasional rumbles of in himself are extrapolated quickly—too quickly—to nightmarish extremes.

There are many variations of the flight-alienation-failure pattern. In *Le Cheval blanc* an inn of that name is the locus of half-comical, half-pathetic "fugues," including yet another incarnation of Léopold—a black-sheep uncle back from a long colonial escape, living in brutish alienation as a night watchman. In *Chemin sans issue* two Russian sailors (inspired by Vladimir and Sasha of Porquerolles) enact a low-keyed, half-comic flight into Riviera decadence. *L'Oncle Charles s'est enfermé* chronicles the family schlemiel's flight into the attic, where he gleefully threatens his brother-in-law with a damning secret he has discovered. Also largely comic, *Monsieur La Souris* stars a jolly clochard-turned-detective, in the vein of Michel Simon's Boudu in Renoir's great film. A clochard, by definition, is a man in a state of flight, or rather at a particular stage of flight—a sort of prolonged terminal stage. A lively plot involves gangsters, murder, high finance, high society, the Police Judiciaire, La Souris's abduction, an exciting chase, and a delightful sequence in which Lognon, the melancholic detective from the Maigrets, shadows La Souris all day long, the whimsical clochard leading him to the banks of the Seine and settling down with a liter of wine and a pile of old newspapers which he meticulously reads for hours. *La Maison des sept jeunes filles* is a wholly comic bagatelle in which the flights are mostly the escapades of the daughters of a harassed petit-bourgeois father.

Suppressed flight is an important subcategory of flight in Simenon's fiction: characters gloomily, or ragingly, or meekly *stuck* in their surroundings. Noteworthy among these are the novels in which the oppressive power—the prison keepers, so to speak—are domineering women. Mme. Pontreau in *Le Haut mal* was an early example. In *Les Demoiselles de Concarneau* Guérec is nurtured and stifled by his two sisters, who conspire to prevent his flight into marriage, and bring him back home, where he wastes away. The title characters of *Les Soeurs Lacroix* are dreadful creatures who hate each other and tyrannize a lugubrious upper-middle-class antifamily.

In *Le Coup de vague*, another pair of tyrannical sisters deliberately destroy the nascent, fragile family that their "nephew," Jean, has just formed with his beloved Marthe. He is in fact the illegitimate son of one of the sisters, an easy victim of their possessive manipulation "for his own good." The story, which is set in Marsilly and mentions La Richardière, includes some fine descriptive passages of the mussel-gathering industry that Simenon knew well.

Il pleut, bergère... is a remarkable variation on the tyrannical female and flight motifs. It is written, with great effectiveness, from a child's point of view—Jérome, who sits for hours by the window observing the apartment across the way and establishing an unspoken, secret communion with the child who lives there, whose father is an anarchist in hiding from the police and from the hostile, conservative neighbors. Jérome is impressed by flight and rebellion because he is himself oppressed by a nasty, vindictive aunt, who, virulently antiradical, antilabor and antichild, betrays the hounded anarchist. The child's sympathetic identification with the tormented household he observes is moving and brilliantly dramatized. Simenon's own identification with the observing child is also clear, both from the tone of the narrative and from the numerous details from his own childhood which he attributes to Jérome. It is astonishing that a novel so sympathetic to thirties political turmoil was published in 1941, though written in 1939.

One more major theme recurs in many of these novels, and throughout Simenon's career: the theme of justice, or more often, of injustice. The injustice may be that born of prejudice: the injustice which the larger community perpetrates upon an alien minority. This is a subject arising in Simenon's fiction as far back as some of the early *Matin* stories, and which finds dramatic expression in *Chez Krull*, which is about a German family long settled in a French town but regarded with a suspicion that turns to violent hostility when their weak-willed son, who timidly follows girls on the street, is wrongly suspected of rape and murder. The long climactic scene, when the rabble reviles and attacks them, is a brilliant dramatization of mob injustice.

The more frequent injustice in Simenon, however, is not that of the mob but of the judicial system. Though his concern for justice doubtless had deep roots in Liège, ranging from the "little people" myth to sibling resentments, his explicit preoccupation with official injustice was most likely an outgrowth of his crime fiction. From writing about cops and robbers, he began at some point reflecting on the implications and realities of criminal justice, an interest that he maintained all his life and which took many forms in his work. The perennial conflict between Maigret and the judicial apparatus is a prominent version of the theme.

In the straight novels, a frequent narrative strategy is to present a double version of a real or alleged criminal situation: the official version as it appears in the dossiers, and the "real" version as experienced by the subject, drawing attention to the discrepancy — sometimes gross, sometimes subtle — between the two. In *Cour d'assises* (published in 1941 but written on Porquerolles in 1937) the hero, Petit Louis, is a small-time crook who gets marginally involved with big-time gangsters and implicated in a murder he had nothing to do with. Simenon develops an interesting double narrative which describes simultaneously what Petit Louis is actually doing on the fateful day, and what he will be accused of doing, or what he will be incapable of proving he has done or not done in terms of the prosecutor's dossier; ". . . suddenly he was made to relive his whole life, but it was not the way he himself had lived it!" All sorts of details are scraped up to make him look bad, including his relationship with his hostile mother. Simenon — on a much less substantial level — anticipates the celebrated judicial situation in Camus's *L'Étranger*. In the case of Petit Louis, character definitely is *not* fate. He is a jolly imp, and his destiny should have been to hang around in the sunshine, bowling and joking and doing strongman tricks. Simenon places him on Porquerolles for a brief respite before the catastrophe, drawing from the sunny side of his own experience and personality before delving into the darker side for the continuation of his story. *Les Rescapés du Télémaque* is likewise a threatened miscarriage of justice, in the investigation, long after the fact, of a case of cannibalism in a lifeboat after a shipwreck. It is a psychological story of sibling tension (as in *Pietr-le-Letton* and *La Maison du canal*), superimposed on a crime story (tracking down the real murderer to clear the innocent suspect), with a grim "doomed-ship" adventure in the background.

Simenon deals with the theme of justice most subtly in one of the best books of this period, *Les Inconnus dans la maison*, especially well known because of the film made from it in 1941, starring Simenon's good friend Raimu, with a screenplay by a later friend, Henri-Georges Clouzot. (An English version with James Mason and Geraldine Chaplin, *Stranger in the House*, was made in 1967.) The story, based on an actual trial in Reims, takes place in Moulins, a small provincial city in central France, where the hero, Loursat, once a lawyer, now lives as an alcoholic recluse in his big house where, since his wife left him years earlier, he has raised his daughter, Nicole.

There are two intertwined actions. One has to do with Nicole's social life: a group of young people who live a decadent, small-town jazzy life peppered with minor misdemeanors, often meeting upstairs in Loursat's house (shades of the Caque, upstairs at the Renchons). Nicole is in love with Manu, a frail and tormented lower-class youth. During one of their complicated misadventures, the gang brings in a youth hurt in a drunken automobile accident, who is later shot to death. At this point, the wheels of the Simenonian injustice apparatus begin to turn, as Manu is accused of the crime (which in fact has to do with an uninteresting involvement of the victim with professional gangsters).

The second action is Loursat's. For years he has been sitting in his study drinking red wine and reading books, ignoring the shenanigans upstairs, stubbornly isolated both from his household and from his erstwhile peers and relatives in the community, whom he scorns as petty social climbers, snobs, and dishonest businessmen and professionals. He is one of Simenon's most interesting dropouts — unconventional, honest, intelligent, and disillusioned. His name is significant: there is a bearish quality about him. Indeed, he has been hibernating for years, and his action, in essence, is coming out of his lair to take up the defense of the victimized young Manu, to protect him from the class prejudices that have already condemned him. Loursat comes back to life, rekindling a dormant love for his daughter, nurturing human sympathies — and a sense of justice — deeply engrained but long buried in his character, reactivating his professional skills, and making a firm and effective commitment rare in Simenon's fiction. The archchronicler of dropping out, Simenon did not often conjure up a vision of dropping back in in such positive terms. André Gide was moved to the highest praise:

> I have read your astounding *Inconnus dans la maison*. Hadn't felt such lively interest in a long time . . . The repercussion of the story on the lawyer is splendid. You're on the right path. The subject of the book is there. Bravo!

In the books written from 1934 to the end of the decade Simenon established most of his themes and techniques, though many counterpoints, variations, extensions and exceptions would appear in future novels. This phase enhanced Simenon's reputation as a serious novelist, and also confirmed his position as a special "case." By World War II an impressive confraternity of Simenon fans had emerged. There were private admirers, such as Carl Jung, and the distinguished novelist Georges Bernanos. Less distinguished, but more demonstrative, was the novelist Claude Farrère (pseudonym of Edouard Bargone), who wrote to Simenon:

Have I already told you that you have one of the proudest, one of the noblest talents that I know? ... There are imbeciles who say, "Simenon, the manufacturer of detective stories..." You have the gift of bringing things to life, and of compassion, and a great thirst for justice.

François Mauriac took notice of him in 1937, writing to him that he knew most of his books, did not appreciate his detective stories, but recognized that he was gifted. He urged him to work on stylistic details, though acknowledged that, in a deeper sense, he had "style." In the press, in spite of some dissident voices, the dominant note was favorable, and the "Simenon case" was discussed, sometimes with admirable insight; and that odd contest among critics endured, each claiming that he has now discovered what no one else was aware of: that Simenon is not *just* a writer of detective stories. Thérive maintained his analytical enthusiasm, particularly in the long essay in *Le Temps* of January 5, 1939, reviewing *La Marie du port* and *Le Suspect*, but evaluating Simenon's situation in general. It abounds in superlatives: "Really, what a great novelist, this M. Simenon!"; "...his personal gift, one of the most extraordinary to have appeared in France." But Thérive also shrewdly pointed to that "goût du malheur" (taste for unhappiness) in which Simenon drowns his plot and characters in *Le Suspect*.

Two recurring motifs were particularly significant among the critics. One was the sense of great *potential* in Simenon — Simenon seen as still cutting his teeth but expected to come out some time with a truly great work. Brasillach, an early supporter, squarely adopted this line in a 1939 article in *Le Matin*: "If someone is capable of some day writing the great novel of our period, we gladly admit that there is every chance that it will be this young man ...", Brasillach ended his essay on the note of the Simenon "case," which here became the Simenon "adventure": "We would like to see him look toward something else ... since we are attentively following his adventure, which is the most curious literary adventure of this time." The other motif in the press was Simenon's aloofness from literary coteries, from what is often labeled "l'esprit de cénacle." His friend Lucien Descaves of the "Sans-Haine" movement wrote:

> He is a happy man who does not wheel and deal, and one can say that it depended on him to occupy the higher literary rank that he deserves; he needed, to achieve this, simply to produce less and to frequent more often the literary "cénacles" which make literary reputations.

François Porche in *L'Époque* similarly pointed to the disadvantage to Simenon's reputation of his having come up from the bestseller lists rather than through the literary circles. This was an evaluation that Simenon took to readily: the rugged, self-made novelist eschewing the literary in-crowd. The interaction between that view on the one hand and the encouragements of that very in-crowd on the other created tensions with which Simenon struggled off and on for some years.

One of Simenon's more persistent admirers in the late thirties was Count Hermann von Keyserling, a minor but respectable German man-of-letters who seems to have "discovered" Simenon around 1935 or 1936, and engaged him in frequent correspondence, which had a limited effect because of Keyserling's torturous handwriting, which Simenon gave up reading after a while. He was flattered enough at Keyserling's interest, however, to send him voluminous parcels of his books, and at least once to visit him at Darmstadt. Flattered, but also suspicious, Simenon had the impression that Keyserling was studying him as a guinea-pig in a laboratory.

> Two years ago, Keyserling insisted on seeing me, to study me a little like a guinea-pig. I finally went to spend a few days in Darmstadt. I fear that I disappointed him, for what he saw arrive was a big, muscular fellow who declined his vodka and whose chief concern was to maintain his equilibrium. A big, *timid* fellow in the bargain. Timid or *impudent*.

The combination of admiration and illegibility on Keyserling's part, and timidity and impudence on Simenon's, is perhaps a curiously apt résumé of Simenon's relationship with "literary" people. Keyserling admired *L'Assassin*, calling it "lugubrious and sinister" and using the English word "harrowing." He felt that Simenon was at his best with quick sketches rather than carefully composed longer works. He appreciated his "rapid strokes of the pen," and saw him as creating a new style "which is very much your own." Like other highbrow admirers, he declared that Simenon had the wrong public, and that his books had "depths which I suppose a good many of your most diligent readers do not even suspect." He called him a "prodigy of nature," and summed him up as an "imbécile de génie."

Simenon's top connection in the republic of letters was, of course, André Gide. According to Simenon, the initiative for their meeting came from Gaston Gallimard, in response to Gide's desire. It is unclear how often they actually met; in their correspondence there are more frustrated plans for meetings than records of actual meetings. Gide's enthusiasm was spontaneous, energetic and generous. Having made his own discovery of Simenon, he acted on it with the intellectual vigor and curiosity that characterized his whole life. He would procure mountains of Simenons, devour them at his phenomenal reading speed, re-read them, make extensive marginal notes, mention them in his journals, read them aloud to his guests and family, and write about them to the author.

> I have just read one after another nine of your latest books . . .

Beyond that, I wanted to backtrack, and I picked out from the Fayard collection, which I had just procured in its entirety, *Le Fou de Bergerac*, and *Au rendez-vous des terre-neuvas*, which I did not yet know . . . Those which you have published in the last two years astonish me, particularly *Le Cheval blanc* which I had just finished last night, and certain passages of which I have just read out loud to Jean Schlumberger, then to Roger Martin du Gard . . .

In his journal he records:

I read especially German and English works; but have just devoured eight books of Simenon in a row, one per day (second reading for *Long Cours, Les Inconnus dans la maison*, and *Le Pendu de Saint-Pholien*).

Later yet, Gide was spreading "acute Simenonitis" to his entourage:

You would have laughed to see us all in the same room immersed, Richard Heyd in *Lettre à mon juge*, Jacqueline H--- in *Il pleut, bergère* . . . , Jean Lambert, my son-in-law, in *Le Haut mal*, Catherine, my daughter, in *Le Bourgmestre de Furnes*, and myself in twelve of your older novels, reread in two weeks . . . Gallimard was kind enough to send us fourteen of your books, and, in addition, we scoured the bookstores here for all the available Fayards (to think that I had never read *Les Fiançailles de M. Hire!*), Add to that the volumes of the new series, either bought here, or sent by you (thanks!), immediately devoured . . . I was full of you and still am.

Gide, thus, was fascinated by Simenon, recommended him right and left, planned articles, lectures, and eventually a small critical work on him (none of which, unfortunately, came to fruition), and asked many questions. Like Keyserling and some of the literary critics, he felt Simenon was radically under-appreciated and had the wrong public: ". . . the strange misunderstanding which has set in in respect to you; you are considered a popular writer and you do not at all address yourself to a mass audience." Gide found Simenon puzzling as an artist: "I do not understand very well *how* you conceive, compose, write your books." This enquiry began, in effect, a prodding process which, for several years to come, counterpointed Gide's continued praise, and was part of his repeated encouragement to rise higher, to do better: "Vous nous devez des merveilles," he was writing in 1942, and was consistently one of those persuaded that Simenon would soon come out with his "big book."

Simenon was clearly affected by Gide's prodding and responded with a long letter from Nieul in January, 1939. He explains that he had determined to be a writer since the age of 12, and "since the age of 18 I know that I want to be some day a complete novelist, and I know the 'oeuvre' of a novelist does not begin before forty, at least." He was about to turn 36 when he wrote this, and whatever merits that assertion has about novelists in general, as regards Simenon it points to expectations, to a sense of working up to something. Indeed, the letter continues with a summary artistic autobiography, emphasizing the conscious stages with which he viewed his evolution: apprenticeship with the commercial work, deliberate postponement of maturity with "semiliterary" works (the Maigrets), and now an ascent toward true maturity with the "romans-roman."

His account of what slows down his progress is his answer to Gide's question about how he goes about composing his novels: he has to put himself wholly into the skin of his characters, live their lives fully and continuously while he is writing. This is so strenuous that he can only sustain it for a limited period. He hopes to extend that limitation little by little, both by writing for a longer period—maybe as much as a month—and by learning to get fully into several different characters, for so far he has only been able to handle one.

He deplores the fact that a writer cannot use a "life model" the way a painter does, and finishes answering Gide's "procedural" question by introducing some of the terms that he will repeatedly use for his method of composition: getting into a trance-like state ("me mettre en trances") that enables him to slip into his character's personality; "l'état de grâce" (the state of grace) which is basically a theological metaphor for the trance condition; staying with it, not letting go ("rester dans le bain") for if he loses his grip for an instant the novel is lost forever; and, similarly, "souffle" (or wind), an athletic metaphor indicating how long you can keep going without running out of breath. He acknowledges his inability to revise: "Since I don't know how the thing is put together, I know even less how to tinker with it." He examines his situation as a writer—his own analysis of the "cas Simenon"—in a tone of agitated earnestness:

> Intelligence frightens me terribly . . . I try to feel rather than think. Or rather to think with . . . (?) here we are! I would be hard put to say with what! A Rembrandt painting, a Renoir . . . A little piece for harpsichord or violin that Bach would *piss* as a musical exercise for his kids.

This sense of worried earnestness recurs not long afterward in another letter to Gide:

> Although the whole summer I felt empty and unable to recover the thread of my work, I have now written three novels in three months, out of the blue, and if I hope for their quick publication, that is because I am eager to know if, as I believe, I have finally arrived at a beginning of plenitude, at having every creature and every "clique" in its place in the little world that I seek to create.

Gide, for his part, continued his "enquiry" for the next decade, providing much encouragement and some well-placed criticism.

If at the beginning of the thirties, then, Simenon was riding the crest of one wave in his career, at the end he was riding another, more complicated one. Rummaging about his sensibility, memories and experience, he had produced an imposing series of straight novels which established, reiterated and modified a whole set of fictional preoccupations. Encouragements abounded, publicly and privately; everything was conspiring to say, "go! go!"; and he himself responded variously by reflections and utterances on his craft, by groping aspirations, by a paradox of worry and self-confidence.

He had also, however, decided to revive Maigret and to try other forays into the detective genre.

XI

MAIGRET'S RETURN
AND THE WAR YEARS
1939-1945

When Simenon abandoned Maigret in 1933, Arthème Fayard received his decision as if he had had a fit of lunacy and was killing the goose that laid the golden eggs. But Simenon really meant it. He had written *L'Écluse numéro un* as the last Maigret; the popular-demand factor prodded him to write *Maigret*, but when it first appeared as a serial in *Le Jour*, he prefaced it with a strong statement swearing that this was the last. What made him change his mind?

The initial reason was doubtless financial. The straight novels did not yield as high or as reliable a return as the Maigrets, and part of their sales was always attributable to a persistent identification of Simenon as the creator of Maigret, or as the man who had *stopped* writing Maigrets — a factor that could not be counted on forever. Furthermore, one should note the date of the announced Maigret revival; 1939 was the year of the birth of Marc Simenon and the beginning of the Second World War. The man who wanted to look youthful for his son also wanted to take no financial chances. Hard times threatened: a golden-egg goose in a corner of the barnyard might not be a bad idea.

But there were other factors: the "recreational" theory, for example, which Simenon often adduced. The idea is that the straight novels took an enormous psychological toll out of him, and at the same time his deeply-engrained work-ethic made him uncomfortable if he remained very long without writing. He found that writing Maigrets was a pleasant diversion. "I discovered a formula that enchanted me: hard novels and Maigrets— Maigret becoming an exercise, a pleasure, a relaxation." For example, tense with anticipation of divorce and the birth of his second son, "I typed *Mon Ami Maigret* to calm myself." Another factor we might call "easeful identification with Maigret." As Thomas Narcejac, Simenon's first book-length critic, pointed out: "In age and experience he had caught up with his hero . . . and no longer needs to ensure his verisimilitude by thinking him through. Maigret . . . becomes an artist, a connoisseur of souls, like Simenon"—a perception Simenon later ratified: "Little by little, indeed, we ended up resembling each other a little." Thus Maigrets were a way for Simenon to hedge his bets both financially and artistically.

Actually, Simenon had been writing Maigret and other detective short stories off and on since 1936, beginning with "L'Affaire du boulevard Beaumarchais," in another reader-participation gimmick in *Paris-Soir Dimanche* of October 26. Thus, the Maigret fans were deprived of their hero for only 31 months, not the eight or ten years usually assigned to his absence. From 1938 to 1941, Simenon published 43 detective stories, of which ten are Maigrets, for the pulp publisher Offenstadt, most of which, together with a few others, were collected by Gallimard in three hefty volumes in the early forties: *Le Petit Docteur, Les Dossiers de l'Agence O*, and *Les Nouvelles Enquêtes de Maigret*, to which should be added *Signé Picpus*, which contains a few more short stories.

These stories of the thirties do not constitute a substantive re-entry of Maigret, however. The Maigrets and the non-Maigrets alike are very light pieces of little import either to the Maigret saga or to Simenon's literary career, written probably for easy money, in the same spirit that he was tossing off his newspaper pieces right and left. Some of them are not without charm and interest. "Stan-le-tueur" is a good mystery turning on the identity of a murderous Polish gang: a preliminary study for *L'Outlaw*, which goes to show, if nothing else, that Simenon *could* rework material if he wanted to. Individually, these stories present a very sketchy Maigret; collectively they convey the impression of the original Maigret holding his own as a personality—or of Simenon keeping in practice for the real revival later. Sometimes, as in "L'Auberge aux noyés," Maigret slips into an uncharacteristic deductive armchair-detective role. Maigret is often retired and encounters cases by accident, as in "Tempêtes sur la Manche," "Le Notaire de Chateauneuf," or "Mlle. Berthe et son amant." In "Une Erreur de Maigret" he has an outburst of hard-boiled violence as he slugs a sleazy, unctuous pornographer. "L'Amoureux de Mme. Maigret" finds the Maigrets living, of all places, on place des Vosges and involved in a spy story underlying a neighborhood fracas. "La Vieille dame de Bayeux" takes Maigret to Normandy and the familiar situation of a fancy family covering up murderous shenanigans.

Most of the other detective short stories—without Maigret—are in three series. In *Les Dossiers de l'Agence O*, Inspector Torrence from the Maigrets has set up a private detective agency, though the most prominent investigator and mastermind of the agency is a photographer named Monsieur Emile. The *Petit Docteur* series features a young country physician practicing in the Marsilly-Nieul area, named Jean Dollent and modelled on the Simenons' real-life local doctor at La Richardière, Dr. Edouard de Béchevel. Dollent is another fling at the armchair mode, and part of the fun lies in his sprightly and impish personality, and in his cavalier way of insinuating himself into criminal investigations: a descendent of Arsène Lupin and Rouletabille.

The third series was called *Nouvelles Aventures policières*, but was collected as *Nouvelles exotiques* when published by Gallimard along with *Signé Picpus* in 1944. They combine the exotic and the detective mode and, with one exception, are basically comic. The exception is "L'Escale de Buenaventura," a tropical gangster story of sex, violence and big money. "Un Crime au Gabon" is a comedic mystery presided over by a smart but lazy colonial commissaire, who anticipates the crime and substitutes blanks for real bullets, assuring a happy ending. In "L'Enquête de Mlle. Doche," a jewel theft is cleared up on a liner in the South Pacific, leaving young lovers to live happily ever after. "Le Policier d'Istambul" resolves an exchange of identity problem between a rich man and his valet. "La Ligne du desert" sends Inspector Nordley of Scotland Yard through Egypt and the Sudan on the heels of a master-criminal: all turns out well in the end, to the extent even that Inspector Nordley—violating all detective traditions—marries the heroine. Simenon's best story of these years is a crime story, though not a detective story: "Le Châle de Marie Dudon," composed with Maupassant-like neatness and telling the story of a poor woman who observes a wife poisoning her husband in the wealthy house across the way. She considers blackmailing the wife, but hesitates, and when she finally decides finds it is too late: the body has not been buried but cremated, leaving no evidence.

The real Maigret revival began at the end of 1939 when Simenon wrote *Les Caves du Majestic*. As far as the public was concerned, it began in 1942 with the Gallimard volume entitled *Maigret revient...*, which includes *Les Caves du Majestic, La Maison du juge* and *Cécile est morte*, followed by four more volumes in 1944. The public, which had been buzzing with a steady background clamor, was ready for it. Claude Farrère was perhaps acting on its behalf when he almost got into trouble with the authorities by sending a telegram to the Police Judiciaire: "Commissaire Maigret missing. Very worried." These volumes constitute a "second movement" of the Maigret saga which has tended to get lost in Simenon criticism: commentators who refer to the "earlier" and the "later" Maigret tend to leave out this "middle" Maigret, which is a mistake. If one is to take Maigret seriously at all as literature, two of these stories are first-rate.

In *Les Caves du Majestic*, the narrative pacing, suspense and construction all work admirably, hand in hand with deft characterization and convincing scene setting. The scene is an extensive elaboration of one which Simenon had created more cursorily in the first Maigret, *Pietr-le-Letton*: the inner workings of the swank Majestic Hotel in Paris. As Maigret sniffs his way into the case, detective and reader alike experience total immersion in the disciplined hecticness of this labyrinthine infrastructure. Maigret observes the prime suspect, who is the coffee man — the sweet raté Donge, who bicycles to work from his suburban cottage early every morning. A puncture on the fateful morning of the crime caused a key delay. Reconstituting route, timing and behavior, Maigret, in a charming scene, gets himself a bicycle and pedals along behind Donge, comes to know his pathetic little household and his unhappy life history. The humble bicycling of the commissaire symbolizes well enough the sympathy of the mender of destinies for this wrongly accused little man.

Cécile est morte is also a splendid tale and a kind of festival of Maigret items. The murder of an avaricious, crippled old woman in a popular neighborhood outside Paris engenders an ideal cast of characters and situations to bring out Maigret at his best. Simenon knows this and soon saddles him with an American criminologist studying his "method":

"I should like, first of all, to know your ideas on the psychology of criminals."

Maigret, meanwhile, was opening his mail, which he had taken from his desk.

"What criminals?" he asked as he read.

"Why . . . criminals in general . . ."

"*Before* or *after?*"

"How do you mean?" . . .

"I ask you if you're talking about criminals *before* their crime or *after*. Because, obviously, *before* they are not yet criminals. For thirty, forty, fifty years, sometimes longer, they are people like everybody else, no? . . . Why does a man commit a crime, Mr. Spencer? From jealousy, greed, hate, envy, more rarely need. In short, impelled by some human emotion or other. Now these emotions, we all have them, to some degree or other" . . .

[1 3 9]

"I understand your thought. But the state of mind of the criminal *afterward?*"

"That doesn't concern me. That's a matter for juries and prison directors. My role is to discover the guilty. And to do that I have to be concerned with their state of mind *before*. I have to consider whether such-and-such a person might have been capable of commiting such-and-such a crime, how and when he committed it."

The colloquy continues a bit later over a marvelously described lunch of coq au vin, cêpes bordelaise and Beaujolais—after an unfortunate stop at a bistro where Maigret has a "calva" and Spencer a glass of milk:

"In a large glass, *patron!*"

"The milk?"

"No! the calva!"

The mystery is well developed, and its suspenseful unravelling is in the best manner of detective writing. If Simenon is a maverick who does not play by any of the rules of the various detective genres, he manages in *Cécile est morte* to have his cake and eat it too: to provide an expertly satisfying "mystery," and at the same time to indulge his divergent tendencies.

The other full-length Maigrets of this period, unfortunately, are not as good. *La Maison du juge* is a murky tale of a reclusive retired judge with an insane, nymphomaniacal daughter, courted by a naive young mussel-gatherer (we're in Simenonian mussel country here, providing some good local color). *Signé Picpus* is an equally off-the-wall plot starring a clochard, Mascouvin, who has been enlisted to play the role of a deceased husband so that the widow can continue to collect the proceeds of an inheritance.

A considerably better story, *L'Inspecteur cadavre*, finds Maigret once again essentially in a private-detective role, investigating the problems of one of those upper-crust provincial families with dismal secrets. His class consciousness, and Simenon's, become sharply activated; there are references to thirties labor unrest and retaliatory activities of the gentry. Maigret is sympathetic to the "little people" and outraged at the corrupt gentry, but says at the end, "Tout s'arrange": people like that always manage to fix things up.

Félicie est là is much jollier, as Maigret, back on duty, investigates the shooting of an old man in a housing development by prying information from the maid, Félicie, who thinks, wrongly, that a nephew whom she secretly loves is guilty and is protecting him. Maigret intuits the truth, partly by his ability to imagine sympathetically Félicie's life with her employer, and her poverty-stricken childhood in Fécamp. Most memorable is a marvelously comic sequence in which Maigret, who is keeping watch all night over the endangered Félicie, picks up a live lobster, has all sorts of trouble with it while making important phone calls, and gets Félicie to cook it with a homemade mayonnaise — all to Inspector Lucas' dismay, who had his eye that same lobster. The chapter indeed, is entitled "The Night of the Lobster," and includes such sequences as:

"Ouch," Maigret growled on the telephone.

"What?"

"Nothing ... It's the lobster ... I'm listening."

Since the lobster won't stay still, Maigret puts it delicately on the floor and growls, "don't move."

"Huh?"

"I was talking to the lobster ..."

. . .

"Say, couldn't you hop over here?"

Maigret hesitates, his foot encounters the lobster: "I can't now ..."

. . .

He says a few words to Lucas, who contemplates the lobster with a morose eye.

. . .

Holding the lobster behind his back: "Tell me, Félicie, I have an important question."

She is already on the defensive.

"Do you at least know how to make a mayonnaise?"

Haughty smile.

"Well, make one immediately, and put this fellow on the stove."

. . .

Lucas eyes the lobster with just a touch of rancor.

The chapter concludes: "Maigret closes the door carefully, and takes up his place in the kitchen, near the window, after having turned off the light and glimpsed once more the red lobster shell on the table."

The Maigret revival coincided closely with the outbreak of the war. The Simenons had returned to Nieul with the newborn Marc at the beginning of the summer of 1939 and, except for one or two trips to Paris, stayed in the area for about a year. On September 3 he was in La Rochelle having a drink in a café with Annette de Bretagne when the declaration of war was announced. His first instinct, back at Nieul, was to pull out all the flowers in his garden and plant vegetables. He wrote Gide that he alternately threw himself at his garden and at his typewriter: both, it might appear, precautionary measures. For several months he was expecting once again to be called to arms in Belgium. But this was the "drôle de guerre" period when nothing happened.

When the real war started in May, Simenon hastened to Paris, wearing his garrison cap from his military service, and reported to the Belgian embassy, which was in chaos, receiving contradictory orders from Brussels, where the Blitzkrieg was under way. Léopold III's swift surrender obviated the call-to-arms issue. Instead, the embassy asked Simenon to return home and take charge of Belgian refugee services in La Rochelle. He was given authority to requisition lodgings for the multitudes fleeing the advancing German armies, and bristled when a lady of his acquaintance asked him to send her only "respectable people" ("des gens *bien*"). When a small flotilla of Ostend fishermen put into port, with women, children and all their household goods, he persuaded them, only with difficulty, to clear the military harbor, sail to a small nearby port, and accept housing there. He observed them well and memorialized them six years later in *Le Clan des Ostendais*.

By June 22, it was all over: France had capitulated, Pétain set up the Vichy government, and Simenon found himself in occupied territory and retreated to Nieul to provide for his household. They did not remain long, for it was a strategic area and the R.A.F. began bombing the nearby port of La Pallice. They scurried inland into the Vendée, where they set up temporary quarters in a small farmhouse in the middle of the forest of Vouvant. It was there that, having injured himself while whittling a stick for Marc, and feeling persisting chest pains, he consulted the nearest radiologist at Fontenay-le-Comte. The man told him he had a heart condition and about two years to live, a diagnosis Simenon accepted with remarkable serenity. About two years later, he casually mentioned his condition during a bridge game which included a doctor, who urged him to go to Paris for verification with an eminent specialist. He made the clandestine trip (travel was not normally authorized for foreigners) and learned that the radiologist had misread the X-rays and that his heart was in splendid shape. Marcel Pagnol and Jean Cocteau were with him to comfort him, then to celebrate, and even to keep a look-out for German patrols that might have molested him.

The farmhouse in the middle of the forest was too small, and later in the fall of 1940 the Simenons moved into town at Fontenay-le-Comte, where they lived for nearly two years in a small Renaissance château, Terreneuve, once frequented by the poets of the Pléiade and possibly by Rabelais. In the summer of 1942, advised that Fontenay's damp climate was bad for Marc, they moved back to the country, into a farm on the edge of the village of Saint-Mesmin-le-Vieux. With an orchard, plenty of vegetables, three cows, chickens, turkeys, geese, ducks and goats, as well as beehives set up against a sugar shortage, Simenon felt reasonably capable of providing for his family.

He had some trouble at the beginning of the occupation, in particular a disagreeable confrontation with a gentleman from the French Jewish Affairs Office, whose function it was to ferret out Jews and turn them over to the Gestapo. He proclaimed blandly that "Simenon" came from "Simon" and that "Simon" was a Jewish name; besides, he said, he could smell a Jew at ten paces, and gave Simenon one month to produce birth certificates going back three generations to prove he had no Jewish blood. Appalled and frightened, Simenon wrote to his mother, who spent weeks trudging about town halls and parish offices, miraculously producing all the required certificates, which the Jewish-Affairs gentleman pocketed, still glowering with suspicion.

Subsequently, however, the war years were a calm period for Simenon, in contrast with his agitated life in the thirties. Little Marc often at his side, he tilled his fields and looked after his stock, fished, hunted mushrooms and snails, and rode around the countryside in his buggy. He got along well with the local farmers, who took to consulting *him* on agricultural problems; and he had an affair with an attractive widow. Never remotely inclined toward political activism, he had little to do with the resistance, but occasionally helped out with provisions of wine and food, and, later, by lending his car to British parachutists on commando raids.

By August of 1944, Paris was liberated and the Germans began to pull out of the Vendée. According to Simenon, he was in danger of reprisals from German columns retreating past his farm, and escaped with his household into the backwoods. However, according to Boule and Tigy, it was not the Germans but the Free French forces that threatened him for inexplicable reasons, since, though not an active resistor, he could hardly be accused of collaboration. In any event, they spent several days hiding in a remote meadow, and the only upshot was that Simenon caught a bad case of pleurisy which sent him on a long convalescence to the resort of Les Sables d'Olonne. Breaking his announced intention to read no more fiction, he spent his enforced leisure going through the collected works of Proust, Balzac and Zola, and wrote most of the stories that were later collected in *Le Bateau d'Émile*.

By the summer of 1945 war and pleurisy were both over and Simenon went back to Paris, while Tigy packed things up at Nieul in preparation for a yet unspecified resettlement. Ever a hustler, he found quarters in the Claridge Hotel on the Champs-Élysées, where he lived for two months with his new secretary. He renewed contact with old friends and made new ones: Raimu, Gabin, Charles Spaak, Pierre Lazareff, now publishing the new daily, *Libération*, and Marcel Pagnol, newly married and elected to the Académie Française. Near the Claridge, he took to frequenting Le Vernet, a night spot run by the chansonnier Jean Rigaud, who introduced him to Justin O'Brien, Gide's biographer and professor of French at Columbia University, then a colonel in the United States Army. Simenon, Rigaud, and O'Brien spent many evenings of drinking and carousing at the Vernet till closing — "a trio of extremely merry fellows." Colonel O'Brien's kind treatment of some drunken soldiers who abused him provided Simenon with what he interpreted to be his first taste of the *real* America.

Gide was in Paris at that time, and the two were frequently in touch, as they had been throughout the war, but had trouble getting together. The Gide-Simenon correspondence records a series of letters, telephone calls and "pneumatiques," which finally yielded a two-day excursion to Fécamp in Simenon's car. Nothing, unfortunately, is recorded of what they talked about — only Simenon's pleasure in the trip: "I have kept a wonderful memory of the two days that you were willing to share with me. . . ." Subsequently, Gide tried to arrange for Simenon to meet the distinguished author of *Les Thibaut*, Roger Martin du Gard, evidently unsuccessfully: if Simenon was to have literary friends, it was to be on his own terms.

If the slower wartime metabolism reduced Simenon's output, the reduction was nonetheless on a Simenonian scale, which means he still wrote a lot. He revived Maigret with six novels and a fistful of stories. In straight fiction, though writing less, he maintained his momentum. He continued his sporadic rumbles of literary self examination with public and private utterances. In addition, he made an important new departure: autobiographical writing. The autobiographical impetus had been prefigured at the beginning of 1937, when, discontent in the swank apartment on boulevard Richard-Wallace, he vividly resurrected the discontents of an earlier period with *Les Trois Crimes de mes amis*.

A prefatory paragraph explains that he thought he had written a novel and found that it was an autobiography. Autobiographical ghosts had been floating up steadily from the depths to populate his fiction, and all of a sudden it ceased to be fiction. Hyacinthe Danse, Deblauwe, and the pathetic little Klein who hanged himself in the church of Saint-Pholien appeared bearing their real names, along with the Caque and the *Nanesse* and the cynical wheeler-dealers of World War I. Among them trots a personage infrequently called Simenon, he, perhaps, something of a fiction. Behind him is a more mature commentator, who serves to excoriate the moral failure of the times.

Simenon's artistic destiny was always to be haunted by the autobiographical coordinate, and its twisted subtleties were soon pressed on him more insistently by the misdiagnosis at Fontenay-le-Comte, giving him two years to live. Until the *Mémoires intimes* of 1981, the *only* context in which Simenon ever mentioned this episode was perfectly cheerful accounts of how he came to write the childhood memoirs which were later published (in 1945) as *Je me souviens*. Expecting not to live long, he wanted to provide Marc in the future with an account of who his father was, where he came from. The project took on considerable dimension for him. Interviewed in Fontenay in the spring of 1941, he told a reporter that he now had ceased writing fiction:

"At the moment, I am working on my life work ["l'oeuvre de ma vie"]. [He] went to a drawer and pulled out a large notebook on which he read: 'Pedigree of Marc Simenon, together with portraits of various uncles, aunts, cousins and friends of the family, as well as anecdotes about his father (1940).'"

"How many volumes?"

"I don't know yet. Perhaps fifteen or twenty."

"The publication date?"

"Probably after my death. I work on nothing else than this."

He was overstating the case, but it is clear that the autobiography loomed large in his consciousness. In 1942 he was quoted as announcing *Pedigree* as "the supreme realization of my art."

Soon the informal memoir turned into a fictionalized "work in progress" about his relatives, his childhood and his adolescence. He appropriated the title of the original memoir and called it *Pedigree*, and, in contrast with his normal writing procedure, worked on it off and on for over two years, and perhaps tinkered with it for more. The result, published in 1948 as fiction, is a chronicle of Liège and his early life, most memorable not as a story but as a display of portraits and scenes. The most fictive element in *Pedigree* is the story of a young anarchist, Félix Marette, who weaves in and out of the central account of the Mamelin (i.e., Simenon) family. Félix, sourly antifamily and antisociety, is a foil and a parallel to Roger, Simenon's alter ego. He is yet another projection of what Simenon felt or feared he might have become. Like Simenon, he escapes to Paris, not a seeker, though, but a fugitive from a bomb attempt. His narrative link to the Mamelin saga is the outcast Uncle Léopold, an anarchist of a different category, who helps him out. The predominantly gloomy or caustic tone of *Pedigree* is due in large part to what Simenon correctly identified as its exorcising function: drawing to the surface the ghosts of the past, and the attendant resentments, anxieties, and conflicts.

> When I wrote *Pedigree* . . . I had cause to breathe a sigh of relief when I finished it. I said to myself: I'm through with all those people! Now that I have made them flesh and blood in a book, they will no longer be in my way, and I shall be able to write about new characters.

(He was later to attribute the same motivation to his friend, the painter Bernard Buffet: ". . . with cruel brush strokes, he strove to rid himself of his ghosts.") Gide had much to do with the progress — or inhibition — of *Pedigree*. He received several drafts, beginning with the original memoir and suggested fictionalizing it. Simenon's later abbreviated version of the Gide involvement was that Gallimard (probably Claude, the son) dropped in one day and left with the handwritten manuscript of the memoir. He gave it to Gide to read, who responded:

It interested me immensely, but stop! Do not write in a personal form. Don't write by hand, either. Do as you usually do. Take your typewriter and write it in the form of a novel.

"I said to myself," Simenon goes on, "why not? All those 'I's' were bothering me. And it turned into *Pedigree*."

Pedigree appears in the correspondence more frequently than any other single book of Simenon, largely because it was the only thing Simenon ever wrote that had compositional continuity and the only manuscript he ever seems to have circulated for comment. Gide at first responded that he missed the qualities that Simenon normally excels in: "a striking, haunting vision of the lives of others . . . creating living, gasping, panting beings." A few months later, he was more favorable: "If you don't flag, you will soon produce a great book. Bravo!" The following summer (1942), responding to the fictionalized *Pedigree*, he found further improvement, praising in particular the portraits of Désiré and Léopold. There was silence for two years, but at the end of 1944 he was presumably responding to further installments of *Pedigree* when, proferring more praise, he added:

> The major objection that one could make against you is your almost exclusive preference for depicting the weak-willed ["abouliques"]. You'll be ahead of the game when you learn to depict others too, showing that men of power, "heroes," are also *driven* beings. And you yourself are quite the opposite of an "aboulique," and you prove it; that, indeed, is the reason why I have such great expectations from *Pedigree*.

In this concern with weak and strong wills one certainly hears the author of *Les Caves du Vatican* and *Les Faux-Monneyeurs*, and behind that of *L'Immoraliste* and the youthful semi–Nietzscheanism of *Les Nourritures terrestres*. His sketchy reasoning as regards Simenon is interesting: Simenon limits his field unnecessarily by dwelling on characters "driven" by a failure of will; the limitation is unnecessary because Simenon has plenty of will; since he has plenty of will *Pedigree* can be made into a great book. Gide adds that the publication of *Pedigree* should be deferred. Simenon, for his part, initially responded to Gide's encouragement with deference and gratitude:

> I agree with you completely about *Pedigree*. There are even times when I ask myself if it wasn't a mistake — other times, to be sure, when I cherish once again this long and slow work . . . I have no intention of publishing it — nor anything else that I may write — before our meeting, from which I anticipate . . . not only a deep joy but also a great benefit, and perhaps a great peace.

Simenon's last word to Gide on *Pedigree*, when it was published in 1948, was that he was pleased by the reviews. Gide's last word was that, in contrast with another batch of Simenons he had just reread in one gulp and found admirable, *Pedigree* continued to seem boring to him, "but you probably did well to write it."

The war years, then, were for Simenon a time of self-examination in the form of autobiography, of receptiveness — alternating with anxiety — toward Gide's prolonged hum of interest, and an amplified sense of moving from one phase of his literary development to another. In this last category, he had always been on a merry-go-round with the critics, who were themselves addicted to proclaiming new Simenon breakthroughs. In an essay in 1943, "L'Age du roman," and again in a virtually identical interview in 1945, Simenon explained once more how his career had been one of waiting for the right moment to move into serious, mature fiction. That moment came during the occupation as he approached the age of forty: "I had reached the age when one writes novels. . . . Now, I envision an imperceptible progression, a very gradual ascent." A bit recklessly, he then related his personal history to the history of literature, proclaiming that the age of the novel was at hand.

This was the beginning of occasional incursions into literary history, a spinoff of his period of self-examination. In this case he was taken up by the critic André Billy, who received his announcement with some skepticism, because he had heard it before; attacked his notion of literary history ("what authorizes him to proffer such gross nonsense?"); but eventually praised some of his books and regularly followed his career for the next three decades. The first "book" about Simenon — not really a book but a pamphlet by Raymond Queneau in 1942 entitled, comprehensively, "Simenon: ses débuts, ses projets, son oeuvre" — was entirely predicated on Simenon's sense of literary escalation and aspirations toward excellence. He is quoted extensively, comparing fiction with painting and citing Courbet and Renoir, who strove to reach a point where they "provided each centimeter of flesh with its own life. That is what I would like to do with words." Whatever he may have ended up grasping, Simenon at this time was at a vigorous stage of reaching; the early forties were a high point of his literary ambition.

After all the fanfare, it may be surprising that few, if any, subsequent studies of Simenon's work note any new departures among the 1940–45 novels. It is true that nothing stands out as marking a major new phase, but there is considerable evidence of more attentive writing, more carefully structured patterns of symbolism, better sustained points of view. Most of the themes are familiar, but new variations emerge, and some new character types. There are more "men of power," which might be attributable to Gide's advice, except that most appear in novels written before Gide's letter, and, besides, the strong characters have a way of ending badly too, and tend to be surrounded by familiar ratés.

The title character of *L'Aîné des Ferchaux* is introduced as a strong-willed man who has made a fortune in Africa, but the story, set in Panama, is of his old age, decline, and increasing sense of powerlessness. His major project is writing a disillusioned memoir, in which it is tempting to see an ambiguous analogue to Simenon's autobiographical ferment. However, the central character turns out not really to be Ferchaux but his secretary, Maudet, one of those desperately ambitious young men in Simenon who are usually headed for a fall. An interesting variation of the father-son motif develops, the son killing the father, almost ritualistically, and succeeding him as a man of power. But it is an ironic success: Maudet ends up a disillusioned big shot, living in luxury but painfully aware of the sterility that governs his life.

François Donge, in *La Vérité sur Bébé Donge*, is also a strong character in a story examining the assault of weakness on strength. This theme is dramatically capsulized in the opening scene when his wife almost succeeds in poisoning him with arsenic in his coffee. The scene is effectively narrated twice: first omnisciently, then through his eyes. Her background is as murky and troubled as his is solid and normal: she is one of Simenon's deficient outsiders looking with helpless yearning at healthy "belongers." The core action is the transformation in François's character engendered by a new, powerfully compassionate understanding of his wife.

Le Cercle des Mahé is one of those novels that pleases by a more carefully coordinated structure of action, characterization and symbolic pattern (the last suffering perhaps from excessive explicitness) than is customary in Simenon. The setting is Porquerolles; its languid, hot, sensuous atmosphere, evoked in some splendid descriptive writing, is itself the nucleus and repository of the symbolism, associated, not unlike Thomas Mann's Venice, with love and death. The protagonist, Dr. Mahé, spends much time vainly fishing for the "péquois," a prized fish difficult to catch, and feels almost a vague, mythic conspiracy to thwart his quest among the people of the sea, possessors of an elusive secret or truth or reality, associated with his equally vague attraction to an adolescent girl—a sexual motif rather delicately underplayed in a manner unusual for Simenon.

On the other side of the symbolic fence is Mahé's ordered life in Saint-Hilaire, like Gustav von Aschenbach's in Munich: the "circles" of the title, the restrictions on life imposed by position, profession, security, and by "family" in the form of a domineering mother and the meek little wife she picked for him, who hates Porquerolles and turns her back to the sea. Mahé's impulse is to break away from it all into the Porquerolles principle—a flight, in short, attended by desire, anxiety and guilt. He sails out alone, looks overboard at the alien, sensuous, dangerous and inviting world of the sea; and a combination of sunstroke, fascination and a sort of

Liebestod suicidal impulse sends him pitching into the sea, where he drowns. The story flags a bit in the middle, but otherwise is an original and successful variation of the Simenonian flight.

A more "classic" version of the flight theme, and one of the better known, *La Fuite de M. Monde*, also reflects a more artful, rounded style than Simenon's preferred "bare" manner. At the very beginning, Mme. Monde reporting her husband's disappearance is described with an unexpected sequence of metaphors: "She fumbled in her handbook with black-gloved fingers, dry as ebony, precise as the beak of a bird of prey," etc. Much later, when Monde accidentally runs into his first wife in Nice, she is described in a most unusually orotund, highly imaged sentence:

> It was an expression that was so much her own, and only her own, that the years evaporated, and he recognized her in her totality, just as he had known her: a fragile little animal, defenseless, paralyzed by fear at the slightest noise, who knows itself incapable of escaping, and who, immobile, pulls its head in slightly, and, with astonished gentleness, watches the wickedness of the world swooping down upon her.

There is also a whole sequence of sea images — of diving, plunging, immersion — associated, as in *Le Cercle des Mahé*, with escape from a constricting environment. The story itself is summed up in the title: a wealthy wholesaler suddenly leaves home and business in Paris and seeks "something" — freedom — in Marseilles and Nice. He gets some sex, a lot of low life, and a sense of revelation. At the end he recovers his original identity, but only, perhaps, by having lost it, and at the cost of hopeless resignation. Simenon, in a depressed mood years later, took to observing the eyes of apparently serene friends, and intuited something like despair behind them; these were the eyes of M. Monde after his return, and he feared he himself had them too.

There are other flight novels of one sort or another. In *Le Bilan Malétras* the title character is also a meticulously well-ordered type, whose breakaway occurs when he impulsively strangles his mistress in a fit of jealousy. In *Les Noces de Poitiers*, an unhappy young couple flees the provinces and a domineering mother to find more unhappiness in Paris; Simenon's brief career with Binet-Valmer's Ligue is transposed to highlight his protagonist's pathetic failure. *Le Fils Cardinaud* is an *anti*flight novel, like, much later, *L'Horloger d'Everton*. That is, the protagonist stays firmly planted and the flight is his wife's. He is a full-fledged Désiré type — punctual, methodical, deferential to his boss at the little insurance office — and what is touching about him and makes this, in fact, an excellent story, is his determined application of his principal asset — methodical diligence — to bring back his errant wife. He is an attractive innocent, whose innocence is signified in a well calculated sequence of religious images (which makes critics inclined to that sort of thing pounce on it to demonstrate that, underneath it all, Simenon has not strayed far from the faith).

There are two novels in the recurring "rural degeneration" category. Best known is *La Veuve Couderc*, highly — indeed, extravagantly — praised by André Gide, who compared it, to its favor, with Camus's *L'Étranger*. It seems closer to Mauriac than to Camus as it depicts the sordid but interesting life of the willful widow Couderc ("Tati") and her ill-fated affair with a weak spirited youth, in a brilliantly imagined psychological situation, to which the form of the novel does not do full justice. Much less interesting in the rural blight vein, *Le Rapport du gendarme* is a house-built-upon-sands story: a troubled past that suddenly returns (after a sojourn in the tropics) to wreck the equilibrium of the heroine, Josephine Roy.

Le Voyageur de la Toussaint features another *naïf*, Gilles Mauvoisin, who inherits money from an eccentric uncle in La Rochelle, as well as a complicated situation of family hatred, poisoning, class prejudice; ostracism, cruelty, violence, scandal, blackmail and much more. He sensibly comes to the conclusion that he doesn't belong: an outsider suddenly thrust into the position of an insider, who finds that his true self is to remain an outsider.

La Fenêtre des Rouet is a good novel that has received less attention than it deserves, in contrast with others frequently more highly touted. It deals centrally (rather than incidentally) with that recurring motif: a character's sense of exclusion and of observing with intense yearning what he is excluded from. A fine opening scene describes the middle-aged Dominique's feelings about her own body, together with her reactions to the young couple she rents a room to, whom she hears making love. They are one of the touchstones for her life of exclusion and desire. Others are more general: the bustle of life in the streets, people sitting at cafés, pretty girls and the men who ogle them. She envies it all, and is left out of all. The chief of these touchstones is the wealthy family across the street, whose movements she observes through their windows month after month, correctly identifying a deadly conflict between the lower-class Antoinette Rouet, embodying youthful vitality and sexuality, and the morbidity, sterility and oppressiveness of the family she has married into. Dominique imaginatively lives out Antoinette's struggle for liberation, even as it takes the form of implicit murder in withholding the medicine her sickly young husband needs to stay alive. The narrative weakens toward the end, as Dominique's identification with Antoinette becomes overstated, too explicit and repetitive. It is nonetheless a remarkable study of a rather special kind of voyeurism.

In addition to these novels, a number of the short stories collected in *Le Bateau d'Émile* of 1954 and *La Rue aux trois poussins* of 1963 were written in this period. Simenon completely forgot many of these and was quite astonished when one of his secretaries discovered them in the files. Given his work method, it is surprising that he has made no more of the genre: he wrote many but never thought of himself or promoted himself as a short-story writer. Malcolm Cowley was perhaps right in making a categorical distinction between the talents of the novelist and of the short-story writer, regardless of actual length, and seeing Simenon as "a true novelist" by instinct. Some of the stories, however, are quite good, and by their very nature often avoid the structural problems that sometimes plague his novels — particularly the tendency toward dead-end departures, marginal developments, and superfluous characters.

"Les Demoiselles de queue de vache" is a miniaturization of *Le Coup de vague*, much simpler and far less somber. "Le Petit Restaurant aux Ternes" picks up the same theme of exclusion as *La Fenêtre des Rouet*, drawing from Simenon's vivid recollection of the loneliness of Christmas Eve in Paris. "La Révolte du canari" and "L'Épingle en fer à cheval" draw from Simenon's childhood and adolescence, as does "Le Matin des trois absoutes," which depicts a choirboy terrified by a criminal, almost as vividly as the famous opening of *Great Expectations*. "Le Docteur de Kirkenes" draws from the trip to Lapland. There are plenty of ratés: "Le Mari de Mélie," "La Rue aux trois poussins" and "Le Destin de Monsieur Saft," among others. There are a number of stories of seafarers, a milieu Simenon often depicts well: "Le Capitaine du 'Vasco,'" "La Femme du pilote," "Le Bateau d'Émile," "Le Comique du 'Saint-Antoine.'"

Before Simenon left for America in 1945, a new, important shift in publishers was in the works: the move to the Presses de la Cité, with which Simenon has remained to this day. The shift was important because it was symptomatic of one aspect of Simenon's existence as a writer — the financially successful, worldly, self-confident side, pooh-poohing literary coteries and the praise of the elite. The Presses de la Cité in 1945 was a newcomer to French publishing, a small outfit founded a few years earlier by a young Danish immigrant named Sven Nielsen. He and his wife had run a tiny operation almost singlehanded: legend has it that Nielsen would personally wrap up his book shipments and wheel them to the post office in a handcart. An ambitious and bold businessman, he decided at the liberation, against all advice, to "go American." This meant abandoning traditional French printing and binding formats for jazzier packaging: the expensive, paperback sewn bindings were replaced by cheaper glued cardboard bindings, then by the mass-circulation paperbacks that are now so familiar. Nielsen's Presses de la Cité was a phenomenal success, whose bold, if risky, capitalization policies paid off and created a veritable empire. "My dream," Nielsen declared, "is to do like General Motors, which manufactures several makes in competition with each other."

Nielsen's first contact with Simenon was in 1944, when he published a detective story by a Norwegian writer named Arthur Omré. The translator who handed him the copy observed, "It's a real Simenon." Nielsen responded by sending the manuscript to Simenon, on the long shot that he might get a blurb. Simenon, convalescing at Les Sables d'Olonne, liked the book, which is called *Traqué*, and sent back, not a blurb, but an extensive preface. What was happening, unbeknownst to both Simenon and Nielsen — to say nothing of Omré — was an astonishing coincidence between Simenon's commercial side and his "literary" side. His preface, whatever its relevance to *Traqué*, clearly reflected the rumination about the direction of his own work and its relation to the history of the novel that he had been expressing in various other contexts. He found the spirit of Omré's book indeed akin to his own work, and both, manifestations of a new unconscious confraternity of writers, scattered in various corners of the globe, reflecting a new conception of man: "man himself, man and his relationship to the world." When he talks about such things, he remains intolerably vague, but what was significant was his urge to identify a development in literary history, however fuzzy, of which he considered himself a part.

Nielsen was more than grateful for the preface, and when Simenon came to Paris after the liberation the two met and became friends. Nielsen would have liked a Simenon novel for the Presses de la Cité, but Simenon said he was bound to Gallimard, but gave him the handwritten manuscript of the original "Pedigree" — the straight memoir — which Nielsen published as *Je me souviens* in 1945. A year later, from America, Simenon signed on definitively with the Presses de la Cité. His friendship with Nielsen doubtless played a role, as did his desire for a more personal, custom-tailored publisher. He was ill at ease among the literati at Gallimard, and, at one particular publishing party around this time, asked himself what the devil he was doing there. An equally important factor, probably, was money: Nielsen was a go-getter who speculated in Simenon by offering highly advantageous terms, one of which, most likely, was that the straight novels would be marketed as vigorously as the Maigrets. The change from the high prestige of the N.R.F. to the hard sell of the Presses de la Cité — occasioned in the first instance by a very "literary" preface — signified a complex evolution in Simenon's career.

Thus, as Simenon was preparing to leave for America, he was preparing also to join a firm that thought of itself as pepping up French publishing by injecting into it the spirit of American enterprise. There was an American thread in his destiny, whimsically adumbrated by the faddish Americanism of the "bal anthropométrique" and reflected in Maigret's oblique connections with the harboiled school. It was soon to culminate in Simenon's great enthusiasm for America itself.

XII

AMERICA
1945–1950

In the summer of 1945 Simenon was busy making arrangements for the trip to America and went to considerable trouble to leave as soon as possible. The war had just ended and transatlantic travel was authorized only for official business. However, the semblance of official business was procurable: Simenon went for the purpose of "making official contact with American publishers and the American press." He got Canadian visas for Tigy and Marc, but Boule had to be left behind. By the end of summer they were in London, registered with something called "the Pool," waiting at the Savoy Hotel for more than a month until the call came to rush to Southampton and board a steamer. Letting no grass grow under *his* feet, he wrote some off-the-cuff articles on life in postwar London for *France-Soir*, reporting that the fancy hotels were filled with people on "official" missions—like himself.

In October, they clambered aboard a tiny Swedish freighter, together with some thirty trunks and crates (he was anticipating a long stay), and bounced their way across the Atlantic for twelve days, sometimes in ten-meter waves. Justin O'Brien was at the pier to meet them in New York and, in spite of a dockers' strike, managed to get the thirty trunks hauled off and the Simenons settled in a luxury hotel. The O'Briens were among their first American friends, and his impression of their charming Greenwich Village apartment and their country house in Massachusetts was highly favorable. Indeed, his immediate response to New York and to America this time was that same sense of "exaltation" he had felt 23 years earlier on arriving at the Gare du Nord to start a new life in Paris. America was his third major enthusiasm, after Paris and Porquerolles.

From the moment of my disembarcation in New York, I felt at home. Not the slightest disorientation. I might even say no curiosity. Everything seemed logical to me, natural, and the very skyscrapers were simply in their proper place.

He was clearly in a receptive mood. He liked the motels and drive-in restaurants, pizzas and supermarkets. He liked rough bars in Brooklyn with their drunken Irishmen saying, "Have another on me." He acquired a taste for Pabst Blue-Ribbon (and even for its singing commercial), and sometimes for dry martinis. He liked Coney Island and the Brooklyn Bridge, and was impressed by the saga of American immigration reflected in Little Italy, the Jewish Lower East Side, and Chinatown. He admired the American idea of "a job," comparing it favorably with the European idea of "a career," and, later, in Martha's Vineyard, was pleased by hotel staffs consisting of students on vacation—some from wealthy families—swimming or golfing with the guests on their off-hours. He compared the American bourgeoisie with the European and, hating the latter, was surprised to find himself at home with the former: "It doesn't have the arrogance and the pettiness of the high bourgeoisie which I've known in Belgium and in France." In short, he liked American democracy, and American individualism.

No less aware than anyone else of the paradoxes and contradictions of American culture, he nonetheless recognized in one major stream of the American experience an original and dynamic version of the myth of the "little people." His newspaper reports to *France-Soir* reflected his enthusiasm—a complete turnabout from his articles ten years earlier. He emphasized the wonder felt by Europeans arriving from their war-ravaged continent and contemplating the abundance in American stores, lights on Broadway, the panoply of restaurants. He refuted preconceived notions of the frenetic pace of American life: people are calmer, automobiles slower in New York than in Paris, and there are just as many "flâneurs" (strollers) on leisurely, casual walks. Also, he predicted, quite accurately, a forthcoming "Americanization" of Europe.

Toward some aspects of America Simenon took a more ironic stance. At American parties he found an odd tendency for men and women to separate, and was bemused by what he considered the widespread American institution of being "on the wagon." It goes without saying that he thoroughly observed and investigated American women. New York was full of beautiful and elegant women. When he took them out to dinner, they invariably ate steak, and when he took them home they kissed him good night and told him to call again. After an appropriate number of "dates," they would invite him up for a nightcap:

> She installs you in an armchair with a whiskey and tells you, "I'll be back in a moment." The moment lasts about half an hour, during which you hear lots of running water. When the young woman appears, she is wearing a peignoir and her skin is fragrant with soap. That evening, everything is permitted, as well as subsequent evenings, if you both feel like it.

He found little prostitution, except on the slum level. On the other hand, he was delighted to discover the call girl, invariably beautiful, impeccably dressed, and very expensive.

The Simenons did not stay in New York long. His English being rudimentary, Tigy's and Marc's nonexistent, he decided French Canada would provide a good transition from the Old World to the New. They went to Montreal in late October, and soon found their first American home some thirty miles from the city, on the shore of Lake Masson, near the village of Sainte-Marguerite. It was called Esterel; the main house was of stone, with a handsome, vast living room looking toward the frozen expanse of the lake, a gigantic fireplace, and rustic furniture. A Canadian reporter visiting him a few months later found that he was already well known in the village and the countryside, and would stop repeatedly on his walks to chat with the local farmers, talking trout-fishing, weather and crops, just as he had at La Richardière and at Saint-Mesmin. Though he took frequent trips to New York, he was pleased with Sainte-Marguerite, where "the snow is much gayer than the sunshine of the short summer." Life was good to him. He had his wife, his six-year-old son, and a private tutor for the child. In New York, he had found himself a ravishing redhead, with whom he considered having "tender and perhaps durable" relations, and who called him, in French phonetics, "D'jord'ge." He also had a secretary, but that was another story.

One of Simenon's *France-Soir* articles begins:

> When I finished the last article, my secretary, who is Canadian (indeed, French Canadian 100%, if not 1000%) pinched her lips and looked at me with her dark pupils like boot buttons. When I asked what crime I had committed, she said: "It is untrue that Ottawa is an English city, since one third of the population is French."

The black-eyed secretary was a young woman named Denyse Ouimet who had been recommended to him by Rudel Tessier, an associate of his Canadian publisher. Tessier had known Denyse as a bright, competent woman when they both worked for the Canadian Information Service and, eager to please Simenon, who needed a French-speaking secretary, urged her to consider working for him. At that time she was in Philadelphia with the British

Information Service and not particularly interested, but, as a favor to her old companion, agreed to call Simenon in New York. When she identified herself, he seems to have answered something that amounted to "so what?" Feeling trifled with, she was about to hang up when his tone turned suddenly to profuse apology and irresistible charm. He asked her to lunch at his regular New York hangout, the posh Brussels restraurant; still miffed and uninterested in the job, but drawn by the charm, she relented and agreed to lunch.

Denyse Ouimet was from Ottawa, and spelled her Christian name with a "y" because of her grandmother, who admired the god Dionysus and felt the "y" provided a nice dionysiac touch. (Simenon, less impressed by Dionysus and given to changing his women's names, turned her into plain "Denise.")

> My father held a high government post in the Canadian Parliament. From an old Canadian family, he had inculcated into us as children the love and respect of the English and the French language. My mother . . . came from an important family in my country.

Or, if one prefers:

> Her father was a bureaucrat, her brothers are bureaucrats, her spinster sister is a bureaucrat, and she herself was one, in the British consulate, when I met her.

To her parents' dismay, she had left home to work for the information service, and by war's end considered herself an "emancipated" woman, with a promising business career. Before boarding the train to meet Simenon, she found a copy of *Liberty Bar* and read it on the way, saying to herself, "Not bad, Simenon."

The accounts of their first meeting given respectively by Simenon and by Denyse Ouimet pretty much agree as to the events, though diverge sharply in interpreting them. Simenon, delayed by traffic, arrived at the Brussels an hour late. Denyse had two old fashioneds, became irate again, and thought of leaving, but realized she had left her cash at her hotel. (In *Un Oiseau pour le chat*, for some reason, she makes much of the fact that she only had a $3000 check with her, a month's salary—which seems indeed strikingly high for 1945.) She waited it out and was rewarded by the appearance of Georges Simenon, who strode toward her "rubbing his hands as if under a faucet," full of gracious apologies. Like his previous American dates, she too had a steak and was dismayed when Simenon ordered the waiter to pass on to dessert before she was half way through it. Otherwise the lunch went well, Simenon talking constantly and exuding charm, though irritating her with his total self-assurance.

When she left for a subsequent appointment, he insisted on accompanying her, and they strolled through Central Park. They passed by a mother duck and four ducklings paddling on one of the ponds, which they were both to remember long afterward. She felt "an extraordinary charm, an undeniable warmth behind his somewhat brusque manner," and was astonished to find how intensely she was attracted to him—that she was, indeed, falling in love. From his point of view, years later, it was also at that duck pond that "I was touched by a certain weakness in her, a confusion that translated itself into proud declarations about her family, her past, etc. . . ." In any case, Simenon urged her to join him again at the Drake after her meeting, since he had no plans that evening and hated being alone. She said "maybe," vacillated after her appointment, but ended up back at the Drake, intending only to chat and then join friends for dinner. Simenon pressed hard, "with his sharp and deep look, with that sort of weightiness of his whole body that I have known in no other man, a sort of deep magnetism." The upshot was that they spent the evening together, walking about New York. Gifts were exchanged spontaneously:

> He stopped in front of a store window, . . . examined a rust-colored necktie that went well with the suit he was wearing. I went in and bought it . . . I remember that it cost me $8.50.

Or:

> Suddenly stopping in front of a necktie street-vendor, three for a dollar, she triumphantly announced that she was making me a present of them. At that period, I only wore Sulka or Charvet neckties, which were the most exclusive in the world.

At another store, later, he bought her a ceramic duck and four ducklings, in remembrance of Central Park. They meandered to the Village and went to hear the black singer Josh Whyte at a little night spot she knew well. Simenon asked her if she came here often, and, more surly: was it with other men? They lingered long, danced to "The Man I Love," or "It's Been a Long, Long Time," and necked heavily. Quite smitten, she nonetheless said she had to catch the last train to Philadelphia. He managed to make her miss it, and they both spent the night at the Drake. Their love-making was intensely passionate, and they both declared their love and their happiness (though later Simenon was to declare that her orgasmic passion was feigned).

He called her often in Philadelphia, asking her to sing "The Man I Love" (or "It's Been a Long, Long Time") and persuaded her to return to New York a few days later. While the reunion was even more passionate, it was also undermined by the first episode of heavy drinking by both and jealous hostility about her past by Simenon. Learning that her first lover's name had been Georges, he angrily determined she would never call him by that name, and they settled on "Jo." The upshot of the men-in-her-past issue was that he supervised the burning of all her love letters, and had her get rid of all the clothes, and even luggage, that might have served for previous liaisons. She claimed that he made her burn even her father's letters, which he denied. He saw her as a troubled young woman, but full of verve and passion, and fell in love with her. She saw herself as a capable, well-adjusted woman with a promising future, and fell in love with him.

Whether she struggled to stay away from him to pursue her career, or she was out of a job and he bailed her out, she came to Sainte-Marguerite pretending to be his secretary. Simenon had it all worked out: she would have her room in the log cabin that also served as his study, and their affair would begin in earnest. He had already declared to Tigy that he was in love, but gave no names, and there was an awkward moment when Tigy took to speculating aloud about Simenon's new love and supposed it was some cover-girl type. Otherwise, the household suffered minimal disruption and the liaison progressed with sustained passion and increasing commitment. They often got together with the only close neighbors, Montrealers named Mandeville, and it was Nina Mandeville who was the first to guess that Simenon's new love was Denyse.

Tigy, more or less, accepted Denyse, and spent a good deal of time away, occasionally in Europe (though not nearly as much as Denyse's book would lead one to believe). The liaison became generally known and acknowledged: Simenon and Denyse, for instance, received separate invitations to a French embassy reception in Ottawa. "Denise" slipped into the functions of mistress of the house, and Simenon celebrated the new union with a surprise Champagne dinner for the two of them. Denise, wearing one of Tigy's evening gowns, hastily adjusted. Afterward, they dashed into the freezing night to admire the aurora borealis. Both were riding high: however acrimonious the tone of their later accounts, neither ever denied being thoroughly in love. "What happened to me? I fell in love — with a love that was passionate, violent and at the same time very tender." He saw her as the only woman who had ever combined sex and love for him.

Shortly after Denise had taken over the reins at Sainte-Marguerite, Simenon announced that he was going to write a novel. He had written no fiction since his arrival. Just before leaving Paris, he had written two Maigrets: the charming and humorous short story, "La Pipe de Maigret," in which a young runaway steals his favorite pipe, bringing out to the fullest Maigret-as-father figure, and leading from trivial mischief to the investigation of a real crime — a matter of stolen diamonds; and *Maigret se fâche*, written quickly at the request of Pierre Lazareff, who was launching *Libération*. In this story, Maigret, brought out of retirement once again, discovers skeletons in the closets of a rich, squalid family — with a touch of the Gothic when Maigret observes the villain at night prowling about an abandoned kennel beneath which he has imprisoned his son. These appeared together in book form only in 1947, and were the first Maigrets from the Presses de la Cité.

The first straight novel that he gave to Nielsen was the one Denise watched him write in the winter of 1945–46: *Trois Chambres à Manhattan*. He was still with the autobiographical instinct he had followed during the war, but now drew from recent events, for *Trois Chambres* is a transposition of his relationship with Denise. In effect, it merges two autobiographical lines: the recent experience of falling in love, with its positive and fulfilling quality, and the familiar "dark" side from the inner self and the distant past. Simenon was beginning to write with sunny enthusiasm to his friends that he had at last found true love; yet when he fictionalized the story, he darkened everything, like a photographer deliberately underexposing.

His hero, Frank, a successful actor suddenly plunged into the world of the ratés, meets Catherine (Kay, which Mme. Simenon spells "Kaye" in her book) late at night in a dingy coffee shop into which, as despondent and aimless as he, she has wandered. They go through many of the same movements—physical and emotional—as Simenon and Denise, and Denise, reading the chapters as they came out of the typewriter, was uncomfortable in recognizing herself in certain aspects of Kay. The bars and stores and streets she and Simenon had wandered in and out of during the first few days were all there, but the hotel where Frank and Kay consummate their love is not the Drake but a third-class establishment like a hundred others in Simenon's fiction. Frank's fits of jealousy, usually after drinking, his sadomasochistic prodding into the men in her past, his insults and cruelty, followed by tears and repentance, are very much like similar scenes Denise describes in *Un Oiseau pour le chat*. In *Trois Chambres*, Kay weathers Frank's abuse, his tendency petulantly to destroy the precious tenderness that they have nurtured, and, after the crisis has peaked, immediately becomes motherly.

Simenon himself later had mixed feelings about *Trois Chambres*. He considered it his first, and perhaps only, love story, and designated it as the book he would choose if he had to flee and could take only one of his novels. Rereading it on the occasion of a new edition, he wrote, "Unhappy with the style, but how I rediscovered the beginning of my love for D.!" His friend the novelist Pierre Benoit wrote to him that he had never read anything as beautiful as *Trois Chambres*. Jean Renoir liked it and passed it on to Charles Boyer, who was also impressed and considered playing Frank in a film version, but thought it would never get past the censors of the Hayes Office. (Marcel Carné directed a film of *Trois Chambres* in 1965.) André Gide, on the other hand, was not enthusiastic:

> . . . I expected a great deal, but you do not keep your promises—or at least what you made me hope for: a novel. It's very fine to discover

love at your age, but that prodigious gift of sympathy which enabled you . . . to live in another person, to become another, is here replaced by personal experience, almost by confession; and that which is new to you is not at all new in literature.

Trois Chambres was also the occasion of Denise's undertaking to deal with Simenon's ways with alcohol. He has contradicted himself about the relationship between his drinking and his writing. In an interview in 1979 he stated that when he started writing the Maigrets and the straight novels, he would drink only coffee, and later tea; and he refuted "a legend cooked up by my second wife that I used to write on whiskey." Elsewhere, however, he says he wrote *Pietr-le-Letton* on two shots of "genièvre" every morning, and continued this system for a long time. He also repeatedly acknowledged that, in France, he always wrote with two or three bottles of red wine, but stopped in his forties, and from then on frequently found himself on the wagon, along with the other Americans he had bemusedly observed there. To Maurice Restrepo in 1952 he wrote that he was a fairly heavy drinker, "and one of those who, having had a drink or two, found it difficult to stop there." For that reason, he added, he and his wife decided from one day to the next to cut out all alcohol. A reporter interviewing him two years later in Arizona found him strictly on Coca-Cola, and a *Time* correspondent in 1951 reported him writing with a pot of coffee at his side.

On the other hand, his son John, his close friend Dr. Jean Martinon, and others attest that both he and Denise were consistently heavy drinkers. Denise's account is that, when she first observed him at work, he would ensconce himself with a bottle of whiskey. The next time he announced he was about to start a novel (which she remembers as *Trois Chambres*, though in that case it is impossible to identify what she would have observed him writing before), she proposed tea as a substitute and sat outside his door, handing him hot cups. He weakened after the fourth cup and said he couldn't go on, but she put a heating pad on his stomach and said, "My poor love, stay quiet a little, without speaking, it will pass." Eventually he went back to work and emerged triumphant with the first chapter. He corroborated this account in *Quand j'étais vieux*, but retracted it vehemently later on.

Two months after bringing his straight fiction to America, Simenon also brought Maigret. *Maigret à New York* is the first Maigret composed on the new continent, and Simenon went all the way by bringing the commissaire himself there. Simenon's curiosity about how Maigret might respond to a place like New York makes him disregard the implausibility of Maigret abandoning his gardening and fishing to steam three thousand miles on a disagreeable private-eye engagement. True to his method, and on the footsteps of his creator, he immerses himself into the city's high life and low life, and emerges with a colorful array of characters: show-biz people, vivid locals from a Bronx neighborhood, a marvelously sloppy and dilapidated alcoholic detective who helps him, and an amusing duo of the "Federal Police" to whom Maigret grumbles things like, "I never deduce anything" and "I am not intelligent."

In the spring of 1946 Simenon's endemic restlessness emerged, and he announced, "We're leaving." They leafed through brochures and decided to summer in a small seaside resort in New Brunswick, Saint Andrews by the Sea. Here, in rapid succession, he wrote *Maigret et l'inspecteur malgracieux* and two straight novels. The first, *Au bout du rouleau*, may obliquely reflect the recent bout with the alcohol problem, for its sullen young protagonist is a bad drunk who becomes increasingly more hostile the more he drinks, especially toward his hapless mistress, and who yearns for father surrogates but rejects them when they appear.

Le Clan des Ostendais, one of Simenon's only two war novels, depicts the dogged struggle for physical and spiritual survival of those Belgian fishermen who had taken refuge in La Rochelle, where Simenon helped them. The opening scenes, describing the arrival of the trawlers and the disembarcation, are brilliant. The tension between the French townspeople and the northern intruders, and the cohesion of the clan in an alien environment, are well dramatized, as is that touching cameo of a very old grandfather carried off the boat on his chair at the beginning, and back again at the end—with shades of Simenon's own "Vieux-Papa." The narrative, however, suffers from not being clearly enough structured around its central theme, which is—or should have been—the almost epic will of the clan's leader, Omer, to lead his people to escape both the Germans and the inhospitable French townspeople.

The installation at St. Andrews by the Sea was quite temporary and punctuated by happy excursions through the Maritime Provinces in a secondhand Oldsmobile: "It's summer," Simenon wrote; "everything is lovely, especially the Gaspé Peninsula, which, with its white fishing villages, resembles Brittany." By August of 1946 he was ready to break loose from French Canada and explore the United States in earnest. The plan was to hug the Atlantic coast as closely as possible from Maine to Florida. Tigy and the tutor had the Oldsmobile and went their own route, while Simenon, Denise and Marc meandered slowly in an old Chevrolet groaning with his possessions (he never travelled light).

During the less interesting stretches of the three-thousand-mile drive, Simenon, playing with the radio dial, stumbled upon another excrescence of American culture, the soap opera, which rang a bell for the ex-prodigy of pulp fiction, who briefly became an afficionado of things like "Stella Dallas." He dashed off a series of articles on "America by Car," published that November in *France-Soir* (now run by Pierre Lazareff). He cast "my wife" in the role of European snob—complaining about food that all tastes like cardboard and the like—and himself as the open-minded, if frequently ironic, interpreter of the "real" American way of life and its values. They reached Florida late in the fall, where Tigy was waiting for them in Sarasota, intending to spend the winter with Marc, but soon, in fact, making an extended stay in Europe.

Simenon found a beach house at Santa Maria Island, near Bradenton Beach on Tampa Bay, which became home for four or five months. Denise wrote: "Bradenton Beach! To this day, I have tender memories of it." On Christmas night, they gamboled on the beach, plunged in the gulf, emerging covered with phosphorescent droplets, and made love, murmuring "Merry Christmas, my wonderful love" to each other as the churchbells rang at midnight. Their love continued passionate, and their commitment firmer. If he was later to say he must have been out of his mind, that only confirmed the intensity of his feeling. At Bradenton Beach, everything was in maximum harmony. He felt he had discovered the "real" Denise:

> What a difference between the artificial young woman, playing multiple and unpredictible roles . . . and the D. of [Bradenton Beach]! The transition was slow, sometimes stormy. It began with her giving up make-up and agreeing to let her hair grow long.

When Tigy came back from Europe, previous tensions abated and she partook of the harmony: "The two are no longer defensive, and call each other by their first names."

It was about this time that Denise began to take on—or to appear to take on—the functions of agent, financial and legal mastermind, and builder of the Simenon empire, establishing an image that was to be widely publicized after their marriage. Later, Simenon was to dismiss the Denise-the-superwoman notion as his own generous fabrication to build up her needy ego; but for years he repeated to generations of reporters that in Denise he had five women: a wife, a mistress, the mother of his children, the supervisor of his household, and his business manager. From Denise's point of view, it was all true: she looked after Simenon's interests with unstinting energy and efficiency.

From his point of view, it started with her messing up his files in Sainte-Marguerite, continued in Florida by his giving her some correspondence to translate into English, then letting her make some phone calls in English; later by giving her a chance to negotiate a Hollywood contract, which miraculously turned out o.k.; then after that by skeptically watching her as she appropriated business matters and engaged in interminable, laborious, and inefficient communications which could have been performed briskly in a tenth of the time. That she did not endear herself to publishers indicates either that Simenon was right in considering her inept, or that she was right in seeing herself as an effective custodian of his interests. This squabble, like the who-drank-more-than-who one, went public in later years, taking on dimensions disproportionate to its interest. At Bradenton Beach, in the winter of 1946–47, all this was in its infancy, and Denise-the-passionate-mistress overshadowed the other roles.

In January they took a trip to Cuba, where Simenon's sexual adventurousness included her for the first time. Looking for a nightclub in Havana, they wandered into a brothel, where they were taken in hand by two friendly young girls who performed erotic acts for them. Simenon joined in, and coaxed Denise in too. (He later claimed that the penchant for voyeurism and group sex was hers, not his.) *Life* magazine, in a feature on Simenon ten years later, reported, among his household artifacts, a picture of a Cuban prostitute, autographed "in gratitude for help and advice Mr. and Mrs. Simenon gave her."

Except for the Cuban escapade, Simenon and his two households stayed at Bradenton Beach until April of 1947, when he announced they were packing up and heading west. He bought a brand-new, light-blue Packard (or Buick) convertible upholstered in red leather, and headed with Marc and Denise across Louisiana. Tigy stayed in Florida, to join them when they had found the next spot to settle in. They drove through the endless south-central plains and were heading for Phoenix, Arizona, when Simenon took a wrong fork and landed in Tucson.

> It was sunset. The beauty of the place, the festival of changing colors on the mountains made me hear a voice within me that said, "This is it, my friend!"

Settling down, like moving on, was usually a matter of instantaneous decision for Simenon. The next morning they went into the first real-estate agency they encountered, were enchanted by the first house proposed to them, in an area called Snob Hollow, and moved in almost immediately. It was a vast hacienda owned by the widow of a certain Judge Keegan (or Kingham), who took an instant liking for the couple and was untroubled by their irregular status. Tigy arrived soon afterward, took the master bedroom, and continued to get along remarkably smoothly with Denise. When Simenon threw a big party some time later, the invitations read: "Monsieur and Madame Georges Simenon and Mademoiselle Denise Ouimet have the honor to invite you. . . ." The little household was rounded out, as it were, by the reappearance of Boule, who had been left in Paris on salary all this time.

They stayed at Snob Hollow almost a year, until the spring of 1948, when Simenon adopted the don't-fence-me-in spirit of the place even more heartily by moving into a remote ranch in southern Arizona, "Stud Barn," a dozen miles from the Mexican border, near the tiny village of Tumacacori, while Marc and Tigy occupied a remodelled schoolhouse. Among Simenon's joys was plunging again into the world of horses, riding daily to get the mail at Tumacacori, or going on long treks through the desert with Marc. As was his usual practice, he mixed effortlessly with the locals, and made friends with Indians and Mexicans. Sympathetic to the wetbacks whose evasive trail brought them by his ranch, he would give them food and drink, even leaving supplies in sight when he was absent. He put his own sentiments into the mouth of a minor character in one of the Arizona novels: "Poor devils who are looking for work and are hypnotized by dollars. For these, I always keep a can of sardines and a bottle of beer."

Other times, he found himself on the other side of the fence, deputized and called out on a manhunt for a convict escaped from a nearby penitentiary. Life in the wide-open spaces clearly had its little adventures. Once, they had gone across the border to dine when cries of "agua! agua!" sent them hurtling toward home in the Packard under a torrential rain which was rapidly filling the dry arroyos they normally drove across. They made it to within six miles of Stud Barn, where the last arroyo had turned into a roaring river. They stripped, swam across, and walked home naked in the moonlight: "We were a pair of coyotes and real coyotes must have been looking at us."

Plunged for so long into the American wilderness, Simenon perplexed some of his friends. Vlaminck wrote to him:

We've been wondering for some time what's happened to Simenon . . . Does life over there really satisfy you wholly? Are you finding your nourishment? Of course, I'm not speaking of material nourishment.

His answer is unrecorded, but would certainly have been a thunderous "yes!" To Gide, he was writing, "I am so happy here, so perfectly adapted to the horizons, to the people, and to objects, that I am loath to leave." He finds it hard, he added, to imagine a world of literary cafés and publishers' offices. Not that his social life was inactive. He fell in easily enough with the local habits of dropping in for drinks at all hours of the day or night, and proposing to go on to someone else's ranch — which might be a matter of a hundred miles or two. Friends dropped in from California and even from Europe. Jean Renoir, who was then in Hollywood, came by for a joyous reunion and introduced his new Brazilian wife, Dido.

A measure of Simenon's contentment in Arizona for over two years was that he left for only two trips, both to Hollywood. One was an impulsive dash to a big bash at Romanoff's given by Alexandre ("Sasha") de Manziarly, the French Consul General in Los Angeles, where he became friends with Charles and Oona Chaplin. Denise seems to have been quite impressed, if one is to judge by the names she drops in her account of the affair: "Rosalyn Russel" (sic), Betty Grable, Claudette Colbert, and Charles Boyer, "whose invitation to dance I declined with a smile." Simenon was disconcerted to find the "old" neurotic Denise reappearing in this context, as opposed to the "new," "real" Denise he felt he was carefully nurturing. The second trip was for film negotiations and a warm visit with the Renoirs. Otherwise, Simenon found sufficient social stimulation in his corner of Arizona. His extravagant libido was regularly assuaged by trips across the border to Nogales, where he became a well-liked habitué in one of the better brothels. Denise sometimes waited for him in the car, and in time was invited into the parlor, where she met the girls and they all chatted amiably about what a dear man Simenon was.

At the beginning of 1949, Denise was pregnant, so that by May they abandoned remote Tumacacori for Tucson once again and safe medical facilities. The situation was changing. Enduring love, long cohabitation, and now a child all pointed toward divorce and remarriage. Tigy became more bitter, and only reluctantly, and for Marc's sake, agreed to sue for divorce in Nevada, and to disagreeable terms giving her custody of Marc but enjoining her to reside no more than six miles from Simenon. Simenon was contemplating his next removal to set up the new household of the future and settled on Carmel, California, sending Tigy, Boule and Marc ahead, while attending to the birth, on September 3, 1949, of Jean-Denis-Chrétien Simenon—"Johnny"—to whom he dedicated the book he was just finishing, appropriately entitled *Un Nouveau dans la ville*.

Simenon found Carmel "unique," a "fairy-tale town," and rented a spacious, split-level villa across the road from Robinson Jeffers' tower. Relations with Tigy, in her own nearby villa, were cool, but Denise, as he perceived her, held her own as the natural, calm, healthy woman he hoped was her "real" self. In May, Tigy spent six weeks in Reno, at the end of which Simenon and Denise arrived, and 27 years of marriage were ended. That evening he whiled away the time at the gambling machines, one of which suddenly exploded in a geyser of silver dollars, which Denise interpreted as a sign that his divorce day was his lucky day. The next morning they were married for ten dollars by a justice of the peace in a slick cowboy outfit. They considered settling in San Francisco, the American south, or Europe, but for the moment, for no particularly cogent reason, flew to New York to think it over.

In contrast with his matrimonial life, Simenon's literary life during his first five years in America was considerably less agitated than before. The nagging self-questioning of his literary situation—where am I in the literary world? What am I up to? Where am I going?—abated in the later forties. He gives the impression of having reached calmer literary waters where he swims about comfortably, alternating Maigrets with straight novels and asking fewer questions. The earnest exchanges with André Gide simmered down in the forties. Gide was unenthusiastic about *Pedigree* and some of the postwar novels, but never diminished his encouragement or his expectations of great things to come:

> I am still waiting for you to bring to a *novel* with many characters the perfection and mastery which you have so often manifested in the construction of a single character.

"Novel" is italicized because Gide, correctly, does not consider *Pedigree* a novel. He felt his faith justified with the publication of *La Neige était sale* later in 1948, which he saw as pointing to "an extraordinary resurgence." Gide's last letter to Simenon, not long before his death, closes: "Dear Simenon, I love you dearly and embrace you very hard." For over a dozen years, Gide had never ceased considering Simenon an important novelist.

In the France of the forties, the public agitation over Simenon was also less than it had been in the thirties, but he was still adequately making waves, and was still, obsessively, a "case": "Le Cas Simenon" (*France-Socialiste*, Aug. 1, 1942), "Le Cas Simenon" (*Le Soir* of Brussels, April 3, 1940), "Le Cas Simenon" (*Vérité*, Aug. 1, 1945), "Le Cas Simenon" (*Arts et Lettres*, Dec. 12, 1945). It is clear that nobody knew what to do with the man. As someone—probably Brendan Gill—remarked, Simenon suffered from an embarrassment of niches. "A novel which is not merely a detective novel," the *Paris-Soir* reviewer writes of *Il pleut, bergère...*, as if that were a revelation. *Gavroche* in 1946 situated Simenon midway between Conrad and Sartre, while *France Illustration* in 1948 oddly reported him as secluded in Arizona writing what may be his "first novel." His autobiographical works, Gide notwithstanding, were well received, and he was reported as among the authors whose books were most often stolen.

Since his move across the Atlantic, Simenon's reputation in the English-speaking world became an important category. The pyrotechnic debut of the Maigrets had quickly spread to England and America, but the reviews were at best jaunty, and by 1935 he had mostly dropped out of sight. His repeated literary escalations of the thirties passed unnoticed, and none of the straight novels was translated during that decade. It was not until the forties that some of the early straight novels were translated, and some of the earlier Maigrets that had been skipped, but the "new" Maigret did not get into English until *Les Vacances de Maigret* (French 1948, English 1950, American 1953). Because of the shortness of Simenon's books, two or three of them, not always from the same period, were often published together.

His biggest early breakthrough was with *La Neige était sale*, which was published in 1950 by Prentice-Hall, within a year and a half of the French, in a translation by Louise Varèse, the wife of the composer Edgard Varèse (who both became friends of the Simenons). The fastest and oddest Simenon translation was of a short story, "Le Petit Tailleur et le chapelier," whose first appearance in print was in English as "Blessed Are the Meek" in 1948 in the *Ellery Queen Magazine*, where it won a prize as the best mystery story of 1948. A French translation of the English version appeared soon afterward in *Mystère-Magazine*, while the original French version was not published until 1950 in *Maigret et les petits cochons sans queue*. Meanwhile, however, Simenon had expanded and transformed the original story into a novel, *Les Fantômes du chapelier*, which turns the mystery story into a psychological novel. In the story, a tailor learns that the hatter across the way is in fact a murderer terrorizing the town; in the novel, the point of view is changed to the murderous hatter, whose behavior is minutely observed, and whose background is extensively explored.

Simenon's success in America in the forties was not outstanding, though *Newsweek*, in 1946, did report that he had "invented one of the greatest detectives of fictional history," and then "turned to more serious writing," but did not elaborate. A San Francisco *Chronicle* review of *L'Homme qui regardait passer les trains*, which Reynal and Hitchcock had just published in 1946, said, a bit cryptically, "Georges Simenon . . . represents the literature of sensation at its closest approach to 'accepted' literature." Otherwise the tone of the American reviews in the forties tended to be consistently more ironic and hostile than it had been in France.

On the other hand, Simenon, most likely through his friendship with Justin O'Brien, got an early foothold among the American literati when he was invited to lecture at the Institut français at the end of 1945, where he gave an account of his development as a novelist and his ideas on novel-writing, published soon afterward in the scholarly *French Review* as "Le Romancier." He described his apprenticeship with the pulps, his move up into semi-literature, and his serious work as the search for "l'homme nu." He sketched out a stylistic theory of "mots matière" — words which somehow have the weight, substance and three-dimensionality of objects — and defined the essence of fiction as finding a situation which takes a character "to the maximum of himself."

Between his departure from Canada in the summer of 1946 and from California in the summer of 1950, Simenon, whenever he settled down, immediately recovered his normal writing rhythm: three straight novels at Bradenton Beach, seven in Arizona, and two in Carmel — with a sprinkling of Maigrets and some short stories. Many of these books dramatize an urgent need to understand — not so much the understanding as the need, or not even the need as the urgency of the need. In *Lettre à mon juge*, the need to understand is also the need to communicate and to explain: the explanation a condemned murderer urgently seeks to convey to his judge, who happens to be Coméliau, the morally obtuse magistrate of the Maigrets. The novel is another demonstration of the discrepancy between what official justice understands and what can be understood by a deeper probing into the human psyche. The condemned man is a country doctor, Alavoine, who has strangled his high-strung wife for complex motives: jealousy not so much of present as past infidelities, and hatred of the superficially wordly woman she has been (the "other" Martine) in contrast with the "real" scared innocent he has found in her.

When Denise read *Lettre à mon juge* hot off the typewriter at Bradenton Beach she was dismayed to find that Martine, like her, had an abdominal surgical scar, and that Alavoine had much in common with Simenon—was "pursued by the same 'phantoms' as he." Indeed, the parallels between the fictive and the real couple are clear, including some details of their courtship. Furthermore, Alavoine's first wife, in her sexlessness, may be a transposition of Simenon's view of Tigy, while Martine reflects what Denise was becoming, or already was, in his eyes: a compulsive organizer, concerned with money and status. (And what further complexity is to be attributed to the fact that Martine comes from Liège, or to Alavoine's dominating mother?) Writing a story about the inadequacy of justice in respect to psychological complexity, Simenon drew from manifest and latent traits in his own character — needs, desires, fears, resentments, failures, and much anger — and in the character of some women in his life, beginning with his mother. As was often the case, he sifted out the brighter part of his experience, leaving the darker part, in the thematic structure of his novel, as the object of understanding — that which so urgently needs to be known and communicated.

Simenon's biggest success of the forties was *La Neige était sale*, a tour de force which, against all expectations, manages brilliantly to transform one of Simenon's most odious characters (which is saying a lot) into an object of some compassion, certainly understanding, and possibly even admiration. It might seem to qualify as a war novel because it takes place in an unidentified country occupied by an unidentified enemy (Simenon has stated he had a small Austrian town in mind). There is a "Gestapo," but some details are more reminiscent of Simenon's Belgium during World War I than of France during World War II, and the names of the occupied tend to be vaguely Germanic (Kromer, Friedmaier, Holz, Lotte).

The protagonist, Frank, is an extreme case of alienation, manifested as brutality, adolescent posturing ("craner" is the French word, which recurs like a Leitmotiv), sexual domination and contempt, and that special Simenonian sullenness of which he is one of the more vivid and profound examples. The underlying action is his humanization through awareness and love, brought out by a brilliant focussing on his inner life, in minute detail, as he *experiences* his aggressiveness, his need, and the birth of love. The trajectory of the novel is from mindless darkness to understanding, enriched by the kind of symbolic patterning that Simenon had experimented with in the early forties. Frank has wronged an innocent girl who loves him, Sissy, in a particularly perverse act of sexual brutality. At the end, he is awaiting execution for having murdered an enemy officer in an act, not of resistance, but of boredom. Sissy and her father, Holz, visit him, forgive him, and love him, so that, figuratively, he acquires a wife and a father.

The paternity motif is the most important of the symbolic patterns: Holz, who has accidentally witnessed the murder, begins to play the role of father, and also of witness—something which Frank desperately needs. Another recurrent symbol is his childhood dream of a cat stuck in a tree, wounded but afraid of being rescued—an image that applies mostly to himself but refers also to Sissy. The snow of the title is clearly an emblem of innocence sullied, derived from a casual remark Denise had made about the wintry landscape of Sainte-Marguerite. *La Neige était sale* was widely praised by the French press when it came out in 1948, and Simenon received hearty encouragement from his friends. Renoir was very enthusiastic and wrote several excited letters proposing to film it, transposing the action to an unnamed American city which would be immediately recognized as Boston: "Can you imagine the shock in America if your action took place, say, in Boston? . . . the film could make a fortune." The project, however, fell through. Simenon himself wrote a stage version which was produced with some success in Paris in 1950, later broadcast as a radio play, and made into a film by Luis Saslavsky in 1952.

Les Volets verts was based on Simenon's good friend, the actor Raimu, who had died in 1946, and whose struggle from music-hall routines to stardom Simenon had observed with empathy and admiration. He felt Raimu was a man to whom success had come too late, leaving him bitter, cantankerous and sardonic toward the sycophants who clustered about him. But Simenon liked that aspect of Raimu and identified with it. When Maugin, the Raimu figure and protagonist of *Les Volets verts*, expresses contempt for the pretentious habitués of Fouquet's and Le Café de Paris, he is clearly speaking for Simenon, who expressed identical feelings. Indeed, in some ways, *Les Volets verts* is more interesting as an unstructured series of self-projections than it is either as a novel or as a transposition of Raimu. Maugin's fits of alcoholic jealousy, his inability to perform without drinking, his boat called the "Girelle," his learning of a heart condition that leaves him not long to live: these clearly suggest Simenon as much as Raimu. The details subserve the deeper parallel. Simenon empathized with Raimu's situation, as he saw it, of success clouded by disillusionment, defeat-in-success.

The division between the strong and the weak that appears in some of Simenon's work had always suggested aspects of himself. The more beguiling perspective on that division, as his friend Vlaminck recognized, had always been that of a Simenon who moved among the strong and the successful, but wrote about the weak and the defeated. Prodded perhaps by Gide, he had begun to explore, rather than to stereotype, some strong-willed characters. In Maugin, he created a complex example of weakness-in-strength particularly relevant to the paradoxes of his own personality.

In two of the novels of this period, Simenon plunged into the Arizona life he was relishing, coming up, as was his wont, with tales darker than the life he was living. *La Jument perdue* (which he originally entitled *La Rue des vieilles dames*, alluding to Snob Hollow) concerns a rancher named Curly John, whose life has been soured for 38 years by the assumption that his old partner Andy had tried to defraud him and plotted against his life, but who obtains evidence that his suspicions may have been wrong. The novel displays some psychological subtlety as John comes to understand Andy, and, more importantly, the complexity of his own feelings about his friend-enemy. *Le Fond de la bouteille* depicts gentlemen ranchers as besotted alcoholics living in absolute inertia. There is a vivid description of the Santa Cruz river in flood, cutting off the ranches: Simenon's merry gambol with Denise across flooding arroyos is transfigured into a depiction of ravaging nature. *Un Nouveau dans la ville*, with an unspecified American setting, is a feeble story about an outsider in a small town hiding out from big-time gangsters.

Of the novels of this period, one, *Le Passager clandestin*, reverts to the exotic settings and depicts a likeable but listless and melancholy Englishman, Owen, and the emergence of his sense of fellow-feeling, in counterpoint to his alienation and solitude, for the stowaway of the title and the young Frenchman he is seeking, who lives an idyllic life in the Tahitian backwoods. The other novels take place in France. The only memorable scene of *L'Enterrement de M. Bouvet* is the opening one, when an old man who had been leading a quiet life drops dead on a Paris sidewalk. *Le Destin des Malou* is very centrally a quest for understanding and a search for a father by Alain Malou, who seeks the truth about his father's financial success, personality and suicide. The father that he finds, a real "man" underneath a worldly, successful one—is not unlike a certain image Simenon has of himself.

Les Quatre Jours du pauvre homme depicts Lecouin's weak struggles for financial and moral survival in Paris, his downfall from corrupt success, and his son's suicide when he learns the truth. Written less than a year after the publication of *Pedigree*, it shows that Simenon's project of ridding himself of his family ghosts was not working well, for *Les Quatre Jours* is as full of the dark phantoms of Simenon's Liège as dozens of his earlier books. The stronger and more affirmative characters that had begun to appear have all vanished here, leaving the world entirely to knaves, *naïfs*, and *naïfs* struggling vainly toward knavedom. Simenon was expanding his repertoire, but the fascination with failure remained strong.

XIII

SHADOW ROCK FARM
1950 - 1955

If the forties were a comparatively low-keyed phase of Simenon's career, the fifties marked a return to the effervescent, hard-sell spirit of the thirties, although, paradoxically, he began the decade by settling down for five years in Lakeville, Connecticut — his longest continuous residence yet. These were among the happiest years of his life: he had a beautiful house, loved his wife (despite some chronic misgivings), adored his two sons — and even more the daughter that was born there, made lots of money, had innumerable friends, and became more famous than ever. Virtually everyone attested to his good humor, calm energy, and alert contentment; even Denise found nothing very ominous to report from those years: "Doubtless we never had such a feeling of being in our own home as in Shadow Rock Farm." Simenon wrote:

> Here, in our old bulwark of a house of Shadow Rock Farm, I am spellbound, convinced that it is for life, for I integrate myself naturally into the life of a country to which, for the first time perhaps, I have the illusion of belonging. An intimate and warm universe, into which we are all integrated.

And Renoir, whatever Simenon may have written to him, wrote back that "the optimism that emanates from your letter makes us see *la vie en rose.*"

The Simenons had drifted into Lakeville more or less by accident and bought Shadow Rock Farm from the writer and journalist Ralph Ingersoll. It was originally an eighteenth-century (not seventeenth, as Denise whimsically dates it) sawmill, which Ingersoll over the years had expanded into an 18-room, multilevel mansion. It was situated on some fifty acres of rolling country, with woods, rocks, cliffs, meadows, two trout streams, and a swamp. "It is a snug, sunny, and affectionate-seeming house," Brendan Gill reported in a 1953 *New Yorker* profile:

> "This is the twenty-sixth house I have lived in," Simenon says, while pell-mell over his face rush expressions of amusement and chagrin at the huge past and pleasure in the huge future.

For Tigy and Marc, he rented another house at Salmon Creek, eight kilometers away. He delighted in his routine of several trips to town a day, heartily greeting the townspeople, stopping for a beer sometimes, or chatting about tomorrow's weather like an old-timer. He cleared his swamp, fished, raised tulips, and pursued a running battle with the beavers who persisted in damning up his trout streams. He attended P.T.A. meetings and, in the evening, frequently played bridge, or watched a newfound toy, television, where he followed the McCarthy hearings and was dissuaded from applying for citizenship.

Pastoral and working periods in Lakeville alternated with whirlwinds of social activity, connected with friendship, business, publicity, or all three. They took frequent trips to New York, stayed at the Plaza (where Simenon came away with one of their do-not-disturb signs, which became part of his writing paraphernalia for the next quarter century), frequented the Stork Club, the Copacabana, Sardi's, and the familiar Brussels: a resurgence of his Paris life of the thirties which he was later to attribute to Denise's needs. In New York, his friendship with the Varèses flourished: "I adored strolling around Greenwich Village with him, where he knows every nook and corner and talks about it with delicious enthusiasm." At one point, he took to riding around the city in police patrol cars — the New York Police Department evidently responsive to the whims of the creator of Maigret.

One of his New York projects was to attend to Marc's sexual initiation. This came up, most likely in a spirit of *épater l'Américain*, at a party in Lakeville for his New York publishers, then Doubleday. John Sargent, at that time a Doubleday editor engaged to Neltje Doubleday, was there with his high-society fiancée. Denise, presumably primed by Simenon, announced that Simenon was about to initiate Marc to sex and wondered if Sargent could recommend a good cathouse. It appears that Sargent found what was wanted and the project went through. Miss Doubleday, however, was much scandalized — all the more when Denise explained how profitable she found it that her husband constantly went out with other women, because he would always come back full of new tricks for her.

Things were hopping. In Lakeville, he became friendly with dozens of nearby residents, including James Thurber, whom he met at the barber shop. Interviewers descended on him regularly from the American and European press. He gave lectures at several colleges, including Yale, where he was introduced by Thornton Wilder, who became a friend and a fan. October, 1954 found him in Washington at a benefit dinner for the Cancer Fund, along with Rex Stout, Frederick Dannay and a battalion of other mystery writers. To an adulating young Liégeois who remarked he was busy "conquering America," he gave a snappy cameo of his busy-ness:

> It's been hard, but now I've carried the day. One of my plays will appear on Broadway; last week, grand gala opening of *La Marie du port*; launching of *The Heart of a Man [Les Volets verts]* which is listed every week among the best-sellers; a television series of my works.

No matter that no Broadway play ever materialized, that the television series floundered and that *The Heart of a Man* was not on the best-seller list: the young Belgian may have misunderstood, and the impression of Simenon's pace and lifestyle was doubtless accurate enough. At the parties, everyone found Simenon charming and wry: "the expression that comes closest to being habitual with Simenon is one of rueful merriment," Brendan Gill wrote. Among the visitors at Shadow Rock Farm were Henriette, who had exchanged her first-class ticket for second class and was suspicious that her son was spending too much money; and Josephine Baker ("Oh, that one again!" Boule commented). The most important domestic event was the birth of Marie-Georges (Marie-Jo), on February 23, 1953.

To replace, or supplement, old admirers, new ones emerged, One was Anaïs Nin, who never met him (surprisingly, since she was a friend of the Varèses and of Henry Miller), but repeatedly recorded her enthusiasm in her diaries. In 1948, she was praising Simenon's extraordinary ability to identify the "early formation" and "germination" of "an impulse of self-destruction." Later, she wrote, "He is my favorite storyteller. He has a good story to tell, and he works subtly at characterization." She considered him "the best of the realists, better than Zola or Balzac," and praised "the sulks so well portrayed by Simenon," and how "Simenon has described a hundred times a man awakening to his total disconnection from the life he is living." Such a devoted admirer was ill-rewarded when, in 1953, struggling to make a living writing screenplays, she tried to get an option on one of Simenon's books: "I wrote to his wife. I received a curt reply that only agents were given options."

It may well have been Anaïs Nin who brought Simenon to the attention of Henry Miller, and Miller who initiated a correspondence with Simenon. "Dear Monsieur Simenon," Miller wrote in 1954, "please add my name to the incalculable list of your devout admirers the world over!" Simenon's answer has vanished, but a month later Miller wrote again, this time in French, announcing that he had spread the word at the Big Sur and elsewhere, and that a dozen of his friends were now Simenon fans. He considers him unique among French writers and finds a certain "tenderness" in his work which is usually lacking in French literature. Simenon sent him large parcels of his books, and Miller praised them all. He appreciated in particular *Les Quatre Jours du pauvre homme* because it reminded him of his own years in Montparnasse: "The most wonderful, accurate picture of Paris, the people, the types, the streets, the manners, the food, etc. etc. etc. etc."

Another admirer who emerged in the fifties was Thornton Wilder:

Chère Madame et cher et joyeux maître!

... I'm so enthusiastic about the works of Georges Simenon that I give them away — I shower them on every guest — I rejoice in sharing them. The gift of narration is the rarest of all gifts in the 20th. Century ... Georges Simenon has *that* — to the tips of his fingers.

"Condensed life — life — life," Wilder wrote of two works he had just read.

One of Simenon's most assiduous correspondents in the fifties was Maurice Restrepo, a rich Colombian who had once lived in Paris, and was fascinated by Simenon, whose works he collected. Both shared an alcoholic problem which, in this case, Simenon acknowledged, though putting his own struggle in the past and giving Restrepo advice. There were other Simenon admirers the world around: John Cowper Powys, W. Somerset Maugham, C.P. Snow. Maigret fans included the likes of T.S. Eliot and Claude Rains; and William Faulkner, asked if he ever read mystery stories, answered, "I read Simenon because he reminds me something of Chekhov." Religious readers found religion in his works — like Marcel Moré, who wrote an article on Simenon and religion in 1951, and the Jesuit Father Jean Mambrino, who entered into a long correspondence with Simenon, who was brought vaguely to acknowledge that there might be something to the alleged religious undertones. One person, at least, seems *not* to have been a Simenon fan in those days. Henriette was reported in 1952 to be "frightened by her son's lifestyle and his novels, which she considers of dubious morality." She was quoted as saying to him: "You must have an awfully black soul to see people in such an evil light." Simenon was alleged to have answered, "Mother, if I wrote about myself, it would be even worse."

In addition to the private admirers, Simenon's public visibility increased considerably in the fifties. In America, he was elected to the American Academy of Arts and Letters, and was president of the Mystery Writers of America. In France, a 1954 cartoon in *Les Nouvelles littéraires* showed the cabinet of the Republic of Letters: Jules Romains Labor, Mauriac Justice, Malraux Fine Arts, Camus Moslem Affairs, and Simenon — holding a bag of money — Finance. From 1950 through 1959 he published 28 straight novels and 23 or 24 Maigrets, and the favorable reviews far outnumbered the pans on both continents. His difficulty in getting away from the "father of Maigret" image continued to be reflected in announcements that he has written something other than a detective story. *The Saturday Review*, reviewing *Lettre à mon juge*, explained: "Perhaps inevitably, Simenon decided to abandon the static form of the detective story and write novels of the eternal conflict of good and evil." Or, as an Oklahoma newspaper headlined: "Whodunit Writer Turns to Straight Novel."

His American residence began to be often mentioned, as was the praise Gide showered upon him, perhaps because Justin O'Brien, reviewing *La Neige était sale* in 1950, quoted Gide. Phrases such as "first-rate achievement," "a great Simenon," "powerfully written," "a powerful writer" are not infrequent, though complaints of just-missed masterpieces recurred: "The manner . . . could have made a masterpiece of this book if M. Simenon had wanted to." And his phenomenal productivity continued to be a subject of awe or wit: "Simenon is like a magazine; he keeps coming out as if he were afraid that the postoffice would clamp down on him if he missed an issue." Simenon was commanding attention on a variety of levels: Professor Otis Fellows in the *Saturday Review*, Charles J. Rolo in the fashionable *New World Writing*, and, appropriately, *The Arizona Quarterly* paying tribute to "Simenon's Psychological Westerns." Harvey Breit interviewed him for the *New York Times*, feature articles appeared in *Life* and *Look* and Brendan Gill wrote an elegant "Profile" in the *New Yorker*. Gill astutely pointed out that

> his appeal is to both ends of the reading scale, and not to the middle, where the hubbub is. He is the darling of intellectuals, and among the readers of pocket books is nearly as well spoken of as Caldwell and Spillane . . .

His high-brow admirers feel

> he should be dealt with as an artist and not as an industry. They hold that any resemblance between him and General Motors is unintentional, coincidental, and too bad.

Claude Mauriac rightly included Simenon as one of his examples of modern "alittérature": the notion that "literature," particularly in modern times, is a word that tends often to accrete pejorative meanings from which many writers seek to dissociate themselves, so that what they write is "alittérature." The pattern fits Simenon like a glove. In the fifties, book-length studies of Simenon first appeared, beginning with Thomas Narcejac's *Le Cas Simenon* in 1950 (the term was only a little over fifteen years old at that point). Narcejac is comprehensive, literate and enthusiastic, but surely hyperbolic in placing Simenon above Camus. Other, lesser books followed, based mostly on interviews: André Parinaud in 1957, Léon Thoorens in 1959; and there is even a Soviet monograph in 1955 on "The Socio-Psychological

Novels Published from 1933 to 1955 by Georges Simenon," by Mariya Nikolaieva Agafonova.

Simenon himself again pondered his own sense of his literary situation. As before, he tried to identify "steps" in his literary development, but tended to be more haphazard about locating them. In an interview for *Combat*, for example, he cited *Trois Chambres à Manhattan, Lettre à mon juge, Antoine et Julie*, and *Feux rouges* as marking various stages: "In successive steps I went from the theme of resignation . . . to that of accommodation with oneself and with life. . . ." To Maurice Restrepo he wrote: "I am slowly advancing toward what I want to write." In an open letter to Jean Cocteau ("Jean, mon vieux frère"), he adopted an uncommonly lofty view of art: "Art, to my eyes, is never a miracle, but the fruit of patient labor, and above all of a renunciation." In the Brendan Gill "Profile" Simenon introduced a new category for his writing, distinguishing not only between Maigrets and hard novels but between hard novels and half-hard novels. This is perhaps the same distinction that he was making for Parinaud, to whom he described "two-step" novels in contrast with "one-step" novels: in the former he wrote a draft of the next day's chapter by hand the previous evening, while the latter were typed straight off each morning. It is not clear how regularly he maintained this practice, what the upshot was in the finished product, or which novels are which. He eventually abandoned the handwritten system because it led to temptations of fancy writing.

Simenon gave a full and intelligent accounting of his literary self in Carvel Collins' interview for the celebrated series of literary interviews which launched *The Paris Review* in 1953. Simenon, whose interview appeared in 1955, was among the first batch of writers. Here too he expressed a sense of literary progression, but with candid diffidence:

> When a novel is finished I have always the impression that I have not succeeded. . . . I want to try again. . . . I consider my novels about all on the same level, yet there are steps. After a group of five or six novels I have a kind of—I don't like the word "progress"—but there seems to be a progress. There is a jump in quality . . .

He proposed that twentieth-century readers suffer from much anxiety and that what they want in fiction is not so much escape as reassurance that they are not alone in their anxiety. He describes the usual genesis and development of his novels: a dimly perceived scene that becomes populated with a few vaguely conceived characters. Then some idea or theme, which he speculated he has been carrying around unconsciously for some time, attaches itself to the scene and to what will become the main character. I have such a man, such a woman, in such surroundings. What can happen to them to oblige them to go to the limit?" He emphasizes his sense of artisanship, and wishes he could carve his novels in a piece of wood with his hands.

He concludes: "I will never write a big novel. My big novel is the mosaic of all my small novels." The *Paris Review* interview showed a rather well developed aesthetic, and was itself a step upward in the seriousness with which Simenon took his work. In a letter to Jean Mambrino, on the other hand, he was more diffident about his literary direction: "I am nearing fifty. I see nothing definite in the past. My last novels nonetheless allow me to hope that I am approaching what I always have felt without defining it too precisely."

If he made categorical distinctions between commercial and serious writing, it did not follow that the serious work did not have its commercial side, and even less that he neglected it. If his high-brow admirers winced at the idea of the Simenon "industry," he himself was not at all above it: "The factory is going full blast," he wrote to Renoir in 1954, referring mostly to Hollywood negotiations, and Denise speaks of "l'enterprise Simenon." In the mid-fifties, estimates were that about three million Simenons were sold every year, and he calculated that by 1957 about 80 million copies of his patronymic works had been sold.

His best sellers in America by 1958 were *La Neige était sale* (850,000), *Le Temps d'Anaïs* (430,000), and *Lettre à mon juge* (350,000). He never used standard contracts with publishers, but wrote his own, which were short, simple, and profitable. The Presses de la Cité still considers him a "draconian" negotiator. He had never settled for the 10 percent royalty, but exactly how much he got remains a secret. (*Paris-Match* reported that he had in effect reversed roles and would decide what percentage the *publisher* was to receive.) Furthermore, at some point he began to reserve for himself all ancillary rights and to sell only the straight publication rights, and only for a limited period.

He brought a certain relish to financial negotiations, and certain convictions: "I considered that the existing norms were more profitable to publishers than to authors and that, in some way, I was fighting on their behalf." While this may appear flippant coming from the multimillionaire author, it isn't. On the footsteps of Dickens arguing with his publishers, Simenon repeatedly protested against the swindling of writers by profit-minded publishers, though he himself always did well and was on friendly terms with all his publishers. The hard bargaining sometimes boomeranged. He or Denise negotiated a fat twenty-book contract with Doubleday in the fifties, but at its expiration it was Doubleday that did not want to renew, finding Simenon's short novels difficult to market and his terms exhorbitant. Doubleday found its best profits in their Crime Club series, which they pushed; but this annoyed Simenon, who, in the sixties, switched back to Harcourt, Brace, where he was to be taken over by Helen and Kurt Wolff, who became good friends and promised to promote the straight novels. In England in the early fifties, he found his definitive publisher in Hamish Hamilton, with whom he has remained since.

Basking in his successful, scintillating, and cozy life at Shadow Rock Farm, showered with love and admiration, Simenon, in the fiction from this period, relentlessly pursued his exploration of alienation and misery. *Pedigree*, printed and reprinted, still did not succeed in exorcising the ghosts of Liège: Lakeville was their counterweight, leaving them perhaps all the freer to pursue their somber and violent destinies. Who knows? If their creator had been living in melancholy frustration, maybe he would have been inventing lives of plentitude and fulfillment. He once declared, "As soon as I became successful, I loved only the humble, those who bow their heads." He also declared, about the novels of those years, that in them "one would search in vain . . . for a reflection of my state of mind." For a while he worried that his happiness, in contrast with previous marital and other discontents, might be a handicap for his work, but concluded that, "on the contrary, it has gained in humanity."

In *Tante Jeanne* the heroine returns after fifty years to the small-town constrictions and the deteriorating family she had escaped as a young woman, which includes such familiar Brüll types as her sister-in-law, who locks herself up in her room and keeps a secret hoard of liquor. *Marie qui louche* is a tragicomedy, the comedy provided by tone, style, and often dialogue, the tragedy (using the term very loosely) by the action, which takes two lower-class provincial girls to Paris, where the pretty one, Sylvie, winds up rich but miserable, holed up in a mansion with her old friend, the squint-eyed Marie of the title. Both of these novels are flight novels, demonstrating, as so often, the futility of flight.

In *Une Vie comme neuve*, the event that sends a man exploring the limits of his being is a mere traffic accident: an accountant, Dudon, is hit by a car in Paris and comes into a new phase of his life in the hospital, anticipating Simenon's more famous *Les Anneaux de Bicêtre* twelve years later. The opening description in minute detail of Dudon's movements and consciousness on the fateful day, is superb virtuoso writing, as is the record of his perceptions after the accident, as he swims in and out of consciousness. He struggles to escape from the shame and guilt that constitute much of his inner life, but, again, escape is futile. Unfortunately, the narrative development of this theme does not live up to the brilliance of the beginning.

The pressure to reach the limits of his being is exerted on the Simenonian hero in two opposite directions: forward, in a foreground action that propels him to the outer edge of his being, and backward in flashbacks to the inner — usually childhood — causes of that being. The latter frequently takes on psychoanalytic colorations of varying degrees of explicitness.

One of the most ample of these psychological explorations, and one of

Simenon's biggest successes from the Connecticut years, was *Le Temps d'Anaïs* (originally entitled *L'Auberge d'Ingrannes*). It is appropriate that it was the text chosen by a group of psychoanalysts to demonstrate Simenon's susceptibility to psychoanalytic interpretation, and that the real hero of the book is a psychiatrist. He is the man to whom the protagonist, Bache, arrested for murder, feels he can explain everything, with a chance of being understood, in contrast with judges, lawyers, police officials, his wife, his mother, the press, and the public in general. Bache is engaged in a solemn quest to understand himself: his compulsive attraction to "tainted" women (the "Anaïs" figures, referring to the nymphomaniac he knew in his early adolescence and watched on the beach with innumerable men, including his own father), and the true motives of his murder of the sleazy con-man who has betrayed and cuckolded him. He concludes that his real motive was neither jealousy nor revenge, but his stunned revelation of failed manhood, the result of a chain of causes and events going back to adolescent sexuality.

Le Grand Bob is also a search for an inner truth, the key to a secret, but this time carried on from the outside by an amiable narrator, Charles, who wants to find out why his vacation acquaintance, Bob, who had always seemed an easy-going bon-vivant, has committed suicide. The psychological logic of the explanation is not convincing, but the book is unusual in its gentleness, and also in its depiction of deliberate choice rather than fatality: Bob, it turns out, has *chosen* at every step the life that he leads and departs.

L'Escalier de fer depicts the more familiar, darker Simenonian atmosphere. Etienne is an anxious and alienated little man who discovers his wife is poisoning him. His desperate loneliness had been provisionally relieved by his marriage, which, by the same token, made him painfully vulnerable: a classic masochist pattern. The iron staircase of the title becomes a symbol of noncommunication, a conduit of threats instead of comfort, of hate instead of love. *L'Escalier de fer* elicited boundless praise from the excitable Thornton Wilder: "I think it is a wonder.... Amazed. Amazed. Oh, Georges, vous êtes *ÉTONNANT*."

In *Les Témoins* the theme of judicial imperfection is taken up from the inside — i.e., from the point of view of a judge suddenly stricken with a mildly troubled conscience. He realizes that circumstantial evidence in a murder case over which he is presiding weighs much more heavily because of class prejudice than it would, say, if he himself were accused, as he imagines he might be in a prolonged meditation about his frigid, invalid wife dependent on medicine for survival. His wife does, in fact, die, and the whole issue, rather effectively, remains in an ambiguous, hypothetical realm.

The enormous role which alcohol plays in many of these novels is striking—always a symptom, never a cause. The protagonist of *Antoine et Julie* suddenly feels the ominous "déclic" that sends him on a drinking binge and puts him on a merry-go-round of shame, guilt, contrition, anger, despair and further drinking. Its graphic, detailed description of drunken behavior—barely making it up the stairs, fumbling with the key, etc.—and its somber intimacy brought high praise from Henry Miller: "Everything is so terribly familiar, yet few writers are able to express this everyday, intimate, universal realm of thought and sensation."

In Lakeville, Simenon wrote four novels with American settings—four and a half, if one includes *Crime impuni*, which begins in Liège in something very like Henriette's boarding house, and ends in Arizona. It depicts the conflict between two Jewish students: Elie, the schlemiel-loser-raté, and Michel, the rich, strong-willed Romanian whom he resents. Two of the Lakeville novels, *Feux rouges* and *Les Frères Rico* were issued by Doubleday in 1954, together with the Arizona novel, *Le Fond de la bouteille*, in a triple volume under the title *Tidal Wave*, which met with some success.

In *Feux rouges*, alcohol again plays a central role. It is a powerfully sustained account of an American couple's Labor Day trip, interrupted when Steve (which some French editions persist in spelling "Stève") drinks too much, and his wife, Nancy, angrily leaves the car and, unbeknownst to him, is raped shortly afterward. His progress through dense traffic along dismal highways, drenched in drizzling rain, with frequent stops at roadside bars, is described with wracking intensity. Simenon wrote to Wilder:

> It's probably the novel which cost me the greatest effort, that is, the greatest nervous tension ... It was a question, indeed, of living for ten days with the rhythm of the open road, without ever letting go. At the end, I was as exhausted as if I had driven for ten days on those same roads, in the midst of the Labor Day traffic.

Steve's rapid alcoholic deterioration is well done: his slurred language, his sentimental fumbling to display pictures of his children at bars, his attempts later at a laconic, Gary-Cooperish style. In an unlikely coincidence willingly accepted by the reader, Steve unknowingly befriends his wife's raper, pours his heart out to him, and elevates this hardened outcast to a symbol of liberation and free-wheeling individualism. But the impetus toward revolt and liberation, falsely glamorized in the vicious Halligan, is exorcised, leaving Steve primed for successful reintegration at the end. It is a flight novel, the flight arrested and reversed in mid-trajectory. Perhaps the upbeat ending reflects Simenon's contented life at Shadow Rock Farm.

Les Frères Rico was probably the most successful of Simenon's American-setting novels, receiving a good press on both sides of the Atlantic and adapted by Hollywood in 1957. Simenon himself set a high store by it in the *Paris Review* interview, summing it up as the story of a man who may be very good but will sacrifice anything to maintain the situation he has achieved: "I tried to do it very simply, simply. And there is not a single 'literary' sentence there, you know? It's written as if by a child." It is the story of Eddie Rico, who, with his brothers, has won his stripes with "The Organization" and has chiseled out a minor mafia domain for himself on the Gulf coast of Florida (the setting comes from the months at Bradenton Beach). Eddie is dislocated from his comfortable life when his younger brother, Tony, leaves "The Organization," and Eddie is sent on his trail, never admitting to himself that he is the point-man in his murder until, in a highly charged scene, Tony fiercely confronts him with the real truth of the situation. Forced to participate in the murder, Eddie returns home, his domain intact, his moral being shattered.

Of the Lakeville novels, *La Mort de Belle* is the one most explicitly set in that environment. It was highly praised by Miller, and may be another that Simenon had special regard for: it is most likely the one referred to in a letter from Renoir early in 1952, alluding to something Simenon had written him about an "important novel in progress." It effectively records what Eddie Rico so fears—a gradual exclusion, a casting out from the community. Spencer Ashby, through whose eyes the action is viewed in a well-sustained point of view, is comfortably established in a small Connecticut town (he appears to be based on a teacher of American history at Hotchkiss Simenon came to know). A teenage girl, Belle, is staying with them for a couple of months, and is raped and strangled in her room one night.

Little by little, the unimaginable happens: suspicion begins to fall on Ashby himself as the police are unable to find the culprit. Ashby begins to explore his own psyche and wonder whether there is that within him which *could* have perpetrated such a deed. Reflecting on his identity, he concludes that, in spite of appearances, he had never really "belonged" after all; there was always something of the suppressed pariah in him. In an unexpectedly sensational but powerful conclusion, Ashby drinks heavily, takes out a secretary of loose morals, and, finding himself impotent in the back seat of his car, strangles her. He becomes what others have begun to suspect him of being, or what he *thinks* others have begun to suspect him of being.

The last of the American novels actually written in America, *L'Horloger d'Everton* is a particularly clear-cut example of the Simenonian novel of "understanding"—of ferreting out and pondering the essential truth behind a traumatic situation. The truth-seeker is Dave Galloway, a gentle watchmaker in a small New York State town. The incident is his son Ben's running off with a girl and being tracked down by the police for robbing and killing a man. The basic action of the novel is Dave's "finding" his son, literally and figuratively, and understanding his destiny.

Simenon returned to Europe only twice during his ten years in America. The first trip, in the spring of 1952, was occasioned by his election to the Belgian Royal Academy. Officially, he scorned such literary folderol but was doubtless secretly pleased, as he was on those occasions when arcane murmurs of his candidacy for the Académie Française were heard, or vague talk of a Nobel prize. During the crossing on the *Île-de-France* Boule was sick, Simenon had a good time, and Denise a middling one. He refused to let her dance with anyone else, but he himself took up with a pretty woman nicknamed "the little baroness." This led to another group-sex experience reported by both Denise and Simenon. The little baroness one night appeared in their cabin and took off her clothes. Simenon followed suit, and Denise was persuaded to join in. Simenon, in top form, passed from one to the other for an hour. As he was about to climax with the baroness, she cried, "No! For her!"—and he slipped back to his wife. He periodically mentioned this as an example of remarkable generosity and assumed Denise's appreciation was as great as his, which appears not to have been the case.

Arriving at Le Havre, they were greeted by fans chanting, "Sim-e-non! Sim-e-non!" The French-Canadian Denise is reported to have wept as she landed on French soil, and made the front page of *France-Soir* with a gallant declaration that she had been waiting three hundred years to return to France. It was a time for grand gestures. On the way to Brussels, Simenon paused at the frontier to carry his wife in his arms into his native country. The first stop was in Liège, where he arrived a day early and, alone, paid a surprise visit to Henriette and was moved to rediscover the old furniture of his childhood but—resentful of disloyalty from any of his women—was annoyed to find it side by side with "Père André's," Henriette's second husband, now deceased. His old friend Victor Moremans had organized a tight schedule of receptions, interviews, and reunions with figures from long ago. "My little Sim! . . . I hadn't hoped . . ." a white-bearded Joseph Demarteau said, embracing him warmly.

In Paris, the Simenons were fêted in a whirlwind of galas. There was a visit to the Préfecture de Police and the offices of the P.J., where a cast-iron stove was kept in honor of Maigret. Marcel Achard gave a dinner with many Simenon intimates: Benoît, Pagnol, Fernandel, the critic Joseph Kessel, Maurice Garçon, and others. They took a quick trip to Milan and were received by Simenon's Italian publisher, Arnaldo Montadori. On the way back, they stopped for another flamboyant gala at Pagnol's estate overlooking Monte Carlo, where another old friend, Jean Cocteau, appeared—the last arrival, in a studied grand entrance, proclaiming, "Mes chéris, je suis là!" Then back to Paris, where Nielsen gave a commemorative dinner at the Boule Blanche in remembrance of the "bal anthropométrique." Simenon was in high spirits to the last day, when he made love to three or four women while Denise was packing the trunks. "That is sexuality in its pure state," he commented. He acknowledged having been caught in a "sexual frenzy" throughout this trip.

The second trip was in the fall of 1954, mostly for promotion in England. Denise was "radiant," Simenon evidently morose amid reporters, critics, and, at Oxford and Cambridge, academics — except at a party at Hamish Hamilton's where he took to chasing an attractive girl up the stairs. There was another whirlwind visit to Paris to see the Renoirs and the Pagnols, and to take Denise on the footsteps of his early Paris days and show her the hotels he first stayed at, the bar where he had the twelve croissants, etc. They were back at Shadow Rock Farm by mid-November, and seemed well ensconced for an indefinite period.

Toward the end of February, Hamish Hamilton ("Jamie") visited Lakeville and, by way of conversation one evening, asked him what it was that kept him in America. Simenon gave various answers, but, shortly afterward, announced to Denise, "We're leaving." When she asked for how long, he answered, forever, and asked how long it would take her to pack. On March 19, 1955, the five Simenons and Boule boarded the *Île-de-France*, while Tigy stayed behind to pack at a more leisurely pace. He retained Shadow Rock Farm for a number of years. Five years later, he was writing about his ten-year stay in America:

> The only years of my life that I would like to relive, Sainte-Marguerite, New Brunswick, Florida, Arizona, Carmel, and finally that Lakeville house which I kept, for no reason, for sentiment.

XIV

CRACKS UNDER
THE GLITTER
1955-1963

If Simenon's return to Europe appeared to be a whim born of restlessness, it was also a recognition that something was changing, and that, whatever it was, it should be marked—or preempted—by a major relocation: that, after all, had always been his mode of manifesting change. The specific change was a deterioration of his second marriage and his personal contentment, which would be gilded over for many years—for the public and for most of his friends—by the appearance of ever-expanding success and self-satisfaction. This pattern, of course, had been with him all his life. Its most characteristic manifestation was the incongruity between his energetic and triumphant life and the bleakness of most of his fiction. But that itself pointed to a sort of two-track existence, in which plenitude and lack persistently cohabited—all the way back to the teacher's pet of Liège seething with inner resentments, and the cocky adolescent achievements overlaying shame, guilt, and discontent.

The return to Europe and the life that followed it manifested amply the triumphant track. The Simenons disembarked with 17 trunks, a white Dodge station wagon, and a poodle named Mister (whom journalists, when he later won first prize in a dog show, took to calling "Mystère," on the assumption that he had something to do with Maigret). After a brief stay in Paris they drove the Dodge down to the Riviera and settled for the summer in Mougins in a vast hilltop villa surrounded by rhododendrons, cypresses, pink laurels and eucalyptus. In the fall they moved to another mansion, the Golden Gate, in Cannes, where Marc became a full-time member of the household: "Tigy writes me a charming letter to tell me that, at his age, she can no longer be useful for Marc, and that he needs his father." Tigy dropped out of Simenon's life, remaining distantly cordial and, eventually, taking up residence in the house at Nieul, where she still lives.

Simenon and Denise remained based on the Côte d'Azur for almost two years, pursuing their scintillating, busy, busy life, and travelling a great deal. They hobnobbed with the cinema, literary and social elite and gave enormous parties at the Golden Gate. They could repeatedly be found at the George V in Paris or the Savoy in London, on occasion in Rome or Venice, and even Brussels and Liège. One summer, evoking the past again, he packed up his whole family on a rented yacht for a waterways cruise in Belgium and Holland. He was, of course, busy with literary and para-literary work, turning out some twelve novels during those two years, escalating the publicity and interview hoopla, and amiably cooperating with film and television projects, and even a ballet. A newspaper report of early 1956 gave this account:

> "But, tell me, this year not only are you making your first steps in the movies [?], but you have written your first ballet."
>
> "That's true. There too, I allowed myself to be seduced. One day I get a call from Roland Petit: 'You absolutely must write me a ballet.' — 'Tell me what that is.' 'O.K., I'm coming down.' He hops on the night train, shows up at my place and goes back the next day with four pages that I had typed during the night, after he had glowingly explained to me what a ballet was."

Among his Riviera friends was Henri-Georges Clouzot, who, like Renoir, was always teeming with plans for Simenon films which came to naught. Simenon, sincerely uninterested in cinematic adaptations except for the money, smiled on his friends' projects but was hardly disturbed if they failed to materialize. He did once agree to write a screenplay of one of his novels for an American producer on the condition that he would not have to reread the book. Someone else did and provided him with a summary; but nothing seems to have come of this project either.

In 1956 Simenon and Denise decided that Switzerland was the best place, geographically and financially, to settle in and opted for the Lausanne area. In July of 1957 they found what they wanted, which was Echandens, a lordly château in Noland, which was to be home for almost seven years. French women's magazines took to giving awed descriptions of it. *Marie-France* reported that the entire ground floor was devoted to the "usine

Simenon": the library filled with Simenons, his study (with the 75 pipes, the red-leather pot for the five dozen finely sharpened pencils, the solid gold ball from Cartier's, which Denise had given him to gratify his tactile sense), Denise's office, followed by that of Joyce Aitken (the efficient young woman who became her principal deputy, in time taking charge of Simenon's "secretariat," an office she holds to this day). *Elle* added a description of the interphone system which it dubbed "l'interphone de l'amour," because its reporter heard Denise from upstairs say, in a gentle voice, "My love? Is everything o.k.? See you in a little while."

The staff was commensurate with the installation, and grew from six in 1957 to eleven by 1961. Denise was in charge, and Simenon claims to have been appalled by the petty military discipline and the instructions to the staff never to walk in the garden, knock on his door, make any noise, address him when they passed him, or even look straight at him. Nonetheless the bright side of his two-track life hummed along nicely. In 1957, Jean Renoir wrote to him: "Nature has given you the gift of enjoying life, of getting drunk on it, without taking away the faculty of isolation, necessary for creators."

His unstinting admirer Henry Miller dropped by in 1960 and was an exuberant witness to the bright side.

> . . . I saw him relaxed, care-free (or was he playing a role?) I saw the husband and the father, and the friend who put himself at my disposition, like a debonaire monarch, highly civilized.

> . . . The baby was cutting his teeth, the cook was throwing a fit, Mme. Simenon had not had more than two or three hours of sleep . . . Our man Simenon, for his part, was there like a bird in his nest. He had only to whistle, and he was provided with everything . . . As we say in America, he's leading the life of Reilly, what in France is called "une vie de Cocagne." . . .

> With Simenon, I've had the kind of conversation that I most appreciate: I mean talking for the pleasure of talking . . . no axes to grind, no goals to reach, no convictions to impose. I noticed I was listening as I would have to organ music. I was especially impressed by the extent of his knowledge, without the least ostentation. . . .

> That's a mature man, a man who has tasted of everything and has extracted its juices . . . one who neither judges nor condemns, who is constantly in harmony with the rhythm of life.

Simenon introduced Miller to Charles and Oona Chaplin, who were neighbors in Lausanne and had become close friends. In an open letter to Blaise Cendrars, Simenon sees the four of them — Cendrars, Miller,

GEORGES SIMENON

Chaplin and himself—as a sort of confraternity of life-exuding, creative nonconformists.

One thing Simenon clearly had in common with Miller—and Chaplin and Cendrars as well—was hyperactive sexuality. Regular "affairs," as one usually understands the term, are rare or unrecorded. What Simenon tends to mention is the off-beat quickie: the secretary, for example, whom, on an impulse in mid-dictation, he ventured to masturbate. She reached a quiet orgasm, and the dictation continued where it had been interrupted—a ritual repeated daily for several weeks. This experience was the origin of one of his more bizarre novels of alienation, *Les Complices*, where Joseph Lambert causes a frightful accident, in which a busload of children perish in flames, because of inattentive driving while masturbating his secretary.

Simenon's residence on the Riviera was also his "striptease" period. He took to frequenting the striptease clubs of Cannes and made friends of many of the performers. He was particularly intrigued by an amateur stripper who was aroused by her own performance to the point of orgasm, and left the audience, the orchestra, and Simenon breathless. He saw her night after night, got to know her and made love to her, but concluded that her orgasms in public were more intense than those he provided. His experience with this girl, telescoped with others, was the origin of *Strip-Tease*, which he wrote in 1957, originally at Clouzot's suggestion, who wanted to make a film on the topic. As so often, he transposed the tone: from benign and cheerful curiosity in life to sordid melodrama and disintegration in fiction.

Financially, the Simenon factory was unquestionably humming. Somerset Maugham, who visited Simenon several times, proffered advice on how to get maximum benefits on movie rights—advice that Denise applied with gusto but which Simenon came to regret as he acquired a reputation for being too expensive. Heady statistics pop up here and there, of uncertain accuracy but doubtless reflecting well enough which way the wind was blowing: 200 million copies printed, translations in 28 languages, 11 million dollars in royalties alone, a Simenon published in the world every three days. In 1960 he "leased" Maigret to the B.B.C. for seven years, reputedly for $2,800,000 (though he felt the contract had been thoroughly botched by Denise in drunken negotiations with a dubious agent). Rupert Davies was signed on as the British Maigret and spent some time with Simenon learning to get into the skin of the commissaire: he had particular difficulty visualizing just how Maigret behaved toward Mme. Maigret when he walked into his apartment, and settled for a pat on the behind.

In spite of his professed indifference to movies, Simenon acceded to be president of the jury of the Cannes film festival of 1960 and revealed himself as a judge of unshakeable convictions. He decided immediately that *La Dolce vita* deserved first prize, easily talked Henry Miller (who was also on the jury but spent most of his time playing ping-pong and voted perfunc-torily with Simenon) into supporting him, then stubbornly proceeded to convince the others, brooking no compromise or alternative. Denise seems to have been hyperactive in the festival hoopla, competing with the stars for last entrance to screenings; Marcel Achard wrote to Simenon, "I hear that people are calling the Festival '60 the Denise Festival."

Thus, on one level, life for Simenon was bubbling right along. He was extolling his wife and the principle of "the couple" and "the family" to every reporter that came along. "We Are Crazy Enough to Still Be in Love," subheadlined one interview, the headline of which is "Those Extraordinary Simenons." "When I am asked my profession," Simenon declared, "I answer 'husband and father.' If I am asked my hobby, I add, 'novelist.'" The birth of another son, Pierre, in May of 1959 reinforced his familial idealizations; he was steadily working his way toward the realization of that occasional day-dream, frustrated by Tigy, of a patriarchal old age, surrounded by his own clan—his personal recreation of the Simenon clan of long ago.

Such was the glitter on the surface. Simenon was not unlike F. Scott Fitzgerald, who, in 1923, gave an interview entitled "What a 'Flapper Novelist' Thinks of His Wife." "She is the most charming person in the world," Fitzgerald said of Zelda; "she's perfect." What was really happening underneath has been amply recorded since. It is probably no accident that, in 1973, Simenon was reading Nancy Milford's *Zelda* and "felt queasy," struck by Zelda's thirst to excel and, failing that, her urge, as he saw it, "to destroy her husband."

Indeed, Simenon's marriage, always turbulent, began to fall apart at Echandens. In *Un Oiseau pour le chat*, Denise accuses him of verbal abuse and physical violence, accompanied by heavy drinking. She provides an ac-count, for example, of taking refuge in Boule's room as Simenon banged on the door, calling her a whore and threatening to kill her, until the arrival of Dr. Pierre Dubuis, who realized Simenon was a sick brute and put him to sleep with an injection. Simenon, for his part, denied the charges of ver-bal and physical abuse and eventually produced an avalanche of counter-charges: her proclaiming before members of the staff and "looking at me hatefully, 'I know I've been a whore, that I am one, and that I shall be a whore all my life'"; of her bringing the staff, again, to witness Simenon drunkenly snoring on his bed, saying, "There's your boss"; of her bored or hostile responses to tender sexual advances; of keeping an embarrassed Italian television crew for interminable drinks and ending up dancing the can-can on a tabletop; and much more.

This is all heavy artillery from a late stage of their own thirty-years' war. Whatever the accuracy of Denise's allegations, Simenon earlier did acknowledge, on occasion, violent impulses in himself:

Even as a child, as far back as I can remember, I was so sensitive that I would often sob all alone, or clench my fists with rage and powerlessness — and it still happens to me at the age of fifty-eight.

He wrote, referring to marital disputes, "at least one time I took my pistol out of its case." There was an angry man, and an angry child, in Simenon's psyche. Some of the adolescent sex had, explicitly, been a mode of revenge rather than pleasure. Denise's rejection of his sexual advances doubtless hurt him but, even more, angered him; and what he saw as gestures of tenderness and desire may themselves have had a strong component of anger.

Denise's accelerating nervous tension was beyond question, and probably beyond anything Simenon may or may not have done. If she attributed it all to overwork and his fits of hostility, others had seen her as always somewhat overwrought, and increasingly so in this period. To Helen Wolff, she appeared clearly deranged in the early sixties, and was an interference, not a help, in business dealings. Simenon's view of her problem moved from kindly to hostile. In the kindly view, Denise had a neurotic compulsion to excel, to prove herself all things to all men; striving for this muddled perfection but inherently weak, she drove herself deeper and deeper into neurosis; he himself tried to "save" her by cooperating to build up her achiever image, but this was a mistake.

The hostile view is that she was a psychotic case from the start; that she, not he, was the alcoholic; that she insinuated herself into business affairs for which she had no competence and muddled them; and that by the early sixties he was still foolish enough to feel love and compassion for her, but that her predominant feeling toward him was hate. The hostile attitude developed in subsequent years.

At the time of her breakdown, her tiredness and its effects were the dominant notes. "Denise has been very tired this end of the year," he wrote to Renoir, "and has been to the clinic for a series of tests. These revealed only a depression caused by too much worry and work." Marcel Pagnol responded to "sad news" about Denise, likewise attributing her condition to overwork and depression. Simenon seemed genuinely baffled as to the immediate causes of her moods: "What did I say to provoke this painful crisis? I don't know. I search in vain. She is there, defeated, exhausted, and everything I say offends her, wounds her." "Yesterday, I thought we were returning to the surface. This morning, everything has to start again from scratch."

It was in 1958 — at a point, that is, when marital tension was beginning to accelerate toward crisis — that Simenon wrote *Le Passage de la ligne*, a curious autobiography of and by a fictional character, Steve Adams, who makes his way from the provinces to wealth and power in Paris. In a slapdash conclusion compressed into a few pages, Steve makes a bad marriage, explicitly in 1950 — "the most troubled period of my life." The fact that he flees his wife, who seeks his money by legal assaults, is an odd instance of fiction anticipating life, as is Steve's voluntary abandonment of luxury and glitter to live very modestly in a Norman village. On the last page of the novel, Steve reveals that he is consulting a psychiatrist, prompting further speculation as to how that fits into the events of the next few years in Simenon's life. Is it a further sign of the times that another novel of 1958, *Dimanche*, is a detailed account — almost instructions — of how to poison one's wife without getting caught?

The marital crisis of the late fifties and early sixties was the major manifestation of a more general discontent and unhappiness, amply documented. During this period, Simenon experienced the unthinkable — writer's block. He began a novel one day, but at midmorning ripped up his first chapter — something which had never happened before. He was crestfallen, alarmed — perhaps came close to a nervous breakdown of his own, fearing his creativity had suddenly vanished. He remained discouraged and listless, then forced himself to a breakthrough with *Maigret aux assises* (which is dedicated to Denise). Actually the gap between it and the previous novel was only four months: writer's block on the Simenonian scale would be a coffee break on any other writer's.

Nonetheless, he felt in a rut and was highly dissatisfied with his work during 1959-60. He would write a Maigret, for example, feeling it should have been a regular novel — a waste of sorts. He wrote at least one novel by hand, *Les Autres*, explaining that he "did not have the courage to type it out in the morning," and gave it to Denise to type. The typewriter suited him better: the only mildly interesting aspect of *Les Autres* is that it is the hero's own fictionalized version of his troubles with his dismal family, which he had previously written as a more intimate autobiography but destroyed when a "famous writer" he had sent it to found it indecently exhibitionistic. The relation to Simenon's writing problem is oblique but intriguing.

After the Cannes festival, he decided to write a novel "full of sunshine," but abandoned it after three pages. Instead, he wrote what he considered his best Maigret, *Maigret et les vieillards*, but inexplicably broke out into tears in mid-composition. The "sunshine" novel seems to have been *Le Train*, which he had uncharacteristically put aside for weeks because of his problem with the central character, Marcel. Separated from his wife and child during the southward rush of refugees at the outbreak of World War II, Marcel is "liberated" from despair by an encounter with a group of refugees — notably a Jewish "woman in black" — in a freight car as it rolls through the pastoral countryside. This is the "sunshine" element. Notwithstanding the sensual and communal values of this new ethos, the old has its rightful claims too:

Marcel finds his wife and child, returns home, and picks up his petit bourgeois life. The woman in black shows up a few years later as a resistance fighter and, in a dramatic ending, is shot after unsuccessfully seeking Marcel's help.

Simenon's bad literary mood led him sometimes to feel neglected by the press, misunderstood even by his well-intentioned critics, and bitter about the public's preoccupation with his money-making — merely a winner "in the literary lottery." He felt sometimes he was not so much a writer as a kind of movie star, and felt like giving it all up: "So what if in twenty, thirty years my novels are mouldering in attics." (Shortly after this, however, he could also write, "Certainly, I believe in the importance of what I do, otherwise I would not have written for forty years.") On October 12, 1960, he finished the lugubrious novel *Betty*, which was originally to be called "The Nightmare" and was based on the ramblings of a woman he met at a bar in Versailles, depicted in the book as an alcoholic, voyeuristic, exhibitionistic, depressive, paranoid nymphomaniac, who begins low and ends even lower.

The 1959–61 notebooks, which were published in 1970 as *Quand j'étais vieux*, were both effect and transcription of his discontents. Restlessly fidgeting about aborted novels and the value of his fiction, he turned once again to private autobiography, this time mostly not memoir but journal of daily life and feelings. He felt old; eight years later, when he published the notebooks, he no longer felt old and gave them his intriguing title, *When I Was Old*. Later, he was to retract the tone of some of these pages, claiming that Denise read over his shoulder and prevented him from being candid, and eventually retracted the whole work. However, if it cannot be taken wholly at face value, neither can the retraction written in later bitterness.

If he was sometimes filled with self-doubt about his work, he had not abandoned his periodic efforts to account for himself as a novelist and for the role of fiction in human affairs. Those efforts eventuated in a long essay published as a small book in 1959, entitled *Le Roman de l'homme*, which itself contributed to his literary gloom because little attention was paid to it. He was vexed that only *Paris-Press* reviewed it, and at that only to tell the "Charlie Chaplin story." The Charlie Chaplin story, which he had already told several times, was that he and Chaplin were chatting one evening, when the conversation turned to the expanding need for psychiatric practitioners and institutions. Chaplin said that, in that respect, the two of them were very lucky: whenever they started going round the bend they made a film or wrote a novel, and "we even get paid for it!" The anecdote was not so much meant to explain the mystery of art as to dramatize that there *was* a mystery by giving one whimsical causation. In a fit of annoyance,

Simenon retracted the story not long afterward: "I am a happy man. I do not write ... to cure my complexes." (On the other hand, he repeated in dozens of interviews that, indeed, he started a novel precisely because of a certain restlessness, because he "doesn't feel well in his skin.") *Le Roman de l'homme* expressed again Simenon's view that the ultimate motive for literature is fear, and fiction a mode of confronting threats and anxieties. It contains a rapid sketch of literary history to the present, in which fiction, after having dealt with gods, heroes, rulers, nobility, and ordinary man, is ready to deal with "naked man." The literary history may be skimpy, but the case for Simenon's place in it, though not explicit, is pointed enough.

The literary discouragements and domestic turmoil of the turn of the decade did not, in the end, make this period any less fertile than the preceding ones. The breakthrough from writer's block, among the straight novels, was *L'Ours en peluche*, which is not hard to read as a reflection of Simenon's inner turbulence. Dr. Chabot is a highly successful and desperately unhappy physician, who feels his social, professional and financial successes as masks, and also as betrayals of the "little people" from whom he came. His secretary-mistress is a sort of Denise type who betrays him with a medical student. Chabot hesitates between murder and suicide, and, almost by accident, opts for the former. Simenon, in one of his rare interpretations, insisted that, psychologically, the two are virtually interchangeable. Chabot is a Simenon might-have-been: a doctor, a dropout, a doctor-dropout. It contains some good scenes and characterizations, but is not as good a novel as Simenon seems to have thought, when he complained that critics were ranking it "lower than what they call my great books"; or Nielsen, who told Marcel Achard that it was probably Simenon's masterpiece.

L'Ours en peluche was written in 1960. It is tempting to take *En cas de malheur*, written four and a half years before, as an earlier exploration of the same personal problems that reached crisis proportion at the turn of the decade. Here too the protagonist, Gobillot, is a highly successful man — a top lawyer — examining the cracks beneath his success. The format is ingenious: Gobillot, whose fame rests on defending "impossible" cases, decides to open a dossier labelled "Me," and proceeds to extract the *real* truth from himself with the same tenacity he uses to pry the truth from his clients, who always start out hedging. While the problem Gobillot seeks to elucidate in himself — his sexual obsession with a twenty-year-old nymphet — does not at all correspond to Simenon's problems, the circumstances of Gobillot's life do — most notably his wife, full of nervous energy, ambitious, a perfect hostess, and utterly tolerant of his affairs. Gobillot is a well-realized character who, however, would work even better in the narrative logic if he were more disagreeable. Perhaps the reason he is not is that Simenon did put more of himself into him than usual. Gobillot thinks and feels like a sensible, compassionate man but behaves like a childish cad—a bit like Simenon.

Simenon's two unquestioned masterpieces of this period "frame," so to speak, the turn-of-the-decade crisis: *Le Président* of 1957 and *Les Anneaux de Bicêtre* in 1962—as if he had produced one "big book," then slipped into a funk, and emerged triumphant with another. Both, once again, deal with successful men plunged deeply into a revaluation of their lives. The genesis of *Le Président* is well-documented: a series of free associations prompted by an etching of a seaside landscape, leading to recollections of a stay in Normandy years before, an old house, remembered speculations about who might live in such a place, and ending with thoughts of Georges Clémenceau, who had finished his days in a country house in the Vendée.

He decided to write a novel about a distinguished ex-premier, flipping, as usual, through telephone directories to give him a name but leaving him anonymous, and consulting his atlases for a hometown, and settling on Evreux in Normandy, which he proceeded to look up to find every possible statistic about the town. Then, on the indispensable manila envelope, he sketched out the old man's present entourage: secretary, cook, maid, nurse, and a chauffeur who would likely be a government spy keeping the old man under observation—each of these provided with a detailed biography. Finally he considered how such a man might be spending his time, and concluded that, obviously, he would be writing his memoirs, and that in these would be some items embarrassing to the present generation in power. The old man himself would be resentful of his loss of power. And thus a plot began to develop. What emerged was a fine novel with a steady point of view and a subtle, suspenseful plot.

The premier's former protégé, Chalamont, is about to form a new government. The old man, who had once sworn that Chalamont would never become head of government, is in possession of an incriminating document, and is hesitating whether or not to sabotage Chalamont. He listens avidly to the hour-by-hour radio reports during the critical evening. Tension mounts as he hears someone snooping about, evidently looking for the incriminating document. He expects Chalamont to come, but he doesn't, and the government is formed. The old man wonders if Chalamont's people have spirited the document away, but it's still there: *that*, in a distinction of Jamesian subtlety, is what upsets him. The government agents have merely photocopied it, and Chalamont has formed a government anyway, unheedful of what he might do. His influence has been discounted; they consider him, he feels, already dead.

The old man could still release the document and probably create enough scandal to bring down the new government. He hesitates, and his reasons for hesitating are what is Jamesian: using his weapon would be true to his past as a man of power and authority; not using it is true to his present dissociation from the whole power-success ethos. Like so many Simenon heroes, the premier, dislocated from the world he has known, enters into a new one; but the change is both gradual and, until the renunciation at the very end, ambiguously incomplete. Alert withdrawal has become part of his daily routine, but he is still drawn to the outer world. He fidgets as he contemplates making his devastating phone call: "His fingers, his knees began to tremble, and his nerves, as usual in such moments, did not obey; the machine, suddenly in neutral ("à vide"), was turning over with uncontrolled accelerations"—a fine image of frustrated power, dynamism wildly expended in the void.

Les Anneaux de Bicêtre was Simenon's biggest success from these years, partly because it too is a fine novel; partly perhaps because Simenon, modifying his celebrated routine, spent 24 days composing it and ten revising it; and partly also because he went about "launching" it with exceptional determination, circulating advance copies widely—including to 200 doctors, some of whom, it is said, assigned the book to their students to give them a perspective on hospital life from the patient's point of view. It is also the novel for which he did the most preparatory research. It records the aftermath of a stroke, and at least three different specialists provided him with extensive documentation. He went in person to the hospital, observed the physical setting, took note of a patient's field of vision in a particular room, and asked the puzzled head nurse about such details as when the garbage was taken out. Dismayed to find there was no chapel with a bell, he took pains to ascertain that bells from a nearby church could be heard: the bells were the core image of the novel and provided its title.

Les Anneaux de Bicêtre is again a summing up and a questioning of a successful life: Maugras, a powerful newspaper publisher, who has collapsed in the men's room of the famous Grand Véfour restaurant where he meets monthly with other successful friends. When the novel appeared, Simenon was hotly pressed to concede, and equally hotly denied, that Maugras was modelled on Pierre Lazareff, who had had a stroke at the Grand Véfour. Much of Maugras's background is clearly not Lazareff but Simenon, including a love of Porquerolles and—an intriguing parallel to Simenon's way with literature—a feeling that he has no journalistic talent but a certain "flair" and a strong interest in people.

Maugras's diminished physical condition, as he awakens in the hospital to the sound of the bells, endows him with perspective and insight, and a feeling that the agitations of big business and high society are meaningless. What are real are his immediate surroundings, his thoughts and memories, and the "little people" from which he comes and whom he rediscovers in the old men from the nursing-home section of the hospital, whom he can observe from his window. He resists intrusions from the outside world — his wife, his friends — to which he does not want to be rehabilitated. Yet he feels an overwhelming solitude, and gradually returns to the world, burdened, however, by a sense that what he is recovering is mere agitation designed to avoid difficult questions and troubling answers.

Human isolation, ubiquitous in Simenon, is even more predominant in the novels of this period — either self-imposed as withdrawal or imposed as exclusion or both. *La Boule noire* depicts a placid Connecticut supermarket manager whose failure to be accepted in a country club alienates him from his "community" (Simenon became interested in the English usage of that word), and reveals to him that he has been so all along.

Le Petit Homme d'Arkhangelsk also records, with much finer tuning, both the *process* of alienation, and the inherent alienation which that process reveals. Jonas Milk is a mild and sensitive Jewish refugee (modelled in part on the Charlie Chaplin film persona), reasonably well-integrated in a small French town, but married to an unbridled young nymphomaniac, who runs away with her hoodlum lover. Suspected of murder, he tries to explain the nature of his feelings for Gina, which are tender and gently accepting, but is totally misunderstood by the authorities, then by the townspeople, who see him as a dirty old man. Denied the social communion that had become a necessary component of his inner fulfillment, he commits suicide — a noble, failed attempt at spiritual survival. Jonas Milk's relationship with Gina is an instance of a recurring theme in Simenon — sexual debility in respect to a highly-sexed woman.

The oversexed Simenon was mostly suspicious — occasionally appreciative — of oversexed women, and usually compassionate toward undersexed men: in *Le Veuf*, for example, where the impotent and alienated Jeantet marries the prostitute he gives shelter to after she has been mauled by a pimp. There are rare novels of shared and equivalent passion: *La Chambre bleue*, a tautly constructed narrative, is one; another is the static and low-keyed *La Porte*, in which the love between a crippled veteran and his devoted wife is punctuated by his jealousy, turned harmless because he recognizes and analyzes it as unfounded.

There is, of course, more bad sex than good in Simenon, as in *La Vieille*, where destructive and self-destructive sexuality is a component of a more pervasive degeneration. The theme of degeneration is relentlessly enforced by two interesting, if grotesque characters: Sophie, a potentially vigorous and healthy young woman in a degraded environment of slumming friends and sordid parties, and her strong-willed grandmother who has wrecked two marriages and ended up as a kind of evil spirit whom Sophie resists in an uneven struggle between Eros and Thanatos. Despite some psychological interest, *La Vieille* doesn't work as a novel. Neither does *L'Homme au petit chien*, meandering and ill-construed and, it turns out at the end, a repeat of the psychological situation of *Le Temps d'Anaïs*. Narrative and structural weaknesses also plague *Le Fils* in its exploration of the father-son theme.

Le Nègre, on the other hand, is a minor work with much firmer plotting, centered squarely on a likeable raté, who keeps repeating, "One of these days I'll get them." His chance comes when he finds himself in a position to blackmail some shady characters, but loses his chance. His life has been a catalogue of half-humorous humiliations, culminating, after he has flubbed his fortune-making plot, in his getting drunk and, on the way home, stumbling toward a sleeping dog to embrace him as a fellow pariah: the dog bites him.

By the time of his return to Europe in 1955, Simenon's literary reputation had reached a certain plateau where it remained fairly steady. Personal admirers continued lavishing their praise. Marcel Achard, now writing on the letterhead of the Académie Française, replaced Gide as devourer of large heaps of Simenons: "I've been in the country for ten days going through my annual Simenon cure.... You are truly a master." Renoir had high praise for *Les Anneaux de Bicêtre* and *Pedigree*, and wrote a brief appreciative essay in 1961 which was never published. Marcel Pagnol wrote to him, "You are a great creator of characters, sometimes in a dozen lines." More book-length studies appeared: Bernard de Fallois in 1961; Quentin Ritzen (Dr. Pierre Debray), also in 1961, with the psychobiography and moral-thematic analysis *Simenon, avocat des hommes*, which disturbed the brooding Simenon of those years; Anne Richter's study of the alienation theme in 1964, *Simenon et l'homme désintégré*. The periodical press continued mixed, as always, but more favorable than not. The influential *Figaro* called *Le Petit Homme d'Arkhangelsk* "a great Simenon"; *Le Président* was widely admired (by Robert Kemp, for example, in *Les Nouvelles littéraires*); and in England and America too the press tilted favorably.

The translation of *Pedigree* came out in 1962 and was a best-seller in England, listed under fiction in the *London New Daily* and nonfiction in the *Birmingham Mail*. *Les Anneaux de Bicêtre* in 1963 was the occasion for a widespread revaluation or reinforcement of Simenon's niche in the literary hierarchy. The review in *Le Monde* was preceded by a long essay reexamining the "Situation of Georges Simenon" and identifying his serious work as "romans-tragédies"; *Bicêtre* signals with particular emphasis "the serious side, the earnestness, even the inwardness of Simenon."

The most prestigious endorsement came from François Mauriac in the *Figaro littéraire*, who placed *Bicêtre* in the Christian *memento mori* tradition and found "the agnostic Simenon" a "better preacher" than most pious works. It was quickly translated and widely commented abroad, again often in the context of reappraising Simenon's literary position. The Berlin *Tagespiegel* concluded that "he is a serious novelist who indeed knows the problems, the methods, and the potentials of modern epic and modern prose." The *Times Literary Supplement* said, "M. Simenon writes wonderfully well about sickness," and the *New York Times* put *Bicêtre* on its "Bear in Mind" list. The *Washington Post* again described the reverse pattern of Simenon's career — from commercial to serious work — contrasting it favorably with the more usual pattern — literary success subsequently exploited in various money-making ventures. It identified the new Kurt and Helen Wolff connection at Harcourt, Brace — a publisher "with a reputation for sponsoring fine writers" — as marking a major upward step. In the *Atlantic Monthly*, William Barrett, while warning against an overreaction by Simenon admirers rescuing him from the detective-story image, nonetheless found *Bicêtre* "a psychological novel of considerable depth and power," and Simenon's "real strength . . . in his uncompromising and candid grasp of life"; "we never feel that he is faking." Thus a high-brow coterie was keeping up a thirty-year campaign to rescue him from indifference among their peers, and from the Maigret image among the general public.

XV

THE LAST MANSION
1964-1987

The Simenons moved out of the château of Echandens in the winter of 1963. They had known for two or three years that they would have to leave because of the projected Geneva–Lausanne superhighway and a new railroad yard right under their windows. Denise feared they would not find anything nice enough in the area, so that, for the first time in his life, Simenon decided to build. His marriage was floundering, and, prone to compensate with mighty mansions for restlessness and threats of disintegration, he now envisioned and realized the mightiest of them all, and the last one.

He found a magnificent property just outside the village of Épalinges, where he often went because of his recently acquired passion for golf. The design was his: a scaled-up, ultramodern version of a simple Picardian or Breton farmhouse, plain white with a slate roof. It had enormous rooms and windows, thick walls, heavy steel doors with rubber facings, a glass-domed swimming pool, and an impressive panoply of conveniences, such as laundry chutes in each bathroom converging on a six-machine room. C. Day Lewis visited Épalinges in 1967 to interview Simenon on the occasion of the English film version of *Les Inconnus dans la maison* and told Simenon he found everything "shipshape" — an expression that pleased him; Day Lewis, sitting in one of the spacious rooms and looking at the spectacular panorama, felt it had "the feel of a room in an ideal-home exhibition." He tried to evaluate the man in his surroundings: "The *joie de vivre* is there in the occasional sunbursts of laughter which break through his talk: I am not so sure yet about his inner serenity."

In later years Simenon looked back on Épalinges even more sourly than on his châteaux of Cour-Dieu and Echandens: "I admit it without shame, I started drinking. I felt alone, in an immense house, with much personnel, and children who kept asking questions." He never strolled on his lawn to relish his incomparable view, and got fed up with the authentic Louis XV furniture he had bought. There were *some* happy memories, such as the first Christmas, in 1964, "a Christmas full of joy, without a shadow, except, perhaps, in a corner of my heart." He frequented some neighbors, the Chaplins still chief among them, but also such luminaries as David Niven and James Mason. Among his most frequent guests were his numerous doctor friends.

A new friendship flourished in the mid-sixties with Federico Fellini, with much warmth and loudly proclaimed mutual admiration. Simenon felt that they had much in common, in particular a certain anxiety, a dissatisfaction, and a tendency to be haunted by "ghosts" which both sought to exorcise in art. There was frequent correspondence between them. In 1969, Simenon sent Fellini lavish praise of the *Satyricon*, and in 1977 of *Casanova*: "I am dazzled and deeply moved," he telegraphed, then sent another telegram to say he hadn't expressed half of his admiration. Fellini, for his part, wrote to Simenon of his "limitless talent and superhuman power and discipline," and sought in him "a companion in work, and, in life, a point of reference which never deludes and provides strength."

If the Fellini friendship showed a familiar Simenonian effervescence, the general tenor of his life during the Épalinges years was more subdued. There was a sense of incipient, gradual withdrawal; his public image was less jaunty; in 1967 he declared:

> I am above all a man who has worked a great deal, who continues to work, and who would be in despair if he could not do so to the end of his days.

> I hope to write many more novels. I would like to live to a very old age for two reasons: the first is that that is the only way of running the whole gamut of man. The second, more personal, that I would like to see all my children grown up and see what direction their lives are taking.

Georges Simenon was taking stock of old age. He took fewer recreational and promotional trips. An exception was the unveiling of the Maigret statue at Delfzijl organized by the Dutch authorities. The last extensive family trip was a Mediterranean cruise to Sicily, Greece and Turkey in 1964.

His deepest preoccupation was with his family. He yearned for and sporadically achieved the paterfamilias ideal that tickled his fancy, as his

Christmas ebullience indicates. One of his favorites in his painting collection was a seventeenth-century Dutch painting showing a patriarch at a long table, surrounded by young men, women and children. But troubles with Denise cast an increasingly long shadow, peaked to a series of psychiatric crises, and ended in a definitive and acrimonious break. The "psychiatric" phase had begun at Echandens, and was to envelope both Denise and the troubled Marie-Jo.

In the course of 1962 Denise was in contact with a Dr. Durand, the head of a psychiatric clinic near Lausanne, Prangins, which in her book she calls "Les Chênes" (and Durand, Dupont). Whether she or Simenon initiated the contact is part of the controversy between them, but the result was that in June of 1962 she was advised to take, and acquiesced to, a rest cure. Stays at the clinic alternated with stormy returns home, and she did not get better. She perceived her experience at Prangins as a sinister conspiracy initiated by Dr. Durand, who was after Simenon's money, and eagerly accepted by her husband, who wanted to get rid of her. She felt manipulated and virtually imprisoned there. Feeling herself hounded as a medical case, one of her reactions seems to have been to spread the word that Simenon was very ill and had to be handled with kid gloves, which caused some alarm among the children, particularly the impressionable Marie-Jo.

Dr. Durand announced to Simenon that Denise was troubled by the notion that Boule, in her absense, had become mistress of the household. With much sorrow, Simenon agreed to drop his most senior servant and mistress from the staff, and sent her to work for Marc and his family in Paris. (Denise, for her part, denies this and countercharges that he dismissed Boule with a grotesquely small pension.) Simenon reports wild episodes of Denise moving in a cot to sleep in Pierre's room, and the child becoming frightened, running through the vast mansion and hiding, while his mother would rouse the staff to help find him. Worse, Denise took Marie-Jo on a vacation and is alleged to have shocked the adolescent by masturbating in front of her and lodging a cancerous secret in Marie-Jo's fragile psyche, not at all appeased by her father's dangerous love for her. (Denise denies the incident, though accepts that Marie-Jo *believed* that such a thing happened. This is the episode she succeeded in having excised by court order from Simenon's *Mémoires intimes* of 1981.) By the summer of 1964 Denise, in practice, was no longer a member of the Épalinges household. She was either at Prangins, or setting up various temporary homes in Switzerland and, later and more permanently, in France.

The two principals of this ill-fated marriage have amply explained their positions, in print, with an astonishing disregard for privacy. The truth, most likely, was that the real Denise was the worldly and ambitious young woman Simenon had made a date with at a luxurious New York restaurant.

The unadorned Denise was his invention, a role he managed to make her play in a Florida fishing village and an Arizona ranch. In Hollywood and New York, the real "real" Denise would be reactivated. Lakeville was a holding action, and Europe an abandonment of the project. Going to the other extreme, he showered her with preposterous luxury and put her into a milieu where he himself functioned with jaunty detachment but she was out of her depth, and ended up resenting her for being neither what he wanted nor what she wanted.

Most likely, and understandably, she could not fathom what he wanted. One factor in the disintegration of the relationship was probably Simenon's evident need for attention, which elicited a warm, sometimes extravagant response toward those who provided it, and a resentment toward those who didn't. Denise at the beginning fed that need as admirer and devotee, passionately dedicated to his manifold desires and undertakings. With the years, she turned from a Simenon-absorbed loyalist to a self-absorbed neurotic. As a result, he turned against her, though long maintaining the illusion that he was trying to help her. The mutual accusations of alcoholism are most likely both accurate: given their situations and temperaments, heavy drinking is not hard to imagine.

Vestiges of the perfect-marriage façade lingered for some time. In 1969, Simenon complained to Dennis Drysdale, who was working on an enormous Simenon dissertation, "What am I going to do alone in this house?" When Drysdale suggested that his wife might find it quieter now that the children were gone and might return, Simenon wryly and radically understated the situation by saying she had achieved an independent life "she might prefer not to give up." Even close friends were not kept informed of the real turmoil, but only of periodic and temporary medical problems. Achard in 1964 was hoping that Denise would "very quickly be completely back on her feet"; Renoir in 1967 wrote, "we are happy to know Denise is better"; in April of 1968 he was still signing off, "Kiss Denise"; in February, 1969, he still headed a letter, "Dear Georges, dear Denise." Thus disintegration was far more advanced than most people knew except psychiatrists, though perhaps not quite as abysmal as both Simenons later reported it to be.

Throughout these crises, through good times and bad, Simenon always reserved ample space in his life for his children. Marc, of course, was an adult by the sixties, married and then divorced, with two children, and attempting a career as a film producer. Johnny finished his schooling and went off into various apprenticeships. Pierre was a growing boy. The closest, and most delicate, relationship was with Marie-Jo. When she was a flirtatious little girl just before the blue-jean era, he took pleasure in buying her pretty dresses and having her hair done up in a coquettish nineteenth-century manner. He taught her to swim and, at the *thés-dansant* of the Bürgenstock, to waltz. "Tennessee Waltz" became their song, partially replaced later when she was a guitar-strumming adolescent by Jacques Brell's most Belgian of songs, "Le Plat pays," which would being tears to Simenon's eyes.

When she was eight Marie-Jo had coaxed him into buying her a gold wedding ring, from which she was never separated. Whatever her troubles with her mother, toward her father she behaved with a classic and acute Electra complex. Most of her letters begin, "Mon grand Dad," or "Mon grand vieux Dad," and end with "ta petite fille, Marie-Jo"; one of her last letters to him was headed (in English) "You, Daddy, my 'Lord and Father.'" She was the only one of his children who he felt took an interest in his work and might herself become a writer. She indeed read a great deal of his work, and sometimes imagined herself as the companion and helpmate of his career that she might somehow have been. Other times she had outbursts of rebellion and hostility, and, when she was 17, ran away from Épalinges provisionally to lead an independent life in Paris.

From early adolescence on she was repeatedly under psychiatric care at Lausanne, Cannes, Paris, and Prangins, where her mother's Dr. Dupont took her under his wing. Simenon, considering his psychiatric knowledge and interests, was astonishingly unheedful of feeding her father fixation. Evidently more gratified than alarmed by her pathological adoration, and accustomed to accommodating and worshipping women around him, he blindly let his daughter take her place among them. It is noteworthy that, while his fiction is full of in-depth studies of father-son relationships, there is not a single instance of a father-daughter relationship of any significance.

Henriette Simenon was coaxed into visiting Épalinges twice. During her second visit, after a loud crash in her room, she was found under a wardrobe that had fallen on top of her. She handed Simenon four little satchels of gold coins and explained that she had been trying to hide them on top of the wardrobe, which toppled. The coins were the accumulation of all the money Simenon had been sending her periodically, which she said she wanted to keep for the children. For her ninetieth birthday in 1968 Simenon went to Liège. She was still sprightly and, interviewed on Belgian television, signed off with a rendez-vous for her hundredth birthday. Two years later, however, she died at the Hôpital de Bavière where Simenon had been a choirboy. He was at her bedside for several weeks.

> She smiled at me, with that smile I knew so well, both a bit ironic, incredulous, which affirmed the unshakable confidence she had in her own judgment. "Why did you come, son?"

Simenon stayed by her, saying little, meditating on past and future generations, parents and children, husbands and wives, men and women. The attending physician reported his behavior to be that of a model son, but, inviting him to dinner, was taken aback by his conversation, which revolved around his urgent need to find some women to sleep with, and, surprisingly, complaints about Marie-Jo as a whacked-out, irresponsible teenager.

Advancing age, domestic stress and bad luck in the later sixties afflicted Simenon with a variety of intestinal, pulmonary and orthopedic problems. The most persistent ailment was chronic dizziness, while the most anxiety-provoking was a prostate condition from which he feared the worst of fates — impotence. If these were years of tribulation, they also brought a more than counterbalancing comfort, and the definitive love union which had been eluding him all his life. Later in 1961, Denise hired a new chambermaid, an Italian woman named Teresa, about whom, at the interview, Simenon had a premonition. For many months she merely exchanged vague courtesies with the master, but once he walked in as she was bending over dusting a table and silently took her. It was an exceptionally intense consummation for him, and he intuited the same for her. Abashed, Teresa offered her resignation, which Denise brushed off lightly. (Denise's countervailing version is that she caught Teresa eavesdropping and fired her, but was persuaded to relent.)

Sporadic sexual relations recurred, but the turning point did not come until Denise was away at Prangins, when Simenon slipped in the bathtub at Épalinges, breaking seven ribs, and called for help long and loud, but vainly because of the impenetrable soundproofing. Eventually it was Teresa who rescued him, and he has repeatedly described how calmly and gently she took charge of the situation, stayed by him at the hospital, and helped him through a difficult convalescence. This experience cemented a relationship which acquired mythic dimensions for him. Henceforth, she was at his side almost all the time, at first moving a cot into his bedroom every night, and eventually sharing his bed. (Marie-Jo's comment was "Why not me?") Above all, his union with Teresa made him feel what he had been missing all his life.

> I met Teresa who, for me, replaces all the women who aroused my curiosity and who brought me a little bit of that tenderness which I needed and which I now enjoy every day.

> I cheated, during my first two conjugal experiences, to obtain that tenderness which was not granted me.

> Slowly, I was going to say insidiously, love came into me, a bit more day after day, and it was the kind of love of which I dreamt since my adolescence.

Tenderness was the first factor activating the cult of Teresa, and the second was the sense that "she was the first being in the world not to have 'taken' something from me, but to have 'given.'" Mistress and companion, Teresa clearly became also nurse and mother; he was candid about it:

> After all, it's my turn to have become a child, that is, to have a pressing need for human warmth, night and day, and she knows only she is able to provide it.

If Denise had come a long way from the creature who crouched behind his door to hand him cups of tea and fallen into a solecism that ignored him, Teresa was awesomely attentive: "Even when I went to write my chapter of a novel, she would remain seated, attentive to the clicking of my typewriter."

At Épalinges, from 1964 to 1972, Simenon wrote 13 Maigrets and 14 straight novels, then abruptly brought his career as a novelist to an end. The themes are mostly further variants of the Simenonian repertoire. A more persistent exploration of matrimony is perhaps discernible — either of bad marriages, or of seemingly good ones in which flaws are brusquely discovered — but this is hardly a new departure. Some of the novels show a preoccupation with adolescents that draws more on his relationship with his growing children than, as in the past, on his recollections and transpositions of his own adolescence. Finally, his three most acclaimed novels of this last period present a more optimistic outlook than the prevailing somberness and pathos.

The first straight novel from Épalinges, in October of 1964, was his most triumphantly affirmative one: *Le Petit Saint*. It was perhaps a sort of antidote to the vast mansion and the spirit it represented, and to Denise's extravagant pretentions. The book had been incubating for some time, and he had decided to set it in "la Mouf," the swarming, colorful and sordid rue Mouffetard where he and Tigy used to prowl in their early Paris explorations and where he had once found an appropriate derelict for the cover photograph of *Le Charretier de la "Providence."* "This was the setting I chose for the novel to come, which would perhaps be sordid, but which I willed to be optimistic, and it was."

He felt the need once more for on-the-spot research and took a quick trip to Paris, staying at the George V as usual, and rummaging around the tenements of the rue Mouffetard while his taxi waited. *Le Petit Saint* is hardly a story, but rather the loosely narrated biography of a fictional character. It is predominantly a *sensory* biography, tracing the history of Louis's sensual perceptions from infancy to old age, with the most weight and density apportioned to childhood. Louis — who acquires his sobriquet as a schoolboy because of his gentleness and timidity — passes his childhood amid Simenon's most impressive display of colorful squalor. His mother is a vegetable hawker on the rue Mouffetard — a vigorous, vulgar, and engaging woman who loves sex and denies herself none of it.

A sexuality that encompasses both the earthy and the bizarre is very much part of the child's sensual environment: the mother's frequent lovers and the shenanigans of siblings in a crowded bedroom, as well as philandering neighbors observed by the attentive, happily voyeuristic child. The content is squalid but the perspective is gay. Everything is transfigured by an untroubled sensuousness, and the sexual component blends easily into the larger sensuality. The most exciting childhood event is the first time he is allowed to accompany his mother in her predawn preparation, and follows her and her pushcart to Les Halles, as she bellows out greetings, spoofs and insults. Les Halles is in full animation, and the pyramids of foodstuffs shuffled about by carters and haulers, traded by retailers and wholesalers, are a marvel to the child. Although this is an urban novel, nature, in fact, plays a preponderant role. Time is marked not by human artifacts but by natural processes:

> They counted the seasons ... by the succession of vegetables and fruits in her cart, cherries, strawberries, the first peas and the string beans, the peaches which cost less at the peak of summer heat, apples in the fall, cabbages and salsifis in winter.

The book is one of Simenon's rare historical fictions, a turn-of-the-century period piece; but the historical and cultural events that mark change, hence time — particularly technological developments like the metro, the gas and electric systems, and the Eiffel Tower — seem to exist only to be displaced by the natural time of seasons, and the larger rhythms of existence. A turning point in Louis's development is occasioned by one of his mother's lovers: a lively, warm-hearted Czech who gives the child a box of crayons for Christmas — reminiscent of Simenon's traditional Christmas gift for many years at Liège. This is the beginning of Louis's discovery of painting, which in time develops into a full-fledged career.

It is almost incidental that *Le Petit Saint* turns out to be the portrait of an artist. It is not really art that counts, nor the genesis and growth of a vocation that is portrayed, but rather the prolongation of the sensory history. As Louis himself points out at the end of the novel, the image of himself that he has maintained throughout his long life is that of a little boy. He is a *primitif* in life as well as in art; the only painter Simenon associated with him is Renoir, "who kept his child's soul until he was seventy-eight." Simenon, however, is less adept at transposing the childhood innocence into its adult prolongation than in portraying the actual childhood years, so that the novel is somewhat lopsided and trails off perfunctorily. Simenon set great store by *Le Petit Saint*. Nudged by Nielsen for a statement to accompany display copies, he came up with, "Finally, I've written it!" Later, he amplified:

> For at least twenty years I have been trying to exteriorize a certain optimism that is in me, a delight in the immediate and simple

communion with all that surrounds me ... For the first time I was able to create, in *The Little Saint*, a perfectly serene character, in immediate contact with nature and life.

Another first-class novel of this, his final period, is *La Mort d'Auguste* of 1966, in which Marcel Achard saw "a certain modest tenderness" not unlike the tone of *Le Petit Saint*. As in the earlier novel, Les Halles plays an important role, here signalling the passage of time, for the action is contemporary, precisely when the decision has been made to dismantle the majestic wholesale market and relocate it in the suburbs. It is the passing of an era, as is the death of the old man who is the title character. He is the founder of a once modest restaurant near Les Halles that has risen with the years to discreet stardom and prosperity, retaining always the principles of honest, solid craftsmanship that were transplanted from the old man's peasant origins and successfully nurtured in the capital.

The old man dies suddenly in his restaurant at the beginning of the novel, while he is showing some old photographs to young customers. He leaves three sons, one good and two bad: the simple, industrious, authentic Antoine who follows in his father's footsteps and works with him in the restaurant; a stuffy, pretentious magistrate; and a wastrel trying to lead a jet-setty, decadent life. These two resent the irony that Antoine has fared better sticking with the restaurant than they have in their dubious ambitions. The well-articulated plot revolves around their greedy eagerness for the inheritance, leading to dreadful scenes of frustrated avarice and Antoine's outburst of disgust: "Couldn't we at least wait till after the funeral?" This greedy, corrupt and vacuous world, however, does not succeed in negating the solid values represented by Auguste and Antoine and the community of decent folks around them.

This sense of community is richly amplified by the warm communion of the old man with the "little people" of the neighborhood, portrayed in flashbacks and reaching a moving crescendo as his funeral procession winds through the heart of Les Halles. As in *Le Petit Saint*, a principle of nature emerges, but less insistent, less exuberant, more elegiac, and impotent to redeem time: "In a few years, Les Halles would disappear; the pavillions would be taken away, like children's toys...." Antoine's loving and constructive relationship with his father is one of Simenon's most affirmative presentations of the ubiquitous father-son motif, stemming from his idealized vision of his own relationship with Désiré, and perhaps now with his own sons.

La Mort d'Auguste is a sort of mini–*Buddenbrooks* — the rise and decline of a family, centered on the consciousness of a pivotal figure (Antoine, Thomas Buddenbrooks), who is both the heir of the family's strengths and a sensitive witness of its impending disintegration. It is a good sociological study, tracing the larger trajectory followed by several generations, and documenting the details of Auguste's and Antoine's daily social and economic life; one learns much about the restaurant business in the best naturalist tradition.

The third important novel of this period, *Il y a encore des noisetiers* of 1969, also reflects a certain optimism. A wealthy retired banker, Perret-Latour, thrice married, enacts the theme of generational continuity and of family, lost and recovered. The important offspring is a granddaughter who comes to see him, pregnant by a man she refuses to marry, but happily determined to have the child. In a bizarre yet touching development, Perret-Latour works things out so that the child is born in great secrecy, and has himself registered as the father: the scene at the town hall, with puzzled and embarrased officials, is done with great finesse and a delicate touch of humor. Nature, once again, plays a reinforcing role and provides the title, when Perret-Latour, his mind stirring with generational thoughts, has his chauffeur drive him along the banks of the Marne:

> I've always lived in cities ... Suddenly I regret it. I should have bought a piece of land with a farm ... Maybe it would have been good for the children. I observe a hedgerow and suddenly I recognize the leaves of a small tree. I look up and I see hazlenuts, still green. Thus, in spite of airplanes, superhighways, livestock raised on chemical products, there are still hazlenut trees.

Perret-Latour is a well-fictionalized portrait of the older Simenon: he has led a glamorous, agitated life but now realizes that it is the little things that count; he has been lucky in his finances but feels money is unimportant; he is even endowed with a housekeeper who attends him tenderly. One of his recurring dreams has been to be a patriarch, surrounded by his family, an ideal which he achieves only obliquely, and, so to speak, symbolically, in antithesis to the family alienation and fragmentation that is part of his real life. Jean Renoir in 1969 spoke of a book in which Simenon had put "the maximum of yourself," which is very likely *Il y a encore des noisetiers*, and later that year wrote enthusiastically about it, and spoke of making a film.

The other novels of the Épalinges period are of lesser stature and, by and large, much gloomier. Among the portraits of parent-adolescent relationships, the most remarkable is *La Disparition d'Odile*, clearly modelled on Marie-Jo in her restlessness and moodiness, and fictionalizing her running away from home to Paris some time before Marie-Jo did just that. The first two-thirds of the story is seen through her brother Bob's eyes (doubtless much like Johnny) as he follows her stumbling footsteps through bars and boyfriends in Paris. The last part of the novel retraces the story through her own eyes and leads up to an attempted suicide. She is clearly seeking parental figures, and finds one in a doctor silhouetted in the background. Her real father, a successful writer of popular history, hides in the attic with his books and his wine and is psychologically absent, though she comes to recognize him as a decent fellow after all.

Le Confessionnal portrays two attractive, candid, wholesome and warmly loving adolescents, who successfully resist the threat presented by his deteriorated family and receive the blessing of her admirably cheerful and nurturing family: the triumph of family over antifamily. Conversely, in *Novembre* a torpid antifamily weighs oppressively over youth in one of Simenon's duller tales. Bad marriages continue to proliferate, or mediocre marriages founded on the desperate need to ward off loneliness. In *La Cage de verre* one of those sad little losers, protected from absolute solitude only by his humdrum marriage and his dog, is enticed into the apartment of the seductive woman across the hall, where, finding himself impotent and full of long-simmering self-hatred and frustration, he shoots her. *Les Innocents*, though it deals with a wife's unfaithfulness, is more cheerful, because husband, wife and lover are all considerate and capable of deep and genuine emotion: no one means harm.

The worst marriage—perhaps in all of Simenon—is portrayed in *Le Chat*. "I've never written anything more cruel," Simenon himself declared, while Achard wrote to him that it was "one of the most dreadful works, but also one of the most extraordinary, that you have written." It has indeed a considerable grotesque power. Its starting point was Henriette's second marriage, with M. André, toward the end of which the two cooked separately to preclude poisoning, and communicated only by little notes. The same situation exists between Émile and Marguerite Gouin in the novel, here precipitated by her allegedly poisoning his cat and he, in revenge, plucking all the feathers from her parrot, who, now stuffed, overlooks the dismal household.

They are a thoroughly ill-matched pair: he, gruff, vulgar, virile, down-to-earth, and proletarian; she, pretentious, frigid, prudish, nagging, and from an upper-middle-class family enriched by cookies merchandized as "délices de France." There is little action: mostly his escapade to an old prostitute friend for 11 days of relief from domestic suffocation, but from which he returns, evidently driven by an inexorable and malign destiny—something like a Freudian thanatos—and by her pathetic weakness, the masochistic helplessness that is her ultimate weapon.

In *La Prison*, another marriage is suddenly revealed as hollow when the wife commits a crime of passion, revealing a dimension of character from which her emotionally flabby husband has been excluded. *La Main*, reverting to a Connecticut setting and opening with a superb description of a New England snowstorm, also portrays marital dissatisfaction. A small-town lawyer envies the glamorous Madison Avenue career of an old classmate, and fails to look for him when he gets lost in the blizzard, triggering guilt, paranoia, psychosis and, in the end, murder—a demented act inadequately accounted for by the analysis of his envies and resentments. In *Le Déménage-ment*, a low-level clerk, mildly dissatisfied with his lot, overhears titillating conversations next door of shady deals and highpowered sex. Vaguely—almost somnambulistically—yearning for new dimensions in life, he wanders into a gangster underworld where escapade turns into hell.

In *Le Train de Venise*, another mild man in a dull marriage finds his life totally disrupted, like Malouin's in *L'Homme de Londres*, by coming into possession of a satchel filled with money. Lecouin, in *Le Riche Homme*, is also stuck in an unsatisfactory marriage, but vigorously—though ultimately tragically—finds his way out of it in his very genuine love for a young servant girl. His efforts to assert the authenticity of his love both to his cronies (who merely josh him) and to the reader are depicted with subtlety. For the last time, Simenon returned to his beloved La Rochelle setting, and once again provided a convincing tableau of the mussel-gathering industry.

Simenon's reputation was well settled in its endemic ambiguity, and the last phase of his fiction did little either to elevate it or to diminish it. *Le Petit Saint* was widely reviewed, but more highly praised in America than in France. *L'Express* liked it for the wrong reasons—as an elucidation of the mystery of art, which it isn't. The *New Yorker* wrote, "Gabrielle is unforgettable. Everyone who reads this story of Parisians struggling to live, and enjoying the struggle, will feel happier—much happier"; and Harry T. Moore praised it in the *Saturday Review*, rightly objecting only to the feeble conclusion. Similarly, *La Mort d'Auguste*, for unfathomable reasons, was better appreciated across the ocean than in Europe: perhaps the French were wearying of "le cas Simenon" while the American intelligentsia, prodded by Helen and Kurt Wolff Books, were still in the process of discovering him. Maeve Brennan, in the *New Yorker* again, wrote a long analysis of *The Old Man Dies* and attributed to Simenon "an unsentimental, untiring, ungrudging sympathy that allows all his characters to move about freely, just as they have to, just as they do."

When Simenon decided in 1970 to publish his 1960–63 private journals as *Quand j'étais vieux*, the results for his reputation were mixed. The book was vigorously promoted by Johnny, who was considering a career in publishing and was doing a stint at the Presses de la Cité. Journalists flocked to Épalinges to learn more about the celebrated author who had begun to reveal all. Some reviewers saw it as a privileged admission into the fascinating private world of a public figure and an insight into the secrets of creativity, while others found much of it banal or embarrassing. It was soon translated into English. The *Times Literary Supplement* devoted a long and fairly favorable review to it, as did the *New York Times*, which summarized,

"Simenon's is a shrewd, lucid mind, not a deep one." The Manchester *Guardian*, on the other hand, read it as the expression of "a sort of male menopause," while the *Sunday Telegraph*'s succinct comment on his sexual avowals was "humph!"

Simenon's last novel was a Maigret, *Maigret et Monsieur Charles*, written in February of 1972. It was the story of a rich, good-natured bon vivant with a taste for call girls, done in by his morbidly neurotic, alcoholic wife. The following summer, Simenon was slowly, much more slowly than usual, incubating a new straight novel, a difficult one. "I was intending to put all my human experience into it, and that is why I hesitated so long before starting it." On September 18 he finally decided to get to work on the book, which was to be entitled "Oscar," or "Victor." He went to his study, wrote one or the other of these names on his manila envelope, and, for much longer than usual, mulled over the details of his protagonist's background and situation. By lunch he still hadn't touched his typewriter. Disgruntled by a telephone call about Denise's financial demands, he tried again, without success. The following day he told Teresa he had decided to cease writing. At the same time, he decided to put Épalinges up for sale. To emphasize his resolution, he had his passport designation changed to "sans profession."

Within a month he had bought a comfortable but ordinary seven-room duplex on the ninth floor of a building on avenue de la Cour in Lausanne. He took a few pieces of the sumptuous furniture and some of the paintings, stored the rest, sold all his cars, and kept only one servant. Épalinges remained for sale, reportedly for three or four million Swiss francs, until Simenon decided to keep it after all, in the event his children might want it. Johnny and Marie-Jo had flown the coop, he to Harvard business school, she unhappily seeking her identity in Paris. Simenon had made a clean sweep of fiction and of luxury, of hustle and bustle:

> I have traveled the continents. I've had what is known as an eventful
> life. I've spent nights dancing or making love with women I didn't
> know. Of all that, nothing remains, except perhaps a capacity for
> feeling intensely my present existence.

The process of narrowing circles that had begun in the sixties was much accelerated after he left Épalinges. He never travelled, except for emergencies, spent his occasional "vacations" nearby in Valmont, received many visitors but was just as content talking about chicken raising with Yole the cook, and, mostly, enjoyed being with Teresa, who was at his side night and day. Later in 1973, he changed residences once more, following, literally in this case, his trajectory of downward mobility. Feeling insecure on the ninth floor because of possible power and elevator failures, he bought a small, eighteenth-century house he had observed across the courtyard. It had a living room, a master bedroom, a room for Pierre and another for Yole, and a fireplace as a hedge against the energy crisis. Outside was a tiny garden with some lilac bushes, a bench, a very old cedar of Lebanon, and many sparrows which he and Teresa spent hours watching through the glass doors.

Very rapidly, the core of his daily existence was reduced to utter simplicity, based on total communion with Teresa. In the fall of 1979, he was saying, "Not only do I feel better than ever but I also think I am more lucid and more serene than in any other period of my life." He divided his life into three periods: childhood, followed by many years of chasing after an electric hare, and now serene simplicity and recovery of childhood joys. The electric hare period was utterly inane and he was grateful that it was over. Literature had been part of it, though his mood varied on this subject: "Novels? Paper. Little black spots on it . . . words, words, always words. Might as well copy out the dictionary." He took pains to establish Joyce Aitken and the "secretariat" at the other end of town, visited it only once, and stalked out, appalled at the rows upon rows of Simenon it contained. Yet, in the very description of this episode he comments, "I disown nothing.... On the contrary, I am happy to have written so many novels."

Sometimes he was in a much friendlier mood toward his work. One summer morning in 1974, for example, musing about the innumerable times he was asked how he went about composing a novel, he decided he "felt like having some fun" by play-acting, so to speak, the engendering of a novel. He imagined himself taking a walk and, for no apparent reason, evoking the Liège slums of his childhood where coalminers lived. He then imagined a miner named Hubert, peaceably married to a solid woman with expressive eyes. He has a vague anxiety about certain looks his pals at the bistro give him, and one day comes home early to find his wife in bed with one of his friends. He says nothing, and life on the surface goes on as before; but everything of course is changed. Simenon spun out his demonstration story step by step, not knowing where it was leading him, but left it unfinished. (He made a similar experiment three years later, developing from day to day a much more extensive, and rather lively and suspenseful "mini-roman.")

Nor did Maigret disappear entirely from Simenon's life, for he dreamed about him. In one dream he saw Maigret with a battered straw hat hoeing in his garden at Meung-sur-Loire, and felt he knew every nook and cranny of his little house intimately. Later, Maigret went to play cards at his usual café; he no longer went fishing because the water was too polluted. A few months later he was moved to take a touching farewell of the character who had made him famous:

I leave him on the banks of the Loire, where he must be retired, like me. He digs in his garden, plays cards with the townspeople and goes fishing. As for me, I continue to practice the only sport I am still allowed: walking. I wish him a happy retirement, just as mine is happy. We've worked together long enough that I may, with a twinge of emotion, bid him farewell.

Simenon's tranquility was broken principally by periodic tussles with Denise — or now, once again, Denyse. Their last two meetings were turbulent. By her account, at the first one he granted her "total sexual freedom," but warned her that 97 percent of the men she might sleep with would be interested only in seeing what Mme. Simenon was worth, and another 2 percent to boast of having slept with Mme. Georges Simenon. At the second meeting, he began abusing her again, but she defended herself by threatening to bash his head in with a large stone ashtray. Eventually she moved to Avignon, where she went into extensive analysis with a man who subsequently became "a teacher and then a friend," and who sent Simenon a bill for 80,000 Swiss francs. She sought a divorce, which Simenon was unwilling to grant because her financial demands were too extravagant. She sued him but lost, claiming her own lawyer had been bribed. According to him, she tried blackmail, threatening to publish devastating revelations if he did not settle 48,000 Swiss francs a month on her. He refused, and nothing much happened until her unflattering memoir, *Un Oiseau pour le chat*, appeared in 1978 — which he interpreted as the threatened blackmail and claimed was ghostwritten.

A far more terrible by-product of the broken marriage than these spats was in store. Marie-Jo was living listlessly in Paris, intermittently receiving psychiatric attention. She toyed with the idea of an acting career, enrolled in a theater school, and got some small parts. She wrote poems, songs, autobiographical meditations, and many many letters to her father. In May of 1976 she took an overdose of sleeping pills, but changed her mind in time, recovered, and seemed for a time relatively stable. Simenon bought her an apartment on the Champs-Élysée in the very building that had once been the Claridge Hotel, where he had stayed so often. In an ill-considered analogy, and evidently innocent of its connotations, he compared having one's own apartment to getting married. (One recalls that he himself had settled briefly into a sort of household at the Claridge with his secretary at the end of the war.) In March of 1978 she visited the little house in Lausanne for the last time. She sang "Le Plat pays," and songs she had written to the melodies of "Tennessee Waltz" and "Blowin' in the Wind." Three weeks later in her Paris flat she shot herself through the heart with a .22 caliber rifle. She left all her writings and tapes to her father, and asked that her ashes be scattered in the garden under the cedar of Lebanon. Among her papers was a copy of her mother's recent book, annotated, according to Simenon, with comments and refutations. Simenon was crushed and felt he would never be the same.

Before the trauma of Marie-Jo's death, and — in time — afterward, Simenon's life was serene. Having abandoned fiction in 1972, he never again returned to his typewriter, but within three days of moving into the avenue de Cour apartment he found the perfect substitute: the cassette recorder. In contrast with the typewriter, it was "more a toy than an instrument of work," and dictating into the machine was effortless, the diametrical opposite of the agonizing strain of writing fiction. Yet the recorder served the same need for psychological exploration and for exercising his deep-bred work ethic: as with writing before, he came to feel ill-at-ease when he stopped dictating for too long. His project was clear from the start — to talk about whatever came into his head.

Though at first he had not intended to publish, a relentless compulsion made him send the tapes to Joyce Aitken, who turned them into typescripts, and these to the faithful Presses de la Cité, who turned them into books. He dictated fairly regularly from February of 1973 to October of 1979, producing 21 volumes, or 3828 pages in a large format. In addition, in the spring of 1974 he dictated *Lettre à ma mère*, which is not a part of the series — an interesting project to evaluate his mother's character and come to terms with his own feelings about her. By the tenth volume, the genre, difficult to label, was fixed, sensibly enough, simply as "Dictées."

The structure of the "Dictées" is the freest of association, and the content is daily life, reminiscences of the past, general comments on the world, nature, and the human condition, reflections on writing, and family affairs — particularly his response in the last volumes to the shock of Marie-Jo's suicide. By far the most important component of the "daily life" category is Teresa; the "Dictées" are in part a continuing hymn to her presence, as reflected in several of his titles: "Hand in Hand," "In the Shelter of Our Tree," and "Woman Asleep." His general reflections, randomly prompted by reading, conversations, and television news and documentaries, sometimes have a Montaignean quality, particularly in their skeptical, anti-anthropocentric spirit.

Simenon expresses outrage at hierarchies, governments, social regimentation, acculturation, technology, commercialization, nationalism, authority, marriage, vanity, patriotism, industrialization, colonialism, neocolonialism, capitalism, gerontocracy, bureaucracy, marketing, packaging, advertising, academies, men of letters, literary circles, critics, decorations, uniforms, ceremonies, cocktail parties, and much, much else. As for reminiscences, the largest proportion and the best are of his family, childhood, and adolescence in Liège, and are almost all mellower than those in previous autobiographical writings. Simenon felt that he was communicating with all sorts of people — particularly "little people" who responded with letters about what he had written and about their own thoughts.

As Denis Tillinac astutely observes, Simenon had dramatized in many of his novels a lack of communication deeply embedded in human nature, and had forcefully depicted struggles to overcome that lack. The "Dictées" are motivated by the same sense of noncommunication and consequent urgency to surmount it, but fail insofar as it is the dramatization of the problem that is of interest, not the facile solution Simenon ended up with. Federico Fellini, for one, was not disappointed with the "Dictées," but read them with an "alert curiosity, a lucid fervor, an enjoyable and troubled participation ["una partecipazione divertita e dolente"], a tense, anxious waiting from page to page."

In February of 1980 Simenon abandoned his tape recorder for the pen (his usual medium for autobiography) and for over a year wrote an enormous autobiographical work which was published at the end of 1981 as *Mémoires intimes*, to which he appended Marie-Jo's various writings. He appears to have been motivated by several factors. One was to write a more or less definitive autobiography, in chronological order, and to include all sorts of details — mostly having to do with Denyse and with his children — which he had omitted or only hinted at previously. Another, closely related, was the publication of Denyse's book, which at first he did not deign to respond to, but which he now wanted to refute. A third factor was the death of Marie-Jo, which activated once again that impulse, going back to *Je me souviens*, of wanting to communicate a self-portrait as a legacy to his children: many portions are addressed to them, in the second person. The book demonstrates how much importance he attached, at the age of 77, to his children, and, in contrast, how little to his books.

He worked on the *Mémoires* with extraordinary tenacity, organizing an entirely new schedule of steady writing from two to eight in the evening, or later, with Teresa — shades of Sainte-Marguerite! — bringing him cups of tea to keep him going. This book, which runs to 753 tightly packed pages, is enormously detailed and, sometimes, uncomfortably intimate. Its perceived sensational, exposé aspect gave it a much larger readership than the "Dictées," though the reviews on both continents were not enthusiastic. It did win him yet another in the long series of distinguished admirers of his work — the 94-year-old Arthur Rubinstein, who lived nearby in Geneva and wrote to express his admiration and make a lunch date. Simenon has sworn to all comers that this would be the last work to be published in his lifetime.

A few weeks before the publication of the *Mémoires*, Denyse Simenon, under the pseudonym of Odile Dessane, published a *roman à clef* entitled *Le Phallus d'or*, which constitutes a sort of refutation of, or revenge against,

Simenon's increasingly explicit hostility in the later "Dictées." It imagines the death of an 80-year-old multimillionaire known as "The Old Guy" ("Le Vieux") of an unspecified profession. His character is evaluated by his children, his ex-wife, his estranged wife, his secretary, his former cook (with a lifelong adoration for him), some acquaintances, and two prostitutes. The universal consensus is that the Old Guy was an egocentric monster, incapable of love, whose claim that he slept with 10,000 women points to sexual deficiency, and whose order with a celebrated jeweler for a solid-gold replica of his phallus provides the title. The most disagreeable character, after the Old Guy, is the intended recipient of the phallus, an Italian chambermaid who has hoodwinked him for his money, and who is roundly dismissed by the heirs after they search her luggage to recover pilfered valuables. The children are thunderously platitudinous, including a daughter who committed suicide because her psyche was maimed by the Old Guy.

This book, together with Simenon's autobiography, has all the makings of a finals match — Intimate Memoirs vs. Golden Phallus — of which the "Dictées" and *Un Oiseau pour le chat* were the semifinals. Simenon wins, but the sport is somewhat unseemly, and — like bearbaiting or gladiatorial combat — rather surprising in this age.

XVI

THE MAIGRET SAGA

Regardless of his own and others' efforts to transcend his association with the Maigrets, Simenon kept writing them as long as he kept writing straight fiction. Maigret's third, and definitive, incarnation took place immediately after the war, lasted for a quarter of a century, and yielded about fifty short novels and a few short stories. This was the "Presses de la Cité" Maigret, after the original 19 "Fayard" Maigrets, and the intermediate "Gallimard" Maigrets just before and during the war. From a pyrotechnic phenomenon Maigret had become an applauded revival; now he turned into an institution.

During all three phases, the evolutionary process initiated soon after the creation continued steadily: that is, the sustained elaboration, the fleshing-out, of a sketchy figure conceived in a moment of lucky inspiration, whose potential Simenon may have subconsciously intuited, but whose amplitude he certainly did not anticipate. Even a good part of Maigret's evolution may have been more subconscious than deliberate, and occasionally in danger of being thwarted by Simenon's more flippant commercial impulses. The first revival of the late thirties, indeed, had been off to a mediocre start, a relapse into the pulp world of Simenon's early days.

Nonetheless, the definitive postwar Maigret, taken together with earlier selves, constitutes a substantial presence, whether he is minimally or maximally evaluated as a literary creation, or somewhere in between. Minimally, Maigret is one of a score of famous detectives in a minor popular genre: that, indeed, is pretty much the status that he — and his creator as well — has for most of the public the world around. Maximally, Maigret is considered as a sort of émigré from a higher literary realm wandering in the world of detective fiction, which he transfigures.

This is the view of Simenon's first book-length critic, Thomas Narcejac, himself a writer of detective stories, who asserted that the detective story is not a serious genre, like the novel, because the novel is predicated on character, the detective story only on plot. Simenon, he was arguing in 1950, wrote only novels, and no distinction was to be made between Maigrets and non–Maigrets.

The *New York Times'* Anthony Boucher took a similar position on occasion. Other readers and commentators — as well as Simenon himself — hold an intermediate view that the Maigrets *are* detective stories, more casually written than the straight novels, but related to them by interwoven threads that provide, to some degree, a certain texture or coloration of seriousness. Simenon himself and others have often pointed out a tendency to treat the same theme "lightly" in a Maigret and more substantially in a straight novel. Furthermore, as we have seen, during his depressed period, Simenon occasionally would aim for a straight novel but, with some discouragement, would reduce the subject to a Maigret.

The elaboration of Maigret — the "fleshing out" process — took many forms. One was the accumulation and reiteration of personal details about Maigret himself and his surroundings, an enterprise, familiar in all famous detective series, which doubtless afforded Simenon much pleasure and delighted generations of Maigret fans. Maigret has good eyesight, can fall asleep virtually anywhere, but tends to be short of breath when climbing stairs and suffers from claustrophobia. His files are disorganized, he often leaves his badge at home, but straightens pictures on walls. He is no good at picking locks, and has never learned to drive a car, fearing that his mind might wander and he would forget he's at the wheel (Mme. Maigret, however, is learning). Maigret, indeed, uses many fewer police cars than might be expected, preferring taxis, and even buses where, like his creator, he likes to ride on the platform (as history moves on, he considers himself lucky when he catches one of the few remaining platform vehicles).

His pipes, of course, continue legendary, though he may be discovered once smoking a cigarette, and once a cigar. He reads psychiatric treatises, but finds them impractical in his work. He reads Alexandre Dumas, but does not read detective stories. Similarly, when television makes its way into his world, he watches westerns and grade-B movies, but dislikes detective shows. He and Mme. Maigret often go to the movies on rainy afternoons, seemingly indifferent to what is playing. On the other hand, he is not unknowledgeable about high literature. One of his inspectors describes a suspect's quarters:

There are books in every corner . . . Engels, Spinoza, Kierkegaard,

Saint Augustine, Karl Marx, Father Sertillange, Saint-Simon . . .
Does it mean anything to you?
"Yes," Maigret answers.

Maigret has two families, two households where he snuggles in comfort and warm intimacy: his home and his office. Home is the fifth floor of 130, boulevard Richard-Lenoir, Paris XIème, which he shares with the celebrated Mme. Maigret. She frequently worries about his getting wet and cold — for good reason, since he often catches cold. She is from Alsace, they first met through a mutual friend at the beginning of Maigret's career, and he first kissed her on a bench at place des Vosges. He never calls her Louise nor she Jules. He calls her Mme. Maigret, and doesn't use terms of endearment because he considers her and him to be the same person. She cooks for him, of course, abundantly, even when the odds are that an investigation will keep him from coming home. She gives him grogs when he has a cold, and can be found knitting him a blue scarf. He tends to be undemonstrative, but his affection and appreciation are pervasively implicit and occasionally rise to consciousness and articulation: "He had rarely been so eager to go home and find his wife's tender and gay eyes"; and, a little later, at a restaurant, he says, "nothing in a restaurant is better than at home."

Maigret's home life is an epitome of quiet integration, of belonging. Yet their belongingness is a state of mind rather than a social fact. In practice, they seem not at all to belong to society at large. The only people they see are the Pardons twice a month, Maigret's doctor friend with whom he exchanges ideas on human character, justice, and the like. Occasionally there's a visit from Mme. Maigret's sister and her husband, who tend to overstay their welcome. That is probably the only sour note. The Maigrets seem to be an idyll of the perfect couple *in vacuo*, utterly self-sufficient. All his life Simenon mused about this ideal, dramatized it and enacted its absence for half a century, and claimed he had found it in old age. The Maigrets' paradoxical belongingness-in-isolation is accentuated by their having no children (except for a daughter who died in infancy), which is a great sorrow to them.

Maigret's other family is the Police Judiciaire, where his lack of progeny is compensated for by his inspectors, whom he repeatedly calls "mes enfants," or "les enfants," as in, say, "au travail, les enfants" (let's get to work, kids). Professional teamwork is as unruffled at the quai des Orfèvres (P.J. headquarters on the Seine) as is domestic harmony at boulevard Richard-Lenoir. Maigret's associates acquire Homeric epithets: le *brave* Lucas, le *petit* Lapointe, le *gros* Torrence, and the ancient usher, le *vieux* Joseph; in the course of the saga, they develop personalities that seem less perfunctory than they are because of the charm of recognition the sympathetic reader feels every time they are described.

Lucas, the senior inspector, is chubby ("grassouillet") and can sometimes pass as Maigret's double; Janvier, as every Maigret fan knows, is a family man, often useful because he looks least like a cop, the best stenographer on the team, and developing a pot-belly; Lapointe is the most junior of the inspectors, the most eager to please and to try to imitate Maigret (we find him developing a Maigret-like intuition, and, at the end of the saga, he also has acquired a family). Others on the team are mere names, arising whenever more personnel are needed: Neveu, Janin, Lourtie, Vacher.

There is the big boss, the director of the P.J., sympathetic to Maigret and often mediating between him and the political higher-ups in the Préfecture de Police and the Ministry of the Interior. (There are indications that Xavier Guichard, a real-life P.J. director, had been Maigret's mentor in his early days and a sort of father figure to him — perhaps adumbrating Maigret's own paternalistic character. But the anonymous "grand patron" has replaced Guichard in most of the stories, and, much later in the fictional chronology, Maigret grumbles about a new director who knows nothing about real police work, "except maybe from novels.")

There are the experts, who have little personality but whom one thinks one knows intimately because of the regularity of their appearance and the reliability of their reports: Dr. Paul, the police physician whose autopsies are often the first clue Maigret has to go on (Simenon was friendly with a well-known real life police physician named Dr. Paul); Moers, the ballistics and general lab man who can identify the tiniest speck of anything (confusingly replaced at one point by a certain Gastine-Renette). One should add Maigret's foreign associates — Pyke of Scotland Yard and O'Brien of the F.B.I., who give him a hand when he needs it.

Finally, there is the memorable Inspector Lognon, who, by bureaucratic organization and by personality is emphatically *not* a member of the team, but desperately wants to be. He is merely a precinct detective, and not of the elite P.J., who happens to show up in numerous stories, assiduously pursuing clues, getting gunned down and beaten up by thugs, and invariably having the rug pulled out from under him when Maigret, though full of compassion, solves the crime. He is the raté among the cops, ever unlucky, always anxious and melancholic even in his diligence, and, on top of it all, saddled with a nagging, bedridden, incontinent wife. He doesn't drink, which is perhaps one of his problems. Oddly, his drabness and melancholy add a touch of color and comedy to the saga.

Among the small personal details that accumulate around Maigret, probably the most insistent (other than the pipes) are those having to do with food and drink, and one can do no better than draw up a kind of Rabelaisian catalogue. Maigret can be found eating ris de veau, blanquette de veau, tête de veau en tortue (a Belgian speciality), tripes à la mode de Caen, filet de hareng, sole dieppoise, bouillabaisse, maquereaux au four, coquille de langouste, homard à l'américaine, escargots, rillettes, goat cheese, baba au rhum, coq au vin blanc, skewered robin redbreasts, and kilometers of andouillettes. Among Mme. Maigret's dishes are fricandeau à l'oseille (one of his favorites), pot au feu, raie au beurre noir, pintadeau en croûte, and quiche (one of which is getting cold in an extended sequence at the beginning of *Maigret et le client du samedi*). Not to be ignored either are Mme. Pardon's boeuf bourguignon, cassoulet, couscous, brandade de morue, and rice pudding.

Maigret eats not only amply and well, but also knowledgeably. In *Le Voleur de Maigret*, for instance, we find him in a restaurant serving La Rochelle specialities such as "mouclade" and "chaudrée fourrasienne," which he correctly identifies to the impressed *patronne* as "an eel soup with little soles and cuttle fish." Gastronomy gives Maigret warmth, charm, and, so to speak, human substance; we enjoy watching him eat. His eating habits make him one of "the people," unlike the epicurean Nero Wolfe, who is merely a snob. (When the *New York Times* claimed that Maigret ate better than Nero Wolfe, Rex Stout testily riposted, "Nonsense. The Wolfe/Breme diet is altogether more stimulating than *cuisine bourgeoise*.") But in both cases, the intention is to enliven and particularize the detective-hero, to make him more intimate to the reader by repeated exposure to his habits.

If Maigret's eating habits invite comparison with such golden-age holdovers as Nero Wolfe, his drinking is more in the I-can-hold-my-liquor-with-the-best-of-them vein of the hardboiled school. He is most famous for his glasses of draught beer (most memorable as washing down sandwiches during long interrogations at the quai des Orfèvres), but he will drink anything alcoholic, even when he doesn't like it, such as whisky (Scotch *and* Bourbon) or champagne. Cocktails are not up his alley, but he will not turn down a very dry martini. He often drinks cognac ("une fine") and keeps a bottle in his office, usually for suspects or witnesses in need, but occasionally for himself. Among other brandies are marc (though he once couples it with kummel as another drink he dislikes—which does not later keep him from savoring a 130-proof bottle), armagnac, many a calvados, and, at home, prunelle and framboise. Sweeter stuff is also not to his liking, and, celebrating a promotion, he once got drunk on mandarin-curaçao—but this is a younger Maigret viewed retrospectively. (Once in a while he can also be caught with a hangover.) Among apéritifs, pernod is the most frequent, but he will also indulge in such things as picon-grenadine.

The catalogue of wines is long and begins with the glasses of white wine, innumerable as the beers, drunk hurriedly at the bar ("sur le zinc"). With or without meals, he drinks, among other wines, Beaujolais, rosé de

Provence (to wash away, incidentally, the taste of a Tom Collins), Chateauneuf-du-Pape, Chianti, Sancerre, and Vouvray. His drinking sometimes alarms his friend Dr. Pardon, who advises him to cut down, just as it is alleged to have alarmed British church authorities monitoring the BBC Maigret series, who counted the number of drinks per program and found it excessive.

Simenon goes further than provide Maigret with an accumulation of personal traits and habits: he provides him with an entire biography. Reaching back to the Marquis de Tracy days, Simenon has Maigret born and raised in the village of Saint-Fiacre in the Allier, which is a transposition of Tracy's château of Paray-le-Frézil. Maigret's father, Evaride, was the bailiff of the estate and is modelled on the lanky, steady-paced overseer of Paray-le-Frézil. Both hint at paternal dignity and filial respect, and are thus shadowy recollections of Désiré Simenon — associations causing a father-son theme to flicker over the Maigret saga, reflected in Maigret's frequent paternal attitude toward victims and criminals alike, in his relationship with his "boys" at the P.J., and, negatively, in the disappointment of his childlessness.

Maigret's principal given name is Jules; by way of amplification but perhaps also because of authorial forgetfulness, he is later saddled with such additional names as Amédée, Anthèlme, Joseph, and François. No one except boors ever calls him "Jules" (it's either "Maigret" or "M. le Commissaire"); gentle fun is poked at his American hosts in *Maigret chez le coroner*, who insist on slapping him on the back, urging him to "have a drink," and calling him "Julius." Maigret lost his mother as a child, attended the local school and was a choirboy. He had a few friends and a few enemies, some of whom show up later as "clients" at the quai des Orfèvres. He attended the lycée in Moulins, from which he graduated with a sufficiently distinguished record to get him into medical school at the University of Nantes, which he attended two years, forced to withdraw by financial problems ensuing from the death of his father. Like his creator, he occasionally muses about his missed career as a doctor — and particularly as a potential psychiatrist, which relates closely to his notion of a "mender of destinies."

Abandoning medicine, he comes to Paris, much like Simenon, staying in a tacky hotel until, at age 22, he joins the police force. He starts at the bottom, patrolling the streets, then moves through various branches: railroad stations, department stores, the vice squad ("brigade des moeurs"), which he hates. (He has particularly grim recollections of the Gare du Nord.) He becomes a precinct clerk at some point — in the 11th arrondissement at the beginning of his career in some accounts, but, in *La Première Enquête de Maigret*, at the quartier Saint-Georges of the 9th, from which he is promoted to the P.J. (In one short story that hardly seems canonical, "Vente à la bougie," he is mysteriously in charge of the "brigade mobile" of Nantes.) Except for the flashback of the *Première Enquête* and many flashforwards to a retired Maigret, he is a "Commissaire divisionnaire" in the bulk of the stories, in theory supervising his family of inspectors, but in fact usually joining them in the leg work—an implausibility in real police work, as Simenon readily acknowledges, but a necessity for effective story-telling. In the last novel Maigret is offered the directorship of the P.J., but prefers to stay where he is. Where he is is often close to retirement, an event which he frequently muses about—one of several characteristics that put him on the edge, rather than at the center, of police officialdom.

The accumulation of personal details gives Maigret a certain density, and they themselves are reinforced when they are related to Simenon's own experience and personality. Thus, as we have seen, young Maigret's arrival in Paris parallels Simenon's, as does his delight in bus platforms and sunny café terraces. They share childhood memories of choirboy duty, and Maigret once lived near place des Vosges. When Maigret furnishes his retirement home at Meung-sur-Loire, he had the same impulse as Simenon at La Richardière to scour the countryside for antiques to furnish it. Maigret, like Simenon, considers himself a collector of men, as he laconically answers the crooked art dealer in *Maigret et le fantôme* when the latter tells him, "You'll have trouble understanding me, you're not a collector. . . ."

Autobiographical elements often signal some measure of literary seriousness in Simenon, and the Maigrets, on their own level, are no exception. The wife in *Maigret et l'homme du banc* surely reflects some of the petit-bourgeois pettiness Simenon attributed to his mother. The teenagers of the Parendon household in *Maigret hésite* (written in 1967) plausibly reflect the behavior of his own children in their "modern" hostility to stuffy elders. Maigret's queasiness at using first names with his chummy F.B.I. counterparts sounds like a version of the Simenon "pudeur."

The personal details are the superficial indicators of that process of amplification in the Maigrets, of which deeper manifestations are Maigret's psychology and his philosophy. Maigret's psychology, like any psychology, is an epistemology: it has to do with truly *knowing* people—discovering the substance beneath the appearance. His philosophy has to do with justice, likewise a justice more substantive and more human than official justice. Thus both psychology and philosophy boil down to a matter of fellow feeling, of human sympathy, which is itself the core of the famous Maigret method. Maigret's sense of himself is elegantly summarized in the last chapter of *Maigret et les vieillards*:

> He did not take himself for a superman, did not consider himself infallible. On the contrary, it was with a certain humility that he

began his investigations, including the simplest of them. He mistrusted evidence, hasty judgments. Patiently, he strove to understand, aware that the most apparent motives are not always the deepest ones.

If he did not have a high conception of men and of their possibilities, he persisted in believing in man. He sought out his weak points; and when he finally put his finger on them, he did not proclaim victory, but, rather, felt a certain despondency.

Maigret's strong psychological orientation is often manifested as an explicit interest in psychiatry. In this same novel he reads in a medical journal that an exceptional schoolteacher, novelist or policeman may be in a better position to delve into the human psyche than a doctor or a psychiatrist, and is piqued only that the policeman is put in third place. He repeatedly discusses the medical and psychiatric aspects of crime with his friend Pardon, whose very name echoes a Maigret-like compassion. In *Les Scrupules de Maigret*, we find him consulting a psychiatric textbook and musing about such headings as "neurosis," "paranoia," and "persecution complex" ("Do you have a difficult case?" Mme. Maigret asks him, to which he shrugs his shoulders and answers, "A bunch of lunatics!").

In *Maigret tend un piège*, Pardon introduces Maigret to a psychiatrist with whom he has a lengthy discussion about the case at hand—appropriately, since this is one of the most "psychiatric" of the stories. Not only does it provide a psychiatric explanation for a murderous stalker of women (he has a possessive mother and a possessive wife), but Maigret's strategy to trap him is predicated on a psychiatric hypothesis about his behavior. *Maigret se défend* likewise opens with a psychiatric discussion between Maigret and Pardon on whether an absolutely evil mentality is possible. The discussion is occasioned by an incomprehensible plot to smear Maigret, and the answer is no, there is no motiveless malignity: the explanation lies in understanding the deeply neurotic though brilliant mind of a sexual pervert, whose problems originate in sexual fear and whose tendency is to find the most involuted way of dealing with them. The question of pure evil shows up again in *Un Échec de Maigret*.

Maigret also seeks Pardon's help in *Le Révolver de Maigret* to determine whether the principal suspect is insane or bluffing insanity. The question of the insanity plea recurs in the Maigrets—article 64 of the penal code, with which that eccentric lawyer in *Maigret hésite* is obsessed (his name is Par[en]don), and which he discusses extensively with Maigret. *Maigret et la grande perche* is perhaps the most oedipal of Maigret's cases: the solution of a murder follows from understanding the suspect's adolescent problems with his father, and his devotion to a vicious old mother. In *Maigret et le tueur* the criminal turns out to be a pathetic young man whom a childhood incident has turned into a random, pathological killer. In *Maigret et le clochard*, the commissaire finds his way to a solution by reflecting on the phenomenon of "victim" psychology, a theory that turns up also in *Maigret à Vichy*.

Maigret plays a straightforward role of psychiatrist-father confessor to the pathological young killer of *Maigret et le tueur*, and, more extensively, to the hapless young Planchon in *Maigret et le client du samedi*, who unburdens himself for hours at Maigret's apartment (while Mme. Maigret's quiche gets cold). It is particularly clear in this story how Maigret's sympathetic response to the underdog is highlighted by the generous sprinkling of personal details: he is nursing a cold, he sleeps late, he has just acquired a television set, the clocks at the P.J. are, as always, twelve minutes slow, and so on.

The explicit psychologizing is, for the most part, a mode of Maigret's wide-ranging (though by no means indiscriminate) human sympathy and comprehension. The recurring motif in French criminal fiction of an understanding, sometimes an identity, between detective and criminal — the Arsène Lupin tradition that Simenon himself had played with in the pulps — is transposed to a different and higher key in the Maigrets. Again and again Maigret, having caught his quarry, feels a burst of compassion, if compassion has not been with him all along. If criminal investigation is a contest, it is one he finds little pleasure in winning, as he once ruefully muses while watching bowlers on the green, envying their satisfaction when they make a nice shot: "Whereas for us, when we've put the final period to an investigation . . . it's prison for a man, sometimes death."

He is often pleased when he can let someone off the hook — as in *Le Révolver de Maigret*, or *La Folle de Maigret*, or *Maigret aux assises*, where he engineers last-minute testimony that disculpates another one of those harassed, weak-willed young men whom he has paternally taken under his wing. When, more commonly, arrest is necessary, it is often made reluctantly — extremely so, for example, at the end of *Maigret en meublé*, where he is forced to arrest an Enoch Arden character who has returned after twenty years and found his beloved married. The two crimes for which he must be arrested are incidental to the "human" truth of the situation. Lapointe, uninformed about the details, congratulates Maigret on the arrest:

> Maigret stood in the doorjamb, his pipe clenched between his teeth, and Lapointe wasn't sure that he had clearly understood what he had mumbled as he left.
>
> "It had to be done."
>
> Lapointe turned toward Vacher: "What did he say?"
>
> "That it had to be done."

[2 2 5]

"*What* had to be done?"

"Arrest him, I suppose."

And young Lapointe, gazing at the door through which Maigret had vanished, said simply, "Ah!"

In *Maigret et le marchand de vin*, Maigret gently coaxes the unfortunate culprit to his apartment for another reluctant arrest.

A recurring manifestation of Maigret's humanity is his accessibility, implausible for a high-ranking officer but, again, necessary for the fiction. The troubled souls who try to reach him rarely fail; on some occasions, when they *have* been kept away, Maigret regrets it, as in *La Folle de Maigret* (and, earlier, *Cécile est morte*). *Maigret et son mort* opens with a man making desperate phone calls to Maigret, saying he is in imminent danger. Unable to respond quickly enough, Maigret soon finds the man murdered; in the subsequent investigation, Maigret's diligence—indeed, his passionate intensity—in piecing together the victim's personality and history is a direct result of the urgency of the telephone appeals, and of a sort of instantaneous intimacy between detective and victim. In this case the title is quite apt: "Maigret and *his* Dead Man." One reviewer called it "a genuine masterpiece."

Maigret's reputation for compassion becomes itself a motive force in several stories. *Le Révolver de Maigret* gets under way when one of Dr. Pardon's patients, who turns out to have committed a crime, asks to be introduced to the commissaire. In *Maigret et le client du samedi* the disconsolate young Planchon virtually seeks Maigret's advice as to whether or not he should kill his wife and her lover. The most intricate version of this motif is *Le Voleur de Maigret*, where the ambitious, high-strung young Ricain, who *has* murdered his wife, pretends to seek out Maigret's sympathetic understanding but is merely tangling up the evidence. Maigret's sympathy for certain criminals surfaces in innumerable little episodes depicting his chumminess with a wide variety of pickpockets, minor gangsters, good-natured whores, burglars, petty embezzlers, etc. Compounded of irony, affection and a kind of professional comradeship, his feelings accumulate into a sense that these are *his* people—a version indeed, of "the little people."

This kind of affection, for example, pervades the inquest of *Maigret et le voleur paresseux*, where the victim is precisely one of those petty burglars, well known at the P.J., and even admired as a sort of artisan in his craft. Maigret's tenacity in solving the case is largely motivated by sympathetic puzzlement as to why anyone should murder such a fundamentally innocuous little truant. The title character of *Maigret et l'indicateur* is in the same vein: a good-natured fellow on the fringes of the gangster world, cheerily nicknamed "La Puce," who moonlights as a police informer. A more eccentric version is M. Louis in *Maigret et l'homme du banc*, a meek, hen-pecked, middle-aged man who has lost his job but found a surefire way of robbing department stores, and who gets murdered for his loot.

On the other hand, Simenon's sympathies are not indiscriminate; he can also break out in unequivocal anger and outrage. His sympathy for La Puce is counterbalanced by his unambiguous revulsion against the murderous couple he sends to prison at the end, taking visible satisfaction in watching them bestially turn against each other to save their skins. In the unusually violent ending of *Maigret au Picratt's*, Maigret feels no remorse when the sleazy blackmailer, pornographer and murderer, Oscar, is shot while resisting arrest (though young Lapointe, who did the shooting, feels un-detectivelike anguish).

Maigret is very hostile to the brutal American gangsters of *Maigret, Lognon et les gangsters*, egged on by warnings that he's in over his head with such people and should drop the case. "Je les aurai" (I'll get them), he keeps repeating — and he does, in another violent ending in the hardboiled man-ner. At the end of *Mon ami Maigret* he feels a sense of relief as he slaps one of the supercilious young murderers and calls them "sales gamins" (nasty kids), the same expression he uses about the degenerate young soldiers ar-raigned, but not convicted, in *Maigret chez le coroner*. His most dramatic hos-tility, perhaps, is in the appropriately titled *Maigret en colère*, when he finds out the culprit had tried to bribe him. Trembling with outrage and banging on his desk, he yells at the man repeatedly, "I order you to shut up!"

Maigret's social philosophy echoes his psychology and revolves around one central principle: *do not judge*. His spontaneous sympathies and revul-sions are subjective, essentially aesthetic responses to people's attitudes and personalities, not moral judgments of their actions. Indeed, his most per-vasive distaste is against those who appropriate to themselves the right to judge: the judges and the whole judicial apparatus which he serves. If one asks why he chose to serve it, he asks himself the same question, and broods about the moral implications of his profession — sometimes solemnly, as to Dr. Pardon at the beginning of *Une Confidence de Maigret*, or more playfully as he looks at himself in a mirror in the penultimate chapter of *Mon Ami Maigret*:

> "There you are, monsieur le commissaire divisionnaire!" ... Lots of people with an uneasy conscience trembled at the sound of his name. He had the power to interrogate them till they cried in anguish, to put them in prison, to send them to the guillotine ... He had trouble con-ceiving that all that was serious; it was not so long ago that he was wearing short pants and was crossing his village square on brisk morn-ings, his fingertips numb with cold, to serve at the mass in the little church lit only by candle light.

Maigret's world is not one that accommodates a principle of justice: the word is meaningless, not because the law is fallacious but because official judgments are based on false knowledge — the superficial ordering of facts and deeds — not the probing into men's souls that leads to understanding, not judgment. Thus, as in some of the straight novels, the justice theme in the Maigrets consists of exposing the discrepancy between official judgments and the truth. In time, Simenon developed a very active preoccupation with questions of criminal justice, criminal psychology, penology, the insanity plea, and the judicial apparatus. He fully adopted his commissaire's views.

It is no accident that the functionaries of the judicial apparatus are almost invariably of the upper classes — the ubiquitous juge d'instruction Coméliau who is Maigret's bête noire, or the young upstart judge Angelot with the handshake of a tennis player, or the obnoxious prefect in *Maigret se défend*, who asks for Maigret's resignation (and also plays tennis: tennis is the representative sport of such people, as bowling on the green is of the "little people"). What is wrong with these officials is precisely what is right with Maigret: they know their cases only from bureaucratic dossiers, he from feeling his way into the very substance of people's lives — the texture of their environment, the quality of their inner selves. As Maigret complains to Pardon in *Maigret aux assises*, historians dedicate their entire lives to studying a famous person, researching the minutest details, "in the hope of reaching a little bit more truth." But for himself, he goes on, "They give me a few weeks, if not a few days, to penetrate a new environment, to hear ten, twenty, fifty people of whom I had known nothing until then, and, if possible, sort out the true from the false."

The nonjustice dispensed by judicial officials echoes the prejudices, the duplicity, the hypocrisy and the sheer meanness of their class, which frequently play a major narrative, as well as thematic, role in the Maigrets. Maigret's disquisition on justice in *Une Confidence de Maigret* is a prologue to a story of a miscarriage of justice stemming from pure class prejudice. Josset, a capable man from a humble background is accused of murdering his unfaithful, uppercrust wife. For Judge Coméliau, as for Mme. Josset's circles, Josset's guilt is a foregone conclusion, but not for Maigret, who carries on his personal investigation, deeper and subtler than the official one, and concludes that Josset most likely is innocent, but cannot prove it.

In several stories that motif takes the form of the coverup: Maigret advised not to investigate certain cases too closely because they involve "highly placed" individuals or families, as in Maigret's retrospective first inquest, *La Première Enquête de Maigret*, which gives Maigret his first taste of the futility of justice and sends him into his first reflections on his fanciful role as a "mender of destinies," and his first thought that he should perhaps resign

The Maigret Saga

from the police. Maigret is repeatedly called upon to deal with upper-class scoundrels, whose skeletons in the closets he normally discovers, and whose moral turpitude arouses his contempt: the vindictive greed of the uncooperative cookie-factory magnates in *Maigret et les témoins récalcitrants*, for example, which shocks him into recollections of childhood innocence — "It occasionally happened that he would grasp at childhood memories and, confronted with certain realities, would be shocked like an adolescent."

In some stories the justice/class theme is presented with more variables: the judges in *Maigret aux assises* and *Maigret et l'affaire Nahour* are exceptionally scrupulous and conscientious; the judge in *Maigret a peur* is an old university friend who, confronted with a case in which suspects and victims are all from a decadent, lugubrious family of local gentry, squirm uncomfortably at having to open an inquest against them; *Maigret chez le ministre* deals with a coverup, but the "ideological" issue is modulated in that the victim is himself an unusually attractive cabinet minister; in the really aristocratic milieu of *Maigret et les vieillards*, Maigret feels totally out of place but not at all hostile; in *Maigret à l'école*, he has to deal with a situation of threatened clan injustice against an alien, suspected schoolmaster.

There is a notable "sunny" side in the Maigrets, and its function is both to highlight and to counterbalance the murky confusion in which the criminal action takes place. It takes many forms: Mme. Maigret's ubiquitous presence in the background, the familial atmosphere at the P.J., the eating, the drinking, the bus platforms, and, periodically, Maigret's anticipated or projected retirement — fishing, puttering, gardening at his little country house at Meung-sur-Loire. The variable interplay between "darkness" and "sunniness" is often an underlying structure of the stories. *La Patience de Maigret* opens at Meung:

> The day had begun like a childhood memory, bright and delightful. For no reason, because life was good, Maigret's eyes laughed as he ate his breakfast, nor did Mme. Maigret's eyes sparkle less gaily across the table from him ... What a wonderful Sunday! A stew simmered in the low-ceiling kitchen with the blueish tile floor ... Even his wife's apron with little blue checks enchanted him by its freshness, by a sort of innocence, as did the sunlight reflected from one of the panes of the credenza.

There follows a dismal story of murder, cruelty and deception. Having unraveled its threads, Maigret, in the last chapter, comes back to the "sunny" world: "The world began to live again around Maigret. He heard the street noises once again, saw the reflections of sunlight, and slowly savored his sandwich." At the very end, when Maigret has disposed of the vicious criminals at the bottom of the case, the bucolic note on which the

[2 2 9]

story had opened comes full circle as he looks out his office window and sees a fisherman on the banks of the Seine:

> He had called him "his" fisherman for many years, even if it likely was not always the same. What mattered was that there should always be a man fishing near the pont Saint-Michel.

In some stories, the "sunniness" may be specks of relief here and there from the prevailing "murkiness," as in *Maigret et les témoins récalcitrants*, where he finds it positively refreshing to deal momentarily with a professional petty burglar that takes him away from the ugly upper-middle-class crime under investigation. Some stories, on the other hand, take place largely in the "sunny" medium, and the criminal element, as regards the dominant tone, is in the background. The premise — and the title — of *Maigret s'amuse* points to exactly this construct: Maigret is on vacation and follows a P.J. investigation from newspaper reports, playfully sending in anonymous hints to his boys as to how they should proceed. *Le Client le plus obstiné du monde* (one of the shorter pieces included with *Maigret et l'inspecteur malgracieux*) opens, continues, and closes in bright Parisian sunshine, with Maigret drinking innumerable glasses of white wine and coming home with a bunch of violets for Mme. Maigret. Simenon must have been himself in a sunny mood when he wrote these stories in 1946, for another one in the same volume, *On ne tue pas les pauvres types*, is also full of sunshine, and deals with a mild little man who, having won three million francs in the lottery, had been leading a double life — a secret apartment, a mistress, and a flock of canaries — until someone murders him for his money.

The celebrated Maigret method had been well enough established and expounded in the earlier Maigrets, so that the later offer mostly amplification. Inspector Pyke of Scotland Yard — like others before him — comes to study the method, keeping close on his heels throughout *Mon Ami Maigret*, and is reported in a later novel to have concluded that there is no method. There is no method because Maigret works largely by improvisation, and also because "method" connotes "logical system," not intuition. In *Une Confidence de Maigret*, Maigret explicitly defies the French "logique" and "bon sens" that have led to a detestable, class-biased miscarriage of justice. Elsewhere he broods about a wretched suspect, "All the rational arguments pointed to him. He was the logical culprit, but the commissaire mistrusted rational arguments."

In principle, Maigret gets on the right trail when the "déclic" occurs — something undefinable that clicks in his consciousness — though it is not always clear when it has occurred in practice. The "déclic" is intuitive, as is the rest of the procedure — or the procedure, perhaps, is a series of "déclics." A nice example occurs in *Maigret et le fantôme* when, questioning a witness from a classy milieu, he suddenly intuits that her origins, like his own, are among "the little people." He seeks the "real self" beneath appearances, and, in *Maigret voyage*, specifically identifies his quest, like Simenon's, as a search for "l'homme tout nu," which, in this case, means delving under the artifacts of the idle rich to discover what makes them tick.

After intuition, imagination often takes over: little by little, the victim or the criminal becomes his intimate in imagination, if not in actuality. An excellent example is *Maigret et la jeune morte*, where he imaginatively reconstructs the texture of the victim's life, helped by Mme. Maigret, who explains feminine psychology to him and, with considerable detail and subtlety, what circumstances might make a young girl wear certain clothes. Indeed, in this, as in several other novels, Maigret's imaginative side sets him to *dreaming* about the case at hand (not, however, to a solution: he is not a psychic detective). At the end of *Maigret et le corps sans tête*, one of the chief suspects finally becomes a complete character in Maigret's imagination; he can even envision her as a little girl, and he *understands* — all this while talking to judge Coméliau and not even *trying* to make him understand.

It has been repeatedly observed that Maigret's method is much like a novelist's — in particular, like Simenon's. The "déclic" is inspiration, the unexpected trivial stimulus that sets imagination in movement. He is sometimes described very much like Simenon at work: "He needed to stay with his momentum, to cling to the little world in which he was immersed." Before that stage, he is apt to just sit ponderously, appearing unresponsive to any data. This is the trance-like state that is also analogous to literary composition. Queried by a local detective, who asks anxiously if the details he has been providing are useless, Maigret answers, "No, no. It's just that I have to get accustomed to the situation."

Perhaps the most vivid articulations of the Maigret method are the metaphors in which Simenon encapsulates it. There is, for example, a pictorial metaphor: "It was still only the background of the canvas that began to emerge. Most of the characters remained unfocused, imprecise." Or an olfactory image:

> It was one of these affairs with an odor he liked, which he would have wanted to sniff about in a leisurely way until he would be so impregnated with it that the truth would appear of itself.

There is a dramaturgical metaphor, describing how, up to a certain point in an investigation, Maigret is not interested in the characters, but, after the "déclic," "the characters in the play ceased to be mere entities for him — pawns, or marionettes — and became human beings." There is an alcoholic metaphor, as Maigret, brooding about the choirboy case in *Le Témoignage de l'enfant de choeur*, suddenly has the indispensable insight: "Alcoholics are like that. Truths become suddenly obvious to them, which they are incapable of explaining, and which dissolve into vagueness as soon as they sober up." There is a rumination image, followed by one of aspiration and absorption:

> In almost all his investigations, Maigret knew this period, more or less long, of drifting, during which, as his colleagues always said, he appeared to be ruminating.

> During this first stage, that is, when he suddenly found himself face to face with a new environment, with a people about whom he knew nothing, he appeared to be mechanically breathing in the life that surrounded him, and to expand with it like a sponge.

One of the more remarkable things about Maigret is the way Simenon juggled with his creature's social and professional status as he developed him over forty years. In contrast with the dominant detective-story mode — either golden-age or hardboiled — he made his hero a policeman. The principal reason for this is the "meneur de jeu" notion which he repeatedly explained: the detective as a kind of master of ceremonies providing ready entry into the narrative and rapid contact with the characters. Making him a policeman facilitates that function even more. But if Maigret had remained just a policeman he would never have acquired the almost mythic status he holds.

In the police hierarchy, Maigret's rank is high enough to provide a reassuring sense of control and, more important, to reinforce the paternal qualities toward subordinates, victims and criminals that are such an essential ingredient of the Maigret myth. But if his rank is high, his heart, so to speak, points downward, to the "little people." He is their protector; he is one of them. Private detectives, after all, tend to serve the rich people who hire them. Maigret is a public servant in the truest sense of the term. On the other hand, it is clear that Simenon turns somersaults to dissociate him from the judicial apparatus of which the police is necessarily a part. Not only does Maigret wage a persistent guerrilla war with the higher echelons, but a great deal of the time he is acting, in fact, like a private detective: technically, every time he is outside the Paris city limits, which he very often is; or when he carries on his own private investigation, paralleling, contravening, or ignoring the official inquest.

His entry into a case is often personal, not official, as in *Les Vacances de Maigret*, where he gets involved in a hospital case because Mme. Maigret is convalescing from an appendectomy. His constant thoughts of retirement, as well as his actual retirement, put him in a private-detective mode, as do those stories where Mme. Maigret becomes a charming amateur — most notably in *L'Amie de Mme. Maigret*. The stories in which Maigret is *really* a cop acting like a cop are few. Thus he takes his place, after all, alongside

Hercule Poirot and Philip Marlowe—more like the latter than the former, but in a world very much his own.

Maigret becomes famous within his own fictions, which is why so many troubled souls try to get in touch with him. In *Un Noël de Maigret*, he discovers that a bashful spinster across the street is secretly in love with him, and the young boy in "La Pipe de Maigret" steals his pipe to imitate him. For the most part, Maigret's fame serves as a mode of communion with the world at large, a response to his own sympathetic impulses. It is appropriate that one of the witnesses in the last Maigret is an old woman, a former prostitute, who says she remembers Maigret from when he was a young inspector.

In 1950 Simenon used a variation of this motif for the delightful *Mémoires de Maigret*, written as if by Maigret in the first person, who, like Don Quixote, is forced to confront his own fictional self. At the beginning he is introduced to a young man named Georges Sim ("not a journalist, a novelist," Sim rectifies when he is incorrectly presented), who gives him a couple of early Maigrets, which Maigret finds full of annoying little errors and distortions. He is reconciled, however, when he receives an invitation to the "bal anthropométrique," and, in the course of subsequent dialogues, tries to correct more of Simenon's inaccuracies about police work and gives him a long account of his background, his career, his ideas on crime, justice, human nature, destiny, and the like. The tone of the book, chipper and comical at the beginning, becomes serious when Maigret expounds his human compassion for the lower levels of society, and says that he himself might have been a raté. He explains at length his vocation as a mender of destinies: trying to get those who have somehow taken a wrong turn back on the right path.

Simenon created problems for himself, as well as successes, by developing Maigret as he did, expanding or reiterating the serious aspects of his personality and of his vision of the world. He changed the rules of the detective story game, frustrating some readers' expectations by shifting the level of seriousness. Yet the shift is not always consistent or sustained enough to be fully satisfying on the new level. A composite, archetypal Maigret (allowing for innumerable exceptions) starts with a mystery, engaging the reader on a level of pure narrative curiosity. Simenon has a knack for opening paragraphs—hence the cover-design gambit of one of the countless paperback reprint series, quoting the opening lines on the back cover on the assumption that this will entice the browser to buy the book. But then he changes from a "mystery" level to a "psychological" level, with light but potentially complex moral implications. The reader may then become engaged on *that* level, but never lets go of the original mystery-curiosity level.

There is nothing new about this: many a masterpiece functions the same way; *The Brothers Karamazov* is a mystery story. The problem in the Maigrets is that the two levels don't always merge satisfactorily. On the mystery level, curiosity is satisfied, as it must be. But by that time, often, the other level has so tangled the narrative that, looking back on the plot, the reader may feel befuddled, even vaguely defrauded. Retelling a Maigret plot backwards from the solution to the mystery may demonstrate it to be quite outlandish.

Maigret et l'homme tout seul, for example, yields something like this: There once were two young Parisians, Marcel and Louis, infatuated with an attractive girl, and when Marcel finds the girl two-timing him, he strangles her. Louis, arriving shortly after the murder, vows vengeance. Subsequently, Louis rises to business success and a good but unpassionate marriage, while Marcel sinks, leaving his pathetic little wife and daughter and becoming a clochard. Twenty years later Louis runs into Marcel, who is earning a few francs unloading produce at Les Halles, and, true to his vow of revenge, kills him. The police is called in, and a heavy-set commissaire little by little untangles the situation and arrests Louis.

A reader who starts out principally interested in finding out why a bedraggled clochard was murdered at Les Halles and ends up with this explanation may feel frustrated; he might have to reread it twice to understand it — and who wants to keep rereading a detective story? On the other hand, the reader who has become involved on the deeper level may protest that the plot is rather ill-conceived and that the detective-story form in which it is cast is not illuminating of that deeper level; this reader may want to know more about Louis and Marcel and the rest, and less about Maigret and his boys.

To put the matter differently, the detective story genre is predicated on satisfying an elementary sense of justice: catching a culprit. The American hardboiled novels, enacted in a grimmer world, offer only a provisional justice, but offer it firmly. In the Maigrets, however, our sense of justice is ambiguous at best, and often quite denied. Thus basic detective story expectations, still met in the hardboiled school, are frustrated in Maigret. Yet, by and large, the stories do manage to steer a middle course that avoids frustrating either detective story or serious fiction expectations. Because of Maigret's benign and attractive character, both categories of readers readily put themselves in his hands and cozily follow him wherever he leads them. Any tendency to be miffed because of frustrated expectations — high- or lowbrow — is neutralized by the commissaire's reassuring presence.

From the beginning of the Maigret saga to its end — over forty years — Simenon persisted in designating that project as "semiliterary." If, as appears to be the case, the rubric originated as an off-the-cuff remark for publicity purposes (see pp. 79–80 above), it probably remains as the most sensible evaluation of the Maigrets. Simenon went into detective fiction for the money, with a limited feeling for the mainline of the genre. He instantaneously overcame that limitation by his customary energy, agility and self-confidence (you want a detective story? Here you are!). More important, he overcame it by luck, in hitting, at first try, upon the figure of Maigret, so pregnant with possibility.

Having little innate feeling for the detective genre, Simenon very quickly expanded it to accommodate the "nondetective" elements that claimed his interest. Also very quickly he moved from the Maigrets to the straight novels: the Maigrets were indeed a pivotal point in his erratic literary escalation. At the same time, except for a few years in the mid-thirties, he never lost touch with the financial imperatives that had prompted the Maigrets in the first place. Detective fiction — like science fiction later — developed in an age of rapidly expanding mass media: cheap publications, movies, radio, and eventually television. The printed media both fed and remained in competition with the technological ones.

Simenon, intent on getting a good slice of the "popular entertainment" pie, staked his claim in the detective genre, but kept shifting it to accommodate his particular talents, which, in some ways, were not for it. In doing this, he made interesting modifications in the genre, exploring certain thematic possibilities more often underplayed by its major practitioners, among them serious consideration of guilt, justice, motivation, ambition, and domestic relations. In any case, Simenon carved out for himself an ambiguous area of popular fiction — ambiguous both in its relation to its own genre and to serious literature — and ended up with an opus that deserves critical attention, as it has gained vast popular appeal. There is at least a score of first-rate stories — *Les Scrupules de Maigret, Maigret tend un piège, La Patience de Maigret, Maigret et la jeune morte* — merely to start a personal list from the third-series Maigrets. In the aggregate, the Maigrets depict many interesting major characters — beginning with the commissaire himself — and a panoply of delightful minor ones. The saga is possessed of at least these qualities: charm, a generous humanism, and endurance.

XVII

ART AND LIFE

> "I always distrust excessively
> perfect beings."
>
> Commissaire Maigret

It is evident that the most widely known and relentlessly publicized fact about Simenon, other than his fathering of Maigret, was his writing speed, and hence the volume of his production. For sixty years it was the occasion of awe, jokes, skepticism, curiosity and dismay. It was also the object of critical enquiry and, on his part and that of his admirers, of continuing apologetics that came to constitute an aesthetic. One cause for his speed was habit, established in his journalistic apprenticeship and activating innate capabilities which he never changed. At first they were too useful and later too much part of his identity. When he later felt a need to account for his speed, his apologia took three directions. One was a recurring comparison with other speedy and voluminous writers: why just me? Look at Balzac, Lope de Vega, Stendhal! His list is long, and, for various reasons, unconvincing.

A second way of accounting for his speed was the development of an aesthetic, both in theory and practice, which justified it and his habitual writing procedure. The procedure is clear from the numerous accounts he gave of it from the thirties on. Its cornerstone was the enormous mental effort required for literary composition, and the physical toll it exacted. He always felt such anxiety ("trac") that he often took tranquilizers before his stint; he calculated he lost between 600 and 800 grams of sweat per chapter, and always emerged with a dripping shirt (immediately washed for the following day, because he had to wear the same shirt each day of composition to maintain his momentum); his blood pressure soared, he lost weight, vomited, had gas pains, stomach cramps, and dizzy spells. In time, he took special precautions before starting a novel: a medical checkup (for his family as well, to minimize interruptive contingencies), cancellation of all visits and appointments, refusal of all phone calls, and, of course, the famous "Do Not Disturb" sign stolen from the Plaza Hotel. At the end the need to unwind was imperative, and habitually took the form of recreational sex. Denyse, asked if such behavior did not disturb her, explained, "No. Georges might feel like swimming, rolling around in the sand, galloping on a horse; he prefers going out to the girls. I don't see what importance that has."

The cause of this compositional torment was the need to put himself into another person's skin and stick with him long enough to see him through the story. For Simenon, such identification was an effort more of will than of imagination. One time, he was living out a character so intensely that he suddenly walloped Denyse, not, this time, because of anything she had done, but because he was acting out his character. He declared he had no imagination but an excellent memory, which, though questionable as regards the role of imagination, may be a clue to his creative anguish.

What he *imagined* was a situation in which to place a character that had floated into his consciousness, presumably from his subconscious memory. After that, he probably imagined further situations — which is to say a plot — while the character remained alive because Simenon *remembered* him, either as someone he had known or as feelings he himself had experienced. The fictional person was always a potential real person, interesting as such rather than as a component of a work of art. Simenon's creative memory was a reenactment setting off a flurry of overtones, a Pandora's box of associations, many of which were evidently troublesome to him. If he sometimes claimed writing as a therapeutic activity when he felt ill-at-ease, it was a bitter medicine.

The intensely personal identification of author with character, precluding or minimizing aesthetic "distance," accounts for the "trance" and the "state of grace" which were the psychological conditions for creation. Simenon's aesthetic discounts mediation between "inspiration" and finished product, leaving out as many intermediate steps as possible. While the result does not look like surrealist automatic writing, the Surrealists were a *reductio ad absurdum* of the same aesthetic principle. For much of his life, for that reason, Simenon downgraded intelligence — his own and that of others. That is why he always felt uncomfortable with André Gide, and why Descartes was his bête noire. He declared, "Intelligence must not intervene during the writing of a novel," not considering that the key word might be "during," and that intelligence might intervene in revision.

The Simenonian aesthetic is mistrustful of intentionality. "There is no 'because'; 'because' is always false, a word for imbeciles." Hence his insistence that he never knew where his story was going from one day to the next, and, more problematical, his determination not to revise earlier chapters to accommodate later plot developments, or eliminate episodes without consequences. Such retroactive causality seemed artificial to him ("voulu"), and he preferred to risk loose ends and brusque plot developments which seemed to him more authentic. Not that he deliberately sought to dislocate causality in the modernist manner: he did not want to do *anything* deliberately. Periods of smoother plotting and symbolic structuring arose, as in the forties, but were abandoned, probably because he felt them alien to his true being as an artist.

It was, paradoxically, to minimize the principle of mediation that Simenon made much of the physical tools of his craft, preferring indeed to think of it as a craft and not an art or a mental procedure, and deploring that its materials were words rather than substances like wood or paint. He tried to transform his well-sharpened pencils and his typewriter into chisels and brushes. The typewriter in particular, following him around the globe in its special case, was aesthetically important. The several dozen pencils were that many temptations to stylistic reworking and refining, while typewriting provided a rhythm and a momentum of its own, diminishing interference by the writer's meddling intellect:

> Once your typewriter is on its way, it pulls you along. You have to follow. You can't stop to reread the last sentence, to scratch something out, and you plunge forward, leaving indispensable corrections till later.

That is why he abandoned the two-phase method with its handwritten draft and went back to the single draft, typewritten in one morning. The word processor, with its infinite possibilities for revision, would not have been to his liking.

Thus, rejecting intellect and intentionality, Simenon's aesthetic did accommodate a principle of craftsmanship whose origins are obvious enough in the Simenon clan of his childhood, embodied primarily in grandfather Chrétien Simenon, the hatmaker, and in Désiré Simenon with his meticulous job sense. Simenon spent a lifetime dissociating himself from the idea of a "man of letters"—a project that probably started with his dim view of his arty companions in the Caque—and designating himself at every opportunity as a "novelist," by which he usually meant a species of craftsman. Yet craftsmanship, it might be argued, is precisely the quality that his books are most deficient in. Craftsmanship was something of a Simenonian identity myth, like "the little people," "the couple," and "the patriarchal family." He tended to see writers ordinarily thought of as craftsmanlike as tedious fussbudgets. He could not stomach Flaubert and his three-day quests for "le mot juste," and among his beloved Russians, the craftsman Turgenev was his least favorite. It somehow never seems to have occurred to him that an attribute of craftsmanship is the patient working out of details, while speed is not.

In truth, he was possessed of conflicting tendencies: toward order and disorder, discipline and anarchy — that old antithesis between conformity and rebellion that went back to his early childhood, and which in his work emerged as a conflict between an ideal of artisanship in principle, and in practice an aesthetic of unintentionality incongruous with it. One of the doctors interviewing him in *Simenon sur le gril* pertinently suggested an antithesis between "social organization represented by your father and anarchy represented by your uncle [Léopold]." Simenon answered that that was true and began, without transition, to talk about his typewriter:

> Two years ago I decided to type my manuscripts directly on the type-
> writer [i.e., abandoning the two-phase system] in order to be in direct
> contact without passing through the filter of handwriting by pencil,
> which requires a certain pondering, which slows down the rhythm.

In this context, Désiré represents order and craftsmanship and sharpened pencils, which Simenon seeks to ward off by a Léopold-principle lurking in an anarchic typewriter.

The third and most important phase of Simenon's accounting for his speed is the attitude toward art and life — in respect to each other — which he evolved and articulated over the years. At a certain point in his career he identified his literary project as a search for man: the essence of man, man in his innermost self, man stripped down to the core: "l'homme nu." It is not clear when he developed this concept, but his feeling that such had been his quest all along was a retroactive attribution. Some time later, he came to another conclusion: that this quest was dangerous.

The doctors interviewing him in 1968 remarked at one point that he had cited Nietzsche at least three times and suggested it might be an alibi. Simenon was fond of citing Nietzsche, here and elsewhere, as an object lesson in the dangers of probing too deeply into the human condition: the prober risked madness, or something like it — alcoholism, suicide, or at the very least profound unhappiness. He had fastened on Nietzsche probably by accident, but what he had in mind was art, and he was quite convinced that the deeper most artists probed into the human condition, and the more dedicated they were to their art, the more disturbed they became. His examples, in addition to Nietzsche, and also Jung, included Faulkner, Hemingway, Fitzgerald, Gauguin, Van Gogh, Rembrandt, Schumann, Rilke, and Lautréamont. For himself, he felt he was willing to go to a certain depth, but no further.

> I observed that there were certain raw truths, certain secret mechanisms, which it was better not to touch if one wants to keep his physical and mental health. I noted among others the case of Nietzsche, who died insane. Many others found madness in wanting to know too much about human nature. I like life too much to see this sacrifice through to the end.

At one time, he saw his artistic progression in a dental image, as drilling into a tooth closer and closer to the nerve — delaying, then abandoning, the fatal probe into frightful pain.

While this sense of artistic danger was doubtless genuine, the doctors' speculation in *Simenon sur le gril* that the Nietzsche syndrome was an alibi is also valid. It was not an alibi for laziness or lack of determination, nor an alibi masking anxiety about how his books would fare. It was an alibi for a disinterest in art which, in fact, explains much of his behavior as a writer. Simenon saw an incompatibility between life and art and squarely chose the former in a way that is rare for an artist. Many artists see no conflict, and those who do tend to choose art, in practice if not in theory (Thomas Mann, for example).

In one sense Simenon was not an artist. He was a keen observer of people and things and had an immense curiosity about human behavior. He was interested in satisfying that curiosity, not in fashioning well-wrought urns. Destiny and talent put fiction into his hands as an instrument to investigate and understand people. It might have been psychology or psychiatry or medicine, with which he felt affinities; or it might have been philosophy or social work or pedagogy if he had leaned in those directions, which he did not. (It was unlikely to have been police work: that was pure fantasy.) At times, he wishes it had been zoology, and envies Konrad Lorenz, "who devoted his life to studying ducks, geese, crows, etc.":

> If I were capable of understanding snails or earthworms, I would gladly write a novel about snails or earthworms, and I would probably learn more about life and man than by taking my contemporaries as characters.

When Simenon wrote a novel, he was interested in what such and such a person might do in such and such a circumstance, invented situations that would push the character "to the limits of himself," and imagined the causes that might account for his behavior. Having found provisional but satisfactory answers, he lost interest, and felt not the slightest impulse to tinker with his story and make it into a more beautiful object. *That* is the ultimate reason why he wrote so fast: he was curious about what would happen next and what that would reveal about his character. At a certain point he had learned enough and was no longer interested. The real problem is not the speed with which he wrote his first draft — a capability he shared with many writers — but his disinclination to second, third and fourth drafts — which he shared with very few. He wrote for the same reason he made love to so many women, and for the same reason he travelled, mingled with people, rode on bus platforms, acquired a wide range of skills and interests, and set up and dismantled households:

> Suddenly, I realized that I never lived the life of a novelist, in any case such as people imagine a novelist. At bottom, I always felt the need to busy myself with everything in the various houses I lived ... Like a good farmer, when I lived in the country, I would go play cards in a smoke-filled room while my horse waited.

It all had to do with curiosity. That was also the reason why he read, and why he stopped reading novels, preferring the lives of writers to their works. Agreeing to give a long presentation of Balzac on French television, he immersed himself in Balzac's correspondence and talked about the man, not the books. He was much more fascinated by the memoirs of Proust's housekeeper, Céleste, than by *Remembrance of Things Past*, and deplored only that her taped recollections had been edited for publication: he would have preferred the raw transcript. In the thirties, when he occasionally took an interest in theater, he preferred to watch from the wings, which did not signify an interest in techniques, but rather in the actors and other personnel as people, and a lack of interest in the work of art they were laboring to present. When he wrote a novel about Raimu, it was Raimu the professional actor who remained in the wings while Raimu the man was on stage. The Little Saint is a sensuous child prolonged into adulthood, not really an artist, and professional writers appear very rarely.

Simenon lacked the play instinct in art — or, more properly, suppressed it in his straight fiction, until it emerged briefly in those sample novels in the "Dictées," which were totally playful. If he envied painters, he failed to consider that painters "play around" a great deal on their canvasses — trying this, trying that, stepping back to consider the whole, starting all over again, etc. They tinker with paints the way writers tinker with words. All art is part tinkering, and Simenon, to be sure, tinkered too — what else was he doing when he picked up his characters and plunked them into this situation or that? But it did not feel like tinkering to him: it felt like plunging into the human soul, and he preferred to resurface quickly and tinker somewhere else. Yet Simenon *was* an artist, whether he liked it, or — as evidently was often the case — not. That is, he wrote novels which he and others took seriously, some of which were very good.

In truth, he was a paradox — he was and was not an artist: *le cas Simenon*. The nonartist sought to pacify the artist by manifesting a concern for the physical circumstances of writing books—the typewriter, pencils, manila envelopes and the "Do Not Disburb" sign—and for the physical existence of the books: the rows upon rows of editions and translations. The artist justified himself to the nonartist by arguing the therapeutic effects of writing novels, explaining their function as research into human nature, and pointing out that they did not really take up much time; while the nonartist warned ominously that writing them was an ordeal that would drive them both into lunacy. Both won: the nonartist persuaded the artist to give it all up and disappear, but the books remained—works of art after all, transcending, a bit sullenly, their reification on bookshelves.

The novels are an extraordinary series of first drafts—extraordinary in that no one before ever published so many first drafts, and also in that some are so good. Simenon was like a photographer quite uninterested in darkroom work but endowed with a very good eye, who took enough shots that some came out entirely right, while most of them, in any case, had something worth looking at. His reworking of certain themes and characters in successive novels might be interpreted—as he himself once suggested—as the equivalent of further drafts. Something nagged him, and he explored it; then, nagged again, he explored it again. But the effect could be more like a treadmill than the working out of a theme until he had it right; the next "draft" was not necessarily better than the preceding; *L'Homme au petit chien* is a repetition of *Le Temps d'Anaïs*, but inferior to it. When he got it right, it was by luck or instantaneous insight, not by progressive accretion. Furthermore, his enormous success in publishing these first drafts reduced any motivation for reworking them.

Simenon, oddly, never seems to have perceived a connection between his search for man and his sense of craftsmanship, or between either and writers he had admired, except to consider that some of them were driven mad by the search. He viewed his project as idiosyncratic and seems not to have thought of Faulkner and Dostoyevsky, Conrad and Gogol as, like himself, craftsmen in search of human truths. When he proclaimed his distaste for the world of "letters," he meant to dissociate himself from fancy phrases and literary politics, chitchat, prizes and the like. But he was in fact also dissociating himself from art. He had no sense of what Nicholas Delbanco calls "colleagueship," either in respect to his contemporaries or his predecessors. A sociable man in life, in literature he was very much a loner.

The unfinished quality of Simenon's novels accounts for most of their flaws and poses problems for both readers and critics. He sometimes puts the reader into the situation of an untrained psychiatrist trying to interpret the mutterings of a neurotic. The critic often finds himself in the awkward—not to say presumptuous—position of "finishing" Simenon's first drafts as he is trying to comment on them, or merely describe them. Simenon's awareness of this problem is in itself the cause of one of his flaws — a propensity for sudden lumps of authorial explicitness, for explaining rather than dramatizing, precisely to compensate for the fuzziness of too hasty a narrative. For example, the description of the attitude of the French townspeople toward the refugees after the news of the capitulation of Belgium in *Le Clan des Ostendais*:

> Were they ashamed? Who was ashamed, in the final analysis? Ashamed for them? Ashamed of not having held out a hand, of not having addressed them a little sign, as one does for people who have had a misfortune?

Sometimes this authoriality is pure carelessness. Cardinaud, whose wife has run away, gets an anonymous note telling him he is a cuckold, which ends, as quoted, "T'es un pauvre cocu"; the author then explains, "There were spelling errors. Pauvre was written with an *o* and cocu with a *t*."

This is not to say that Simenon cannot carry off an omniscient point of view quite deftly, as in the Dickensian perspective on Petit Louis in *Cour d'assises*:

> What he had no way of knowing was that his actions and gestures already had no more importance, that he was as if momentarily reprieved, that fate, too busy elsewhere, forgot him for an instant, leaving the bridle on his neck, sure to find him again.

Indeed, Simenon can handle a very wide range of points of view: first person (of varying degrees of self-consciousness), third-person (of varying degrees of omniscience), second-person (intimate, or — as in "his mother, you see, your honor, is of another race from you and us" — authorial), interior monologue, *erlebte Sprache*, epistolary, journal, news reporting, etc. He can slide from one to another — sometimes to excellent effect, sometimes haphazardly, absent-mindedly. What is objectionable is lumpish authorial intrusion, or banalities of description ("he had impressive hands") or of characterization intended to compensate for a narrative or thematic inadequacy.

These are sins of commission. A recurring sin of omission is his failure to exploit potentially interesting ambiguities in point of view, his neglect of irony. This is most evident when he comes closest to an enriching irony, but hesitates, or flubs it, as at the end of *L'Homme qui regardait passer les trains*, where the brilliant ambiguity of Popinga's sanity as he plays chess with the psychiatrist would have been enhanced had Popinga been treated more ironically all along. In a cameo scene in *Le Bourgmestre de Furnes*, Terlinck, the powerful but alienated protagonist, decides to keep a visitor waiting:

He checked his chronometer, decided he would make the lawyer wait exactly seven minutes. To kill the time, he slipped the narrowest blade of his jack-knife under his fingernails. Then he considered that six minutes would do and rang.

An ironic tone is undeniable and inviting, but is less effective than it might have been because it does not occur in a context of sustained irony and ambiguity toward Terlinck. We would like *not* to know whether Terlinck is snobbish, or faking snobbishness, or keeping up his spirits in a deteriorating situation, or putting down a tedious fool; but we would like not to know because the author shifts the grounds with ambiguities and keeps us alert — which is almost, but not quite, the case.

Ambiguities, sometimes, instead of being illuminating literary maneuvers, result from an incomplete conception of a character, or a loss of interest. For example, it is ambiguous whether Simenon is justifying the alienated small-town lawyer in *La Main*, or only *understanding* him: but it is an ambiguity of incompleteness, not an invitation to weigh complexities of character. In some instances, Simenon might have resolved point-of-view problems by making somewhat grotesque characters squarely grotesque, allowing a countervailing humanity to emerge from their grotesqueness, rather than vice-versa — as in *L'Oncle Charles s'est enfermé* and Alavoine of *Lettre à mon juge*. On the other hand, one should acknowledge Simenon's admirable hold on point of view even in some minor novels, such as *L'Horloger d'Everton*, *L'Escalier de fer*, *Les Témoins*, *Le Grand Bob*, and the wonderful child's point of view of *Il pleut, bergère*....

Even more evident than flaws of point of view are flaws of structure: troubles with beginnings and endings. The beginning often turns out to be a false start, a fumbling around for the true subject, a misleading emphasis on something that has no important consequences (as *Le Destin des Malou* or *Long Cours*) — a defect again evidently attributable to his allergy to revision. And loss of interest is the most likely cause of his troubles with endings: he gets deeper and deeper into a complex situation to satisfy his curiosity, then does not know how to get out of it and impatiently winds up his story with a perfunctory ending, a weak trailing off, as in *Betty* or *Quartier nègre*. Occasionally, in effect, he disposes of his story by reverting to something like a pulp mode, as with Philippe of *Le Testament Donadieu*.

Sometimes the trouble is that the situation, potentially interesting, has been developed in the wrong direction, as if he were playing a good hand in the wrong suit (Simenon was a bridge player). Less often, it turns out in retrospect to have been an ill-conceived situation to begin with. None of this, of course, prevented Simenon from frequently coming up with brilliant openings and brilliant endings: He had the talent and was merely uninterested in whatever it would take to insure it was used consistently.

Simenon rarely exploits plot for suspense value—which is remarkable for a writer whose fame persists in resting on his detective stories. His skill lies not at all in manipulating the reader, which may be to his credit, though it may also be argued that literature *is* manipulation. Simenon was impatient with structure and once declared it had always been his ambition to write a picaresque novel, "with neither head nor tail," but he never got to it, except for the unpublished *Jehan Pinaguet* of his youth, and perhaps for *Pedigree*.

Narrative dead ends appear in the course of the story as well as the beginning: aborted story lines and characters introduced and then abandoned, for example. Furthermore, one can develop a certain distrust of Simenon's descriptive details, of their relevance to the meaning of the tale. He tends to interrupt his narrative to provide extensive details of various characters' backgrounds, even minor ones—a spinoff of his habit of writing minibiographies on the manila envelopes. Sometimes these were never used in the fiction; when they were, the result might range from brilliant psychological illumination to irrelevant clutter. On the other hand, Simenon is principally a realist, and sometimes a naturalist, and the conventions of those modes accommodate accumulations of factual detail.

Indeed, one can acquire a good deal of information from reading Simenon's novels: how to run a Paris restaurant (*La Mort d'Auguste*), a luxury hotel (*Les Caves du Majestic*), or a country inn (*Le Cheval blanc*, where one also learns how to save a sauce béarnaise about to turn); how to run a retail wine franchise (*Une Vie comme neuve*), a travel agency (*Le Déménagement*), a mussel-gathering business (*Le Coup de vague, Le Riche Homme*) or a cardboard-box business (*Maigret et les braves gens*); how to deal in diamonds (*Maigret et l'inspecteur malgracieux* or *La Patience de Maigret*) or in rare stamps (*Le Petit Homme d'Arkhangelsk, M. La Souris*); how to fish for the péquois (*Le Cercle des Mahé*), how to make a good shot in bowling on the green (*Signé Picpus*), how to poison your wife (*Dimanche*), and, of course, how to run an investigation in the criminal brigade of the Police Judiciaire.

In addition to flaws of point of view and of narrative structure, there are sometimes flaws of dialogue. Usually Simenon was good at it, but in his haste he could leave improbabilities in his characters' mouths. A garrulous old lady like the title character of *La Vieille* is unlikely to have described a frantic search for her father in this language:

> Un soir que ma mère avait eu une syncope alors que j'étais seule avec elle, j'ai couru dans les rues, haletante, et je revois les deux larges baies voilées de rideaux écrus derrière lesquels on devinait une vie mystérieuse.

(One evening when my mother had had a heart attack as I was alone with her, I ran through the streets, panting, and I can still see the two bay windows veiled by unbleached curtains behind which one guessed at a mysterious life.)

As for Simenon's style, it has been a matter of controversy in France for half a century, and aspects of it cannot but be counted among his flaws. He makes elementary grammatical mistakes which, French copy editing being what it is, remain firmly embedded in the texts and occasion periodic lists of bloopers by unfriendly reviewers. He himself was given to asserting that his errors were deliberate and justified by overriding considerations of rhythm and momentum — a declaration that smacks more of bravado than of policy. It is not difficult to draw up one's personal list: One can forgive him his eccentric ways with the imperfect, the pluperfect and the subjunctive, less so his dangling participles ("après avoir en vain essayer de conquérir l'Angleterre, on le croyait victime d'un coup d'état"), failures of agreement ("des problèmes que l'obstination de ta mère soulèvent"), faulty homonyms ("pour qu'elle raison"). His Anglicisms are grating, and perhaps even more noticeable to American ears ("il ... collecta les billets"; "alimonie"; "le complet ... à presser"; "ils se congratulaient"; "l'air conditionné"). Some of his stylistic and punctuational devices become quirky: the obsessive use of the ellipsis (particularly at the ends of sentences...); the rhetorical interrogation point. He has an excessive tendency to personify looks and feelings, as in "The looks of the two men finally crossed. That of the flutist said, 'I couldn't do otherwise'"; or "'You see,' her look said, 'they are good people, perfect neighbors.'"

Simenon's predominant and persistently proclaimed style was the plain style, attributed to Colette's advice in 1923. He prided himself on limiting his literary vocabulary to about 2000 words (though adding that he knew more), and especially on the translatability of his work, which he considered a grass-roots quality, a universal comprehensibility, fusing stylistic principle and the myth of the "little people." Simenon's aversion to "literary" language — "fioritures," "mots d'auteur" — was extreme, and avoiding it was one of the few literary problems that could prompt him to fuss quite as much as a James or a Flaubert. In his depressive moodiness of 1961 he was once nearly nagged to a minor nervous breakdown by a "literary" phrase he had let slip by through sheer weakness of character.

The plain style, which pleases some and leaves others indifferent, is a perfectly respectable literary manner with a venerable ancestry (going back at least to the "trobar plahn" of the Provençal troubadours). Hemingway was a master of one version of it, as Simenon at his best was of another. He could give a paradoxically elegant demonstration of it, as when prodded by an interviewer to describe the very unplain desk he was sitting at: "I would say that it is a round table with a high polish, incrusted with bronze, such as one sees in museums, separated from the public by a red cord." The only problem with Simenon's plain style is the too frequent intermingling and confusion of plainness born of conviction with that born of speed and carelessness. Nonetheless, he can indeed be delicately simple and sparse, as in the admirable description of Maugras's awakening to consciousness in *Les Anneaux de Bicêtre*:

> A chair has crackled, as when someone gets up precipitately, and he must have managed to part his eyes since he sees, very close to him, a white uniform, a young face, brown hair escaping from a nurse's cap. It is not his nurse and he closes his eyes, disappointed. He is really too tired to ask questions and prefers to let himself slide to the bottom of his hole.

Simenon is adept — and unpredictable — at providing vivid, character-revealing little cameos — the weakness and diffidence of Marthe in *Le Coup de vague*, for example:

> Likewise, when she rode her bicycle on the road and a car came toward her, she would turn the handlebars two or three times awkwardly before stopping by the side of the road, out of prudence, and getting off her vehicle.

Simenon's plain style does not preclude figures of speech, sometimes quite apt, like this fleeting sketch of two archenemies: "Amélie and Françoise embraced for a long time, as one embraces after funerals"; or Emile in *Le Chat*, trudging back to his dismal household: "He walked mechanically, his head bowed, without having to pay attention to his way, like an old horse going back to the stable." Not that he always hits it right; he can come up with such dubious images as comparing a scene of Christmas strollers on snowy sidewalks to "slices of bread spread with caviar." But he can also work out an effective, extended conceit, such as that in which Maigret observing a bumbling American police investigation is compared to a kibitzer at a card game hardly able to contain himself.

Simenon is most often praised, rightly enough, for his descriptive ability. Here, as a keen observer and relisher of life with a remarkable memory for detail, he was at home. Bursts of descriptive brilliance sometimes occur as part of a narration, while, at other times, narration is momentarily suspended for a brief tableau. Simenon's descriptive power is most celebrated in its creation of "atmosphere," by which is meant either the compelling vividness of his scene setting — a sense of "being there" — or a congruence between scene (often weather) and theme or character, resulting in meaning. His frequent descriptions of barren construction sites, for example, and the equally barren constructions that arise there echo the barren lives that unfold in them, as in *Le Chat, La Vieille, Le Déménagement, Maigret et l'homme du banc*, and others: the meaning is meaninglessness.

Sometimes the analogy between scene and character is straightforward to the point of banality, though in fact he can be very good even when the analogies are quiet explicit, as in Dr. Malempin's reminiscence of his troubled youth:

> A colorless sky, still impregnated with water; light coming from nowhere, providing no shadows, no relief to objects, emphasizing the harshness of the tones. It was these tones, precisely, those of the countryside that surrounded us, which gave me nightmares, in a literal sense: I feared the dark green which the swampy meadows take on in winter, with frozen puddles here and there out of which sprout nasty little specks of grass; I feared the trees outlined against the sky and especially—I don't know why—the pollard willows; as for the freshly ploughed earth, its brownness turned my stomach.

Or he can be more concise and indirect, as in *Bergelon*, where he objectifies young Cosson's drunken despair at the death of his wife at childbirth:

> The most upsetting thing was that blue spot on a chair, in the half light, that immobile and silent presence of Cécile, and, on the table, the remains of cold cuts on a piece of paper and a drop of red wine at the bottom of a glass, crumbs of bread . . .

Maigret, about to plunge into a world of corruption and betrayal, finds it implicitly prefigured in the flavor of a Parisian fog: "When he emerged from the metro at the Pasteur station, the yellowish fog had thickened, and Maigret recognized its dusty flavor on his lips." Fog, rain, heat, cold, dampness, and sunshine, as well as towns, streets, houses, rooms, furniture, food, bars, restaurants, trees, flowers, meadows, rivers, seas, skies, clouds, jungles, ships—and, of course, markets—habitually correlate, with varying degrees of explicitness or indirection, subtlety or banality, with personalities, states of mind, collective unconsciousnesses, moral conditions, hopes, fears, desires, passions, hatreds, despairs and joys. Yet the same Simenon who cherished his intimacy with the plain style could easily enough revive the fancy style that he started with in his youth. *Maigret se fâche*, for example, opens with a quiet Dickensian and flowery syntactic triad:

> Madame Maigret, who was shelling peas in a warm shade where the blue of her apron and the green of the pea shells made sumptuous spots, Mme. Maigret, whose hands were never inactive, even at two o'clock in the afternoon of the hottest day of an oppressive month of August, Mme. Maigret, who watched over her husband as she might a toddler, was worried.

And if Simenon could produce stylistic arabesques as a teenager, he was still capable of it if he wanted to as an old man. To his tape recorder in 1977 he was describing the happiness reflected in a sleeping woman:

> That happiness, which comes from the depths of her being, that total

relaxation, those uncontrolled tremors, like the ripples on the surface of a lake in beautiful weather, are more eloquent for me than the smiles of the greatest stars. I would not be far from asserting that, to really know a woman, one must have seen her, in the first glimmer of dawn, asleep, her breathing slow and deep, her dreams, unbeknownst to her, reflected on her features.

Simenon's plain style, in short, was a matter of choice, or ideology, which he could abandon at will.

Thus equipped with talent and energy and casual about his limitations and defects, Simenon produced his life's work. As he clearly recognized in mid-career, he would never create the Great Book that Gide and others expected of him, and was quite right in identifying his *oeuvre* as the mosaic of small novels he was accumulating. His recurring themes and character types correspond to certain aspects of his life and personality, and not at all to others, while much remains in that grey, enticing area of conjecture that constitutes the charm and danger of transactions between critics and novelists. If he has persisted, almost in anger, in denying that he ever put himself into his fiction, so sensitive an admirer as Anaïs Nin was convinced of the contrary, and this exchange in the Fellini interview is hardly to be ignored:

> *F. Fellini*: I have this exasperating feeling of always having been interested only in myself.
>
> *G. Simenon*: Well now, Fellini, be reassured, because others are always myself! ["les autres, c'est toujours moi!"]

Quite so: the author's self in a fiction need not take the form of a self-portrait.

A list of Simenon's character types must surely start with the raté. Even strong men like Ferchaux and Terlinck make their way into the world of ratés, while those who escape it tend to retain vestiges that are sometimes almost nostalgic. The early sources of Simenon's preoccupation with failure are many: a mother from whom he felt a lifelong disapproval which, unresisted, would have implied failure in whatever he did or was, and who herself fought a tight battle to erect a meager fortification against failure; a beloved, undemonstrative father who was weak in body and spirit; a galaxy of relatives who were alcoholic or insane or maudlin or brutes or outcasts or diseased or all of these things; an array of poverty-stricken bohemian friends who became models of how not to live. Simenon had a vision of the potential raté in himself, developed an implacable determination to avoid that path, and fastened on commercial writing as a protection against it. On the other hand, for the same reasons, he developed an intense curiosity about the phenomenon of failure and studied the raté in depth and in breadth. He undertook to catalogue and exemplify the infinite variety of ratés in the world.

Commercial turned into serious literature; the protective system, magically maintaining its function, became also a medium for expressing his fascination with the raté. The raté of the serious fiction was the obverse of the invariably successful romantic hero of the pulps. In his own life, he probably came closest to turning into a latter-day, rich raté during the marital-creative crisis of 1960–61, as he was tearing up first chapters, pacing up and down in frustration, and breaking out into tears. He was well on his way to becoming one of those successful, socially integrated personalities whose real lives turn to shambles, whom he had so often depicted in fiction, most notably, in that very period, in *L'Ours en peluche*. An unappreciative mother had been replaced by — as he saw it — an unappreciative wife, reviving ghosts of failure haunting life as well as fiction.

The most widespread kind of raté in Simenon is the unhappy little man leading a humdrum life, oppressed by wife, family, employer, neighbors, or the world at large. When the familiar Simenonian dislocation occurs and he escapes to a new environment, he almost always remains a raté, whether he sinks into the new environment or sheepishly returns to the old. His story can be deeply moving or quite tedious or both; he is almost always viewed with some measure of sympathy, and often with a profound compassion that is one of Simenon's more attractive traits. If "raté" is by definition a negative designation, it nonetheless often serves, in the total mosaic, to discredit the moral shabbiness of its opposite: the world of success and particularly of established social and economic status. Simenon very early acquired and always retained a distrust of the establishment, even if he occasionally courted it, and worked out ways of excluding himself and his friends from the moral pitfalls of success — mostly, at bottom, by emphasizing the positive values of hard work and an energetic capacity for enjoying its rewards.

One variant of the raté *does* embody positive values: the clochard, who became a major divinity in Simenon's mythology. The clochard is the existentially authentic mode of being a raté. The protection from failure that was Simenon's solution in life is never available to his fictive creatures. Their solution should be to become clochards, which would mean freely choosing failure and finding further freedom and true contentment in not yearning for anything else. Simenon was successful even at that: life in the little pink house, with precipitously reduced aspirations, was his way of becoming a clochard. Yet the clochard, being free, does not fit well into the Simenonian universe, which is almost wholly determined. A man is defined and is to be understood by his antecedent history. He is what he has been made, and to understand him is nothing more nor less than to understand his past. This accounts for Simenon's sometimes excessive tendency to provide major and minor characters alike with detailed personal histories. It is also, by and large, the secret of Maigret's success in solving crimes. As for the mender of destinites, it has never been a wholly clear notion logically or metaphysically.

The majority of Simenon's ratés are from the "little people" — as are some nonratés, like the Little Saint. Among his characters in general, even those of a higher station turn out very often to originate from the "little people." Sometimes they feel guilty about having betrayed them and are plagued by a sense of inauthenticity in their achieved environment. There is some discrepancy between Simenon's constantly declared veneration of the "little people" and his manner of depicting them in fiction, where, far from heroicized, they are most often at best pathetic and at worst mean and destructive. There is little of the Zola or Steinbeck spirit in Simenon's fiction, though there is in his nonfiction. The liveliness, tenderness, and solidity which he attributed to the "little people" in his personal mythology frequently appear marginally in his fiction, but not often centrally — another instance of his tendency to darken his vision in transposing it from life to fiction. His mother's snobbish attitude toward the proletariat — a condescension which he loathed — may nonetheless be a factor. The "little people" are the petite bourgeoisie, not the proletariat, but Simenon, having in his own idiosyncratic way risen beyond either class, may have had a tendency to blur them, unconsciously transposing his mother's disdain for the working class and his own for her class into a generalized vision not only of misery and despair but also of degradation and violence.

The alienation of the Simenonian hero is evident, has been amply discussed by everyone, and, in that respect, puts Simenon's work in the mainstream of twentieth-century fiction. Simenon's second great fear, after failure, was solitude. Its most vivid childhood incarnation was his dash after choirboy duty through deserted early-morning streets: "... an anguish ... of being alone, at night, in a deserted street." His sense of the misery of exclusion was strong, and the image of the solitary being yearningly observing couples or families haunted his fiction and his autobiographical work all his life. A good part of his compassion is directed to the lonely:

> what moves me the most in streets, or anywhere else, is to encounter
> solitude. The number of solitaries seems on the increase. I recognize
> them by their gait. You feel that no one is awaiting them, that they
> have no more reason to be at one place than at another. Sometimes
> they stop in front of store fronts where there is manifestly nothing
> to interest them. Perhaps they are ashamed, ashamed of being alone.

The fear of solitude is the obverse of Simenon's sense of immediately "belonging" wherever he went, as it is, of course, of his idealization of The Family and The Couple. These idealizations were personal myths in his life, while in the mosaic of his fiction they served largely to highlight the predominant antifamilies, anticouples and anticommunities that engaged his interest. This contrast echoes that of his childhood between the ideal Simenon family—which was not all that ideal anyway—and the unideal Brülls family.

Simenon's obsessive hypersexuality was doubtless as much a product of his fear of solitude as of his curiosity. Never for an instant was he "uncoupled" since he was twenty. Marriage with Denyse took place within hours of divorce from Tigy, and Teresa was well established as his companion as Denyse was on her way out. Alienation, in Simenon's work, was less a response to the Zeitgeist than an emanation from his personal history. Though Simenon was in the habit of construing his ten thousand women as positive experiences—except for his two wives—the origin of this preoccupation was surely a negative factor: a lack, an absence, a frustration, which he readily enough also acknowledged. It is not incongruous with his view of sex as exploration urged by curiosity: lack, not possession, stimulates curiosity. The lack evidently originated, again, in his sense of neglect by his mother—both of himself and his father—and of her favoritism toward his brother.

After the publication of *Lettre à ma mère* a critic suggested, as Simenon summarized: "Simenon felt himself frustrated by the lack of maternal love. Since then, he has been in search of feminine tenderness." Simenon added, "That is almost true. I have always felt the need to communicate with people, and in particular with 'woman.'" If, as regards literature, such a psychological situation tends often to induce idealized womanhood, that is not the path that Simenon took. The idealized women of the pulps were manufactured dolls that had nothing to do with his inner life. When his inner life was pressed into serious literature, not a single one of these emerged. The only idealized woman is Mme. Maigret, whom, when asked, he acknowledged as his "idéal amoureux." Otherwise feminine types range from admirably competent and loving to grotesquely perverted and destructive: approximately the same range as the masculine types, where the only idealized man, correspondingly enough, is Maigret.

It was in life, not in literature, that Simenon idealized women, even if the idealization took the unusual form of an infinity of quick lays (one tends to infer that his favorite position was from the rear, standing up, and with clothes on—but that is perhaps an accident of what he has chosen to reveal). If the curiosity factor made him experiment with a bit of everything, including Pilar's orgasm-provoking eyelashes on New Year's Eve of 1922, he was probably more comfortable with a blunt, proletarian kind of sex than with sophisticated arabesques. In his fiction, Simenon, otherwise a splendid witness of sensory experience, never portrayed in any depth the sensuality of sex. There are many Cleopatras in his books, but nothing of Enobarbus' immortal appreciation. How much of the Enobarbus spirit there was in

Simenon's liaisons is questionable: "infinite variety" meant something different to him than to Shakespeare. Simenon decided around his mid-sixties that he had found the ideal woman in Teresa, and stuck to his decision with enviable conviction. Throughout, there was a touch, fiercely denied, of that misogyny which quite often accompanies the idealization of women. That too, surely, goes back to Henriette Simenon.

Simenon's antiheroes are created into a burnt-out world, or at best a hollow, factitious one. Typically, they become aware of its falseness and react in a variety of ways. One way, particularly among the younger antiheroes, is sullenness: the snarl, the contemptuous shrug of the shoulders, the rejection of friend and enemy alike, the weakly arrogant "et alors" (so what?), which is their favorite locution. The narrative point of view here is often that of a bad boy about to turn worse: an echo of Simenon's childhood rebelliousness, suppressed by the conformist teacher's pet. The most typical reaction, of course, is flight, real or implicit, which leads usually to a double identity itself a sign of the hollow world, and often becomes an instrument for destroying that world because of the inevitable collision between the two identities, which both collapse. Another reaction to a burnt-out world is masochism, which either stands alone, as in *La Fenêtre des Rouet* or *Feux rouges*, or, classically is coupled with sadism, as in *Lettre à mon juge* or *Au bout du rouleau*. Simenon was fascinated by the intertwining of destructiveness and self-destructiveness—a phenomenon he studied closely, as in *Les Suicidés*, and on occasion brilliantly, as in *La Neige était sale*.

Neither transcendence nor salvation is built into the Simenonian universe, yet both emerge, miraculously perhaps, and become after all part of the mosaic's pattern. There is resistance as in *Le Président*, endurance as in *Le Clan des Ostendais*, promise as in *Le Confessionnal*, reconciliation as in *Feux rouges*, love as in *Trois Chambres à Manhattan*, wisdom as in *Les Anneaux de Bicêtre*, happiness as in *Le Blanc à lunettes*, heroism as in *Les Pitard*, and hope as in *Il y a encore des noisetiers*. There is the triumphant processional of *La Mort d'Auguste*, and the sensuous plenitude of *Le Petit Saint*. This last dramatizes the best bet, the keen sensory awareness which Simenon possessed and cherished, and so frequently imaged forth in novels dark or bright:

> Since my retirement, I often evoke for myself such or such a period of my life, such or such an event in the past. And I ask myself: What remains of it in me?
>
> A lot. I feel rich in memories, but not of things I would have mentioned at the time. My memories, which are now part of my existence, are the sun beams, rain trickling down window panes, the taste of ice cream, long walks alone in various neighborhoods of Paris, with a few stops in an old-style bistro where customers converse without knowing each other.

What has counted in my life is the warmth of the sun on my skin, or of a wood fire in a fireplace in winter, and especially the markets, in La Rochelle, in Cannes, in Connecticut, or elsewhere.

The smell of vegetables and fruits. The butcher slicing into huge pieces of meat. Fish laid out on paving stones.

If I have learned anything in my life, it is that all this is good and important. The rest is mere anecdote and food for newspapers.

NOTES

For the most part, references for Simenon's fiction are to chapters of the books, because the chapters are usually short, there are various reprints available, and the Oeuvres complètes *are difficult to come by. However, for the very numerous references to* Pedigree *and* Je me souviens *in the earlier chapters, it seems advisable to pinpoint the page in the* Oeuvres complètes. *The bold Arabic number before the page number is the volume number. References to other works of Simenon are to the first edition, which is usually the only one. Unpublished letters, except for those to me, are in the Simenon archives at the University of Liège. In a few instances, periodical references are incomplete, or may be in error, because they are taken from clippings in the archives which were improperly dated and which I have been unable to verify.*

The following abbreviations are used for frequently cited works:

Arbre	*A l'abri de notre arbre*	Gril	*Simenon sur le gril*
Banc	*Un Banc au soleil*	Homme	*Un Homme comme un*
Becker	Lucille Becker's		*autre*
	Georges Simenon	Homme nu	*A la recherche de*
Cave	*De la cave au grenier*		*l'homme nu*
Choeur	*Je suis resté un enfant de*	Jour	*Jour et nuit*
	choeur	Jurer	*A quoi bon jurer?*
Cistre	*Cistre Essais 10,*	Lettre	*Lettre à ma mère*
	Georges Simenon	Libertés	*Les Libertés qu'il nous*
	(L'Age d'homme)		*reste*
Dossier	Roger Stéphane's *Le*	L. & S.	Francis Lacassin &
	Dossier Simenon		Gilbert Sigaux's
Fallois	Bernard de Fallois'		*Simenon*
	Simenon	Mag. lit.	*Magazine littéraire,*
Femme	*La Femme endormie*		Dec., 1975
Froid	*Quand vient le froid*	Main	*La Main dans la main*

McCormick	Author's interview of Kenneth McCormick of Doubleday & Co., Dec. 11, 1978	S.	Simenon (followed by a date indicates interview with author)
Mémoires	*Mémoires intimes*	Soixante	*On dit que j'ai soixante-quinze ans*
O.C.	*Oeuvres complètes* (Rencontre edition)	Souviens	*Je me souviens*
Oiseau	Denyse Simenon's *Un Oiseau pour le chat*	Thoorens	Léon Thoorens' *Qui êtes-vous, Georges Simenon?*
Parinaud	André Parinaud's *Connaissance de Georges Simenon*	T.S.	Author's interview of Mme. Tigy (Régine) Simenon, March 9, 1982
Pas	*Des traces de pas*		
Ped.	*Pedigree*		
Petits	*Les Petits Hommes*	Vacances	*Vacances obligatoires*
Playboy	French *Playboy*, Aug., 1975	Vent	*Vent du nord, vent du sud*
Point	*Point-Virgule*	Vieux	*Quand j'étais vieux*
Porte	*Au delà de ma porte-fenêtre*	Vivant	*Tant que je suis vivant*
		Wolff	Author's interview with Mrs. Helen Wolff, Dec. 1, 1978
Portrait	*Georges Simenon, Portrait souvenir: Entretiens avec Roger Stéphane*		
		Writers	*Writers at Work* (The *Paris Review* interviews), 1st. series
Prix	*Le Prix d'un homme*		

Correspondents frequently named: (Jean) Renoir, (Henry) Miller, (Maurice) Restrepo, (André) Gide, (Thornton) Wilder.

Epigraphs

vii   Gide. *Journals*, vol II (Pléiade), 321. S. *Femme*, 122.

Chapter I

1   Arrival. *Homme*, 31–34; *Portrait*, 69; *Porte*, 98. Dec. 11 is date in *Portrait*, Fallois, et al.; in *Mém.* it is Dec. 15.

3   Allergic. *Lettre*, 83. *N.Y. Times*, July 7, 1957.
        Number of works. I take my statistics from Claude Menguy, "Bibliographie de Georges Simenon," *Désiré* #27, 1980. M. Claude Nielsen, S.'s publisher, counts 193 patronymic novels (conversation with author, March 12, 1982).
        Fellini interview. *L'Express*, Feb. 21–27, 1977.

4   Monogamy at 70. *Pas*, 101.

Notes

Chapter II

7   Mother alert enough. *Souviens*, O.C. **17**, 25.
          Ville pluvieuse. *Homme*, 15.
7–8   Désiré & Henriette. *Lettre*, 50–51; *Ped.*, O.C. **18**, 25–26, 30; *Souviens*, O.C. **17**, 25.
8–9   Genealogy. *Souviens*, O.C. **17**, 25–27; *Choeur*, 112.
          Simenon grandparents. *Vivant*, 84–87, 92; *Vacances*, 10; *Petits*, 168; *Portrait*, 21; *Souviens*, O.C. **17**, 37, 43–46. "Kreutz" is "Krantz" in *Souviens*, where the drink is designated as "Kempernar," while in *Vivant*, it is "advocaat."
9   Vieux-Papa. *Vivant*, 89–91 (S. here says his name was Demoulin, which must be a confusion in his mind). Cf. *Souviens*, O.C. **17**, 47–48, et al.
9–10   Other Simenons. *Banc*, 27; *Portrait*, 19; O.C. **17**, 46–47, 49, 132.
10–12   Désiré. *Souviens*, O.C. **17**, 22–23, 30–31, 48–53, 85; *Ped.*, O.C. **18**, 67–69; *Cave*, 15, 128, 175; *Portrait*, 24–25, 53; *Gril*, 16; *Jurer*, 69; *Pas*, 216; S. to Marcel Moré, Aug. 3, 1951; *Les Quatre Jours du pauvre homme*, ii; cf. Becker, 21–23.
12   Social instability. *Portrait*, 20.
          Henriette's father. *Souviens*, O.C. **17**, 39–40; *Lettre*, 23–24.
13   Pots of water, hat & gloves. *Lettre*, 23; *Gril*, 22.
13–14   Brülls. *Souviens*, O.C. **17**, 80, 108–12, 121–29, 202–8, 240–44; *Lettre*, 26, 68; *Portrait*, 14, 31, 32; *Gril*, 22; *Destinées*, 145, 149–50. (In *Vieux* Anna is called Maria.)
16–17   Henriette. *Portrait*, 14, 17–18, 29; *Lettre*, 40, 42–43, 65, 68–69, 86, 90–91, 107, 110, 112; *Souviens*, O.C. **17**, 28, 44, 62, 83, 84, 145, 152–155, 200, 205; *Ped.*, O.C. **18**, 29, 249–51; S., March 4, 1982; *Vieux*, 223; *Femme*, 50–51; *Libertés*, 96; *Playboy*: Raymond, *Simenon in Court*, 178; *Choeur*, 22; *Froid*, 44–45. The returning of the money is reported in *Playboy* as occurring on her deathbed, but in *Lettre* (81), in his home.

Chapter III

18   Weak child. *Souviens*, O.C. **17**, 37, 46, 54–55; *Jour*, 150.
          Money, caca. *Dossier*, 14; *Froid*, 131–32.
18–19   Rue Pasteur apt. *Destinées*, 109–10; *Cave*, 25; *Femme*, 117.
19   Market. *Vieux*, 301; *Souviens*, O.C. **17**, 103.
19–20   Sensory experience. *Homme*, 268; *Banc*, 42, 47; *Vent*, 39; *Choeur*, 23, 34; *Ped.*, O.C. **18**, 212, 286.
20   Rue de la Loi apt. *Petits*, 123; *Vent*, 48–49.
          Domestic tensions. *Souviens*, O.C. **17**, 147, 149–50, 152, 200; *Ped.* O.C. **18**, 278–80.
20–21   Christian. *Pas*, 219; *Souviens*, O.C. **17**, 258; *Portrait*, 38; *Femme*, 126–27; T.S.; Bresler, *The Mystery of Georges Simenon*, 170–72.
21   Other children. *Homme*, 219, 225, 227; Thoorens, 46; *Ped.*, O.C. **19**, 7, 10–11.

Parental sex. *Vent*, 37.

21-22   Relatives. *Vivant*, 101; *Cave*, 50; *Souviens*, O.C. **17**, 95-96.

22-25   Boarders. *Souviens*, O.C. **17**, 166, 232, 179-86, 212-14, 222-23, 209-19; *Ped.*, O.C. **19**, 39-49, 33, 68-71, 67. The first edition of *Pedigree* is that of 1948. The second, in 1952, is the one with the blank spaces.

25   Nursery & primary schools. *Vivant*, 75-76; *Femme*, 120, 127; *Homme*, 230; *Banc*, 47; *Arbre*, 171; *Jour*, 42-45; *Portrait*, 35-36; *Ped.*, O.C. **18**, 243-244, **19**, 112, 84, 115; Piron, "Georges Simenon et son milieu natal" (in *Cistre*, 31-41).

25-26   Choirboy, mornings, Embourg. *Choeur*, 178-79; *Ped.*, O.C. **19**, 78-80, 85-100; S. to Moré, Aug. 3, 1951; *Vacances*, 33; *Froid*, 9; *Pas*, 212; *Homme*, 15-16; *Main*, 157.

26-27   Music, art, books. *Homme*, 198; *Ped.*, O.C. **18**, 317, **19**, 116; *Choeur*, 179; *Vieux*, 170; *Petits*, 79; *Vent*, 76.

27-28   Loneliness, rebellion & conformity. *Writers*, 153; *Vent*, 119.

Chapter IV

29-30   Escape, solitude, dissipated life. *Homme*, 195; *Ped.*, O.C. **19**, 267-68, 139, 144-45, 271-72, 285, 283.

30   Sex. *Femme*, 27-28, 69-70; *Ped.*, O.C. **19**, 236-43, 165-95, 192-95, 234-39, 69, 282; *Banc*, 47; cf. Bresler, *op. cit.*, 24; *Mém.*, 10; *Froid*, 25; *Vieux*, 215-16; *Choeur*, 98; *Vent*, 107-8.

30-31   Alcohol. *Vieux*, 223; *Ped.*, O.C. **19**, 222-48.

Walks, perfect day, fishing. *Porte*, 168; *Vieux*, 282; *Cave*, 172.

31-32   School. *Portrait*, 43-44; *Paris-Match*, Nov. 25, 1955; Piron, *loc. cit.; Ped.*, O.C. **19**, 147, 127, 200-205. (In *Ped.*, O.C. **19**, 202, S. doesn't mention Flemish but says he was at the bottom of the class in German, at the top in French.) The Diction Prize certificate is in the possession of Claude Menguy.

32   War. *Playboy; Trois Crimes*, iii; *Portrait*, 52, 54-56; *Ped.*, O.C. **19**, 135, 222-32, 315-17; *Point*, 33. *Homme nu*, 300; on Dance, cf. straightforward historical account in *Sud-Ouest*, Oct. 30, 1960.

Bakery, bookstore. *Pas*, 216-17; *Life*, Nov. 3, 1958; *Ped.*, O.C. **19**, 296-312.

Painting, sex. *Cave*, 10; *Dossier*, 43.

33-34   Writing vocation. *Portrait*, 44-45; Jean Jour, *Simenon et Pedigree; Playboy*. On "raccommodeur de destinées," cf. *Vieux*, 257, where it is a "sorte de Maigret médecin, psychiatre, etc., sorte de Dieu-le-Père consultant."

34-35   Books. Piron, *loc. cit.; Synthèse*, April 1952, 202; *Portrait*, 46-47; *Ped.*, O.C. **19**, 248-49, 184-87, 206; *Vent*, 154; *Trois Crimes*, iii; *Pas*, 80; *Homme*, 258-59; *Vieux*, 170; *Writers*, 159; *Jurer*, 165-66; *Soixante*, 70-73; Dieudonné Boverie, "Georges Simenon, écrivain liégeois," in L & S, 273-74; *Au pont des Arches*, 39; *Mag. lit.; Gril*, 22; *Vacances*, 8; *Point*, 32.

Notes

35-36   Early writing. *Homme*, 119-20; *Portrait*, 46; *Fallois*, 27; *Notizie letterarie*, July, 1966; *Mém.*, 10; *Jour*, 14; *Ped.*, O.C. **19**, 183.

Chapter V

37-38   *Gazette. Mag. lit.*; S., March 4, 1982; *Gazette de Liège*, June 12, 1920; *Homme*, 16; *Banc*, 21, 164; *Vieux*, 217, 37-38. My list of S.'s subjects comes mostly from leafing through copies of the *Gazette*, 1919-22. Of the Foch interview, this is the account S. has most often given, most extensively in *Main*, 121-23. Elsewhere he has declared that his "start" as a journalist came when he interviewed Foch, wearing a bathrobe, in a hotel room in Liège. On the other hand, if one consults the *Gazette* itself (March 9, 1920), the Foch interview, with Sim's byline, is reported as taking place at the Brussels station.

38-40   Gazette articles. *Gazette.* Nov. 18, 1919, June 10, 1920, July 1, 1920, July 11-12, 1920, June 25, 1920; River series: Aug. 25, 26, 29, & 31, 1922; Jewish peril, Sept.-Oct. 18, 1921; *Vieux; Destinées*, 36; *Revue sincère*, April 15, 1923 (reprinted in L. & S., 302-3); "Simenon et l'antisémitisme," *Droit et liberté*, Dec. 15, 1961; *Dossier*, 21-23; Chaim Raphael, "Simenon and the Jews," *Midstream*, March 23, 1981; Thoorens, 69; Victor Moremans, "Simenon avant Maigret," *Bonne Soirée*, Sept. 24, 1972; *Portrait*, 59-60.

40   *Cinématographie française. Froid*, 90.
     La Nanesse. Trois Crimes, 76-92. Lucille Becker (p. 32) says that he "worked for a brief period for a newspaper, *La Cravache*," but gives no source; I believe she is mistaken about the name of the newspaper and the date. It's called *La Nanesse* in *Trois Crimes* as well as in real life (it began publication on Nov. 27, 1920); *La Cravache* is one of the names Simenon, as a character in the book, proposes for the projected newspaper. I have found no record of any periodical called *La Cravache*. I should point out, however, that Simenon himself seems to be confused, since he thinks that, in *Trois Crimes*, he named *La Nanesse La Cravache* (S. to author, Nov. 7, 1979; in the same letter he states that everything in *Trois Crimes* is related exactly as it happened in life).

41   Rebelliousness. *Vent*, 119; *Gril*, 11-13.
41-42   La Caque. *Portrait*, 41-42; *La Meuse*, Oct. 14, 1953; S. to R. Remouchamps, May 3, 1976; *Porte*, 180-81; *Homme*, 22-55, 222, 16; *Petits*, 23; *Froid*, 136; *Li Clabot*, Feb. 1969; *Point*, 79; *Jour*, 25-26; T.S.; *Trois Crimes*, iii, iv; *Ped.*, O.C. **19**, 208; *Arts*, Nov. 12, 1958; S. to J. Mambrino, in *Cistre*, 218-19. For mellower portrait of the Caque, see Georges Rémy, "Hommage à Georges Simenon," pamphlet of the "Service éducatif de la province de Liège," 1961.

43   *Jehan Pinaguet.* 2, 66. (The ms. is in the possession of Prof. Maurice Piron.)
43-44   "Compotier tiède." In L. & S., 199-301; *Vieux*, 115.

44-45   Régine. *Point*, 152-55; *Gril*, 46; *Homme*, 13, 18-20, 26-27, 306-7; *Mém.*, 12, 16; *Femme*, 29; S., March 4, 1982.
44   Father's death. *Main*, 159-60; *Point-Virgule*, 131-32, 136; *Cave*, 177; *Homme*, 33, 173; *Mém.*, 14. (S. has sometimes remembered his father's death as taking place after his military service, but it was just before; cf. *Portrait*, 66.)
45   Tigy wanted to go to Paris. *Mém.*, 16.
   Military service. *Point*, 132-33, 139-41; *Vent*, 49-50. *Mém.*, 13.

Chapter VI

46   Paris in twenties. *Femme*, 113; *Froid*, 26; *Le Passage de la ligne*, I, v, II, i; *Homme*, 176.
46-49   First impressions & activities. *Mém.*, 22; *Portrait*, 125-26, 74-75; S. to Restrepo, Nov. 1953; *Homme*, 44, 64-67, 69, 204, 79, 46, 62, 38-39; *Froid*, 26; *Cave*, 51; *Vent*, 155-56; *Vieux*, 216; *Point*, 54; *Hommes et mondes*, Dec. 1954, 124; *Petits*, 63; *Destinées*, 113.
49   Binet-Valmer. *Homme*, 35-37, 40-41, 48-49; *Hommes et mondes*, Dec. 1954, 123; *Expansions*, Feb. 1971; *Mag. lit.* Dernière heure, June 17, 1954; *Destinées*, 44. For Plumier, author's conversation with Claude Menguy, Jan. 4, 1981.
50   Wedding. *Homme*, 58-59; *Mém.*, 17.
   Tigy's painting. *Homme*, 90-91; *Vent*, 55; *Vieux*, 216; T.S.
   Chasse aux femmes. *Homme*, 65-66; S. to Restrepo, Nov. 1953.
50-51   Liège friends. *Porte*, 168-69; *La Meuse*, Oct. 14, 1953; *Homme*, 29, 52-54; *Vieux*, 161-62.
51   Haircuts & clothes. *Cave*, 46; *Petits*, 116; *Banc*, 27-28; *Femme*, 113.
51-52   Tracy. *Portrait*, 60, 77-78; *Homme*, 69-85; *Mag. lit.; Main*, 67; *Prix*, 130-31; Gilles Henry, "Comment nait un personnage," in *Cistre*, 147.
52   *Revue sincère.* L. & S., 302-4.
   Georges Ista. *Homme*, 92-93. (He is not named but called, for some reason, "R-----.")
53-54   Erotic pieces. *Homme*, 63-64; "Théodore et la danseuse," *Sans-Gêne*, Sept. 1, 1923; "Trouillet et la nourrice," *Sans-Gêne*, Sept. 22, 1923; "Le Trou de la serrure," *Sourire*, 1926 (date unclear); "Pantomimes," *Frou-Frou*, March 18, 1925; "Un Coeur sensible," *Paris-Flirt*, 1924 (uncertain date); "Partouzes et partouzards," *Frou-Frou*, June 25, 1927; "Sécurité, discrétion," *Frou-Frou*, April 20, 1927.
54-55   Colette. *Portrait*, 72, 73; *Homme*, 89-90; "Le Romancier," *French Review* **19** (Feb. 1946), 218-19; et al.
55   *Matin* stories. May 6, 1924; Aug. 15, 1924; March 29, 1924; Oct. 25, 1924; July 25, 1924; Oct. 23, 1923. Dennis H. Drysdale, *Georges Simenon: A Study of Humanity.*
56   Writing & selling. *Homme*, 89, 93-94.

Notes

Chapter VII

57–58   Places des Vosges. *Main*, 15; *Vacances*, 70; *Homme*, 49, 100–2; S. to author, Nov. 7, 1979; *Vent*, 115–16; *Vieux*, 116; *Destinées*, 118–20; *Froid*, 27; *Mém.*, 121.
58   Friends, parties. *Vieux*, 153; *Homme*, 49; *Vieux*, 39, 224; *Porte*, 108–9. Brothel. *Femme*, 65; *Playboy*.
58–59   Josephine Baker. S., Feb. 19, 1979; S. to Restrepo, Nov. 1953; *Petits*, 42; *Mém.*, 24; *France-Dimanche*, #1498, 1975; Lynn Haney, *Naked at the Feast*, 113–14.
59   Films. *Destinées*, 79–81; *Cistre*, 187.
        Skimming through pulps. *Porte*, 177.
60–61   Fayard. *Nouvelles littéraires*, July 30, 1953.
61   *Dactylo. Homme*, 91; *Vacances*, 71.
        Les Larmes avant le bonheur, 79.
        Menguy. *Désiré* #27 (1980). He leaves out "Simenon," which makes 38.
62   Writing habits. *Vacances*, 71–72; *Homme*, 35, 101–2.
        Fayard. Max Favelli, "J'ai vu naître Simenon," *Gazette des lettres*, Oct. 15, 1950, 59–60; see also *L'Eventail* (Brussels), Nov. 23, 1951, which is mostly a plagiarism of the above; also, "Editeurs, qui êtes-vous?" *Nouvelles littéraires*, July 30, 1953; *Choeur*, 8–9.
62–63   Payments. *Mag. lit.; Expansions*, Feb. 1971; *Homme*, 101. Contract for *Étoile* in M. Menguy's possession.
63   Ballads. *Jurer*, 87, 89–90, 110; *Porte*, 157–58.
        Roman populaire. *Dossier*, 125–27; *Portrait*, 74.
63–64   *A l'assaut d'un coeur*, 71.
64–65   Adventures. *La Gazette des lettres*, April 15, 1952, 53; *Homme*, 101; *Mag. lit.*
65–66   Jarry. S., Feb. 19, 1979; S. to Restrepo, Nov. 1953; *Soixante*, 147–48; *Chair de beauté*, 67.
66   Male prostitute. *Femme*, 140–42.
66–67   Serious & apprentice work. S. to Gide, Jan. 1953, in L. & S., 398; *Homme*, 42, 102; *Vieux*, 14; *L'Express*, Feb. 6, 1958; *Portrait*, 81; *Destinées*, 45–46; *Soixante*, 71; *Mag. lit.; Writers*, 149.
67   Fitzgerald. Letter to Harold Ober, in *F. Scott Fitzgerald*, ed. Mizener (*20th.-Cent. Views*, 1963), 3.
        Balzac, André Maurois, *Prométhé, ou la vie de Balzac*, 75, 98.
68–69   Étretat. *Pas*, 186; *Vieux*, 61; *Homme*, 96, 113; *Mém.*, 23, 495; *Oiseau*, 124. Bresler reports a three-year wait before the consummation between Boule & S. (*op. cit.*, 58).
69   Porquerolles. *Homme*, 106–15; *Point*, 159–68; *Vieux*, 69; *Mém.*, 25; S. to M. Restrepo, Dec. 6, 1953; *Cave*, 30; *Jour*, 97–99.
70   Île d'Aix. *Vent*, 146.
        Style dépouillé. *Destinées*, 97.
70–71   Merle. *Homme*, 281–83; *Mag. lit.; Cave*, 51; *Le Progrès* (Lyons), Dec. 21, 1963; A.G. Raiti, *Simenon, policier de l'âme. Merle rose*, April 1, 1927. (*Le Merle rose* is not to be confused with *Le Merle blanc*, as does Fallois, 30.)

71-72   *Ginette. Vieux*, 51, 260; *Petits*, 141; *Homme*, 120-26; *Pas*, 237; *Science et voyages*, March 19, 1970.
72   *Ostrogoth. Express Rhône-Alpes*, Nov. 1970; *Vieux*, 52; *Homme*, 140-41; *Mag. lit.*
73   Northern trip. "Pays du froid," in *A la recherche de l'homme nu*, 107-28; *Cave*, 173.

Chapter VIII

74-75   Creation of Maigret. O.C. **1**, 10-11, *Homme*, 234-36. Account of creation quoted here is from "La Naissance de Maigret," Preface to O.C. **1**, 10-11. For the rectification of the date of the first Maigret, I follow Claude Menguy's minutely argued reasoning. Doubt as to Sept. 1929 for *Pietr* arises because it would follow that Simenon, having composed it, let it lie about for almost a year, then wrote more of the series, then approached Fayard—a sequence difficult to envision, all the more so since, in the interval, we must imagine him reverting to a large number of straight pulp works and of ancillary detective enterprises. Menguy's identification of *Captain S.O.S.* as the likely product of Simenon's recollection of the images that floated into his head, and his precise dating of the contract for *Train de nuit*, which would explain Simenon's Sept. 1929 recollection for a first Maigret, are compelling, if circumstantial, pieces of evidence. Menguy further points to p. 141 of *Homme*, where Simenon speaks of writing in the cabin of the *Ostrogoth* and, immediately afterward, of composing *Pietr*, which would void the sunken-barge recollection. (However, it is possible to interpret the p. 141 reference more generally, rather than as referring specifically to the composition of *Pietr*.) Details of Menguy's convincing dating are in a letter to author, Jan. 31, 1982, and, in more extensive detail, in a letter to Gilbert Sigaux, Jan. 25, 1982. Menguy's analysis was presented to the colloquium on "Simenon, la littérature policière et Maigret," on Jan. 21, 1982, at the Centre Culturel de la Communauté belge in Paris, and is now available, with further rectifications and details, in his *Simenon au fil des livres et des saisons* (Paris, 1986).
76   Urged by Fayard. M. Robert Toussaint of Fayard believes the Maigret series was Fayard's initiative (conversation with author, March 11, 1982), which does not correspond at all with S.'s account.
Ric et Rac. See Menguy's essay in *Mag. lit.*
"13" series. There has been some confusion as to whether these were written before or after *Pietr*, but the evidence points very strongly to before. See Menguy, in *Mag. lit.* and letter to Sigaux, *Homme*, 224, and *Mém.*, 27. De Fallois's chronology dates them after (p.31), and Ritzen's even later in the winter of 1930-31 (*Simenon, avocat des hommes*).
76-79   *Pietr.* ii, xv.
79   Simenon at Fayard. See *inter alia, Homme*, 141-42; *French Review* **19**

(Feb. 1946), 223–24; Max Favelli, *loc. cit.; Expansion,* Feb. 1971; *Mém.,* 410–11, 493; S. to Restrepo, Oct. 6, 1953; *Le Courrier de Paris,* Oct. 7, 1945; Gilles Lambert, "Les Introuvables de Georges Simenon," *Le Figaro,* Nov. 11, 1980; *Portrait,* 83.

79–80   Semi-alimentary. *Inter alia, French Review,* Feb. 1946, 223; *Portrait,* 83; *Paris-Match,* April 8, 1967.

80–81   Bal anthropométrique. *Paris-Midi,* Feb. 21, 1931; *L'Européen,* Feb. 25, 1931; *Paris Music-Hall,* March 15, 1931; *Sourire,* March 19, 1931; *Canard enchaîné,* Feb. 25, 1931.

81   Deauville. *Vacances,* 139–40; *Point,* 57–62.
     No such thing as detective story. Thoorens, 129.

85   Symons. *Mortal Consequences,* 143.

87–89   *Chien jaune.* i, ii, iii, ix, vii, iv, vi. One of the stories in *Les 13 Énigmes* has the same title but bears no similarity to this novel. In addition to Aymé's preface, *Le Chien jaune* is the subject of a book-length study by Régis Boyer, *Le Chien jaune de Georges Simenon* (Paris, 1973).

91–93   Reviews. *L'Information,* March 3, 1931; *Le Monde illustré,* March 7, 1931, April 18, 1931; *Sud-Ouest Républicain* (Bayonne), March 6, 1931; *Le Matin,* July 26, 1931; *Nouvelle Revue critique,* Sept. 1, 1931, June 10, 1931; *Divan,* April 1, 1931; *Maître-Jacques,* Sept. 1, 1931; *L'Action française,* Oct. 23, 1931, Aug. 11, 1932; *New Yorker,* Oct. 24, 1931, 62–63; *Le Canard enchaîné,* Feb. 10, 1932; *L'Intransigeant,* Feb. 4, 1933, May 18, 1932; *Cri de Paris,* Jan. 24, 1932; *Charivari,* Jan. 9, 1932; *Quotidien,* Jan. 12, 1932; *Quinzaine critique,* March 25, 1932; *Le Petit Journal,* Dec. 27, 1932; *Nouvelles littéraires,* Feb. 20, Dec. 31, 1932; *L'Oeuvre,* March 22, 1932; *Gringoire,* (?) 1937; *Mém.,* 411; *N.Y. Herald Tribune,* Sept. 4, 1932, July 2, 1933, Feb. 5, 1933; *Saturday Review,* Feb. 25, 1933; *Pittsburgh Press,* March 5, 1933; *Denver News,* Feb. 19, 1933; *N.Y. Times,* Feb. 5, 1933; *Sunday Dispatch,* Oct. 1, 1933; *TLS,* Aug. 16, 1934; *Evening Chronicle,* Oct. (?), 1933; *Marianne,* Nov. 28, 1934.

93–94   Fame, real P.J. *Mercure de France,* Feb. 1, 1932; Albany *Knickerbocker Press,* March 12, 1933; London *Morning Post,* Sept. 12, 1933; *Dossier,* 87–88; *Oiseau,* 81.

94   *La Folle d'Itteville. Vieux,* 320; S. to C. Menguy, June 22, 1979.

94–95   "Au fil de l'eau." *Figaro illustré,* May 1932; *Point,* 66.

95   Ouistreham, movies. *Vacances,* 142–41; *Point,* 63–71; Bresler, *op. cit.,* 91.

96   La Richardière. *Point,* 77–80; *Vent,* 116; *Banc,* 148; *Vieux,* 116, 199; *Prix,* 129–30; *Homme,* 268; *Sud-Ouest Dimanche,* Feb. 14, 1982; *Jurer,* 166–65.

96–97   Lifestyle. *Homme,* 144, 146, 108; Achard to S., April 12, 1967; *Vent,* 11, *Pas,* 187; *Marianne,* Jan. 3, 1934; *Charivari,* Dec. 9, 1933; *Mém.,* 32.

Chapter IX

99   Polarlys. *Nouvelle Revue critique,* Oct. 1932; *Mercure de France,* Oct. 1, 1932.

100   "L'Âne rouge" nightspot. *Li Clabot,* Feb. 1969.

102   First "roman dur." S., Feb. 19, 1979.

103   Source of *Hire. Gazette*, July 27, 1919. Cf. *La Meuse*, Oct. 14, 1953.
104   Grandmother Simenon. Drysdale, *op. cit.*, 338.
        Gallimard. *Choeur*, 11.
104-6   Reviews. *Le Crapouillot*, Aug. 1933; *Vie intellectuelle*, Dec. 10, 1934 (This is a quotation from Gérard Walker in *Monde*, Nov. 2, 1934); *Nouvelle revue critique*, Oct. 1933; *Ami du peuple*, May 2, 1933; *Cité universitaire*, Nov. 15, 1933; *La Liberté*, Oct. 1, 1934; *Le Rempart*, Sept. 18, 1933; *Le Matin*, Sept. 22, 1935; *Europe*, Oct. 15, 1935; *Le Matin*, Sept. 9, 1934; *La Liberté*, Oct. 11, 1936; *Le Temps*, May 9, 1935 (reprinted in *Cistre*, 238-42); *L'Humanité*, May 4, 1937; *Journal des instituteurs et institutrices*, Nov. 30, 1935; Max Jacob, letter to S., April 13, 1933 (in *Cistre*, 208-9).
106-10   African trip. *Homme nu*, 43-106, 255-60, 263-71; *Point*, 80-127; *Vent*, 156; *Choeur*, 73-75; *Pas*, 62, 234; *Banc*, 143, 162; *Froid*, 116; *Prix*, 64. S. identifies Wadi-Halfa as on the border of the Congo, but this town is on the northern border of the Sudan, with Egypt, not the southeastern, with the Congo. The *Voilà* series was called "L'Heure du Nègre" and appeared Oct. 8, 15, 22, 24, & Nov. 5 & 12, 1932. It is reprinted in *Homme nu*, pp. 43-106. Other pieces in this same volume, written a few years later, occasionally deal with Africa.
109-10   Mercier lawsuit. *Point*, 115-21; *Courrier colonial*, May 18, 1934.
110   Eastern Europe. *Homme*, 198-201; a very different version of the encounter with the prostitute at Vilna appeared in *Voilà*, April 1933. Trotsky. *Paris-Soir*, June 16-17, 1933 (in L. & S., 302-20).
111-12   Journalism. *Marianne*, July-Sept. 1934, June 24, 1934); *Paris-Soir*, Feb. 6-16, 1936 (reprinted in L. & S., 321-68), Jan.-April 1934; *Voilà*, April 22, 1933; *Le Jour*, Oct.-Nov. 1934; *Nouvelles littéraires*, Feb. 7, 1963; *Pas*, 237; *Destinées*, 84-86.

Chapter X

113   Income. *Expansions*, Feb. 1971. (This is not a reliable source, but these figures, roughly, are plausible enough.)
114   Oustrick, lifestyle. *Homme*, 242-43; *Pas*, 77.
114-15   World trip. *Homme nu*, 159-95, & passim; *Point*, 55; Bresler, *op. cit.*, 102; *Arbre*, 84; *Main*, 62-65; *Playboy; Homme*, 160-61; *Vieux*, 211; *Soixante*, 22; Bresler, *op. cit.*, 119; *Jurer*, 22 ("Adventure Is Dead" was printed in 1945 in *Les Étincelles* in Lyons).
115-16   Cour-Dieu. *Vieux*, 198-99; *Homme*, 146-47, 198; *Vent*, 116; *Destinées*, 122; *Soixante*, 16-17; *Cave*, 174; *Life*, Nov. 3, 1958.
116-17   Richard-Wallace, lifestyle. *Vent*, 116, 99; *Homme*, 145, 228; *Cave*, 77-78; *Vieux*, 310; *Soixante*, 21, 24; *Vacances*, 86-87; *Mém.*, 33-34, 37; *Vivant*, 143-44; *Arbre*, 100-10 (the program prints the French version of the songs); *Banc*, 107; S. to Gide, Jan. 1939, in L. & S., 396.
117-18   Nieul. *Mém.*, 12, 38-41; *Homme*, 145, 229; *Pas*, 63.

Notes

118-19   Relations with Tigy. *Vieux*, 211, 309; *Homme*, 160, 188-89; S. to Restrepo, Nov. 1953; *Prix*, 15; *Mém.*, 40, 107-8; *Destinées*, 48.
119   *Sans-Haine. Le Journal*, Jan. 6, Feb. 10, 1938; *Echo de Thionville*, Feb. 12, 1938.
121   Becker. 74.
      Engineer in gold mine. *La Mauvaise Étoile*, ii.
122   Coffee plantation owner. *Ibid.*, xi.
122-24   *Donadieu. Vieux*, 119 (the Balzac comparison recurs in contemporary reviews: e.g., *L'Intransigeant*, April 21, 1937); Gide to S., Jan. 1939, & March 11, 1948, in L. & S., 401 & 438; *Le Merle blanc*, April 10, 1937; *Figaro*, April 3, 1937; *Le Temps*, May 27, 1937; Henriot to S., Mar. 26, 1937 (in *Cistre*, 211).
123-24   *Marie du port. L'Intransigeant*, Oct. 27, 1938, where Thérive quotes S. The "manifesto" itself appeared as a publicity leaflet issued by Gallimard: *Cahiers d'annonces de la N.R.F.*, Nov. 1938 (reprinted in O.C. **11**, 9-10). *Le Temps*, Jan. 5, 1939; Gide to S., Dec. 31, 1938 (L. & S., 393); S. to Gide, Jan. 1939 (L. & S., 402); *Marie*, ch. ii.
126   *Bourgmestre.* S. to Gide, Jan. 1939 (L. & S., 403, 405). Thérive uses the term "pièce de maîtrise" in *Le Temps*, Jan. 5, 1939.
      Faubourg. Gide to S., May 2, 1948 (L. & S., 440).
129   *Cour d'assises.* x.
129-30   *Inconnus. Le Fait*, Feb. 1941; postcard from Gide, July 8, 1941 (L. & S., 415).
130-31   Admirers & critics. *Gril*, 30; Gide to S., March 11, 1948 (L. & S., 438); Farrère to S., Nov. 27, 1941 (in *Cistre*, 213); Mauriac to S., April 23, 1937 (in *Cistre*, 212); *Le Matin*, Aug. 27, 1939; *Le Journal*, Feb. 25, 1940; *L'Époque*, Feb. 19, 1940.
131   Keyserling. S. to Gide, Jan. 1939 (L. & S., 397); *Writers*, 157; Keyserling to S., Feb. 28, 1937, April 17, 1937, Feb. 25, 1937.
132-34   Gide. For beginning of relationship, see *Paris Review* interview, 157. S. dates this meeting in 1936, but that is almost certainly too early. S. is casual about dates. (In the same context he says he had met Keyserling five years earlier, which is even more improbable.) Quentin Ritzen (*op. cit.*) dates the first meeting with Gide in 1935, which, since he provides no evidence, seems also too early. Gide to S. Dec. 31, 1938 (L. & S., 392-3); *Journals* 1939-49 (Pléiade), 259-60; Gide to S., Dec. 1 & 16 (L. & S., 435-36); Gide to S., Dec. 31, 1938 (L. & S., 393); Gide to S., Jan. 6, 1939 (L. & S., 394); Gide to S., Aug. 21, 1942 (L. & S., 419); S. to Gide, Jan. 1939 (L. & S., 396-405); S. to Gide, Dec. 1939 (L. & S., 412; the novels he is referring to are *Bergelon, Il pleut, bergère...*, and *L'Oncle Charles s'est enfermé* [he has already forgotten the exact title of the last, calling it "L'Oncle Charles a disparu"]).

Chapter XI

136   *Le Jour.* Feb. 19, 1934.

136-37   Recreational factor. *Mém.*, 241; S. to Restrepo, Dec. 11, 1953.

137   Narcejac. *The Art of Simenon*, 118-19 (translation of *Le Cas Simenon*); cf. *Mag. lit.*

137-38   Maigret revival. See Claude Menguy, "La Fausse Sortie de Maigret," *Le Chasseur d'illustrés*, July, 1971, 2-3, and "Simenon chez Offenstadt," *Le Chercheur*, Feb.-March 1973, 14-17. Cf. *Mém.*, 40. Confusion reigns on this subject. In a recent book on Simenon, for example, Denis Tillinac writes of Maigret, "Simenon le ressuscite une première fois en 1938, puis il disparait jusqu'à la Libération pour faire alors un 'come-back' définitif" (*Le Mystère Simenon*, 122). For Gavin Lambert, the "later Maigret" begins in 1949 (*The Dangerous Edge*, 179). Narcejac, on the other hand, sees a firm "later Maigret" in *Cécile est morte* (*op. cit.*, 119).

138   Dr. de Béchevel. T.S.

138-40   *Cécile est morte*. 3, i.

141   *Félicie est là*. vii.

141-43   War. *Pas*, 44, 210; S. to Gide, Dec. 1939 (L. & S., 412); *Vieux*, 78-79, 359; *Mém.*, 71-75, 89-91, 77-78, 32, 108-9; *Destinées*, 122; *Homme*, 150; *Mon Copain*, Feb. 13, 1944; *La Légia*, June 20, 1943; *Point*, 169-79; *Gril*, 51; *Nouvelles littéraires*, Nov. 28, 1968; Bresler, *op. cit.*, 152-54. The standard version of the heart condition episode appears in innumerable texts (e.g., the Preface to the 1961 edition of *Souviens*); see also *Mém.*, 79-83, and *Oiseau*, 171-72.

143-44   Paris. *Porte*, 55-56; *Mém.*, 122-23; *Prix*, 21-22; S. to Gide, June 1945 (L. & S., 427).

144-47   *Pedigree*. *L'Ouest-Éclair* (Rennes), June 4, 1941; *Figaro*, Oct. 23-24, 1942; Jean Jour, *Simenon et Pedigree*, 13-14; "M. & Mme. Bernard Buffet," *Jours de France*, Feb. 14, 1959; *Parinaud*, 388; *Vieux*, 222; *L'Express*, Feb. 6, 1958; L. & S., 414, 450-51; Gide to S., Sept. 19, 1941 (L. & S., 415); Gide, Journal entry of July 6, 1942, p. 126; Gide to S., Aug. 21, 1942 (L. & S., 418); Gide to S., Dec. 11, 1944 (L. & S., 420; Gide had broached the subject of Simenon's preoccupation with losers in the letter of Aug. 21, 1942, in L. & S., 418); S. to Gide, Dec. 18, 1944 (L. & S., 423); S. to Gide, Oct. 6, 1948 (L. & S., 442); Gide to S., Dec. 29, 1948 (L. & S., 442).

147   "L'Age du roman." *Confluences*. nos. 21-24, 1943 (reprinted in O.C. **27**, 267-71); the interview is in *Clartés*, July 20, 1945. Billy: *La Bataille*, Aug. 9, 1945; *Le Figaro*, Oct. 24-25, 1942; *Le Monde illustré*, Sept. 22, 1945.

149   *Monde*, vii; *Vieux*, 251.

150   Critics inclined. e.g., Marcel Moré, "Simenon et l'enfant de choeur," in L. & S., 245-46.

         Gide on *Veuve Couderc*. To S., July 14, 1945 (L. & S., 430).

151   Cowley. Introduction to *Writers*, 12 (originally published in *New Republic*, Dec. 9, 1957).

         "La Révolte du canari." S. says he wrote this story during his early days in Paris (*Arbre*, 173). It was published in *Gringoire*, July 15, 1940.

151-52   Presses de la Cité. *Figaro littéraire*, May 7, 1965; S., March 4, 1982. Preface to *Traqué* reprinted in L. & S., 369-72.

Chapter XII

153   Preparation for U.S. trip. *Prix*, 15-16; *Mém.*, 126-27; *France-Soir* articles in *Homme nu*, 281-86.
153-55   First impressions. *Prix*, 22-28, 37-38, 41, 44-47, 84, 89-92; *Homme*, 302; *Mém.*, 363-64; *Information et documents*, Aug. 1, 1964; *Homme nu*, 306-7, 310-15.
155   Sainte-Marguerite. *Espoir*, 1946 (this is a press clipping in the Simenon files in Liège, with no further indication of the date or the periodical in question). *Prix*, 9, 18; *Oiseau*, 55; *Mém.*, 131-32.
155-58   Denyse. *Homme nu*, 329; *Oiseau*, 9-69; *Vivant*, 159-62; *Homme*, 290-91; *Vieux*, 209; *Froid*, 44-45; *Mém.*, 132 ff. The account of her reading *Liberty-Bar* is hers, but it seems unlikely that it was available at the Philadelphia station in French, while in English it was available only in a triple volume. As to the $3000 check, S. makes it $200 in *Mém.*, 133. On her feigned orgasm, see *Mém.*, 141. On burning letters, see *Oiseau*, 90-91; cf. *Mém.*, 159-60.
159-60   *Trois Chambres*. *Oiseau*, 78-79; *Vieux*, 148; *Réalité*, Nov. 1961; Pierre Benoît to S., Jan. 29, 1957; Gide to S., Feb. 12 & 16, 1948 (L. & S., 436). Denyse says that *Maigret à New York* was the first book S. wrote after her arrival at Sainte-Marguerite, but it is explicitly dated March 7, 1946, and *Trois Chambres* Jan. 7, 1946.
160   Alcohol. *Marie-France*, Aug. 1979; *Vent*, 71; *Vieux*, 224-25; *Express Rhône-Alpes*, Nov. 1970; *Arbre*, 12; S. to Restrepo, Sept. 21, 1951; *Pas*, 139; *Mém.*, 168-69, 278-79; Bresler, *op. cit.*, 193-94; *Nouvelles littéraires*, Feb. 5, 1948; *Time*, July 2, 1951; *Oiseau*, 76-77.
161   Maritimes. *Oiseau*, 85; *Mém.*, 170.
161-62   North-south trip. *Homme nu*, 343-437; *Prix*, passim; *Oiseau*, 102-6; *Mém.*, 174-83.
162   Bradenton Beach. *Prix*, 78-80; *Oiseau*, 106-8; *Homme nu*, 431-34; *Mém.*, 185-90.
162-63   Denise & business affairs. *Oiseau*, 107; *Mém.*, 193, 216, 220, 314, 380. For Denise & publishers: Wolff, McCormick.
163   Cuban brothel. *Oiseau*, 109-13; *Mém.*, 192, 391; *Life*, Nov. 3, 1958. Trip west. *Oiseau*, 119-23; *Prix*, 53-54, 67-68; *Mém.*, 193-204; *Nouvelles littéraires*, Feb. 5, 1948.
164   Tumacacori. *Prix*, 69-75; *Oiseau*, 128-33, 138-39; *Mém.*, 217-20, 236, 208-13, 216, 228-29; *Vieux*, 338; Vlaminck to S., Dec. 11, 1948; S. to Gide, Oct. 4, 1948 (L. & S., 441); Renoir to S., Sept. 11, 1948.
165   Johnny, Carmel, divorce. *Mém.*, 234-35, 243, 247-48, 255-60, 263, 273-79; *Oiseau*, 144-47, 151-54; *Newsweek*, May 1, 1950; *Traces*, 120; *Homme*, 295, 302-3.
166   Gide. To S., May 2, 1948 & Nov. 29, 1950 (L. & S., 440, 448-49).

"Placing" S. *New Yorker*, Jan. 24, 1953; *Paris-Soir*, Sept. 6, 1941; *Gavroche*, Nov. 21, 1946; *France-Illustration*, July 1948; *Ici Paris*, Nov. 18, 1947.

167 "Blessed Are the Meek." *N.Y. Times*, March 19, 1948; *Ellery Queen Magazine*, April 1949; *Mystère-Magazine*, May 1949. American press. *Newsweek*, July 10, 1946; *S.F. Chronicle* quoted in *Multiplying Villainies*, ed. R.E. Briney & F.M. Nevins, 31; *French Review* **19** (Feb. 1946).

168 Denise on *Lettre à mon juge. Oiseau*, 79.

168-69 *La Neige était sale. Mém.*, 202; Renoir to S., Dec. 28, 1950, Dec. 30, 1950, Jan. 29, 1951.

169-70 S. & Raimu. "Raimu le colosse," *Arts*, Jan. 18, 1958 (reprinted in *Cistre*, 263-65); S. to Restrepo, Nov. 17, 1953; Vlaminck, *Portraits avant décès*, 258-62.

Chapter XIII

172-74 Shadow Rock Farm. *Oiseau*, 156-59, 174-76; *Mém.*, 292-314, 317-18, 344-50; S. to Restrepo, Nov. 1953, Jan. 4 & Feb. 8, 1954; *Paris-Match*, March 23, 1953; *Time*, July 2, 1957; *New Yorker*, Jan. 24, 1953; S. to Miller, Aug. 13, 1954; McCormick; *Bulletin de Paris*, June 21, 1956; J. McAleen, *Rex Stout*, 406; Marcel Hichter, "Un Dimanche avec Simenon," *Synthèse*, April 1952; *Froid*, 126.

174 Anaïs Nin. *Diary of Anaïs Nin* (N.Y.: Harvest/HBJ, 1975), V, 44; V, 47; VI, 12; VI, 100; VI, 229; V, 122.

174-75 Miller. To S., March 23, 1954, April 23, 1954 (reprinted in *Cistre*, 223), May 27, 1954, Aug. 11 (1954?).

175 Other admirers. Wilder to S., June 30, 1953, July 15, 1953; Ted Morgan, *Maugham*, 598; *Newsweek*, April 20, 1970; Faulkner, *Writers*, 137. Moré's essay, "Simenon et l'enfant de choeur," appeared in *Dieu vivant* #19, 1951 (reprinted in L. & S., 227-63). The Simenon-Mambrino correspondence is in *Cistre*, 216-22. Henriette's remark in *La Meuse*, March 10, 1952.

175-76 Critics. *Nouvelles littéraires*, June 24, 1954; *Nouveaux jours*, May 25, 1951; *Saturday Review*, Oct. 11, 1952; *Oklahoman*, Feb. 8, 1952; *N.Y. Herald Tribune*, May 28, 1950; *Washington Star*, July 1, 1951; *Le Figaro*, Jan. 30, 1951; *New Republic*, Jan. 5, 1952; *New Yorker*, Nov. 8, 1952; *N.Y. Herald Tribune*, Feb. 22, 1953; *Saturday Review*, Feb. 21, 1953; *New World Writing* (N.Y., 1952), 234-45; *Arizona Quarterly*, an essay by N.J. Tremblay, Autumn, 1954; *N.Y. Times Book Review*, May, 1950; *Look*, Nov. 25, 1953; *Life*, Nov. 3, 1958; *New Yorker*, Jan. 24, 1953; Claude Mauriac, *L'Alitérature contemporaine* (Paris, 1958); Narcejac, *Le Cas Simenon*, 169, 177.

177-78 Literary declarations. *Combat*, Nov. 15, 1959; S. to Restrepo, Nov. 23, 1953; letter to Cocteau, *Arts et spectacles*, Oct. 5-11, 1955 (reprinted in *Cistre*, 243-55); Parinaud, 401; *Mém.*, 202-3, 420-21; *Vacances*, 75; Mambrino, in *Cistre*, 218-19; (in conversation with author, March 4, 1982, S. identified *Lettre à mon juge*, written at Bradenton Beach in 1946, as the first two-step novel); *Writers*, 154–60.

178 Financial success. S. to Renoir, Sept. 19, 1954; *Oiseau*, 195; *New Yorker* "Profile"; *Figaro littéraire*, Feb. 16, 1963. *Life*, Nov. 3, 1958 (cf. *Mém.*, 341, where S. says *Neige* came out with a 2 million printing); *Expansions*, Feb. 1971; *Oiseau*, 174; *Lui*, June, 1967; *Jurer*, 92; *Paris-Match*, April 21, 1960; author's conversation with Claude Nielsen, March 12, 1982; "Sur la propriété littéraire," *Arts*, Oct. 3–9, 1956 (reprinted in L. & S., 373–79); McCormick.

179 Remarks on writing. *Portrait*, 127; *Mém.*, 364; S. to Restrepo, Nov. 1958.

180–82 Comments on books. *Portrait*, 127; *Mém.*, 364; S. to Restrepo, Nov. 1958; Wilder to S., March 4, 1953; Miller to S., June 6 (1960?); S. to Wilder, Aug. 5, 1954; *Writers*, 155; Renoir to S., Jan. 9, 1952. On original of Ashby, see *Mém.*, 364–65; the dates don't coincide, but S. acknowledges a poor sense of chronology; the teacher's den and woodworking hobby are almost identical with Ashby's.

183 Académie Française, Nobel prize. See *inter alia, Ici Paris*, July 17, 1950; *Nouvelles littéraires*, Nov. 28, 1963. *Marie-France* in Aug. 1979 reports a bit hyperbolically that S. has already refused the Nobel prize three times and asks him if he intends to make an exception on the 50th anniversary of Maigret's birth. S.'s answer is that he doesn't intend to change his habits, and immediately changes the subject. See also *Vent*, 30; *Vieux*, 337.

183–84 Trips to Europe. *Oiseau*, 165–73; *Mém.*, 320–34; *Vieux*, 211–12, 268; *New Yorker* "Profile"; *Le Havre*, March 18, 1952; S. to Restrepo, Nov. 9, Nov. 27, 1953; *Lettre*, 38; *Hommes et mondes*, Dec. 1954; *Combat*, Nov. 15, 1954.

184 Leaving America. *Oiseau*, 176–77; *Mém.*, 369–70. Denise states that they sailed on the *Liberté*, but a local reporter has them arriving on the *Île-de-France*.

Chapter XIV

185 Arrival in France. *Paris-Normandie*, March 28, 1955; *Mém.*, 378.

186 Côte d'Azur. *Le Soir illustré* (Brussels), Aug. 28, 155; *Mém.*, 377, 413–17; *Vieux*, 61; *Oiseau*, 180; *Sud-Ouest Dimanche*, Jan. 1, 1956; Renoir to S., March 29, 1957.

186–87 Echandens. *L'Express Dimanche*, Jan. 9–10, 1960; *Dossier*, 89; *Marie France*, June 1958; *Elle*, Aug. 20, 1960; *Oiseau*, 198–99; *Pas*, 153; *Soixante*, 157; *Mém.*, 438, 466–67; Renoir to S., March 29, 1957; Miller's remarks in *Candide*, May 11, 1961 (in L. & S., 268–71); *Vieux*, 148; *Nouvelles littéraires*, Dec. 8, 1960.

188 Sex. *Pas*, 71–72; *Arbre*, 134–36; *Porte*, 69; *Femme*, 144–47; *Mém.*, 576–77.

Finances. *Mém.*, 440–41, 446–47; *Paris-Match*, April 21, 1960; *Le Figaro littéraire*, Feb. 11, 1963; *Liberté* (Clermont-Ferrant), Dec. 9,

1963; *Elle*, Aug. 26, 1960; *Portrait*, 93-94; *Soixante*, 68; *Paris-Match*, April 21, 1960; *Arbre*, 110-11.

188-89 Cannes Festival. *L'Express*, Feb. 21, 17, 1977; *Vivant*, 117-19; Achard to S., June 4, 1960; *Mém.*, 442-43.

189 Surface lifestyle. *Sud-Ouest*, Oct. 30, 1960; *La Vie en fleur*, June 10, 1961; *Figaro*, May 7, 1963; *Elle*, Aug. 26, 1960; *Liberté* (Clermont-Ferrant), Dec. 11, 1963; *Daily Telegraph*, March 2, 1972.
Fitzgerald interview. *Baltimore Sun*, Oct. 7, 1923.

189-90 Marital crisis. *Homme*, 234, 254-55, 189-90; *Oiseau*, 188-91, & passim; *Froid*, 22, 45ff; *Mém.*, 380-81, 393, 404-5, 410, 444-45, 467, & passim; *Vieux*, 313, 184, 182-83, 194-95, 220, 202; McCormick; Helen Wolff, interview with author, Dec. 1, 1978; *Homme*, 189-90; S. to Renoir, Feb. 15, 1960; Pagnol to S., Sept. 19, 1961; *Passage de la ligne*, III, ii.

191-93 Literary dejection. *Vieux*, 13, 14, 77, 107-8, 119-20, 139, 143, 145, 231-33, 375-76, 388-89, 398, 140-41, 160, 177; *Oiseau*, 194-97; Achard to S., June 4, 1960; author's conversation with Gilbert Sigaux, March 15, 1981 (*re Betty*); *Petits*, 94; *Froid*, 46; *Mém.*, 445-46; *Roman de l'homme* (Paris, 1959), 20-21 (this was originally a lecture given at the Brussels World's Fair on Oct. 3, 1958, and published serially in *Arts*, Nov. 12-Dec. 9, 1958).

194-95 *Le Président*. *Life*, Nov. 3, 1958 (predictably, S. has also denied the Clémenceau model: Raymond, *op. cit.*, 20-21); *Le Président*, v. Becker misreads the action as regards the damaging document, thinking it has been taken away, which makes the point much less subtle (135-36; the relevant passage in *Le Président* is in ch. v. O.C. **34**, 398-400).

195-96 *Les Anneaux de Bicêtre*. *Cistre*, 48-49; *Revue de Paris*, Oct. 1963; *Combat*, May 9, 1963; *Le Figaro*, May 7, 1963; Claudine Gothot-Mersch, "La Genèse des *Anneaux de Bicêtre*," in *Cistre* 79-104; *Gril*, 44.

196 "Community." See also, e.g., *La Mort de Belle*.
Chaplin persona. *Vieux*, 149-50.

197 Praise & critiques. Achard to S., undated (probably ca. 1961); Renoir to S., May 22 & June 17, 1963; Pagnol, typescript, Feb. 1961; *Le Figaro*, Jan. 30, 1957; *Fig. lit.*, Jan. 16, 1960; *Nouvelles littéraires*, Nov. 13, 1958; *London New Daily & Birmingham Mail*, Sept. 1962 (exact dates unavailable); *Le Monde*, Jan. 5, 1963; Mauriac: *Fig. lit.*, May 11, 1963 (in L. & S., 283-84); *Tagesspiegel*, Aug. 26, 1964; *TLS*, Dec. 5, 1963; *N.Y. Times*, April 4, 1964; *Washington Post*, date uncertain, 1964; *Atlantic Monthly*, June, 1964.

Chapter XV

199-200 Épalinges, friends. *Oiseau*, 201-2; C. Day Lewis, "The Man Who Isn't There," *Weekend Telegraph*, May 26, 1967; *Le Figaro*, March 20, 1964, Nov. 4, 1965; *Bonne Soirée*, Sept. 24, 1972; *Vendredi, Samedi, Dimanche*, June 8, 1978; *Homme*, 308; *Vent*, 117; *Choeur*, 23;

Notes

	Mém., 458–60, 469–70, 501; *L'Express*, Feb. 21–27, 1977; *Porte*, 58–59; S. to Fellini, Dec. 17, 1969, Jan. 14 & 17, 1977; Fellini to S., Sept. 22, 1969.
200	Lifestyle. *Paris-Match*, April 8, 1967; *Vent*, 168–9; *Soixante*, 56–57.
201–2	Deteriorating marriage. *Mém.*, 473–569 & passim; *Froid*, 46–47; *Oiseau*, 200–46; Drysdale, *op. cit.*, 103, 93; Achard, to S. July 10, 1964; Renoir to S., Sept. 5, 1967, April 2, 1968, Dec. 2, 1968, Feb. 22, 1969. The masturbation incident is described on pp. 495–6, 719 & 721 of the unexpurgated edition of *Mém.* Author's conversation with Mme. Denyse Simenon, March 1982.
202–3	Marie-Jo. *Liberté*, 100–1; *Mém.*, 599, 751 & passim; *Arbre*, 128; *Pas*, 149, 167, 192; *Homme*, 153.
203–4	*Henriette. Mém.*, 516–17, 545–46; *Cave*, 160; *Homme*, 273; author's conversation with Mme. Colette Desruelle, March 21, 1979.
204–5	Teresa. *Homme*, 191, 308, 313; *Arbre*, 44; *Pas*, 74; *Mém.*, 465–66, 468, 510–13, 539; *Liberté*, 127; *Oiseau*, 199; *Femme*, 148; *Main*, 55.
205–7	*Le Petit Saint. Mém.*, 493–94; *Le Monde*, June 5, 1965; *Le Petit Saint*, II, i.
207	*La Mort d'Auguste.* Achard to S., April 12, 1967.
208	*Il y a encore des noisetiers.* v; Renoir to S., March 29, 1969, & May 22, 1969.
	Date of *Odile*. See *Mém.*, 572, 583.
209	*Le Chat. Nouvelles littéraires*, March 1967; Achard to S., April 12, 1967; *Le Figaro*, May 22, 1967.
210	Critics. *L'Express*, June 14–20, 1965; *New Yorker*, Dec. 18, 1965, Sept. 1967; *Sat. Rev.*, Oct. 30, 1965; *Le Figaro*, May 12, 1970; *TLS*, March 24, 1972; *N.Y. Times*, Oct. 24, 1971; *Manchester Guardian*, March 11, 1972; *Sunday Telegraph*, Feb. 27, 1972.
211	Decision to stop writing. *Homme*, 7; *Mém.*, 589; *Newsweek*, Feb. 19, 1973.
211–13	Lifestyle, mood. *Monde*, June 11, 1978; S., March 4, 1982; *Pas*, 282, 243, 91, 93, 190; *Mém.*, 591–92; *Destinées*, 61; Swiss TV interview, Feb. 1975; *Pas*, 117; *Petits*, 35–36; *Jurer*, 45–63, 81–85, 97–107, 123–34; *Homme*, 209–10, 292–93; *Pas*, 32.
213	Relations with Denyse. *Oiseau*, 248, 256–59 (but cf. Bresler, *op. cit.*, 214); *Mém.*, 572–73; *Petits*, 93; *Froid*, 47; *Destinées*, 49–57. Author's conversation with Mme. Denyse Simenon, March 1982.
213–14	Marie-Jo's suicide. *Destinées*, 29–31; *Froid*, 22–36; *Mém.*, 594–733; *Soixante*, 77ff; *Porte*, 56–57.
214	Dictées. *Mém.*, 591; *Homme*, 9, 68; *Jour*, 7–9; *Femme*, 7; *Froid*, 57–58; Tillinac, *op. cit.*, 180; Fellini to S., Oct. 30, 1976.
215	*Mémoires*. S., March 4, 1982; *Nouvel Observateur*, Nov. 28, 1981; *Le Point*, Nov. 16–22, 1981; author's conversation with Claude Nielsen, March 12, 1982.

Chapter XVI

218   Narcejac. *op. cit.*, esp. 15 & 115–17.
     Boucher. *N.Y. Times*, Oct. 11, 1953.
     Same themes in Maigrets & non–Maigrets. *Portrait*, 118; *Dossier*, 46;
     Wilder to S., March 4, 1953.

218–23 Maigret details. Eyesight (*L'Écluse numéro un*, x); fall asleep (*La Maison du juge*, iii); claustrophobic (*M. se défend*, vi); short of breath (*M. et M. Charles*, i); files ("Stan le tueur," iii); leaves badge (*M. et l'homme du banc*, i); straightens pictures (*L'Inspecteur cadavre*, viii); picking locks (*M. au Picratt's*, ix); drive a car (*M. chez le ministre*, vii, *Le Voleur de M.*, i); bus platforms (*M. et l'homme tout seul*; iii, *Le Voleur de M.*, i); cigarette (*M. et les vieillards*, iii); cigar (*Le Révolver de M.*, viii); psychiatric treatises (*Les Scrupules de M.*, iii); Dumas (*M. et son mort*, iii); no detective stories (*M. à New York*, ii); television (*M. et le marchand de vin*, v; *M. et le client du samedi*, iii); movies (*M., Lognon et les gangsters*, v); "there are books in every corner" (*M. chez le ministre*, iii); first kiss (*La Folle de M.*, vi; *M. se défend*, viii); terms of endearment (*M. et le fantôme*, vi); grog (*M. et le marchand de vin*, i); blue scarf (*ibid.*, i); "he had rarely been so eager" (*M. se défend*, iv); nothing in a restaurant (*ibid.*, v); Mme. M's sister (*Mon Ami M.*, i); children ("Le Notaire de Chateauneuf," i; *L'Écluse numéro un*, iv; *M. et l'homme du banc*, iv); Lucas "grassouillet" (*Mon Ami M.*, ii); M.'s double (*Un Noël de M.*, iv); Janvier (*M. se défend*, iii; *M. et M. Charles*, ii; *M. se trompe*, i); Lapointe (*L'Amie de Mme. M.*, iii; *Les Scrupules de M.*, iii; *M. et M. Charles*, i); Xavier Guichard (*Les Mémoires de M.*, i; *La Première Enquête de M.*, ix); new director (*M. se défend*, i); the real Dr. Paul (*Mém.*, 322); Gastine-Renette (*M. se trompe*, iv — but Moers appears in the first chapter); Lognon doesn't drink (*M., Lognon et les gangsters*, ii); ris de veau (*La Folle de M.*, vi; *M. et M. Charles*, i); blanquette (*M. et le marchand de vin*, i; *Un Échec de M.*, ii); tête de veau (*Le Révolver de M.*, ix); tripes (*M. et M. Charles*, iii); hareng (*La Folle de M.*, ii); sole (*M. chez le ministre*, vi); bouillabaisse (*M. et l'indicateur*, v); maqueraux (*M. et le tueur*, iii); langouste (*M. s'amuse*, iv); homard à l'américaine (*Le Révolver de M.*, viii); escargots (*M. et le tueur*, iv); rillettes, goat cheese, baba, coq au vin (*ibid.*, vi); robins (*Mon ami M.*, ii); fricandeau (*La Folle de M.*, iv); pot-au-feu (*M. et M. Charles*, v); raie (*M. et le marchand de vin*, vi); pintadeau en croûte (*M. et l'indicateur*, i); boeuf bourguignon (*M. et le tueur*, i); cassoulet, couscous, brandade de morue (*Le Révolver de M.*, i); rice pudding (*La Folle de M.*, ii); Maigret ate better than Nero Wolfe (McAleen, *op. cit.*, 520); whiskey (e.g., *M. et l'affaire Nahour*, vi; *La Patience de M.*, iii); champagne (*La Patience de M.*, iv); martini (*M. voyage*, v); cognac in the office (e.g., *M. s'amuse*, viii); marc (*M. se fâche*, viii; *La Patience de M.*, ii); calvados (e.g., *La Première Enquête de M.*, iv); prunelle, framboise (e.g., *M. et le marchand de vin*, v; *M., Lognon et les gangsters*, ii); mandarin-curaçao (*Mémoires de M.*, vii);

hangover (e.g., *M. chez le ministre*, iii; *M. a peur*, i); Beaujolais
(e.g., *La Folle de M.*, ii); rosé de Provence (*ibid.*, vi); Chateauneuf-
du-pape (*M. et l'indicateur*, i); Chianti (*M. en colère*, ii); Sancerre
(*M. et le tueur*, ii); Vouvray (*ibid.*, iv); Dr. Pardon (*M. à Vichy*, i;
M. et l'indicateur, iv); British church authorities (*Portrait*, 94);
Évaride Maigret (see *Un Échec de M.*, i, etc.); M's names (see
Menguy, "Maigret proteste" [*Désiré* #20, Feb. 1969]; cf. *M. se
fâche*, i); lost mother (*Le Révolver de M.*, viii); clients (e.g., *M. a peur;
Un Échec de M.; L'Ami d'enfance de M.*); Lycée (*L'Ami d'enfance de M.*,
i); medical school (*M. a peur*, i; *M. hésite*, i; *La Première Enquête de
M.*, v); psychiatrist (*M. hésite*, viii); comes to Paris (*L'Ami d'enfance
de M.*, v); M.'s early career (*La Folle de M.*, i; *M. se défend*, i; *M.,
Lognon et les gangsters*, v; *Les Mémoires de M.*, ii); Gare du Nord (*Les
Mémoires de M.*, v); "Vente à la bougie" (this story is included in
the grossly mistitled *M. et les petits cochons sans queue*; it is the only
Maigret story there); offered directorship (*M. et M. Charles*, i);
sunny café terraces (*Le Voleur de M.*, i); place des Vosges (*M. se défend*, viii); choirboy memories (*L'Affaire Saint-Fiacre; M. et les
vieillards*, i; "Le Témoignage de l'enfant de choeur"); furnishing
country house (*M. aux assises*, i); collector of men (*M. et le fantôme*,
vii; cf. *Destinées*, 152); political wheeling and dealing (*M. chez le
ministre*, v); first names (*M., Lognon et les gangsters*, i).

224 *Les Scrupules de M.* iii.
M. tend un piège. ii.
Un Échec de M. iv.
M. et le clochard. iv. *M. à Vichy.* iii.

225 "Whereas for us." *M. à Vichy.* iii.

226 "Genuine masterpiece." *France nouvelle*, May 28, 1948.

228 S.'s concern with criminal justice. Raymond, *op. cit.*, 113; *Portrait*,
108–22; *Gril*, 383; cf. S.'s articles, "L'Homme devant les hommes,"
in *La Vie judiciaire*, Jan. 1958, and "L'Article 64," in *Le Crapouillot*,
March 1969.
Angelot, prefect. *M. et les témoins récalcitrants*, i; *M. se défend*, i.
M. aux assises. iii.

229 "It occasionally happened." *M. et les témoins récalcitrants*, iv.

230 *Une Confidence de M.* vii.

230–31 Déclic. e.g., *La Première Enquête de M.*, iv (where, one might note, the
"déclic" comes after a number of shots of calvados). Cf. *M. à New
York*, viii.

231 *M. Voyage.* i. Cf. *M. se fâche*, viii.
Dreams. *M. et la jeune morte*, vii; *M. et les vieillards*, vi; *M. et les témoins
récalcitrants*, vii; *Un Échec de M.*, vii.
Stay with momentum. *La Colère de M.*, vi.
Trance-like state. e.g., *M. à New York; M. et la vieille dame*, i.

231–32 Metaphors. *M. et les témoins récalcitrants*, iv (cf. *M. et son mort*, iv); *M.
et l'inspecteur malgracieux*, ii; *M. à New York*, viii; "Le Témoignage
de l'enfant de choeur," ii; *Le Voleur de M.*, v.

Chapter XVII

236   "I always distrust." *M. et le marchand de vin*, ii.
Speedy writers. *Portrait*, 124–25; *Nouvelles littéraires*, Nov. 28, 1963, *et al*.

236–38   Method of composition. *Paris-Match*, April 21, 1960; *Marie-France*, Aug. 1979; *Mém.*, 558, 562–63; *Nouvelles littéraires*, Nov. 28, 1963; *Gril*, 41, 6–7, 28; *Dossier*, 43, 94; *Vieux*, 351; *Newsweek*, Feb. 19, 1973; *Life*, Nov. 3, 1958; Oran *Echo*, March 30, 1950; *Destinées*, 98; *Parinaud*, 403 (cf. *Paris-Match*, Nov. 26, 1955 & *Vacances*, 75); *Pas*, 227; *Porte*, 59; S. to Gide, undated, probably, March 1939 (L. & S., 410).

239–42   Search for man. *Mag. lit.; Homme*, 158; *Vacances*, 82; *Pas*, 124, 76, 65–66 (cf. *Vent*, 25), 219; *Mém.*, 437; *Playboy; Vieux*, 44; *Destinées*, 82ff; Nicholas Delbanco, *Group Portrait* (New York, 1982).

242–49   Techniques & style. *Le Clan des Ostendais*, v; *Le Fils Cardinaud*, iii; *Cour d'assises*, viii; *Le Rapport du gendarme*, iii; *Le Petit Saint*, iv; *Les Bourgmestre de Furnes*, iii; picaresque novel, *Vieux*, 161; *La Vieille*, iv; dismissing grammatical errors, *Parinaud*, 395; *Jurer*, 19; *Mém.*, 7; *M. et le clochard*, viii; *Le Nègre*, iv; *La Cage de verre & Mém.*, passim (for "alimonie"); *Les Frères Rico*, ix, viii; *Les Anneaux de Bicêtre*, iii; *La Première Enquête de M.*, v; *L'Inspecteur cadavre*, i; *Mag. lit.; Vieux*, 360; *Dossier*, 113; *Les Anneaux de Bicêtre*, i; *Le Coup de vague*, ii; *La Veuve Couderc*, iii; *Le Chat*, iv; *Un Nouveau dans la ville*, vi; *M. chez le coroner*, ii; *Malempin*, ii; *Bergelon*, iv; *M. chez le ministre*, i; *Point*, 28.

249   S. in his fictions. The latest disclaimer is in *Mém.*, 421, but is preceded by countless others. Anaïs Nin, *Diary*, V, 254; Fellini interview, *L'Express*, Feb. 21, 1977.

251   What moves me most. *Homme*, 265; cf. 127.

252   Women as positive experiences. e.g., *Playboy; Mém.*, 383.
Simenon frustrated. *Vent*, 105.
Mme. Maigret. *Pas*, 157.

253–54   Since my retirement. *Petits*, 17–18.

BIBLIOGRAPHY OF
THE WORKS OF
GEORGES SIMENON

Claude Menguy has kindly given permission to use his bibliographies (see "Secondary Sources," page 289), supplemented by his chronology of dates of composition of the patronymic works, recently published in a special Simenon edition of *Enigmatika*, number 30 (May–June, 1986). M. Menguy is of course not responsible for any errors that may have been made in transposing his exemplary research.

An asterisk (*) indicates a collection of shorter pieces.

I. Juvenilia

All are signed "Georges Sim"

1921   *Au pont des Arches* (printed at Imprimerie Bénard, Liège)
       "Les Ridicules!" (printed in a few copies for private circulation on the
         Gazette de Liège presses)
       "Jehan Pinaguet" (unpublished)
       "Le Bouton de col" (with H.-J. Moërs, unpublished)

II. Pseudonymous Works

By year of publication: pseudonym, title, publisher abbreviation: AF, Arthème Fayard; JF, J. Ferenczi; MF, Maxine Ferenczi; P, Prima; T, Jules Tallandier

1924   Jean du Perry. *Le Roman d'une dactylo* (JF)
       Amour d'exilée (JF)
       Georges Simm. *Les Larmes avant le bonheur*. . . (JF)
1925   Jean du Perry. *L'Heureuse fin* (JF)

Pour le sauver (JF)
Pour qu'il soit heureux!. . . (JF)
L'Oiseau blessé (JF)
La Fiancée fugitive (JF)
Entre deux haines (JF)
Ceux qu'on avait oubliés (JF)
A l'assaut d'un coeur (JF)
Georges d'Isly. *Étoile de cinéma* (F. Rouff)
Christian Brulls. *La Prêtresse des Vaudoux* (T)
Georges-Martin Georges. *L'Orgueil qui meurt* (T)
Gom Gut. *Au Grand 13* * (P)
  Un Viol aux Quat'z'Arts (P)
  Perversités frivoles * (P)
  Plaisirs charnels * (P)
  La Noce à Montmartre (P)
  Aux vingt-huit négresses (P)
Plick et Plock. *Voluptueuses étreintes* * (P)
1926 Jean du Perry. *Amour d'Afrique* (JF)
  L'Orgeuil d'aimer (JF)
  Celle qui est aimée (JF)
  Les Yeux qui ordonnent (JF)
  De la rue au bonheur (JF)
  Que ma mère l'ignore (JF)
  Un Péché de jeunesse (JF)
Christian Brulls. *Nox l'insaisissable* (JF)
  Se Ma Tsien, le sacrificateur (T)
Gom Gut. *Liquettes au vent* * (P)
  Une Petite très sensuelle (P)
  Orgies bourgeoises (P)
  L'Homme aux douze étreintes (P)
Luc Dorsan. *Nini violée* (P)
  Histoire d'un pantalon (P)
  Mémoires d'un vieux suiveur (P)
  Nichonnette (P)
  Nuit de noces * (P)
1927 Georges Sim. *Défense d'aimer* (JF)
  Le Cercle de la soif (JF, reissued in 1933 as *Le Cercle de la mort*)
  Le Feu s'éteint (AF)
  Paris-Leste * (Paris-Plaisirs)
  Les Voleurs de navires (T)
  Un Monsieur libidineux (P)
Jean du Perry. *Lili-Tristesse* (JF)
  Un Tout Petit Coeur (JF)
Luc Dorsan. *La Pucelle de Bénouville* (P)
Gom Gut. *Étreintes passionnées* (P)
  Une Môme dessalée (P)
X. . . . *L'Envers d'une Passion* (F. Rouff) (date uncertain)
1928 Georges Sim. *Le Semeur de larmes* (JF)

Bibliography

Songes d'été (JF)

Le Sang des Gitanes (JF)

Aimer d'amour (JF)

Le Monstre blanc de la Terre de Feu (JF, reissued in 1933 as *L'Île de la Désolation*)

Le Lac d'angoisse (JF, reissued in 1933 as *Le Lac des ésclaves*)

La Maison sans soleil (AF)

Miss Baby (AF)

Chair de beauté (AF)

Le Secret des Lamas (T)

Les Maudits du Pacifique (T)

Le Roi des glaces (T)

Le Sous-marin dans la forêt (T)

Les Nains des cataractes (T)

Les Coeurs perdus (T)

Christian Brulls. *Annie, danseuse* (JF)

Dolorosa (AF)

Les Adolescents passionnés (AF)

Mademoiselle X... (AF)

Le Desert du froid qui tue (JF, reissued in 1933 as *Le Yacht fantôme*)

Jean du Perry. *Coeur exalté* (JF)

Trois Coeurs dans la tempête (JF)

Le Fou d'amour (JF)

Les Amants de la mansarde (JF)

Un Jour de soleil (JF)

Georges-Martin Georges. *Un Soir de vertige...* (JF)

Brin d'amour (JF)

Les Coeurs vides (JF)

Cabotine (JF)

Aimer, mourir (JF)

Gaston Vialis. *Un Petit Corps blessé* (JF)

Haïr à force d'aimer (JF)

G. Violis. *Rien que pour toi* (JF)

G. Vialio. *L'Étreinte tragique* (JF)

Jacques Dersonne. *Un Seul Baiser...* (JF)

Jean Dorsage. *L'Amour méconnu* (JF)

Gom Gut. *L'Amant fantôme* (P)

Madame veut un amant (MF)

Les Distractions d'Hélène (MF)

L'Amour à Montparnasse (MF)

Poum et Zette. *Des gens qui exagèrent* (MF)

Kim. *Un Petit Poison* (MF)

Bobette. *Bobette et ses satyres* (MF)

Luc Dorsan. *Une Petite dessalée* (MF)

1929 Georges Sim. *Le Roi du Pacific* (JF, reissued in 1935, abridged, as *Le "Bateau-d'Or"*)

L'Île des maudits (JF, reissued in 1935, abridged, as *Le Naufrage du "Pélican"*)

La Fiancée aux mains de glace (AF)
Destinées (AF)
La Femme qui tue (AF)
Les Bandits de Chicago (AF)
Les Contrebandiers de l'alcool (AF)
La Panthère borgne (T)
L'Île des hommes roux (T)
Le Gorille-Roi (T)
En Robe de mariée (T)
La Femme en deuil (T)
Les Mémoires d'un prostitué (P)
Jean du Perry. *La Fille de l'autre* (JF)
Coeur de poupée (JF)
Deux Coeurs de femmes (JF)
Le Mirage de Paris (JF)
L'Épave d'amour (JF)
L'Amour et l'argent (JF)
Luc Dorsan. *Un Drôle de coco* (P)
Georges-Martin Georges. *Une Ombre dans la nuit* (JF)
La Victime (JF)
Voleuse d'amour (JF)
Nuit de Paris (JF)
Jean Dorsage. *Celle qui revient* (JF)
G. Violis. *Trop beau pour elle* (JF)
Gaston Viallis. *Le Parfum du passé* (JF)
Germain d'Ântibes. *Hélas! je t'aime...* (JF)
Jacques Dersonne. *La Merveilleuse Aventure* (JF)
Christian Brulls. *Les Pirates du Texas* (JF, reissued in 1934, abridged, as
 La Chasse au whisky)
L'Amant sans nom (AF)
Un Drame au Pôle sud (AF)
Captain S.O.S. (AF)
Lily-Palace (AF) (date uncertain)

1930 Georges Sim. *Nez d'argent* (JF, reissued in 1933, abridged, as *Le Paria des
 bois sauvages*)
Mademoiselle Million (AF)
La Femme 47 (AF)
L'Homme qui tremble (AF)
L'Oeil de l'Utah (T)
Le Pêcheur de Bouées (T)
Le Chinois de San Francisco (T)
Christian Brulls. *Jacques d'Antifer, roi des iles du vent* (JF, reissued in 1934,
 abridged, as *L'Héritier du corsaire*)
Train de nuit (AF)
L'Inconnue (AF)
Jean du Perry. *Les Amants du malheur* (JF)
Celle qui passe (JF)
La Femme ardente (JF)

Petite Exilée (JF)
La Porte close (JF)
La Poupée brisée (JF)
Jacques Dersonne. *Les Étapes du mensonge* (JF)
Georges-Martin Georges. *Le Bonheur de Lili* (JF)
    Un Nid d'amour (JF)
    Bobette, mannequin (JF)
    La Puissance du souvenir (JF)
Jean Dorsage. *Coeur de jeune fille* (JF)
    Soeurette (JF)
Gaston Viallis. *Lili-Sourire* (JF)
    Folie d'un soir (JF)
1931 Georges Sim. *L'Homme de proie* (AF)
    Les Errants (AF)
    Katia, acrobate (AF)
    L'Homme à la cigarette (T)
Christian Brulls. *La Maison de la haine* (AF)
Georges-Martin Georges. *La Double Vie* (JF)
Jean du Perry. *Pauvre amante!* (JF)
    Marie-Mystère (AF)
    Le Rêve qui meurt (F. Rouff)
Jacques Dersonne. *Baisers mortels* (JF)
    Victime de son fils (JF)
Gaston Viallis. *Âme de jeune fille* (JF)
Jean Dorsage. *Les Chercheurs de bonheur* (JF)
1932 Georges Sim. *L'Épave* (AF)
    La Maison de l'inquiétude (T)
    Matricule 12 (T)
Christian Brulls. *La Figurante* (AF)
    Fièvre (AF)
    Les Forçats de Paris (AF)
1933 Georges Sim. *La Fiancée du diable* (AF)
    La Femme rousse (T)
    La Château des Sables Rouges (T)
    Deuxième Bureau (T)
1934 Christian Brulls. *L'Évasion* (AF)
1937 Christian Brulls. *L'Île empoisonnée* (JF)
    Seul parmi les gorilles (JF)
In addition, nine books may have been published by MF in 1928, but actual publication is not verified; also, seven book-length narratives were serialized in periodicals, 1926–32, but not published as books.

III. *Patronymic Works*

By publisher and year, in approximate order of publication. Each year is divided into straight novels, detective novels (mostly Maigrets), and nonfiction. There is sometimes a discrepancy between the title-page or copyright date and the printing date indicated at the end — which accounts for certain discrepancies in various bibliographies. The date given here is usually the title-page date. In parentheses are date and place of composition; in a few instances these are conjectural. The titles in English are of the translations; when there are two titles, the second is usually the American.

The *Oeuvres complètes* were published by Editions Rencontre, Lausanne, under the editorship of Gilbert Sigaux, 1967–73, in two series: volumes I–XXVIII are the detective stories; volumes 1–44 are the straight novels and the nonfiction.

Editions Jacques Haumont

1931 *La Folle d'Itteville* (Morsang-sur-Seine, on board the *Ostrogoth*, 1931)

Fayard

1931 *M. Gallet, décédé* (Morsang-sur-Seine, summer 1930) The Death of M. Gallet, Maigret Stonewalled

Le Pendu de Saint-Pholien (Beuzec-Conq, winter 1930–31) The Crime of Inspector Maigret, Maigret and the Hundred Gibbets

Le Charretier de la "Providence" (Morsang-sur-Seine, summer 1930) Maigret Meets a Milord, The Crime at Lock 14

Le Chien jaune (La Ferté-Alais, March 1931) A Face for a Clue

Pietr-le-Letton (Stavoren, winter 1929–30) The Case of Peter the Lett, Maigret and the Enigmatic Lett

La Nuit du carrefour (La Ferté-Alais, April 1931) Maigret at the Crossroads, The Crossroads Murder

Un Crime en Hollande (Morsang, May 1931) A Crime in Holland

Au rendez-vous des terre-neuvas (Morsang-sur-Seine, July 1931) The Sailor's Rendezvous

La Tête d'un homme (Paris, winter 1930–31) A Battle of Nerves

La Danseuse du Gai-Moulin (Ouistreham, Sept. 1931) At the "Gai-Moulin"

Le Relais d'Alsace (Paris, July 1931) The Man from Everywhere

1932 *La Guinguette à deux sous* (Ouistreham, Oct. 1931) Guinguette by the Seine

L'Ombre chinoise (Cap d'Antibes, Dec. 1931) Maigret Mystified, The Shadow in the Courtyard

L'Affaire Saint-Fiacre (Cap d'Antibes, Jan. 1932) The Saint-Fiacre Affair, Maigret Goes Home

Chez les Flamands (Cap d'Antibes, Jan. 1932) The Flemish Shop

Le Fou de Bergerac (La Rochelle, March 1932) The Madman of Bergerac

Le Port des brumes (Cap d'Antibes, Feb. 1932) Death of a Harbour Master

Liberty-Bar (La Richardière, April 1932) Liberty Bar

Le Passager du "Polarlys" (Beuzec-Conq, Nov. 1930) The Mystery of the "Polarlys," Danger at Sea

Les 13 Coupables * (Stavoren, winter 1929–30)

Les 13 Énigmes * (Paris, winter 1928–29)

Bibliography

Les 13 Mystères * (Paris, winter 1928–29)

1933 *La Maison du canal* (La Richardière, Jan. 1932) The House by the Canal

Les Fiançailles de M. Hire (La Richardière, fall 1932) Mr. Hire's Engagement

L'Âne rouge (La Richardière, fall 1932) The Night Club

Le Coup de lune (La Richardière, fall 1932) Tropic Moon

Les Gens d'en face (La Richardiere, summer 1933) The Window over the Way, Danger Ashore

Le Haut mal (La Richardière, fall 1933) The Woman in the Gray House

L'Écluse numéro un (La Richardière, April 1933) The Lock at Charenton

1934 *L'Homme de Londres* (La Richardière, fall 1933) Newhaven-Dieppe

Maigret (La Richardière, Jan. 1933) Maigret Returns

Gallimard

1934 *Le Locataire* (La Richardière, fall 1933) The Lodger

Les Suicidés (La Richardière, fall 1933) One Way Out, Escape in Vain

1935 *Les Pitard* (Porquerolles, April 1934) A Wife at Sea

Les Clients d'Avrenos (on board *Araldo*, summer 1933)

Quartier nègre (La Cour-Dieu, summer 1935)

1936 *L'Évadé* (La Richardière, fall 1934) The Disintegration of J.P.G.

Long Cours (La Cour-Dieu, Sept. 1935) The Long Exile

Les Demoiselles de Concarneau (La Cour-Dieu, fall 1935) The Breton Sisters

45° à l'ombre (Il Cavo, Elba, June 1934)

1937 *Le Testament Donadieu* (Porquerolles, July–Aug. 1936) The Shadow Falls

L'Assassin (Combloux, Haute Savoie, Dec. 1935) The Murderer

Le Blanc à lunettes (Porquerolles, spring 1936) Talata

Faubourg (Antnéor, Feb. 1936) Home Town

1938 *Ceux de la soif* (Tahiti, March 1935)

Chemin sans issue (Porquerolles, spring 1936) Blind Path, Blind Alley

Les Rescapés du "Télémaque" (Igls, Tyrol, Dec. 1936) The Survivors

Les Trois Crimes de mes amis (boulevard Richard-Wallace, Jan. 1937)

Le Suspect (boulevard Richard-Wallace, Sept. 1937) The Green Thermos

Les Soeurs Lacroix (Saint-Thibault, Nov. 1937) Poisoned Relations

Touriste de bananes (Porquerolles, June 1937) Banana Tourist

Monsieur La Souris (Porquerolles, Feb. 1937) Monsieur La Souris, The Mouse

La Marie du port (Port-en-Bessin, Oct. 1937) A Chit of a Girl, The Girl in Waiting

L'Homme qui regardait passer les trains (Igls, Dec. 1936) The Man Who Watched Trains Go By

Le Cheval blanc (Porquerolles, March 1938) The White Horse Inn

G7 (*Les Sept Minutes*) * (Morsang-sur-Seine, June 1931)

La Mauvaise Étoile * (Tahiti & Indian Ocean, spring 1935, revised La Cour-Dieu, June 1935)

1939 *Le Coup de vague* (Beynac, Dordogne, April 1938)
Chez Krull (La Rochelle, July 1938) Chez Krull
Le Bourgmestre de Furnes (Nieul, Dec. 1938) The Burgomaster of Furnes

1940 *Malempin* (Scharrachbergheim, Alsace, March 1939) The Family Life
Les Inconnus dans la maison (Nieul, Sept. 1938) Strangers in the House

1941 *Cour d'assises* (Isola Pescatore, Lago Maggiore, Aug. 1937) Justice
Bergelon (Nieul, Sept. 1939) The Delivery
L'Outlaw (Nieul, Feb. 1939)
Il pleut, bergère... (Nieul, Oct. 1940) Black Rain
Le Voyageur de la Toussaint (Fontenay-le-Comte, Feb. 1941) Strange Inheritance
La Maison des sept jeunes filles (boulevard Richard-Wallace, fall 1937)

1942 *Oncle Charles s'est enfermé* (Nieul, Oct. 1939)
La Veuve Couderc (Nieul, May 1940) Ticket of Leave, The Widow
Le Fils Cardinaud (Fontenay, July 1941) Young Cardinaud
La Vérité sur Bébé Donge (Vouvant, Sept. 1940) The Trial of Bebe Donge, I Take This Woman
Maigret revient * includes: *Les Caves du Majestic* (Nieul, Dec. 1939) Maigret and the Hotel Majestic; *Cécile est morte* (Fontenay-le-Comte, Dec. 1940) Maigret and the Spinster; and *La Maison du juge* (Nieul, Jan. 1940) Maigret in Exile.

1943 *Le Petit Docteur* * (La Rochelle, spring 1938) The Little Doctor
Les Dossiers de l'Agence "O" * (La Rochelle, spring 1938)

1944 *Le Rapport du gendarme* (Fontenay, Sept. 1941) The Gendarme's Report
Signé Picpus * includes: *Signé Picpus* (Fontenay, summer 1941) To Any Lengths; *L'Inspecteur cadavre* (Saint-Mesmin, March 1943) Maigret's Rival; *Félicie est là* (La Fauta-sur-mer, May 1942) Maigret and the Toy Village; and *Nouvelles exotiques* * (boulevard Richard-Wallace, winter 1937–38)
Les Nouvelles enquêtes de Maigret * (boulevard Richard-Wallace, Oct. 1936, and winter 1937–38) in Maigret's Pipe

1945 *L'Aîné des Ferchaux* (Saint-Mesmin, Dec. 1943) Magnet of Doom, The First Born

Editions de la Jeune Parque

1945 *La Fenêtre des Rouet* (Fontenay, July 1942) Across the Street
La Fuite de M. Monde (Saint-Mesmin, April 1944) Monsieur Monde Vanishes

Presses de la Cité

1945 *Je me souviens* (Fontenay, Dec. 1940–June 1941 & Jan. 1945)

Gallimard

1946 *Les Noces de Poitiers* (Saint-Mesmin, winter 1943–44)
Le Cercle des Mahé (Saint-Mesmin, May 1945)

Bibliography

Presses de la Cité

1946 *Trois Chambres à Manhattan* (Sainte-Marguerite, Jan. 1946) Three Beds in Manhattan

Gallimard

1947 *Le Clan des Ostendais* (St. Andrews, June 1946) The Ostenders

Editions de la Jeune Parque

1947 *Le Passager clandestin* (Bradenton Beach, April 1947) The Stowaway

Presses de la Cité

1947 *Au bout du rouleau* (St. Andrews, June, 1946)
Lettre à mon juge (Bradenton Beach, Dec. 1946) Act of Passion
Le Destin des Malou (Bradenton Beach, Feb. 1947) The Fate of the Malous
Maigret se fâche, together with "La Pipe de Maigret" (St. Fargeau-sur-Seine, Aug. 1945) in Maigret's Pipe
Maigret à New York (Sainte-Marguerite, March 1946) Maigret in New York's Underworld, Maigret in New York, Inspector Maigret in New York's Underworld
Maigret et l'inspecteur malgracieux * (Sainte-Marguerite, April–May 1946 & St. Andrews, Aug. 1946) in Maigret's Christmas

Gallimard

1948 *Le Bilan Malétras* (Saint-Mesmin, May 1943)

Presses de la Cité

1948 *La Jument perdue* (Tucson, Oct. 1947)
La Neige était sale (Tucson, March 1946) The Stain in the Snow, The Snow Was Black
Pedigree (Fontenay, Saint-Mesmin, Dec. 1941–Jan. 1943) Pedigree
Maigret et son mort (Tucson, Dec. 1947) Maigret's Dead Man
Les Vacances de Maigret (Tucson, Nov. 1947) Maigret on Holiday, No Vacation for Maigret
1949 *Le Fond de la bouteille* (Stud Barn, Sept. 1948) The Bottom of the Bottle
Les Fantômes du chapelier (Stud Barn, Dec. 1948) The Hatter's Ghost
Les Quatre Jours du pauvre homme (Tucson, July 1949) Four Days in a Lifetime
La Première Enquête de Maigret (Stud Barn, Oct. 1948) Maigret's First Case
Mon Ami Maigret (Stud Barn, Feb. 1949) My Friend Maigret, The Methods of Maigret
Maigret chez le coroner (Tucson, July 1949) Maigret and the Coroner
Maigret et la vieille dame (Carmel, Dec. 1949) Maigret and the Old Lady

[2 8 3]

BIBLIOGRAPHY

1950 *Un Nouveau dans la ville* (Tucson, Oct. 1949)
      L'Enterrement de M. Bouvet (Carmel, Feb. 1950) Inquest on Bouvet, The
        Burial of Monsieur Bouvet
      Les Volets verts (Carmel, Jan. 1950) The Heart of a Man
      Tante Jeanne (Lakeville, Sept. 1950) Aunt Jeanne
      L'Amie de Mme. Maigret (Carmel, Dec. 1949) Madame Maigret's Friend,
        Madame Maigret's Own Case
      Maigret et les petits cochons sans queue * (Nieul, 1939, Les Sables d'Olonne,
        1945, St. Andrews, 1946, Bradendon Beach, 1947)
      Les Mémoires de Maigret (Lakeville, Sept. 1950) Maigret's Memoirs
1951 *Le Temps d'Anaïs* (Lakeville, Nov. 1950) The Girl in His Past
      Une Vie comme neuve (Lakeville, March 1951) A New Lease on Life
      Marie qui louche (Lakeville, August 1951) The Girl with a Squint
      Un Noël de Maigret * (Carmel, May 1950) Maigret's Christmas
      Maigret au Picratt's (Lakeville, Dec. 1950) Maigret in Montmartre,
        Maigret and the Strangled Stripper
      Maigret en meublé (Lakeville, Feb. 1951) Maigret Takes a Room, Maigret
        Rents a Room
      Maigret et la grande perche (Lakeville, May 1951) Maigret and the Bur-
        glar's Wife, Inspector Maigret and the Burglar's Wife
1952 *La Mort de Belle* (Lakeville, Dec. 1951) Belle
      Les Frères Rico (Lakeville, July 1952) The Brothers Rico
      Maigret, Lognon et les gangsters (Lakeville, Sept. 1951) Maigret and the
        Gangsters, Inspector Maigret and the Killers
      Le Révolver de Maigret (Lakeville, June 1952) Maigret's Revolver
1953 *Antoine et Julie* (Lakeville, Dec. 1952) The Magician
      L'Escalier de fer (Lakeville, May 1953) The Iron Staircase
      Feux rouges (Lakeville, July 1953) Red Lights, The Hitchhiker
      Maigret et l'homme du banc (Lakeville, Sept. 1952) Maigret and the Man
        on the Bench
      Maigret a peur (Lakeville, March 1953) Maigret Afraid
      Maigret se trompe (Lakeville, Aug. 1953) Maigret's Mistake
1954 *Crime impuni* (Lakeville, Oct. 1953) Account Unsettled, Fugitive
      L'Horloger d'Everton (Lakeville, March 1954) The Watchmaker of Everton
      Les Témoins (Lakeville, Sept. 1954) The Witnesses
      Le Grand Bob (Lakeville, May 1954) Big Bob
      Maigret à l'école (Lakeville, Dec. 1953) Maigret Goes to School
      Maigret et la jeune morte (Lakeville, Jan. 1954) Maigret and the Young
        Girl, Inspector Maigret and the Dead Girl
      Maigret chez le ministre (Lakeville, Aug. 1954) Maigret and the Minister,
        Maigret and the Calame Report

Gallimard

1954 *Le Bateau d'Émile* * (Les Sables d'Olonne, Paris, 1944–45)

Presses de la Cité

1955 *La Boule noire* (Mougins, "La Gatounière," April 1955)

[2 8 4]

Les Complices (Mougins, "La Gatounière," Sept. 1955) The Accomplices

Maigret et le corps sans tête (Lakeville, Jan., 1955) Maigret and the Headless Corpse

Maigret tend un piège (Mougins, "La Gatounière," July 1955) Maigret Sets a Trap

1956   *En cas de malheur* (Cannes, "Golden Gate," Nov. 1955) In Case of Emergency

Le Petit Homme d'Arkhangelsk (Cannes, "Golden Gate," April 1956) The Little Man from Archangel

Un Échec de Maigret (March, 1956) Maigret's Failure

1957   *Le Fils* (Cannes, "Golden Gate," Dec. 1956) The Son

Le Nègre (Cannes, "Golden Gate," April 1957) The Negro

Maigret s'amuse (Cannes, "Golden Gate," Sept. 1956) Maigret's Little Joke, None of Maigret's Business

1958   *Strip-Tease* (Cannes, "Golden Gate," June, 1957) Striptease

Le Président (Echandens, Oct. 1957) The Premier

Le Passage de la ligne (Echandens, Feb. 1958)

Dimanche (Echandens, July 1958) Sunday

Maigret voyage (Echandens, Aug. 1957) Maigret and the Millionaires

Les Scrupules de Maigret (Echandens, Dec. 1957) Maigret Has Scruples

1959   *La Vieille* (Echandens, May 1959) The Grandmother

Le Veuf (Echandens, July 1959) The Widower

Maigret et les témoins récalcitrants (Echandens, Oct. 1958) Maigret and the Reluctant Witnesses

Une Confidence de Maigret (Echandens, May 1959) Maigret Has Doubts

Le Roman de l'homme (Echandens, 1959) The Novel of a Man

La Femme en France (Echandens, 1959)

1960   *L'Ours en peluche* (Echandens, March 1960) Teddy Bear

Maigret aux assises (Echandens, Nov. 1959) Maigret in Court

Maigret et les vieillards (Echandens, June 1960) Maigret in Society

1961   *Betty* (Echandens, Oct. 1969) Betty

Le Train (Echandens, March 1961) The Train

Maigret et le voleur paresseux (Echandens, Jan. 1961) Maigret and the Lazy Burglar

1962   *La Porte* (Echandens, May 1961) The Door

Les Autres (Echandens, Nov. 1961) The House on Quai Notre Dame

Maigret et les braves gens (Echandens, Sept. 1961) Maigret and the Black Sheep

Maigret et le client du samedi (Echandens, Feb. 1962) Maigret and the Saturday Caller

1963   *Les Anneaux de Bicêtre* (Echandens, Oct. 1962) The Patient

La Rue aux trois poussins * (Nieul, Les Sables d'Olonne, 1939, 1940, 1945)

Maigret et le clochard (Echandens, May 1962) Maigret and the Dossier, Maigret and the Bum

La Colère de Maigret (Echandens, June, 1962) Maigret Loses His Temper

1964 *La Chambre bleue* (Echandens, June 1963) The Blue Room
L'Homme au petit chien (Echandens, Sept 1963) The Man with the Little Dog
Maigret et le fantôme (Echandens, June 1963) Maigret and the Apparition
Maigret se défend (Épalinges, July 1964) Maigret on the Defensive
1965 *Le Petit Saint* (Épalinges, Oct. 1964) The Little Saint
Le Train de Venise (Épalinges, June 1965) The Venice Train
La Patience de Maigret (Épalinges, March 1965) The Patience of Maigret
1966 *Le Confessionnal* (Épalinges, Oct. 1965) The Confessional
La Mort d'Auguste (Épalinges, March 1966) The Old Man Dies
1967 *Le Chat* (Épalinges, Oct. 1966) The Cat
Le Déménagement (Épalinges, June 1967) The Neighbors, The Move
Maigret et l'affaire Nahour (Épalinges, Feb. 1966) Maigret and the Nahour Case
Le Voleur de Maigret (Épalinges, Nov. 1966) Maigret's Pickpocket
1968 *La Prison* (Épalinges, Nov. 1967) The Prison
La Main (Épalinges, April 1968) The Man on the Bench in the Barn
Maigret hésite (Épalinges, Jan. 1968) Maigret Hesitates
L'Ami d'enfance de Maigret (Épalinges, June 1968) Maigret's Boyhood Friend
Maigret à Vichy (Épalinges, Sept. 1967) Maigret Takes the Waters, Maigret in Vichy
1969 *Il y a encore des noisetiers* (Épalinges, Oct. 1968)
Novembre (Épalinges, June 1969) November
Maigret et le tueur (Épalinges, April 1969) Maigret and the Killer
1970 *Le Riche Homme* (Épalinges, March 1970) The Rich Man
Maigret et le marchand de vin (Épalinges, Sept. 1969) Maigret and the Wine Merchant
La Folle de Maigret (Épalinges, May 1970) Maigret and the Madwoman
Quand j'étais vieux (Echandens, June 1960–Feb. 1963) When I Was Old
1971 *La Disparition d'Odile* (Épalinges, Oct. 1970) The Disappearance of Odile
La Cage de verre (Épalinges, March 1971) The Glass Cage
Maigret et l'homme tout seul (Épalinges, Feb. 1971) Maigret and the Loner
Maigret et l'indicateur (Épalinges, June 1971) Maigret and the Flea, Maigret and the Informer
1972 *Les Innocents* (Épalinges, Oct. 1971) The Innocents
Maigret et M. Charles (Épalinges, Feb. 1972) Maigret and Monsieur Charles
1975 *Lettre à ma mère* (Lausanne, April 1974) Letter to My Mother
Un Homme comme un autre (Lausanne, Feb.–Sept. 1973)
Des traces de pas (Lausanne, Sept. 1973–March 1974)
1976 *Les Petits Hommes* (Lausanne, April–Nov. 1974)
Vent du nord, vent du sud (Lausanne, Nov. 1974–March 1975)
1977 *Un Banc au soleil* (Lausanne, April–Aug. 1975)
De la cave au grenier (Lausanne, Aug.–Nov. 1975)

A *l'abri de notre arbre* (Lausanne, Dec. 1975–April 1976)

1978 *Tant que je suis vivant* (Lausanne, April–June 1976)

Vacances obligatoires (Lausanne, June–Aug. 1976)

La Main dans la main (Lausanne, Aug.–Nov. 1976)

Au-delà de ma porte-fenêtre (Lausanne, Nov. 1976–March 1977)

1979 *Je suis resté un enfant de choeur* (Lausanne, March–June 1977)

A quoi bon jurer? (Lausanne, June–July 1977)

Point-virgule (Lausanne, Aug. 1977)

1980 *Le Prix d'un homme* (Lausanne, Dec. 1977)

On dit que j'ai soixante-quinze ans (Lausanne, March–July 1978)

Quand vient le froid (Lausanne, Sept.–Oct. 1978)

Les Libertés qu'il nous reste (Lausanne, Nov.–Dec. 1978)

Le Femme endormie (Lausanne, Feb.–March 1979)

Jour et nuit (Lausanne, April–May 1979)

Destinées (Lausanne, Aug.–Sept. 1979)

1981 *Mémoires intimes* (Lausanne, 1980–81) Intimate Memoirs

Readers knowing either the original French title or the title in English, and wanting to know the other may consult the index under either title.

FILMOGRAPHY

Film title, book title if different from film, date of film, director, principal actors. The films are French unless otherwise indicated.

La Nuit du carrefour, 1932: Jean Renoir; Pierre Renoir, Winna Winfried

Le Chien jaune, 1932: Jean Tarride; Abel Tarride

La Tête d'un homme, 1933: Julien Duvivier; Harry Bauer

La Maison des sept jeunes filles, 1941: Albert Valentin. (A film named *Sept amoureuses*, made in the U.S. in 1938 and released in France in 1945 is conjecturally related to Simenon's novella, but the issue is extremely obscure: see Maurice Dubourg's filmography in *Cistre*, 168.)

Les Inconnus dans la maison, 1941: Henri Decoin (screenplay, Henri-Georges Clouzot); Raimu, Juliette Faber, Jean Tissier, Lucien Coëdal

Annette et la dame blonde, 1942: Jean Dréville (screenplay, Henri Decoin); Louise Carletti, Henri Garat

Le Voyageur de la Toussaint, 1942: Louis Daquin (screenplay, Marcel Aymé); Jean Desailly, Simone Valère

Monsieur La Souris, 1943: Georges Lacombe (screenplay, Marcel Achard); Raimu, Aimé Clarjond, Aimos (in U.S., *Midnight in Paris*)

Picpus (from *Signé Picpus*), 1943: Richard Pottier; Albert Préjean

Homme de Londres, 1943: Henri Decoin; Fernand Ledoux, Jules Berry, Suzy Prim

Cécile est morte, 1943: Maurice Tourneur; Albert Préjean

Les Caves du Majestic, 1945: Richard Pottier (screenplay, Charles Spaak); Albert Préjean

Panique (from *Les Fiançailles de M. Hire*), 1946: Julien Duvivier (screenplay, Charles Spaak); Michel Simon, Viviane Romance

Dernier Refuge (from *Le Locataire*), 1947: Marc Maurette; Raymond Rouleau, Mila Panoy

Temptation Harbour (English, from *L'Homme de Londres*), 1948: Lance Comfort; Robert Newton

The Man on the Eiffel Tower (American, from *La Tête d'un homme*), 1948: Burgess Meredith & M. Allen; Charles Laughton, Burgess Meredith, Franchot Tone

La Marie du port, 1950: Marcel Carné; Jean Gabin, Nicole Courcel

La Vérité sur Bébé Donge, 1951: Henri Decoin; Danielle Darrieux, Jean Gabin

The Man Who Watched the Trains Go By (American, from *L'Homme qui regardait passer les trains*, released in France as *Paris-express*), 1951: Harold French; Claude Rains, Anouk Aimée

Brelan d'as (trilogy, of which third part is from "Le Témoignage de l'enfant de choeur"), 1952: Henri Verneuil; Michel Simon

Le Fruit défendu (from *Lettre à mon juge*), 1951: Henri Verneuil; Fernandel, Françoise Arnoul

La Neige était sale, 1952: Luis Saslavsky; Daniel Gélin, Valentine Tessier

Maigret mène l'enquête (partly adapted from *Cécile est morte*), 1955: Stany Cordier; Maurice Manson

Le Sang à la tête (from *Le Fils Cardinaud*), 1956: Gilles Grangier; Jean Gabin

The Bottom of the Bottle (American, from *Le Fond de la bouteille*), 1956: Henry Hathaway; Van Johnson, Joseph Cotten

The Brothers Rico (American, from *Les Frères Rico*), 1957: Phil Karlson; Richard Conte

Le Passager clandestin (Franco-Australian), 1958: Ralph Habib; Martine Carol, Serge Reggiani, Arletty

Maigret tend un piège, 1958: Jean Delannoy; Jean Gabin, Annie Girardot

En cas de malheur, 1958: Claude Autant-Lara; Jean Gabin, Brigitte Bardot, Edwige Feuillère

Maigret et l'affaire Saint-Fiacre (from *L'Affaire Saint-Fiacre*), 1959: Jean Delannoy; Jean Gabin, Michel Auclair, Valentine Tessier

Le Baron de l'écluse, 1959: Jean Delannoy; Jean Gabin

Simenon, arbre à romans (Swiss documentary on Simenon, with a scene from *Le Président*), 1960: Jean-François Hauduroy; Michel Simon

La Mort de Belle, 1960: Edouard Molinaro (screenplay, Jean Anouilh); Jean Desailly

Le Président, 1961: Henri Verneuil & Michel Audiard; Jean Gabin

Le Bateau d'Émile (Franco-Italian), 1962: Denys de La Patellière; Lino Ventura, Annie Girardot, Michel Simon, Pierre Brasseur

L'Aîné des Ferchaux, 1963: Jean-Pierre Melville; Jean-Paul Belmondo

Maigret voit rouge, (Franco-Italian, from *Maigret, Lognon et les gangsters*), 1963: Gilles Grangier; Jean Gabin

Trois Chambres à Manhattan, 1965: Marcel Carné; Maurice Ronet, Annie Girardot

Maigret à Pigalle (Italian, from *Maigret au Picratt's*), 1967: Mario Landi; Gino Cervi

Stranger in the House (English, from *Les Inconnus dans la maison*), 1967: Pierre Rouve; James Mason, Geraldine Chaplin

Maigret und sein grösster Fall (Franco-German, released in France as *Maigret fait mouche*, from *La Danseuse du Gai-Moulin*), 1968: Alfred Weidenmann; Heinz Ruhmann

Le Chat, 1970: Pierre Granier-Deferre; Jean Gabin, Simone Signoret

La Veuve Couderc, 1971: Pierre Granier-Deferre; Simone Signoret, Alain Delon

L'Horloger de Saint-Paul (from *L'Horloger d'Everton*), 1973: Bertrand Tavernier; Philippe Noiret

Le Train, 1973: Pierre Granier-Deferre; Jean-Louis Trintignant, Romy Schneider

L'Étoile du nord (from *Le Locataire*), 1982: Pierre Granier-Deferre; Simone Signoret, Philippe Noiret

Les Fantômes du chapelier, 1982: Claude Chabrol; Charles Aznavour, Michel Serrault

Equateur (from *Le Coup de lune*), 1982: Serge Gainsbourg; Barbara Sukowa, Francis Haster

Secondary Sources Cited or Consulted

Reviews and journalistic articles and interviews, with some exceptions, are not listed.

Becker, Lucille F. *Georges Simenon* (New York, 1977)

Boileau-Narcejac, *Le Roman policier* (Paris, 1964)

Boverie, Dieudonné, "Georges Simenon, écrivain liégeois," in Lacassin & Sigaux (q.v.)

Boyer, Régis, *Le Chien jaune de Georges Simenon* (Paris, 1973)

Bresler, Fenton, *The Mystery of Georges Simenon* (New York, 1983)

Briney, R.E., and F.M. Nevins, eds., *Multiplying Villainies* (New York, 1973)

Bronne, Carlo, *Discours à Simenon* (Paris, 1952)

Casals, J.-C., *Simenon en su obra y en la vida* (Barcelona, 1957)

Cistre Essai 10: (*Simenon*), (Lausanne, 1980)

Collins, Carvel (see *Writers at Work*)

Courtine, R.J., "Simenon ou l'appétit de Maigret," in Lacassin & Sigaux (q.v.)

Day Lewis, C., "The Man Who Isn't There," *Weekend Telegraph*, May 26, 1967

Delbanco, Nicholas, *Group Portrait* (New York, 1982)

Dessane, Odile (pseud. of Denyse Simenon), *Le Phallus d'or* (Paris, 1981)

Drysdale, Dennis, *Georges Simenon: A Study in Humanity* (unpublished dissertation, University of Nottingham, 1973)

Dubourg, Maurice, "Filmographie de Georges Simenon," in *Cistre* (q.v.)

Fabre, Jean, *Enquête sur un enquêteur: Maigret, un essai de sociocritique* (Montpellier, 1981)

Fallois, Bernard de, *Simenon* (Paris, 1961; revised ed., Lausanne, 1971)

Faucher, Jacques, *Les Médecins dans l'oeuvre de Simenon* (Paris, 1965)

Favelli, Max, "J'ai vu naître Simenon," *Gazette des lettres*, Oct. 15, 1950

Galligan, Edward L., "Simenon's Mosaic of Small Novels," *South Atlantic Quarterly*, LXVI, 4 (Autumn, 1967)

Georges Simenon, Entretiens avec Roger Stéphane: Portrait-souvenir (Paris, 1963: transcript of broadcast on French television, Nov. 30, Dec. 7, 14, 21, 1963)

Gide, André, *Journal 1939–1949* (Paris, Pléiade ed., 1954)

_____, and Georges Simenon, *Correspondence*, published in Lacassin & Sigaux (q.v.)

Gill, Brendan, "Profile," *The New Yorker*, Jan. 24, 1953

Gothot-Mersch, Claudine, "La Genèse des *Anneaux de Bicêtre*," in *Cistre* (q.v.)

Haney, Lynn, *Naked at the Feast* (New York, 1981)

Henry, Gilles, *Commissaire Maigret, qui êtes-vous?* (Paris, 1977)

Jour, Jean, *Simenon et Pedigree* (Liège-Brussels-Paris, 1963)

_____, *Simenon, Enfant de Liège* (Brussels, 1980)

Lacassin, Francis, and Gilbert Sigaux, eds. *Simenon* (Paris, 1973)

_____ and _____, eds., *A la recherche de l'homme nu* (Paris, 1976: collection of Simenon's journalism)

Lambert, Gavin, *The Dangerous Edge* (New York, 1976)

McAleen, Robert, *Rex Stout* (New York, 1977)

Magazine littéraire (Dec. 1975: Simenon issue)

Mauriac, Claude, *L'Alittérature contemporaine* (Paris, 1958)

Mauriac, François, "Bloc-Note" of May 11, 1963 in *Le Figaro littéraire*, reprinted in Lacassin & Sigaux (q.v.)

Menguy, Claude, "Bibliographie des éditions originales de Geogres Simenon" (from *Le Livre et l'estampe*, 49–50, 1967)

_____, "La Fausse sortie de Maigret," *Chasseur d'illustrés*, no. 21, (July 1971)

_____, and Pierre Deligny, *Simenon au fil des livres et des saisons* (Paris, 1986)

Moré, Marcel, "Simenon et l'enfant de choeur," in Lacassin & Sigaux (q.v.)

Moremans, Victor, "Mon ami Simenon," in Lacassin & Sigaux (q.v.)

Morgan, Ted, *Maugham* (New York, 1980)

Narcejac, Thomas, *Le Cas Simenon* (Paris, 1950) (translated into English as *The Art of Simenon* [London, 1942])

Olivier-Martin, Yves, *Histoire du roman populaire en France* (Paris, 1980)

Parinaud, André, *Connaissance de Georges Simenon* (Paris, 1957)

Piron, Maurice, "Simenon et son milieu natal," in *Cistre* (q.v.)

Playboy (French), Simenon interview (Aug., 1975)

Raiti, Angela Gabriella, *Simenon, policier de l'âme* (Tesi di laurea, Rome, 1964–65)

Raphael, Chaim, "Simenon on the Jews," *Midstream*, March, 1981

Raymond, John, *Simenon in Court* (New York, 1968)

Rémy, Georges, "Hommage à Georges Simenon," Service éducatif de la province de Liège (1961)

Secondary Sources

Richter, Anne, *Georges Simenon et l'homme désintégré* (Brussels, 1964)

Ritzen, Quentin (pseud. of Pierre Debray), *Simenon, avocat des hommes* (Paris, 1961)

Sigaux, Gilbert (see Lacassin)

Simenon, Denyse, *Un Oiseau pour le chat* (Paris, 1978) (see also Odile Dessane)

Simenon sur le gril (Paris, 1968)

Stéphane, Roger, *Le Dossier Simenon* (Paris, 1961)

Symons, Julian, *Mortal Consequences* (New York, 1973)

Tauxe, Henri-Charles, *Georges Simenon: de l'humain au vide* (Paris, 1983)

Thérive, André, Review in *Le Temps*, May 9, 1935, reprinted in *Cistre* (q.v.)

Thoorens, Leon, *Qui êtes-vous, Georges Simenon?* (Verviers, 1959)

Tillinac, Denis, *Le Mystère Simenon* (Paris, 1980)

Tourteau, Jean-Jacques, *D'Arsène Lupin à San Antonio: Le Roman policier français de 1900 à 1970* (Tours, 1970)

Tremblay, N.J., "Simenon's Psychological Westerns," *Arizona Quarterly* 3 (autumn 1954)

Vandromme, Pol, *Georges Simenon* (Brussels, 1962)

Veldman, Hendrik, *La Tentation de l'inaccessible: structures narratives chez Simenon* (Amsterdam, 1981)

Vlaminck, Maurice, *Portraits avant décès* (Paris, 1943)

Writers at Work, The *Paris Review* interviews, 1st. series, ed. Malcolm Cowley (New York, Penguin ed., 1977). Simenon interview by Carvel Collins

Young, Trudee, *Georges Simenon: A Checklist of his "Maigret" and Other Mystery Novels and Short Stories in French and in English Translations* (Metuchen, N.J., 1976)

INDEX

INDEX

Index

Index

Index

Index